ESSAYS ON MEXICO, CENTRAL AND SOUTH AMERICA

Scholarly Debates from the 1950s to the 1990s

Series Editor
JORGE I. DOMÍNGUEZ
Harvard University

A GARLAND SERIES

Series Contents

VOLUME
7

RACE AND ETHNICITY IN LATIN AMERICA

Edited with an introduction by
JORGE I. DOMÍNGUEZ

GARLAND PUBLISHING, Inc.
New York & London
1994

Library of Congress Cataloging-in-Publication Data

Race and ethnicity in Latin America / edited with an introduction
by Jorge I. Domínguez.
    p.   cm. — (Essays on Mexico, Central and South
America ; v. 7)
    ISBN 0–8153–1491–4 (alk. paper)
    1. Latin America—Race relations. 2. Ethnicity—Latin
America.   3. Social conflict—Latin America—History.
4. Social mobility—Latin America—History.   I. Domínguez,
Jorge I., 1945–   . II. Series.
F1419.A1R33   1994
305.8'0098—dc20   93–47174
                                             CIP

Printed on acid-free, 250-year-life paper
Manufactured in the United States of America

Contents

INTRODUCTION

In nearly all racially and ethnically heterogeneous societies, there is overt national conflict among parties and social movements organized on the basis of race and ethnicity. Such conflict has been much less evident in Latin America. Scholars have pondered the nature of race and ethnicity with regard to both Afro-American and Indo-American societies, though research on Brazil has been particularly prominent. Special attention has been given to the relationship between social class and race and ethnicity.

Charles Wagley sought to understand the diverging criteria for racial classification—physical features, ancestry, or socio-cultural traits. He noted that the United States relied nearly exclusively on ancestry. In Indo-American societies, socio-cultural criteria (including language use) predominated; in them, Wagley thought that "it is only a question of time until such populations may be entirely classed as *mestizo* by social race and social differentiation will be entirely in terms of socio-economic classes." In Afro-Latinamerican societies, he argued, there were few within-country cultural variations and limited attention to ancestry; thus physical traits shaped racial classification, as is evident in the vocabulary employed to describe shades of color along a continuum. Nowhere did the categories have genetic validity, but varying racial criteria were employed everywhere to sort out the place of individuals in society.

For Woodrow Borah, the central question was: "What is an Indian?" He reviewed various attempts to answer it—physical traits, linguistic preferences, cultural patterns, loyalty to an Indian community, political choice. He noted that some intellectuals, bureaucrats, and political activists had a stake in the search "to find Indians." Borah's conclusion was that Indians had disappeared in Mexico as separate ethnic groups, that the search for Indians thus responded to other psychological or political needs, and that the term "Indian" had come to mean poverty-stricken rural dwellers. "Our thinking on Mexico would be much clearer if we abandoned the word 'Indian' ... in favor of the more accurate term 'peasant.'"

Julian Pitt-Rivers criticized acculturation theorists for neglecting to study the society within which acculturation was
alleged to take place, and Marxists (and also Borah and, for Indoamerica, Wagley) for reducing the study of race relations to a
special instance of class relations. Instead, he argued, race relations could only be studied at the local level, where ancestry plays
little role and physical traits are bases for classification mediated
through social relations. Pitt-Rivers had little difficulty finding
locales where "ethnic consciousness" had emerged. He further
argued that in the long term indigenous peoples tended "constantly [to] abandon their Indian identity and becom[e] integrated
into the nation;" such integration led "persons of mainly Indian
physique into the proletariat."

In the studies of the 1950s and 1960s, the focus was on the
society. By the 1980s, the scholarship had shifted to focus on state
policies toward indigenous peoples.

William Bollinger and Daniel Manny Lund sought to understand the relationship between social class and race and ethnicity,
urging Marxist scholars to recognize that factors other than just
social class had to be taken into account to analyze the conditions
of Indo-American and Afro-American peoples in Latin America.
From a Marxist perspective, they focused on the state as an agent
of control over subordinate peoples defined in part by their race
and ethnicity.

"Indians" could be created by the state to serve political ends,
argued George Collier. State indianist policies segmented agrarian workers by indigenous communities, and the latter among
themselves, to blunt their consciousness for concerted working
class political action and also to prevent alliances among indigenous peoples. State policies also concentrated power in the hands
of local-level peasant leaders beholden to the state through clientel-
istic patronage relations. Indigenous local-level leadership remained "factional and impermanent." State-sponsored indianism
sought to secure "political compliance."

By the early 1990s, some indigenous peoples had begun to
develop an ethnic consciousness and to act politically in ways
unexpected from the earlier scholarship. Rodolfo Stavenhagen
focused on the relationship between the "unitary state" and the
"ethnic and cultural diversity of the societies of Latin America." He
noted that political movements of indigenous peoples gathered
force beginning in the 1970s. Intellectuals, church personnel, and
political activists acted to create an ethnic consciousness as a basis
for movement and party formation and for social and political
action. Such action often focused on cultural, legal, and linguistic

concerns as well as on regional autonomy from the state. The new groups forged international alliances to obtain political support and financial resources.

Race and ethnicity are not the exclusive concern of indigenous peoples or of the descendants of African slaves. Gino Germani was one of the premier students of the large and diverse mass European (mainly Spanish and Italian) immigration into Argentina. In 1914, the foreign-born constituted nearly half of Argentina's labor force. The "Argentinization of Argentina," to use Germani's term, was unusually complex and belated by Latin American standards.

A large number of Chinese were brought to Latin America, mainly as indentured servants. Bernard Wong discovered that the Kwantung province-origin Chinese in Lima, Peru, were much more likely than Chinese in New York City were with regard to U.S. culture and institutions to adopt Peruvian speech behavior and to learn the Peruvian way of social interaction; to enter the cliques, clubs, and institutions of Peruvian society; to eschew the formation of a residential "Chinatown" and to intermarry. Wong argues that state policies and social institutions in Peru were much more welcoming to the Chinese than in the United States. The experience of the Chinese in Lima, Wong notes, demonstrates that the Chinese can be assimilated, and that the deterrent to assimilation is found in the host, not in the sending, state and culture.

Takashi Maeyama made a somewhat different point with regard to Japanese immigrants, most of whom first came to Brazil as contract labor. These Japanese immigrants are "an associational people in an unorganizational society." Repressed (though not interned) during World War II, they responded to longer-term challenges by forming a myriad of voluntary associations for sports, religious, recreational, and business purposes. Such associations served to "enforce their identification with an original ethnicity" but also facilitated active participation in Brazilian national life.

There is, finally, considerable research on race relations in Brazil (less so on other Afro-Latinamerican countries), much of it conducted by Brazilian scholars. Florestan Fernandes pioneered much of this research, seeking to understand why Brazilians tended to deny that there might be a racial problem in their country even though race was, indeed, one factor in social stratification. He demonstrated that wealth, prestige, and power were racially concentrated and that such concentration had changed little since the abolition of slavery. Economic growth had reinforced the previous racial distribution of access to goods and opportunities. Color divisions among Afro-Brazilians, however, were barriers to their collective action to bring about changes. In order to forestall such changes, state and elite ideologies fostered the notion that Brazil was a racial democracy—a notion believed even by many Afro-Brazilians.

Fernando Henrique Cardoso analyzed the nature of color prejudice in Brazil. His approach was historical and dialectical, a way to observe history in the making, beginning with a study of slavery and its long-term effects. He emphasized the importance of studying race relations in the context of the totality of Brazilian society, not isolating Afro-Brazilians for the purpose of study. Cardoso also paid special attention to ideologies and the work place as means to understand the contexts for race relations.

Roger Bastide criticized what he called the São Paulo school (including Fernandes and Cardoso) of race relations for omitting the study of black culture. Bastide believed, instead, that blacks did have their own culture and that they had an effect on the shaping of culture in Brazil more widely. For example, he saw Afro-Brazilian religions as a manifestation of "the search for a power effective against the forms of power monopolized by the whites." In that way, black culture had a specificity of its own as well as means of resisting and of influencing the larger culture.

Abdias do Nascimento focused on the place of African culture in Brazilian art. For him, African culture had a clear impact upon the culture of Brazil as mediated by the descendants of the slaves. Such impacts have been evident in the plastic arts, dance, music, theater, literature, and film. In each case, his analysis serves also as a means to criticize the behavior of the Roman Catholic church and the Brazilian state.

Pierre-Michel Fontaine emphasized the utility of a comparative approach to understand race relations, situating the study of Brazilian race relations in a wider context. Fontaine called attention to the similarity of cross-national findings: the continued importance of the legacies of slavery, the absence of "racial democracy" except in the ideology of rulers as a means to prevent collective action by non-whites, the severe economic and status inequalities related to race, the lack of nationwide political activity by non-whites, and a preference for individual mobility over group action.

Carlos Hasenbalg and Suellen Huntington examined the Brazilian claim to racial democracy historically and in the light of a large economic survey conducted in 1976. Racism was found to limit upward mobility for all non-white Brazilians, pointing to a "break" in Brazil's color-class continuum. They showed that racial barriers were not merely a legacy of slavery but that they were re-created during each generation; whites from poor families have had much greater opportunities for cross-generational social mobility. They contend that ideological manipulation has sustained the myth of racial democracy despite the facts of racial inequality; such ideology has emphasized "whitening" as a means of advancement as well as symbolic integration through ritual kinship and the wider culture's acceptance of the Afro-Brazilian heritage in music and dance.

Thomas Skidmore, in turn, has analyzed the international challenges to the persistence of the ideology of Brazilian racial democracy. The ideology developed in part in counter-position to U.S. race relations; by the 1980s, however, the condition of U.S. non-whites had changed in important respects, above all their own collective political activity, for which there was no Brazilian parallel. Another pillar of the ideology had been the benign view of Lusophone race relations; Portugal, however, was the last imperial power with major colonies in Africa. The newly independent Angolan television network, moreover, even claimed that Brazilian television carried racist programs. Skidmore documented the Brazilian government's efforts to suppress ideologically inconvenient information and actions.

George Reid Andrews surveyed the history of black political protest in São Paulo to show that it was not accidental or sporadic but part of a wider ongoing pattern of struggle. He found that middle-class militants consistently experienced great difficulty in bridging the gap between themselves and poor and working-class blacks whom they sought to organize; class divisions within the black population posed systematic barriers to collective action. On the other hand, Andrews also found that "exclusionary regimes" (slavery and the military regime 1964-85) "tended to provoke the most effective" black political mobilization, whereas "inclusionary regimes" succeeded in weakening the impulse toward racial mobilization.

Howard Winant sharply criticized those who reduced racial distinctions in Brazil to mere adjuncts of class categories. He also believed that the efficacy of elite racial management has been exaggerated. Instead, he considered race as a "flexible," not a fixed, category that is discursive and constructed. Racial categories, Winant argues, are "permanently conflictual identities." Race relations were to be found not merely in structural facts but in the ways Brazilians used them to articulate their racial consciousness to each other. Ideology matters indeed, but it is an instrument in the hands of all, not just the elites.

Race and Class in Mexico

WOODROW BORAH

[Woodrow Borah is associate professor of speech in the University of California, Berkeley.]

THE BASIC PROBLEM of this paper* may be posed in a single question: What is an Indian? This question presented no difficulty for Hernán Cortés or any sixteenth-century conqueror. Any of the people found in the New World at the time the white men landed and all of their pure-blooded descendants were "Indians." Furthermore, Indians could be rather easily distinquished from whites or blacks by physical appearance and such cultural characteristics as food, dress, speech, and a separate political organization. But today, rather more than four centuries after the fall of the Aztec capital, the question cannot be handled so easily. Three races have lived side by side in Mexico for a period a century longer than the entire historical experience of European settlement on our Atlantic seaboard. One race, the black, has almost complete disappeared. If one may judge by terms in popular and learned usage, whites and Indians remain, but they have been busy in each other's affairs and a very large group of mixed bloods or mestizos has come into existence. How today can one distinguish Indians from other groups in the Mexican population? And, if one can separate them out, just what is it that makes them "Indians"?

This problem is, of course, hardly peculiar to Mexico but rather is common to most countries of the Western Hemisphere. In the United States, the Bureau of Indian Affairs has met it by holding that an Indian is anyone legally subject to its jurisdiction or descended from anyone who at any time has been legally subject to it. But this solution, although extremely useful to the bureau, cannot be of much value to the scholar. It has, moreover, the very real difficulty of presenting us with legal Indians, one of whose parents may have been born in Hamburg or Brooklyn, and who, indeed, may not have more than a clear sixteenth or thirty-second of Indian blood, if that much.[1]

---

* A paper read at the meeting of the Pacific Coast Branch of the American Historical Association, at Vancouver, British Columbia, on December 29, 1952. This paper arises from observations and impressions during a year's travel and study in Mexico, 1951–1952, made possible by the John Simon Guggenheim Memorial Foundation.

[1] See Frank Lorimer, "Observation on the Trend of Indian Population in the United States," and H. L. Shapiro, "The Mixed-Blood Indian," in The Changing Indian (a symposium edited by Oliver La Farge, Norman, 1942), 13–18 and 20–27.

The Mexican government's statistical services have been faced with this problem in their attempts at periodic counts of the population. The first official census in 1895 classified inhabitants by race, apparently using as the basis whether the individual declared himself to be Indian or was judged to be so by the census reporter. This method was so unsatisfactory that it was dropped in the Porfirian counts of 1900 and 1910. A second criterion, used in all three Porfirian counts, was language. If the individual spoke an Indian tongue rather than Spanish or another Old World language, he could be held to be an Indian; but by this criterion, Mexico had very few Indians, far too few to suit the officials of the Mexican Revolution, which allegedly had been fought to vindicate the rights of a great submerged Indian mass. Accordingly, the census of 1921 again attempted a direct classification by race. Apparently this was done on much the same basis as the count of 1895, and was as clearly unreliable. In the 1930 census, straight classification by race was dropped again, but classification by language was extended to separate out not merely people who spoke only an Indian language, so-called *indigenas monolingües*, but also those who, while claiming knowledge of Spanish, also spoke an Indian tongue. Although the category undoubtedly included traders and others who had learned an Indian language, presumably the bulk of these so-called bilinguals might be held to be Indians even though they were in the process of moving toward exclusive use of Spanish and so ceasing to be Indians in any linguistic sense. The census of 1940 tried yet another approach, and for the first time, in addition to the linguistic classification used in 1930, adopted a classification by cultural traits; that is, by type of clothing and shoegear, the presence of wheat bread in the family diet, and the type of sleeping arrangement. Presumably the family which wears peasant dress, goes barefoot or in sandals, eats corn tortillas to the exclusion of wheat bread, and sleeps on the ground or on a *tapexco* may be classed as Indian. Virtually the same method has been retained in the 1950 census.[2] But this method of classification, since it employs basically economic tests, equates the Indian with the poverty-stricken and declares that that portion of the Mexican population which belongs to the lowest economic level is to be considered "Indian." It is evident that the government statistical services are still groping for a sound basis of classification.

[2] Manuel Germán Parra, Introduction to *Densidad de la poblacion de habla indigena en la Republica mexicana* (México, 1915), 13–14. For the 1950 census, see Mexico, Secretaría de Economía, Dirección General de Estadística, *Septimo censo general de población 6 junio de 1950*, vol. *Oaxaca*, pp. 18, 22, 745–746.

The same problem of defining just what is an Indian in Mexico has also received a great deal of attention from anthropologists, *indigenistas*, and civil servants.[3] They, too, have their difficulties, as may be seen in the experience of the Smithsonian's Institute of Social Anthropology, which after selecting Tzintzuntzan for examination as a Tarascan Indian market town very rapidly came to the conclusion that it was studying mestizos.[4] The basis for classification in this instance was language. The discussions among civil servants and scholars have tended to revolve around four sets of criteria, summarized by Dr. Alfonso Caso in an often-cited article[5] written in an attempt to quiet the disquieting discussion. These criteria are: physical appearance, culture, language, and loyalty.

By physical appearance are meant those somatic traits presumed to be characteristic of Indians; such as stocky build; dark-brown or reddish skin color; high cheek bones; straight, coarse black hair, and so on. This basis for selection suffers from the simple fact that, on the one hand, a substantial number of individuals in so-called Indian centers do not have these characteristics while, on the other hand, they are to be found in millions of Mexicans whom no one would dream of denominating Indians. It is apparent, as Caso himself points out, that there has been racial mixture on so vast a scale that it extends back into the "Indian" centers; and Caso concludes that this set of criteria at best can serve only as an indication rather than proof that an individual is Indian.

Using culture as the basis for distinction involves, of course, the assumption that there are distinct Indian cultures, or at least cultures sufficiently distinct to set their members apart as Indians. Manuel Gamio, who has had a long and truly distinguished career of attempts to improve the lot of the Indians, has proposed that the cultures of the various towns be broken down into traits and that these traits then be studied in order to classify them as to origin—Spanish, Indian, and mixed. If a town's culture showed a majority of Indian traits, the inhabitants of the town could then be known with assurance to be Indians.[6] Aside from the practical difficulty that, before the lengthy studies needed for such determination could be carried out, all of the Indians involved

---

[3] The literature on this problem is enormous. I cite only a few of the pertinent items.

[4] George M. Foster, assisted by Gabriel Ospina, *Empire's Children: The People of Tzintzuntzan* (México, 1948), 30–31.

[5] "Definicion del indio y de lo indio," *América indígena*, VIII (1948), 239–247.

[6] "Consideraciones sobre el problema indígenas," *América indígena*, II (1942), no. 2, pp. 16–23, and no. 3, pp. 15–19.

might have passed over into mestizo category, there is the further difficulty, as Caso points out, that cultural intermingling has been at the
least as prolonged and as deep as racial mixture. This process has gone
so far that many cultural traits considered clear proof of the individual's
being Indian, such as the wearing of the *calzón* and leather sandals, use
of the wooden tipped plow, membership in *cofradías* or *mayordomías*,[7]
are demonstrably of European derivation. I suspect that, were Gamio's
proposed studies carried out, except for the few hundreds of Seris and
Lacandones, no community or group in Mexico could be found to have
retained a majority of preconquest aboriginal traits. Another serious objection to cultural criteria as now used is that they are almost entirely
economic, and so the category measured turns out to be poverty.

Language, the third of Caso's criteria, is really a cultural trait emphasized because of its convenience. There can be no doubt that listing
people who speak an Indian tongue gives us a fairly firm category. Yet
this method gives surprisingly little comfort to those who have what we
might call a vested interest in detecting Indians, for they complain that
it omits many people who should be considered Indians but who have
now switched to Spanish.[8] Caso manages to extend the language criterion
considerably by suggesting that even in the instance of Spanish-speakers,
the language of the mother must be taken into account. Presumably
this device would catch a fair number of recent refugees from the status
of linguistic Indian.

The fourth of Caso's criteria and the one which he declares to be the
most important is psychological: loyalty to an Indian community. This
conception is based upon a shrewd appreciation of the fact that the
dominant unit in the organization of Mexican economic and social life
is the town. Hence the family which lives in an Indian town, accepting
its ways and habits of thought, must be considered "Indian." Furthermore, permanent settlement in an Indian community would bar the
assimilation which a family living in a non-Indian society would be
under heavy pressure to accept. The criterion, however, is subject to
an extremely serious objection: it leaves us with the fundamental
difficulty at one remove, for how are we to rate towns as Indian? And
so the problem still remains.

---

[7] *Ibid.*

[8] See Germán Parra, *op cit.*, 14–15; José E. Iturriaga, *La estructura social y cultural de
México* (México and Buenos Aires, 1951), 93–98; Julio de la Fuente, "Definición, pase y
desaparión del indio en México," *América indígena*, VII (1947), 63–69.

A fifth criterion for establishing what is an "Indian" that has been suggested by a number of scholars for Latin America as a whole is the right to redress for historical injustice. Those groups are Indian, they say, which are entitled to reparation for the wrong of the conquest and for the long burden of depressed status during the colonial period, which has left them living in primitive conditions today. This is an interesting suggestion, and it is made even more interesting by some of its ramifications. Two writers point out that among the Negroes of the Caribbean there are groups living in primitive conditions who qualify for special treatment as Indans on grounds of historical wrong and acceptance of aboriginal customs. On the other hand, groups among the Uruguayan peasantry who live in equally primitive and poverty-stricken conditions, cannot be held entitled to special treatment because, being essentially of European descent, although they undoubtedly can show a long history of depressed status and so of injustice, they cannot exhibit the specific kind of historical injustice needed to qualify as Indians.[9] This conception of redress for historical injustice is, of course, at the root of much of Indian legislation in the United States, and in Mexico it has dictated many of the special pro-Indian measures adopted since the revolution. Yet the criterion cannot be held to provide a workable basis for sorting out Indians from other elements of the population without long genealogical inquiries most likely to be of immediate benefit only to unemployed historians. It suffers, moreover, from the objection that most of the mixed-blood population can make the same claim for redress.

It is apparent that, with the exception of language, none of the criteria suggested provide workable methods for distinguishing "Indians" from the rest of the Mexican population, and that reliance upon all of them is not likely to solve the problem. I suggest further that language, which permits separation on a fairly easy basis (although one that is fast vanishing), does not measure a truly significant difference for anything except the study of language. We are not dealing here with groups so held apart by language, bulwarked by differing governmental structures, economies, and traditions, that they feel themselves to be different and are therefore easily distinguishable. Rather, in Mexico we are dealing with groups subject to the same general government and system of local organization, held in the same general economy, and receiving the impact of the same general cultural influences for four centuries. Within each lin-

---

[9] Oscar Lewis and Ernest E. Maes, "Base para una nueva definición práctica del indio," *América indígena*, V (1945), 107–118, esp. 115–118. See also Manuel Gamio, "Consideraciones sobre el problema indígena en América," *ibid.*, II (1942), no. 2, pp. 16–23.

guistic group there have been, since shortly after the conquest, sufficient administrators, chiefs, traders, and other men of substance necessarily versed in Spanish to serve as channels for a fairly free entrance of Iberian cultural traits. From the Spanish-speaking mass there have come similarly administrators, priests, traders, and businessmen who have had to operate upon and within the linguistically different group and who have served likewise as channels for the infiltration of outside influences. Hence differences in language may have slowed up assimilation but can hardly be said to have arrested it. The matter may be summarized in the simple inquiry whether there exist basic differences in culture—clothing, techniques, religion, outlook, and aspirations—between a Tarascan-speaking peasant and the Spanish-speaking peasant of similar economic and social status living near him, or between an Otomí-speaker and his Spanish-speaking neighbor. I think not, and the attempt of *indigenistas* to include in the category of Indians precisely such Spanish-speaking peasants is evidence to support my judgment. Further evidence is present in the extent to which Spanish has penetrated the Indian tongues. Elsie Clews Parsons estimated that a clear quarter of Zapotec vocabulary is derived from Spanish, and it seems likely that an equal or greater proportion holds for most other Indian tongues.[10]

The difficulty in finding adequate criteria is especially noteworthy since a relatively large and well-subsidized group of scholars associated with government-backed anthropological studies or working in institutes for the advancement of Indians have been searching for a clear means of distinguishing those who should be their charges. Moreover, in Mexico the intellectual movement claiming to vindicate the rights of the Indians by exalting the Indian heritage in the Mexican past and in many instances by reviling the Spanish, has had a passionate interest in proving the survival among the Mexican population of a substantial number of Indians as a separate element of the population.

The overwhelming pressure is thus to find Indians. The fact that there is, nevertheless, difficulty in arriving at a clear definition of an Indian suggests that there is serious difficulty with the whole conception. Indeed, a number of scholars, recognizing that there is difficulty, have suggested that the term be confined to pre-Conquest populations and such cultural traits as can be clearly shown to be of direct descent from them without European admixture.[11]

---

[10] *Mitla, Town of the Souls* (Chicago, 1936), 20–21.

[11] Julio de la Fuente, "Discriminación y negación del indio," *América indigena*, VII (1947), 211–215.

Yet the term "Indian" is in general use in Mexico today, and the question may properly be asked: What do people mean when they use it? The term no longer seems to be racial in significance. It also omits urban populations and appears to be applied exclusively to rural groups. Furthermore, within rural society it is applied to people who are characterized by adherence to older customs in dress, diet, organization of work, religion, speech, and culture in general. These customs on examination turn out to be a colonial amalgam of aboriginal and European traits. The backwardness of the people denominated Indian—and such it is since it vanishes in most instances whenever and wherever economic circumstances permit—is imposed in some instances by isolation but almost invariably by a grinding poverty. It thus appears that the basic criterion is economic, and that the term Indian today designates in Mexican popular and even learned usage the more primitive and poverty-striken part of the peasantry. Similarly, the complementary term *mestizo* has come to mean in rural usage not a mixed blood but a shopkeeper or person of middle class economic position and a mode of life nearer to more recent European, i.e., city customs. The justice of these statements is evident, it seems to me, in the fact that, with few and notable exceptions, the aspirations of the so-called Indians are not to secure opportunities to maintain ethnic distinctness, autonomy within the national structure or even complete freedom from it, but merely to secure an easier life with more conveniences. They are therefore not a separate ethnic group but a depressed group within a single culture which they share with those they envy.

It is thus clear that the term "Indian" which at the time of the conquest denominated groups culturally and racially distinct from the Spanish, has come through the centuries with the blurring of racial and cultural differences, to designate a depressed class within a single society. Clearly behind this change in meaning lies a prolonged amalgamation of races and cultures of a remarkable depth and effectiveness which constitutes one of the most important processes in Mexican history but also one largely ignored by anthropologists and historians. Many of the omissions Lesley Simpson has pointed to lie in this area.[12] I should like to make a few additional comments.

At first glance there is apparent a contrast in the operation of the factors of race and culture. During the entire colonial period, perhaps 250,000 Europeans migrated to the present area of Mexico; since inde-

---

[12] In a companion paper, "Mexico's Forgotten Century," *Pacific Historical Review*, XXII (1953), 113–121.

pendence, perhaps 300,000 more, at a guess, may have settled in the Republic. Although social and economic advantage favored the survival and more rapid increase of their descendants in most of their mixtures, yet no more than perhaps a quarter of the elements entering into the present mixture of races in Mexico is generally thought to be of European origin. The bulk of the remaining three-quarters is thought to be of Indian racial origin.[13] In terms of descent, then, although fundamentally mixed, Mexico is predominantly of Indian origin.

In terms of culture, however, although we are dealing again with a fusion, the proportions are reversed. Most cultural traits are of European origin, so much so that anthropologists studying a number of Mexican villages have commented that they thought they were studying sixteenth-century Spanish towns.[14] The process seems to have been one in which there has been continuing and deeper implantation of European cultural items. Indeed, virtually every new item has been of Old World origin so that the original Indian cultural elements have been steadily reduced in number and importance in folk life.

The implantation of European cultural traits has proceeded at unequal rates: most rapidly and directly in the Spanish cities and areas adjacent to them, more slowly in rural areas farther away from urban centers and with few Spanish settlers, slowest of all in isolated areas far from roads and with almost no Spanish settlers. But in all Mexico there have been few areas so remote that European culture has not penetrated the aboriginal one to form the stable amalgam that we know as colonial. The word colonial suggests further that the development of this mixed culture was fairly complete some time before the rupture with Spain.[15]

Of the agencies that worked to bring about fusing of Spanish and aboriginal cultures in this colonial amalgam, we have, I think, been aware of the work of the church and its *doctrineros*. The few people who have thought about the matter agree that they were probably the most important agency in introducing European elements, not merely new techniques of cultivation, new plants, domesticated animals, the new religion, but also new legends, new ideas of healing and witchcraft,

---

[13] See Nathan L. Whetten, *Rural Mexico* (Chicago, 1948), 52–53.

[14] See, for example, Ralph L. Beals, *Cheran: A Sierra Tarascan Village* (Washington, D.C., 1946), 210–213. George M. Foster, "Report on an Ethnological Reconnaissance of Spain," *American Anthropologist*, LIII (1951), 311–325.

[15] Whetten uses the term "Indian-colonial" to describe this amalgam, which he believes to have been developed shortly after the conquest. *Op. cit.*, 355–356.

new standards of value, and new forms of group organization.[16] On the other hand, they relentlessly extirpated much of the aboriginal culture.

We have not given due weight to the Spanish administrators: *alcaldes mayores, corregidores,* their lieutenants, and other lesser officials, as culture bearers of the European. Such men often settled in Indian towns, bought up lands, opened general stores, and very often in alliance with the native *principales* developed illegal but highly lucrative enterprises, most of which involved introducing new ways and linking the Indians to the general commercial system of the ciites. One of the great values of *compadrazgo* relationships among the Spanish was that they provided bonds for economic alliance that successfully evaded the blood relationship restrictions in the Laws of the Indies. The operations of local officials were so effective in New Spain that the viceregal government never felt it necessary or even desirable to introduce the *repartimiento de mercancias* which was used in Peru to force the natives into commercial activity. I suspect also that the local officials were deriving large enough yields to have little interest in the Peruvian device or may even have opposed it. All of this was, of course, in addition to the tribute of one peso silver a family, which tended to force the Indian population to secure cash either by working for the Spanish or by selling them commodities.

Of surprise to me has been the discovery of the extent to which Spanish, mestizos, and mulattoes, all of whom served as bearers of European culture, infiltrated Indian areas. The unattached Spanish males who descended upon Indian towns to live upon them and enjoy their women were numerous enough to bring forth repeated regulations, none of which seems to have had effect. But, although such vagabonds contributed greatly to the woe of the towns where they chose to pause, they also contributed greatly to the mixing of blood and the introduction of European culture even though it may not have been in terms that the *doctrineros* approved. On a par with such activities and probably indistinguishable from them were those of the *arrieros,* who travelled with their pack trains over a large part of New Spain. On a completely legal level, there was extensive settlement of Spanish merchants and ranchers in the Indian towns. Over a number of generations their techniques and ways of life could not fail to have effect. The role of the hacienda in

---

[16] George M. Foster, "The Significance to Anthropological Studies of the Place of Origin of Spanish Emigrants to the New World," *Acculturation in the Americas* (Chicago, 1952), 292–298; Beals, *op. cit.,* 210–213; Parsons, *op. cit.,* 479–544.

penetrating and remaking the Indian mass has already been mentioned by Simpson.

Thus far I have dealt with some of the European agencies operating to introduce European culture. A number of writers have depicted the Indians as a sullen passive group enduring rape, exploitation, and cultural mongrelization with resentful resignation. Such studies as we now have show that the situation was more often quite the reverse. Within two decades after the conquest, Mixtec merchants were traveling by caravan and in Spanish ships to Sonsonate in Central America to buy the prized cacao and bring it back for sale in their own towns and the great market of Mexico City. Within three decades after the conquest, the Indian trader with his pack animals and Indian attendants, peddling Indian and Spanish wares, became fairly common along the roads of New Spain. Many of the caciques very rapidly adopted Spanish ways, and set themselves up as Hispanized gentry, living on tributes from their towns but developing substantial estates as entailed patrimonies. Another potent agency of mixture must have been the workmen and servants who were drawn into Spanish employment. Many of these remained near the Spanish centers as cultural mestizos who had broken all ties with their towns of origin. But a substantial group must have returned to bring new ways and perhaps new blood to their communities. Even without the operation of these groups within the Indian communities, it seems unlikely that any economy maintaining a large network of local and regional markets with constant travel and interchange would have remained immune to new techniques and new ways. The highly developed *tianguis* or market system, which we know existed, meant that the Indian centers could not remain sealed in a hermetic envelope of self-sufficiency, and never did. The evidence to date, then, shows that the Indians positively accepted and even searched out European cultural traits to adopt.

The rate at which implantation and adoption of European cultural traits took place must have varied widely, but it seems likely that the new mestizo colonial culture was well toward formation in and near the Spanish centers by the late seventeenth century. In the 1690's the Spanish authorities were seriously concerned because many of the Indians of Mexico City had become so completely European in dress that they could not longer be distinguished from Spaniards.[17] In the rest of the country, the new culture would have become dominant by the

[17] Order of July 18, 1692, Mexico City, *MS*, Archivo General de la Nación, Mexico, *Indios*, XXIII, 60–61.

middle of the eighteenth century. By then, or certainly by the end of the eighteenth century, racial mixture had proceeded so far that there were few pure bloods left in the country.[18]

The coming of independence with its freer entrance of Europeans and European wares and ways meant acceleration of change in Mexico. The nineteenth and twentieth centuries have witnessed an even larger amount of mixing of European blood and the steady introduction of more European cultural elements so that the colonial cultural fusion is progressively becoming more European. The political and economic movements of Mexican republican history have greatly speeded up the change. The Laws of the Reform, especially the dissolution of community land holdings, meant weakening the power of towns over their members and so speeded up adoption of new ways. The accelerating formation of the great landed estates, which created a landless and rootless rural working class, must have opened the doors wider to change. The railroads and, more recently, highways have also improved communications so that many communities now find themselves no longer isolated. In recent years the products of the new factories have been offered at sufficiently low prices to work a revolution in dress, travel, and amusement.

I have said that there are certain notable exceptions to the general process of assimilation. In Sonora the Yaquis maintain a tribal organization in opposition to the Mexican state and cling to their traditional ways.[19] In Quintana Roo certain Maya villages containing descendants of peons who retreated into the jungle at the time of the War of the Castes, also have a separate organization. On examination, however, both of these groups show clearly that they have the culture of the colonial amalgam and, in fact, have a distinct admixture of white blood as well. They are mestizos who participated in the general cultural mixing until the middle of the nineteenth century, when they revolted against peonage and seizure of their lands. They have attempted to find a permanent structure for resistance in a romantic reversion to Indianism, setting up an independent, anti-Mexican tribal structure which is a new creation.[20] These groups had lost their ethnic separateness, but,

---

[18] This is the opinion of Sherburne F. Cook.

[19] Julio de la Fuente, "Discriminación y negación," *op. cit.*

[20] For Quinta Roo, Robert Redfield, *The Folk Culture of Yucatan* (Chicago, 1941), 49–57. That the Yaquis were assimilated becomes clear if one remembers that they were part of the Jesuit mission system and continued to be a relatively peaceful group for nearly a century after the expulsion of the Jesuits.

having developed a new one, they may properly be called Neo-Indian. The Huichols also may fall in this category. Some other small groups on the periphery of European penetration are probably truly Indian in the sense of showing an uninterrupted relationship to pre-Conquest cultures. The three hundred Lacandones in the jungles of Chiapas and Campeche and the hundred and fifty Seris slowly dying in Sonora are certainly distinct both in race and culture,[21] but they are insignificant in the larger picture.

Regional loyalties which are beginning to emerge as significant, such as those of the present-day Mixtecos and Istmeños are, it seems to me, proof of the extent of the general assimilative process rather than evidence against it. Regional consciousness tends to supplant loyalties based on language or tribal descent, as in the case of Tehuantepec and Juchitán or the Isthmus in general, where regional attachment obscures a sense of kinship with Zapotecs elsewhere.[22] It is significant that regional consciousness embraces all racial mixtures and classes within the area. Indeed, its most vocal adherents and propagators turn out on examination to be middle and upper class, clearly mestizo, and very often of families recently settled in the region. Furthermore, the major influence in developing regional consciousness and the legends associated with it is the schoolteacher of the national Secretaría de Educación Pública. The new regionalism is proof that in this sphere administration by the federal government has been effective.

With few exceptions, then, it seems to me that Indians have disappeared in Mexico as separate ethnic groups. The search for Indians embodies a romanticism which ignores the sweeping amalgamation of races and cultures that is the most striking feature of Mexican history since the conquest. The term "Indian" has come in current popular usage to designate the most poverty-stricken and retarded dwellers of the countryside. It has to do with economic status, and our thinking on Mexico would be much clearer if we abandoned the word "Indian" to archaeologists and human biologists in favor of the more accurate term "peasant."

---

[21] See Robert Redfield, "The Indian in Mexico," *Annals of the American Academy of Political and Social Science,* CCVIII (March, 1940), 143, for a list of Indian groups outside the Mexican political organization. His list includes groups like the Tarahumara, who are clearly mestizo in culture.

[22] See the comment of Julio de la Fuente, "Definición, pase y desaparición" *op. cit.*

ON THE CONCEPT OF SOCIAL RACE IN THE AMERICAS

Charles Wagley

This paper was written while in residence at the Center for Advanced Study in the Behavioral Sciences.

The present paper is concerned with a limited aspect of race relations in the Americas, namely, with the systems of classification of people into "social races" that have been used in the past and are used today in our American societies. The term "social race" is used because these groups or categories are socially, not biologically, defined in all of our American societies, although the terms by which they are labeled may have originally referred to biological characteristics. (Wagley, 1952, p. 14). Such terms as 'Negro", "white", "Indian", or "mulatto" do not have genetic meanings in most of our American societies; they may in one society be classifications based on real or imaginary physical characteristics; in another they may refer more to criteria of social status such as education, wealth, language, and even custom; while in still another they may indicate near or distant ancestry. Thus, a man with identical physical characteristics might be classed as a mulatto in Brazil, a Negro in the United States ,and perhaps a *mestizo* in Mexico. In this paper, the point of view is taken that the way people are classified in such social races in a multi-racial society tells us in itself much about the relations between such groups. More specifically, the criteria for defining social races differs from region to region in the Americas. In one region *ancestry* is stressed, in another region *socio-cultural* criteria are emphasized, and in still another, *physical appearance* is the primary basis for classifying people according to social race. This produces in each of these regions a different number of social races and different structural arrangements for race relations. The different ways that each region conceives social races reflects the relations between people of diverse biological and cultural origin within a larger society.

13

To understand how these different classifications of social race came about and the different functions they have played in the various nations, it will be helpful to look at some of the simple, and relatively well-known facts, regarding the formation of the populations of our American nations. All of our American nations are multi-racial in some degree. Biologically speaking the population of the New World has been formed by three racial stocks - the Amerindian of Mongoloid derivation, the African Negroids, and the European Caucasoids. Each of these three racial stocks has contributed in different proportions in the various regions of the Americas. The Amerindian predominated in the highland countries from Mexico south to Chile; the Negro formed numerically the most important element of the population in the lowland region from southern United States, into the Caribbean, and on the South American mainland south into Brazil; Caucasoids have contributed in greatest numbers in the northern and southern most extremes of our continents, namely, in Canada and northern United States and in Uruguay, Argentina, and Chile. Yet, everywhere the three racial stocks have each contributed in some degree to the contemporary populations.

Likewise, throughout the Americas, the process of intermixture between the three racial stocks began early - almost at once after the arrival in the New World of the Europeans and their African slaves. In the highland countries, the Spanish *conquistadores* mated freely with Indian women and by the end of the 16th century, people of mixed Spanish-Indian ancestry were relatively numerous throughout the highland countries. Furthermore, in Mexico and also in other highland countries, a considerable number of African slaves were imported to work in the mines and on the plantations, the majority of these Africans were males and they too mated with Indian women. Their offspring added to the racially mixed population and further complicated the types of mixtures present in colonial society.

Likewise, in the tropical and semitropical regions of the Americas, a similar process of race mixture began soon after 1500. At first, the Spanish, Portuguese and even the English mated with Indian women. But since the Indian population was sparse as compared to the highlands and since many tribes were soon decimated as the result of contact with Europeans, such unions were not numerous and did not in general produce a large European-Indian mixed population as it did in the highlands. Still, in certain areas of the lowlands European-Indian populations were important; in Brazil, the *mamelucos,* the children of Portuguese fathers and Indian mothers, became relatively numerous in the late 16th century and in Paraguay where the Spanish *conquistadores* lived as the owners of veritable harems of Indian women, a mixed European-Indian group soon became the most important element of the colonial population. But, throughout most of the tropical lowland region, the formation of a mixed population comparable to that in the highlands awaited the arrival of the flood of African slaves.

From the middle of the 16th century until the end of the 18th century, this region received literally millions of Negroes, mainly from West Africa. The story of miscegenation of the European slave owners with their female slaves is so well known that it need not be documented here. Such unions were probably most frequent in Brazil and in the West Indies between Spanish, Portuguese, and French males and Negro women. This has been attributed, particularly in the case of the Portuguese, to a lack of prejudice —even considerable attraction— toward women of darker hues. (Cf. Freyre, 1946, p. 4). But, the men from these Latin countries were not alone in being attracted to Negro women. The Dutch and the English also mated frequently with Negroid women. Although the laws and social pressure against miscegenation were stronger in the English colonies (and later in the United States) than in the colonies of other European powers, there is no doubt that miscegenation was almost as frequent. This is attested by the large mulatto population which took form in the British Islands and in southern United States. By 1850, for example, about one-twelfth of the slave population of the United States and over a third of the "free" Negroes were said to be of mixed Negro-Caucasoid ancestry. (Frazier, 1949, p. 67).

Miscegenation took place also on a large scale even in those regions which are today predominantly European. In Canada during the 18th and early 19th century, the so-called *metis*, the offspring of French fur traders and Indian women, outnumbered Europeans in western Canada. In Argentina, *mestizos* (Indian-Europeans) greatly outnumbered people of European ancestry until after the middle of the 19th century. In both Uruguay and in Argentina, there were an appreciable number of mulattoes and Negroes during the first half of the 18th century.[1] There have been numerous "explanations" for the disappearance of these people of Negroid ancestry and the large number of *mestizos* in Argentina and Uruguay; an example, is the explanation that they were killed off in the various wars.[2] But it should be obvious that they were almost totally physically assimilated by the great wave of European immigrants of the late 19th and early 20th centuries.

Throughout the Americas, the process of miscegenation between Caucasoids, Amerindians, and Negroes produced hybrid populations. It also produced a complicated social hierarchy in which racial appearance or ancestry was perhaps the most important criteria of rank. At first, this social-racial hierarchy was simple. Everywhere the European whites dominated by force the American Indians and/or the African slaves. In the social hierarchy the European whites were on top and the Indian and African were on the bottom. Caucasoid physical features were symbolic of membership in the "superior" social group, and Amerindian and Negroid physical features were symbolic of membership in the "inferior" groups. But within a generation, the process of miscegenation produced intermediate groups who were intermediate not only in their physical appearance but also in social status. During the early colonial period, it was usual to attempt to describe such people in terms of their mixed ancestry, their intermediate physical appearance ,and their intermediate social position. In order to account for these groups of mixed ancestry, and the intermediate social status accruing to them, it was necessary to develop a profusion of categories of social race, especially in those regions where intermixture of the component racial stocks was greatest.

In Brazil, in addition to the *brancos* (whites), *Indios* or *Indigenas* (Indians), and *pretos,* there were *mamelucos* (Indian-Portuguese), mulattoes (Portuguese-Negro), *cafusos* (Negro-Indian) *cabras* (Portuguese-mulatto) as well as terms for other mixtures. (Cf. Ramos, 1944, p. 205). For Mexico, Aguirre Beltrán has brought together a series of systems of classification of social race or, in other terms, the system of castas that took form in the 17th century; in each of these systems a long series of ancestral types and degrees of intermixture, each with its relative position in accordance with "closeness" to full Spanish ancestry, are listed. Thus ,in the system described by Aguirre Beltrán (pp. 166-172), there are in addition to *bermejos* (i. e., whites or Spaniards) and *indios* (Indians); *negros* (Negroes) divided into two categories; mulattoes, divided into seven categories; and *mestizos,* divided into five categories. Although these were color categories, they also were based upon other anatomical characteristics such as hair, lips, and nose. Ancestry was often specified; a mulatto *morisco,* for example, was specifically "the offspring of a Spaniard and a *mulata" (op. cit., p.* 167). Likewise, throughout the Caribbean region there was a proliferation of social racial categories based primarily on skin color but also upon ancestry. Perhaps the most elaborate of these is the system ascribed to Haiti in the 18th century by Moreau de Saint Mery (1797, Tome I, pp. 68-88). Saint Mery explained the system by attributing to all men 128 parts (almost like genes). Thus, a *blanc* (white) has 128 parts white, a *Négre* (Negro) 128 parts black, and the offspring a *mulâtre* (mulatto) 64 parts white and 64 parts black. In addition, he listed also *sacatra* (8 to 23 parts white), *griffe* (24 to 39 parts white); *marabou* (40 to 48); *quateron* (71 to 100); *métif* (101 to 112); *mamelouc* (113 to 120); *quateronné* (121 to 124) and finally a *sang-mêlé* (125 to 127). (*Op. cit.*, p, 86).[3]

Even within the southern United States, the slaves were often differentiated according to such ancestral types as *mulatto, quadroon* (one quarter Negro ancestry), *octaroon* (one-eighth Negro ancestry) and *mustie* (near white). Although still slaves, these people of intermediate ancestry were considered by their owners to be more intelligent, brought higher prices in the slave market, and received preferred occupation on the plantations. Furthermore, they were more often freed (sometimes by their white fathers), and the "free Negroes", who were relatively numerous, especially in Charleston and in New Orleans, were mainly of mixed ancestry. (Frazier, 1949, p. 76 ff).

Everywhere in the Americas, these early systems of classification of people emphasized ancestry as well as physical appearance as their dominant criteria. They also represented a preoccupation with the intermediate social position of such groups between the dominant Caucasoids and the Negro slaves and the subjugated American Indians. But for several reasons, such elaborate systems of classification soon became unworkable and impossible to maintain. First, they could not possibly be extended in complexity to account for all possible mixtures. As mating took place not only between whites, Indians and Negroes but also between individuals of the growing variety of race mixtures, the number of categories theoretically had to be amplified. According to one system reported for Mexico, the type called *Ahi-te-Estas* illustrates the absurd lengths such classifications could be extended. The *Ahi-te-Estas* was a person born of one *coyote-mestizo* and one mulatto parent. A *coyote-mestizo*, in turn, was a person born of one *chamizo* and one Indian parent and a *chamizo* was the offspring of one *coyote* and one mulatto. (Whetten, 1948, pp. 51-52). Obviously, as mixture between the various types continued, such systems became even theoretically impossible to maintain.

Second, while most of the systems described ancestry, they also implied either explicitly or implicitly that individuals of a given category would share in general a similar phenotypical appearance; that is a person who was a mulatto of one white and one Negro parent would have a physical type intermediate between Caucasoid and Negroid. This was roughly so, as long as it involved mating between individuals of two distinct racial stocks. But, as soon as the situation involved the mating between the intermediate types themselves, physical appearance no longer was so indicative of ancestry. Not all individuals, even offspring of the same parents, who had three white ancestors and one Negro ancestor, for example, had a similar phenotype. The genetic process of transmission of physical characteristics does not work like the combination of chemical elements. Rather the genes of the parents sort themselves out quite distinctly in the different progeny. It was perfectly possible, therefore, to have two individuals both of whom were by the criteria of ancestry *moriscos* (i. e., one Spanish and one mulatto parent according to the same complex scheme mentioned above for Mexico) but who by the criteria of physical appearance could be placed in different categories. If one were dark in skin color, he would be a mulatto (one Spanish and one mulatto parent); the other lighter in skin color might be an *albino* (one Spanish and one *morisco*).

But perhaps the most important reason that such complex schemes were destined to fall out of use was the fact that socio-cultural criteria were not only implied by a term for a category but soon came into play in placing an individual in such groups. In the 16th century, the terms *gaupuchin, criollo,* Negro, and Indian in Mexico described with relative certainty not only a physical type but also the occupation, wealth, education, and language of a group. Similarly *preto* (Negro) in Brazil in the early period implied slave status and *branco* the status of a free man. But soon throughout the Americas, in greater or lesser degree, a conflict began to develop between classification of an individual by either ancestry or physical appearance and these social and cultural criteria. Thus, soon there was the anomaly of those individuals who were in terms of ancestry and/or physical appearance Indians and *mestizos* but who were in terms of language, dress, education, wealth and other social and cultural characteristics Spanish "whites". Or, there were free people of Negroid ancestry and physical appearance who by socio-cultural criteria should be mulattoes or even whites. Clearly a Spanish-speaking individual who was wealthy could not be classed with the people living in an isolated and primitive village despite his Amerindian physical appearance and ancestry nor could a black professor be classed with the black workers on a plantation. Social and cultural criteria became entangled with criteria of ancestry and phenotypical appearance, further complicating and confusing these systems of classifying people by social race.

18

During the 19th century ,and to a certain extent as a reaction to the idealistic creeds of the new American republics, there was a trend everywhere of resolving this conflict between the classification of people simultaneously by physical appearance, ancestry, and socio-cultural status. The conflict became especially acute as abolition came in the regions with a large slave population and as social and economic mobility increased the number of people who were Negro, mulatto, Indian, *mestizo,* or other intermediate types in physical appearance but "white" in accordance with social and cultural status. Everywhere there seems to have been a simplication of the systems of classification of people by social race. Numerous intermediate types based primarily upon ancestry and color disappeared from official usage, but not entirely from the popular vocabulary in many regions and countries. In Spanish America all of the intermediate types of the so-called *"castas"* fell out of general use and such broad categories as *mestizo, ladino,* and *cholo* came to be used. In Brazil, at least such terms as *pardo* (literally "brown") and *caboclo* (meaning any lower class rural person of mixed ancestry) supplanted the more elaborate terms once used for intermediate types. In the United States, although mulatto was used on several occasions as a category in taking the census, the terms for various degrees of Negro-white ancestry disappeared from general usage. But more important a basic difference, perhaps already apparent in the earlier periods, appeared between the different regions and countries in the Americas as to the criteria used in classifying people by social race. And, this difference in criteria has continued into the twentieth century to set the frame of reference for "race relations" in the different regions. This difference consists of making use of, or even of placing greater weight upon, one of the three sets of criteria for classification mentioned above, namely, *ancestry, physical appearance,* or *socio-cultural status.*

Broadly speaking the United States stands apart from most of Latin America in making use of ancestry almost exclusively in defining who is a Negro and who is a white. Curiously, during slavery more weight had been given to social and cultural criteria; despite the fact that many slaves were of obvious mixed ancestry, it was their legal condition that placed them in a slave category. And, during slavery a relatively large group of free people of color had taken form who stressed their intermediate brown color and their intermediate social position between the slaves and the whites. But, by the late 19th century, there was a decided shift in the criteria used to classify people as to social race and the possibility of a social race of mulattoes, intermediate in physical appearance and social position, was precluded. The dominant whites were able to establish a rule of descent based upon ancestry which states that anyone who has a known Negro ancestor is a Negro. This rule became a law in many southern states.

Thus, the system of classification of people by social race was reduced to a two-fold castle-like system of "Negroes" and "whites". Not even the fair skinned individual with Caucasoid features with a remote Negro ancestor can be classed as a "white", although thoroughly adapted in occupation, education, social graces, and economic position to middle or upper class status. This did not prevent a large number of such people, however, from "passing" as whites (i. e., assuming the status of a white by migrating to a locality where one's ancestry is unknown); and it did not prevent the "Negroes" themselves from making use of the other criteria of physical appearance and social and cultural status in determining rank within their own "caste".

The formation of this system of two "caste-like" social races was, of course, the reflection of, and a result of, the pattern of relations between Negroes and whites that took form after abolition. It provided a structure favorable to a system of segregation. With but two groups vis-à-vis each other, without intermediate groups, segregation in schools, housing, public conveyances, restaurants, and other public meeting places was feasible. The difficulties of segregation under another system of classification of people by social race is brought home strikingly if we allow ourselves to imagine the complexities of segregation, if the intermediate position of mulattoes, *quadroons,* and *octaroons* were recognized nowadays in the United States. If segregation on the basis of but two social races is considered costly to the nation, then it would have been prohibitive to provide at least parallel facilities for four or five separate social racial groups. In the United States, by emphasizing ancestry combined with a rule of descent, a system of two caste-like social races with little mobility between the groups has been amenable to segregation and productive of tension.

In the region of the Americas which consists of Mexico and Guatemala, (and this probably also applies to Ecuador, Peru, and Bolivia which have large Indian populations) the classification of people by social race took another form in the 19th and 20th centuries. In this region the emphasis has been placed mainly on the criteria of social and cultural status, almost to the point of ignoring the criterion of physical appearance. Furthermore, except within certain local communities, ancestry as a criterion for membership in a social race has little or no importance. In each of these countries, there continues to be a relatively numerous segment of the population classified as *"indígenas"* or Indians, an intermediate social race called *mestizos* in Mexico and *ladino* in Guatemala, and finally a social race which we might call the whites. The difficulty in distinguishing between Indian and *mestizo* (or *ladino*) on any basis except social and cultural criteria such as language, custom, community membership, costume, and self-identification is well known and need not be restated here. It is enough to say that physical appearance seldom serves as a criteria to classify a person in one of these two groups. Similarly, although a highly educated man in the city might have Indian-*mestizo* physical features, it would be difficult to classify him as *mestizo* or *ladino*. The answer to this lack of emphasis upon physical appearance as a criterion for classifying individuals as to social race is that there is an almost imperceptable gradation of physical appearance from Amerindian to Caucasoid running from the Indians to the whites. This is the result, of course, of a high frequency of miscegenation between Indians and Europeans in the colonial period and, as we shall see, from continued biological intermixture even today.

Yet, something must be said concerning the importance given to ancestry as a criteria for social racial classification in Mexico and Guatemala. It is probably true that in these countries (and in the other Indian countries) ancestry still is an important criterion for membership in the group of "aristocratic families" who claim "pure" European descent, sometimes conveniently forgetting an Indian ancestor in colonial times. Yet such "aristocratic families" form but a small segment of the "whites". But ancestry as a criterion is also important in some regions of Mexico and Guatemala where in local communities it is applied with a force that is reminiscent of the United States. In the region of southeastern Guatemala, in the northwestern highlands of the same country, in highland Chiapas, and perhaps in other local regions where relations between Indians and non-Indians are tense, it is virtually impossible for an Indian *within his own community* to overcome the criterion of ancestry and to become a *mestizo* or *ladino* on the basis of social and cultural criteria. This creates a twofold caste-like situation similar to that in the United States, (Tumin, 1952 and Gillin, 1951). But there is a vast difference between the two situations. Lacking emphasis upon physical appearance as a criterion for social race ,it is easier to "pass"; and it is always possible for an Indian who leaves his home community and who acquires the social and cultural criteria of a *mestizo* or *ladino* to lose his identification as an Indian and to be accepted as a *ladino* or *mestizo*. Furthermore, the emphasis upon ancestry producing a caste-like structure is far from universal within these nations. In other regions of Guatemala, for example, it is possible for, at least, the offspring of a man of known Indian ancestry who acquires *ladino* culture to be classed as a *ladino;* and in Mexico, Beals speaks of whole Tarascan communities which "may gradually shift through time from being Indian to being regarded as *mestizo*". (Beals, 1955, pp. 9-22). There could be no clearer witness to the emphasis upon socio-cultural criteria to the almost total exclusion of the criteria of both

21

physical appearance and ancestry than the fact that *a whole community may change its social race presumably without a change in physical type.*

Like the caste-like system of the United States, the system of social race of Mexico and Guatemala reflects the kind of relationship that has taken form between the various groups. Indians are looked down upon and discriminated against by non-Indians. But contrary to the situation of the Negro in the United States, they are not being identified by the indelible criteria of physical appearance nor are they placed in the "inferior" group by ancestry. There is then a greater possibility for individual, and even whole community, mobility from Indian to *mestizo*. Furthermore, while the system of social race of the United States actually perpetuates itself, the system of Mexico and Guatemala seems to contain in itself the seeds of its own destruction. Miscegenation between Negro and white in the United States only adds to the numbers of the Negro group. In Mexico, intermarriage between Indian and *mestizo, mestizo* and white, or Indian and white generally adds to the *mestizo group*. The offspring of such unions are generally raised within the *mestizo* culture and thus become *mestizos*. And, this system promotes continued racial intermixture; an individual who is an Indian in physical appearance but classed as a *mestizo* on the basis of social and cultural criteria will most probably mate with a *mestizo* and his or her offspring will be raised as such. At least, theoretically, it is only a question of time until such populations may be entirely classed as *mestizo* by social race and social differentiation will be entirely in terms of socio-economic classes.

Finally, in Brazil and in the Caribbean region of the Americas the system of classification of people by social race has taken still another turn. In this region, emphasis has been placed upon physical appearance rather than ancestry or social and cultural criteria.[1] In this region of the Americas there are no striking cultural contrasts, comparable to that between Indians and non-Indians in Mexico and Guatemala. There are religious beliefs and rituals of African origin in some localities, such as Haiti and northern Brazil. And, in some parts of the Caribbean a creole language, partially derived from Africa, is spoken by peasants. These cultural and linguistic traits are often identified with the Negro, but they are hardly limited to those classed as Negroes, being shared by a wide variety of people regardless of social race. The criteria of ancestry seems only to be important in the Caribbean and Brazil, as in Mexico and Guatemala, among those segments of the population who seek to prove the purity of their European derived lineage. For the large mass of people, ancestry seldom acts to place an individual in a particular social race. But the indelible mark of physical appearance, with the highest prestige accruing to Caucasoid features and the lowest to Negroid features, remains as an important set of criteria by which to classify people in social races. Throughout this whole region, such features as color, the shape of the lips, hair texture, and the shape of the nose are closely analyzed in order to place an individual in the proper social race.

But in populations such as those of Brazil and the Caribbean where mixture between the racial stocks has been so extensive, there is a tremendous variety in physical appearance. Although such terms as mulatto, "people of color", and *pardo* (literally "brown") are used to described a wide range of physical types, intermediate between Negro and white; in popular usage, there are a numerous set of more precise terms describing people of intermediate social races. In one Brazilian community, for example, with a highly variegated population Hutchinson lists eight categories and several sub-categories descriptive of people of Negro and mixed Negro-white descent. In this one community individuals are classified as: 1) *preto*, Negro or dark black; 2) *cabra* (female *cabrocha*), lighter in skin color than *preto*, hair less kinky, and facial features less Negroid; 3) *cabo verde*, dark skin color but straight hair, thin lips, and narrow nose; 4) *escuro*, literally a "dark man" but meaning dark skin with some Caucasoid features —generally used for an individual who does not quite fit the three above categories; 5) *mulato*, yellowish skin color, kinky to curly hair, thin to thick lips, narrow to wide nose— sub-types are light and "dark" mulatto; 6) *pardo*, "brown" a classification most often used officially for census and the like, but sometimes applied in common parlance for individuals who "are closer to the white than a light mulatto"; 7) *sarará*, light skin, reddish blend but kinky hair, and Negroid facial features; and 8) *moreno*, literally brunette — "excellent" fair skin, dark curly hair, features... much more Caucasoid than Negroid". (Hutchinson, 1957, p. 120). Similar systems of multiple categories have been reported for other Brazilian communities by Harris (1956, pp. 119 ff.), Nogueira (1955, p. 460), Pierson (1942, pp. 135-136), Zimmerman (1952) and Wagley (1953). Although none have as many category-terms as that described by Hutchinson, all contain from four to seven category-terms.

Likewise, the societies of the Caribbean are characterized by the classification of people by a series of terms describing their social racial appearance and again, as in Brazil, such features as skin color, nose, lips, and hair textures are the diagnostic traits. In the French West Indies, for example, there are such terms as *béké* (white), *mulâtre clair* (or *blanc*) *mulâtre foncé* or *noir* (dark or black mulatto), *câpre* (straight hair but mulatto or Negroid features), *chabin* (rather dark skin but Caucasoid features and light colored hair), *négre* (Negro) and *congo* (very black with "bad" features). (Leiris, 1955 and Debrueil, 1957).

23

Similar systems of multiple categories of social race are reported by Henriques (1953) for Jamaica, by Steward and associates (1956) for Puerto Rico, and by Crowley (1951) for Trinidad, to cite but three examples.

What is distinctive about these Brazilian and Caribbean systems of social race is that they are actually a continuum from Caucasoid through the various degrees of mixed physical appearance to Negroid. They do not in themselves form social groups that interact vis-à-vis one another as to Indian and *mestizo* in Mexico, and Negro and white in the United States. They are a way of describing and classifying individuals acording to physical appearance, but this is but one way that these societies classify people. The position of an individual in the hierarchy of social race combined with education, economic status, occupation, family connections, even manners and artistic abilities places one in his or her proper rank. Each of the categories of social race is divided by socio-economic classes, although it must be said that the largest proportion of Negroes are in the lower classes and the majority of the upper class is white since educational and economic opportunities for mobility have not been generalized. Thus, neither Negroes, mulattoes, *pardos,* whites or any other social race acts as a group nor attempts to improve their situation as a group. This situation is thus less conducive to discrimination and segregation on the basis of social race. Yet given the presence of relatively rigid socio-economic classes deriving out of the colonial period, class discrimination and segregation often functions in a manner superficially similar to "racial" discrimination and segregaton.

In addition, these Brazilian and Caribbean system of social race provide a situation favorable to individual mobility. An individual does not "pass" from Indian to *mestizo* nor from Negro to white. Rather by means of improving his education, financial position, and other qualities capable of modification within a lifetime, he may move up in the class structure while still remaining "low" in the hierarchy of social race. People politely try to ignore such an individual's disability of personal appearance. There is then a noted tendency in such societies to "lighten the skin" of individuals who have the other qualifications for high rank, except personal appearance or social race. Thus, a man who is dark in skin color and who has Negroid features but who is a well placed engineer or physician, for example, may be classed as a *moreno* or a *pardo* rather than as a "dark mulatto" or "Negro". Thus, even physical appearance is often perceived subjectively, distorted by other criteria. Only a sense of the ridiculous prevents Brazilians from carrying out literally their traditional statement: "A rich Negro is a white man and a poor white man is a Negro" and in some degree this applies to the Caribbean as well.

Each of these systems of classifying people by social race produces a very different structural situation for "race relations". Each defines social races in different terms. In Mexico and Guatemala (and elsewhere in the Indian countries) an "Indian" is defined in socio-cultural terms. In the United States, a Negro is defined in terms of ancestry alone. In the Caribbean and in Brazil, social racial types are defined on the basis of physical appearance as modified in their perception by the total social status of the individual. These different definitions of social race have different consequences and thus so-called "race problems" are different problems in each of the three regions. In the United States, the definition of the Negro in terms of ancestry has created two caste-like social races and the race problem of the United States consists of the struggle of the Negroes as a group to achieve equality of opportunity vis-à-vis the whites. But, even if equality of opportunity is achieved by the Negroes in the United States, the continued presence of the two self-perpetuating caste-like social races will provide a situation highly conducive to continued competition and conflict. In Mexico and Guatemala, it might be said that there are also two self-conscious groups —Indians and non-Indians— and that the Indians act to improve their position as a group vis-à-vis the non-Indians. Yet, by defining Indian in cultural terms, the way is always left open for individuals and whole communities to transform themselves from Indians into non-Indians. In the Caribbean and in Brazil, the situation is highly permissive to individual mobility. Social races do not form self conscious groups and "race relations" do not take the form of interaction between "racial" groups. Despite low position in the hierarchy of social races, individuals may improve their total position in society by achievement in other ways. Yet, rigid barriers of socio-economic classes operated to reduce the mobility of all people of low socio-economic status; the "race problem" of this region is to a large extent a problem of socio-economic classes.

Yet, in all of our American societies classifications of social race, however defined, remain as a basis for formal or informal social, economic, and even legal discrimination and often as the basis of prejudice against whole groups. In view of the extensive miscegenation between people of all three major racial stocks and between the various intermediate types and especially in view of the criteria used to define these social races, it is clear that nowhere do such categories as mulatto, Negro, Indian, *mestizo* and even white have genetic validity. But, in the course of our American experience such racial terms have become entangled with social and cultural meanings and they remain as symbols out of the past of slavery, peonage, and cultural differences to plague a large segment of our American people.

NOTES

1   According to the estimate of the Argentine sociologist Ingeneiros (cited in Taylor, 1948, p. 56), the Argentine population contained in 1869 - 350,000 whites; 1,315,000 *mestizos;* 120,000 mulattoes; 3,000 Indians ;and 15,000 Negroes. It was essentially a mixed population.

2   This argument is again brought to life in a recent book, *La Vida Rural Uruguaya* by Daniel D. Vidait (p. 57), Montevideo, 1955.

3   Aguirre Beltrán gives examples of a series of "erudite" classifications which were set down in the early 19th century in New Spain which are as complex as that given by Moreau de Saint Mery. According to Aguirre Beltrán, these systems "fortunately never were carried into practice". (*Op. cit.,* p. 175). Like the "theoretical" system of Moreau de Saint Mery, they do, however, indicate the growing complexity of attempting to take into account the various types of intermixture.

4   In two brilliant essays (1955 and 1957) the Brazilian sociologist, Oracy Nogueira has examined the different consequences between "prejudice of color" (*"marca"* or *"côr"*) in Brazil and "prejudice of origin" in the United States. In my terms, this distinction is between the criterion of physical appearance (Brazil and the Caribbean) and ancestry (United States). I have drawn heavily in this from these two essays but I have attempted to stress the structural consequences of the use of these different criterion rather than their consequences in the type of prejudice.

WORKS CITED

1.—AGUIRRE BELTRAN, GONZALO. *La Población Negra de México,* 1519-1810, México, D. F. 1940.

2.—BEALS, RALPH. "Indian-Mestizo-White Relations in Spanish America", in *Race Relations in World Perspective,* edited by Andrew W. Lind, Honolulu, 1955, pp. 412-432.

3.—CROWLEY, DANIEL J. "Plural and Differential Acculturation in Trinidad", *American Anthropologist,* Vol. 59, No. 5, Oct. 1957, pp. 817-824.

4.—FRAZIER, E. FRANKLIN. *The Negro in the United States,* New York, 1949.

5.—FREYRE, GILBERTO. *The Masters and the Slaves,* New York, 1946, translated by Samuel Putnam.

6.—GILLIN, JOHN. *The Culture of Security in San Carlos,* Middle American Research Institute, Publication No. 16, New Orleans, 1951.

7.—HARRIS, MARVIN. *Town and Country in Brazil,* New York, 1956.

8.—HENRIQUES, FERNANDO. *Family and Colour in Jamaica,* London, 1953.

9.—HUTCHINSON, HARRY W. *Village and Plantation Life in Northeastern Brazil*, University of Washington Press, Seattle, Washington, 1957.

10.—LEIRIS, MICHEL. *Contacts de Civilisations en Martinique e Guadeloupe*, París, UNESCO, 1955.

11.—NOGUEIRA, ORACY. "Relações Raciais no municipio de Itapetinga", in *Relações Raciais entre Negroes e Brancos em São Paulo*, edited by Fernandes and Bastide São Paulo, 1955, pp. 362-554.

12.—NOGUEIRA, ORACY. "Preconceito Racial de Marca e Preconceito Racial de Origem", Annais do XXXI Congr. Internacional de Americanistas, São Paulo, 1955, pp. 409-434; "Côr da Pele a classe social", Seminar on Plantation Systems in the New World, San Juan, Puerto Rico, 1957 (mimeographed).

13.—PIERSON, DONALD. *Negroes in Brazil*, Chicago, 1942.

14.—RAMOS, ARTHUR. *Las poblaciones del Brasil*, México, 1944.

15.—SMITH, T. LYNN. *Brazil: People and Institutions*, Baton Rouge, 1954.

16.—STEWARD, JULIAN, *et al.* *The People of Puerto Rico*, Urbana, 1956.

17.—TAYLOR, CARL C. *Rural Life in Argentina*, Baton Rouge, 1948.

18.—TUMIN, MELVIN. *Caste in a Peasant Society*, Princeton, 1952.

19.—VIDART, DANIEL. *La Vida Rural Uruguaya*, Montevideo, 1955.

20.—WAGLEY, CHARLES. (Ed.) *Race and Class in Rural Brazil*, París, 1952.

21.—WAGLEY, CHARLES. *Amazon Town: A Study of Man in the Tropics*, New York, 1953.

22.—WHETTEN, NATHAN. *Rural Mexico*, Chicago, 1948.

23.—ZIMMERMAN, BEN. "Race Relations in the Arid Sertão", in *Race and Class in Rural Brazil*, edited by Charles Wagley, París, 1952, pp. 82-115.

27

COLOUR PREJUDICE IN BRAZIL

FERNANDO HENRIQUE CARDOSO

The results of the research carried out in Brazil on the relations between Negroes and Whites are contradictory on the question of the degree of reciprocal tolerance existing between these two groups of the population. That is to say that specialists disagree on the intensity of the colour prejudice in Brazil and on the manner in which it manifests itself.

These conflicting opinions on the process of adjustment between Negroes and Whites could, to a certain extent, merely reveal the existence of different patterns of relations according to the country's various socio-cultural regions. The diversity of interpretations could be but the reflection of the varying situations arising from inter-racial daily life. It can thus be shown that Donald Pierson's research on Whites and Negroes in Bahia, or Thales de Azevedo's and Wagley's research on North-East Brazil base prejudice on social class differences rather than on racial or colour differences [1], while the research carried out by Bastide and F. Fernandes on Sao Paulo accentuates the importance attached to reciprocal judgements related to social different-iations which occur as a result of different shades of skin and racial traits [2].

This hypothesis is not, however, acceptable. Recent research and theoretical criticism of the assumptions of Pierson and his continuators seem to refute the interpretations according to which colour barriers coincide with class barriers. Thus, while Pierson states that " the existing prejudice is a class prejudice, not a *racial* prejudice. It is the same type as the very strong prejudice existing within a colour group in the

---

[1] Donald PIERSON : *Brancos e Pretos no Bahia* ; Cia Ed. Nacional, S.-Paulo, 1945 ; Thales de AZEVEDO : *Les élites de couleur*, UNESCO ; Charles WAGLEY : *Races et classes dans le Brésil rural*, UNESCO, Paris, 1952.
[2] Roger BASTIDE and F. FERNANDES : *Brancos e Negros em S. Paulo* ; Cia. Ed. Nacional, S. Paulo, 1950.

United States "[3], Florestan Fernandes and Roger Bastide quite rightly declare that " it is evident that *colour prejudice* exists in the various regions of Brazil and penetrates into all social classes in varying degrees "[4]. The authors pass from this assertion (which, when it was made, did not correspond to a conclusion drawn from scientifically conducted observations) to a radical criticism of the interpretation proposed by Pierson since, according to them, the assertion that colour prejudice is more a form of adjustment between *social classes* than between *races* contradicts the selection of racial differences made with a view to being used to determine the Whites' negative opinion of Negroes. The works of Bastide, Fernandes and Oracy Nogueira (apart from their criticism of the classical interpretation of racial prejudice) show that the existence of a large amount of discrimination and prejudice not connected with the class problem, can be confirmed — in Sao Paulo at least [5].

Octavio Ianni, Renato Moreira and the author of this article carried out a relatively ample survey in four communities of Southern Brazil in order to increase the amount of information available on the behaviour and attitudes of Whites and Negroes in Brazil and with a view to verifying to what extent the analyses of Bastide and Fernandes could be maintained when confronted with other situations in racial coexistence. As guiding principles for this research, it was presumed that the varying social integration patterns in these four communities, the irregular rhythm of the process of their differentiation into social classes, their economic differentiation and the existence of different cultural groups, would involve various intensities of racial prejudice and specific aspects of this prejudice. In a sense, the research implied the " possibility " — although this was not very probable in view of the theoretical considerations pointed out above — that prejudice against Negroes varies from one region to another and may, in certain sectors, coincide with class barriers.

The communities were selected in order to represent entirely opposed situations with regard to the state of differentiation of their economic activity, the coefficient of

[3] PIERSON : *op. cit. ;* p. 402.
[4] BASTIDE and FERNANDES : *op. cit ;* p. 334.
[5] Oracy Nogueira's *Relations raciales dans le Municipe de Itapetininga* has been published in a book which also includes the research carried out by Bastide and Fernandes and whose general title is *Relations entre Nègres et Blancs en Sao Paulo*, Ed. Anhembi, 1955.

Negroes in their population and the proportion of immigrants to inhabitants. Consequently, we selected Porto Alegre which is highly differentiated as far as economic activities are concerned, being Southern Brazil's most industrialized and " urbanized " town and also a predominant zone of European immigration. Pelotas was our second choice because of its large percentage of coloured people and because it was the centre of a typical pro-slave-trade area, due to its dried meat industry. Inversely, the city of Curitiba — although it is also well urbanized — not only has one of the lowest percentages of coloureds but also has not yet come in contact with industrialization. Finally, Florianopolis, apart from being another example of urbanization without industrialization, has the particularity of being a city whose population is basically Luso-Brazilian (while Curitiba has a high percentage of European immigrants). Moreover, it is situated on an island where the slave-trade never flourished on a large scale as it was inhabited by Acorians owning small plots of land.

The results of these surveys have not yet been fully published [6], but the main outline of those that have been completed result in conclusions which are bound to be unexpected : " racial prejudice " acts in all four communities as a fundamental component of the process of inter-racial adaptation ; differences of intensity or forms of manifestation of prejudice are hardly significant. The differences can be attributed to the varying social structures referred to above, for there is no doubt that the " racially prejudiced person " has social functions that vary according to the type of organization and structure of each complete society. Thus, in Florianopolis in the past, the relatively violent domination of the Negro by the White took on a particular aspect, owing to the non-existence of the patriarchal pattern typical of the rest of Brazil — the coexistence of free work with slave work. The non-existence of material conditions capable of assuring the former a *seigneural way of life* caused differences of a racial *nature* between the two to be emphasized, to

---

[6] Only the following works have been pubilshed : F.H. CARDOSO and Octavio IANNI : *Côr e Mobilidade Social em Florianobolis* ; Cia Ed. Nacional, S. Paulo, 1960 ; IANNI : *is Metamorfoses do Escravo* ; Difusao Europeio do Livro, S. Paulo, 1962 ; CARDOSO : *Escravidao e Capitalismo no Brasil Meridional* ; Difusao Europeio do Livro. S. Paulo, 1962. Ianni's survey concerns the region of the Parana during the slave-trade. *Escravidao e Capitalismo* concerns the Rio Grande do Sul during the same period. For the present situation in the Rio Grande do Sul, see CARDOSO : *Os brancos ea ascensao social do negro em Porto Alegre,* referred to below.

compensate for the small inequality existing in social conditions of production as both lived by tilling the land personally and directly. The *lord's* discrimination against the *slave* could more easily be transformed, under these conditions, into the discrimination of the *White* — even the poor White — against *Negroes* as a whole, even the free. Racial discrimination was more easily maintained after the suppression of slave work because abolition naturally could not cause the physical differences to disappear [7]. In Pelotas, on the other hand, the adjustment based on traditional relations has persisted ; in this case, with closer coexistence in the same social space, the basic asymmetry governing their relations runs no risks. Similarly, there are differences in how conscious the Negroes of Porto Alegre are of their situation within a society compared with those of Florianopolis or Curitiba : these differences can be explained by the historical or structural particularities of the communities surveyed. Nevertheless, in all these communities, prejudice occurs in the same form as it is encountered in other regions.

All this goes to show that this phenomenon has its roots in the slave-trade and that it occurs persistently — with no great variations — in the various social situations of racial coexistence found in Brazil today. To be empirically confirmed, such a conclusion doubtless requires new investigations in the North-East where the authors mentioned at the beginning of this article seem to have found different results. However, this is not the fundamental aspect of the question. The greatest problem — from the sociological point of view — consists in determining precisely the relations between class and racial barriers.

The initial aim of the Southern survey was to determine precisely the effects which the position of Whites and Negroes in the class structure could have on the form of value judgements with regard to racial differences. Indeed, although the authors could, thanks to the results of the most recent scientific research and to their own experience of everyday life in Brazil, reject the idea that the existing prejudice is an expression of *class* and not *racial* values, they still had to analyse the connections between the *class situation* of the two and the social restrictions made in regard to their *race*. In our view, a white man's opinion of a *learned Negro* (doctor,

---

[7] Cf. the conclusions of CARDOSO and IANNI : *op. cit.* ; p. 236-237.

engineer or lawyer) would presumably show a more favourable degree of social acceptance than his opinion of a female
domestic servant ; conversely, the opinion of a white street-
porter of Negroes in general would be different from that of
a secondary schoolmaster.

The research based on the different intensities of prejudice
in relation to its structure reveals, to a certain extent, that
the Brazilian situation definitely has something which
distinguishes it from that of North America. When American
authors such as Pierson and Wagley tried to explain the
Brazilian inter-racial coexistence patterns and compare them
with North America's, it was not by chance that they finally
convinced themselves that Brazil did not, in fact, have " racial
prejudice ". As a matter of fact, not only do the ways in
which prejudice occurs vary according to the class situation
of the people involved, but the intensity of rejection of the
Negro varies in relation to his class position[8]. This means
that in Brazilian civilization there is nothing to compare with
the examples of Negroes being rejected by white men *in so
far as they are Negroes,* let alone any other attributes. Oracy
Nogueira rightly points out that, while prejudice in the
United States can be defined as " due to origin ", in Brazil
it becomes prejudice " due to appearance ", defined as follows :
" Any unfavourable disposition (or attitude) conditioned by
culture, relative to a part of the population that is branded,
either because of its physique, or because of its total or partial
ethnical origin, is considered to be racial prejudice ; when
this is based on a person's physical features, his gestures and
pronunciation it will be defined as *due to appearance* ; when
one can presume that the individual is suffering from the
consequences of the prejudice because he belongs to a specific
ethnic group, it will be defined as *due to origin* "[9].

The discovery that, in Brazil, Negroes are rejected as a
result of their physical appearance and not of their ascendance
has been made implicitly by the above-mentioned authors
who have emphasized the essentially sociological character
of this phenomenon among white Brazilians : " Racial prejud-

---

[8] This does not contradict the assertion made above concerning the varying
intensity and force of the prejudice in the various regions surveyed if one
considers that, *for each class situation,* there is a relative uniformity of the
standards of racial coexistence in the various regions surveyed.
[9] Oracy NOGUEIRA : *Preconceito racial de marca e preconceito racial, de
origen ;* in Anais do XXXI Congresso Internacional de Americanistas. Ed.
Anhembi, S. Paulo, 1955, Vol. I, pps. 416-7.

ice is one of the modalities of the phenomenon under consideration (prejudice in general), a modality wherein differences between races (whether real or imaginary) that are ethnocentrically represented, give rise to stereotypes... Thus, it seems to develop as a natural consequence of persons or groups belonging to different 'races' coming into contact, intermittently or continually, each time there is some connection between a specific physical trait and the type of occupation, wealth, standard of living, social position and the education of the persons concerned " [10]. The terms " race " and " racial differences " used in this context explicitly express an opinion of social value and not a biological connotation. Therefore, the same authors add : " The sociological significance of the notion of race has not yet been determined in Brazil. The expression ' coloured man ' (and other equivalent expressions) is used to describe Negroes and half-castes ; nevertheless, people known to have Negro ancestors and having certain very apparent negroid features are frequently considered to be ' white ' and are treated as such " [11].

The definitely socioligical nature of this prejudice and the selection of certain phenotypical features for defining Negroes have not only enabled " passing " (lighter skinned people passing the colour barrier) to take place on a large scale, but have also rendered the interpretation of the relation between class and colour barriers even more complicated. In fact, the existence of light-skinned half-castes who " pass " into the white group and succeed in climbing socially to the middle layers of the population may suggest to the foreign sociologist that there are no prejudices in Brazil.

The interpretation of the problem of the connection between racial and class prejudice in Brazil does not, therefore, depend on the analysis of this process whereby light-skinned half-castes are integrated into the white group ; it is what happens when persons considered as Negroes climb in society that must be examined. This does not imply that the acceptance of light-skinned mulattos is as generalized and free from tensions as it is made to to be. It is evident that the standards of *inter-racial adaptation* — and not *racial conflict* — which characterize Brazilian society, as well as the phenotypic definition of the Negro, enable " passing " to take place more

---

[10] BASTIDE and FERNANDES : *op. cit.* ; pps. 326-7.
[11] *Idem* : p. 327.

easily, but they do not eliminate the white man's subtle discriminations and veiled negative attitudes *vis-à-vis* the " socially white men ". In order to understand the connection between " class " and " race " better, it must be pointed out that the social ascension of persons that are sociologically considered as *Negroes* is more strategic than the social ascension and " whitening " of light-skinned mulattos.

Research carried out on relations between Negroes and Whites in Porto Alegre has enabled the problem to be discussed with this perspective in mind, because historical and sociological reasons have fevoured the forming — in this community — of a lower-middle-class sector within the Negro group [12]. Unfortunately, the results of our analysis do not enable us to hope that ascension is the solution to the " Negro problem ". On the contrary, it appears that even the traditional means of accommodation between the racial groups — which, while implying certain forms of social distance, also enable coexistence to be accepted on a formal basis — tend to break down when Whites are confronted with Negroes whose *social and professional status* is higher than theirs. For this reason, answers relatively favourable to coexistence during work (given in a survey carried out among the white population of Porto Alegre) give place to reticence when interviewees are asked to what extent they would tolerate working with Negroes senior to them [13]. Similarly, the acceptance — by non-coloured people — of the professional services of Negro doctors, lawyers, professors or dentists did not represent more, than 57.8 % of the answers.

It could be supposed — as a criticism of this data — that restrictions on the social acceptance of Negroes expressed verbally do not correspond to the actual attitude, but life histories and testimonies of middle-class Negroes in the Rio

---

[12] The use of slaves in semi-skilled and domestic occupations enabled the Porto Alegre Negroes to finld regular employment after abolition, and, thus, to fight against anomic tendencies within the coloured population. The fight against prejudice and for better living conditions began in this region in the 19th. Century. The Negroes of this city have thus been able to maintain an organized family and economic life and a few families have been able to occupy typically lower-middle-class social positions.

[13] The questions were as follows : " Would you accept to work with persons of another colour ? " " Yes ", 13. 8 % ; " No ", 66. 3 % ; indifferent, 20. 7 %. " Would you accept to work with persons of another colour if they ar senior to you at work ? " " Yes ", 21 % ; " No ", 45. 6 % ; indifferent, 33. 9 %. These results are given by F.-H. CARDOSO : " Os brancos e a ascensao social dos negros em Porto Alegre ", in *Revista Ahembi*, Ano X, No. 17, Vol. XXXIX, August 1960, pp. 583-596.

Grande do Sul enable those conducting the surveys to affirm that their relative isolation generally counter-balances their ascension. Whites belonging to the same social strata maintain formal relations with Negroes during work that are traditionally approved by inter-racial coexistence patterns ; however, they never live with them in their clubs, in family gatherings or in other circumstances that can be qualified as " society life ". On the other hand, middle-class Negroes have avoided their own masses for " class " reasons : as they do not lead the same kind of life as Negro workmen or employees, as they have few professional qualifications and higher intellectual needs, they have not found any possibilities to achieve the social expectations which inspired their conduct. This attitude often causes them to be stigmatized by the rest of the Negro population as traitors to the " race ". Since only a small number are involved, they do not even have the consolation of constituting themselves (with their own clubs, companies and pressure groups) into a social segment, as in the United States, limited by class and caste barriers but enjoying autonomy with regard to social necessities.

Since these results are taken from our survey conducted in Porto Alegre (where a large proportion of the population is of German or Italian origin) it could be thought that this social isolation is a result of the prejudices of the immigrant groups. Yet, on analyzing the answers to our questionnaire, we have been able to confirm that Luso-Brazilian families have slightly higher percentages of racial intolerance than families descended from immigrants in the answers they give concerning work situations. When interviewees are questioned on mixed marriage their reaction is naturally different : in this case, there is an extraordinarily high proportion of negative replies in both groups : answers to a question concerning possible marriage to Negroes (included in the questionnaire set to appriximately 4,000 secondary-school-students) were practically 100 % negative.

Considering these results, it is evident that prejudice against Negroes in Brazil — although based on their appearance and not their origin — nevertheless exists in the form of *racial prejudice*. Stratification into social classes also plays a part in the process of attribution of status. Now, instead of the prejudice giving way to class intransigence, the latter only adds a new dimension to the resistances met by the Negro : not only is he socially " inferior " but he is " inferior " because of his colour. For this reason, if he succeeds in

breaking class barriers, his colour gives away his humble
social origin. This acts like a magnet which draws the weight
of all negative opinion and what may be evidence of a danger
for the White : a Negro who " has left his place ". White
men, realizing the threat which middle-class Negroes present
to their position as the dominant social class, are redefining
their former attitude of racial " tolerance " and are now
denying the latter, who have become their equals socially,
the right to live on equal terms with them.

Consequently, the social ascension of Negroes in a class
society, far from implying the end of prejudice can —
contrary to what has been supposed — mean that a " Negro
problem " is beginning in Brazil in the very form in which
it exists in the United States.

FERNANDO HENRIQUE CARDOSO : *A Brazilian sociologist.*

Mass Immigration and Modernization in Argentina

GINO GERMANI

Harvard University

1. Introduction

CONTEMPORARY Argentina cannot be understood without a thorough analysis of the role of immigration in its development. In the first place, immigration was a powerful factor in the total process of modernization. In the second place, the intensity and volume of immigration caused a substantial re-alignment of the population: economically, socially, and politically. In no other country did the proportion of adult foreigners reach the level that it did in Argentina, where for more than sixty years foreigners represented around seventy per cent of the adult population in the capital city (which contained one-fifth to one-third of the total population of the country), and almost fifty per cent in the provinces which were heavily populated and economically important.

Immigration resulted from a conscious effort by the elites to replace the old social structure inherited from colonial society with a structure inspired by the most advanced Western countries. This plan was based on three assumptions: (1) massive immigration; (2) universal and compulsory education; (3) import of capital, development of modern forms of agriculture and a livestock-breeding industry, and heavy investment in social overhead capital, especially railways.

The principal aims of immigration were not only to populate an immense territory that had a low population density, but also to modify the *composition* of the population. Underlying this aim are other aspects of the plan: education, and the expansion and modernization of the economy. To understand these aims it is necessary to remember the point of departure for the elites which conceived and carried out national organization. Only then can we understand the essential role that immigration played in the transformation of the country, although there were consequences which were unforeseen and undesired.

The revolution that initiated the successful movement for national independence was led by an elite inspired by eighteenth century enlightenment. It was composed of creoles belonging to the upper urban class, especially from Buenos Aires. It was numerically very small, and its Western and modern (1800 style) outlook contrasted sharply with the traditional nature of the vast majority of the population, urban and rural (but mostly rural). The failure of the Independence elite to establish a modern state was basically the result of this contrast. The years of anarchy and autocracy did not fail to teach the modernizing elite a lesson. They saw that a modern national state could only be established on the basis of a transformed social structure and a change in its human composition. This attitude was reinforced by ideas about the role of racial factors and the national character. The intention of many was to modify the "national character" of the Argentine people in a way that would suit the political ideal of national organization to which these elites aspired. It was necessary to "Europeanize" the Argentine population, to produce a "regeneration of the races", to use Sarmiento's expression. Insurmountable limits in the psycho-social characteristics of the existing population made it all the more necessary to physically bring Europe to America (according to the well-known formulation by Alberdi).

2. A Century of Foreign Immigration

One of the first changes introduced by the new regime which replaced colonial rule in 1810 was to open the country to foreigners, thus eliminating the strict isolation enforced by the Spaniards in their colony. The governments of the following two decades stressed the need to attract immigrants. This was especially true of Rivadavia, who took concrete steps to create a stream of European immigration into the country. But these attempts were doomed to failure for the same basic reasons which destroyed the dream of establishing a modern national state soon after formal independence had been reached. Only a limited number of immigrants arrived in Argentina during the first two decades of independence, and in the next thirty years the Rosas dictatorship practically re-established the old colonial barrier against foreigners. In the second half of the century, after the downfall of the autocracy, immigration increased. The promotion of immigration became a formal function of the State, according to the 1853 Constitution. For nearly seventy years thereafter, European immigrants arrived in Argentina in a continuous stream, broken only occasionally by domestic events like the economic crisis of 1890 or by international upheavals like the First World War.

Of the nearly sixty million Europeans who emigrated overseas, Argentina received some eleven per cent, a proportion much smaller than that of the United States, but still considerably larger than that of any other immigration country.[1] But what really makes Argentina a special case is that the six and a half million foreigners who arrived* between 1856 and 1930 found a very small local population, estimated at 1,200,000 in 1856. This meant that for many decades the proportion of the foreign born was higher than that of the natives within many important sectors of the population.

During the first decade after 1853 immigration did not exceed a few thousand per year. But as soon as some of the more pressing internal problems were solved, the inflow of foreigners increased to an annual average of nearly 180,000 in the decade preceding the First World War. After the war, large-scale immigration resumed, deterred only by the great depression of 1930. From 1947 to 1952 there was another large inflow of European immigration, after which it practically disappeared.

Thus, three major periods can be distinguished in overseas immigration. The first stage ended in 1930, the second stage extends through the thirties and most of the forties, and the last stage corresponds to the period of post World War II. It must be noted that after the end of the first stage another stream of foreign immigration was added: immigration from the neighbouring countries, especially Bolivia, Paraguay, and Chile. This process became more important as the demand for industrial labor increased. But in many ways this stream resembles the mass internal migrations, which also occurred in response to industrial development.[2]

In Argentina, as in other immigration countries, not all the immigrants remained. A certain number of them returned to their native lands or emigrated to other countries. Unfortunately, available immigration statistics do not distinguish between permanent and transitory arrivals or departures. The figures for net overseas immigration included in Table I result from the difference between total departures and total arrivals for European passengers travelling second and third class.

TABLE I
NET OVERSEAS IMMIGRATION IN ARGENTINA. 1857–1965.

Years						Net immigration (in thousands)
1857–1860	.	.	.	.	.	11
1861–1870	.	.	.	.	.	77
1871–1880	.	.	.	.	.	85
1881–1890	.	.	.	.	.	638
1891–1900	.	.	.	.	.	320
1901–1910	.	.	.	.	.	1,120
1911–1920	.	.	.	.	.	269
1921–1930	.	.	.	.	.	878
1931–1940	.	.	.	.	.	73
1941–1950	.	.	.	.	.	386
1951–1960	.	.	.	.	.	316
1961–1965	.	.	.	.	.	206

Sources: Alessandro Bunge, "Ochenta y cinco", *Revista de Economía Argentina*, 1944; and information provided by the Dirección Nacional de Estadísticas y Censos.

It must be noted that the idea of permanent immigration is difficult to define. It is well-known that most of the overseas emigrants to South America, especially in the period under discussion, did not intend to become permanent citizens of the new country. Their chief motivation was to save enough money to return to their native villages and buy land.[3] This motive, which affected the assimilation of the immigrants, made difficult the interpretation of migration statistics. In any case, it must be noted that the "return" movement included, in addition to seasonal immigrants and temporary visitors to native lands, a number of permanent returns. These last were probably of two kinds: those returning because of their inability to adjust to social, economic, and personal conditions; and those returning because they had earned the money they desired.

TABLE II
NUMBER OF FOREIGN PASSENGERS DEPARTED FOR EVERY 100 ADMITTED (SECOND AND THIRD CLASS).

Years						Departed passengers
1957–1913	.	.	.	.	.	40
1914–1920	.	.	.	.	.	151
1921–1930	.	.	.	.	.	38
1931–1940	.	.	.	.	.	67
1941–1946	.	.	.	.	.	79
1947–1950	.	.	.	.	.	14
1951–1958	.	.	.	.	.	56

Sources: Alessandro Bunge, "Ochenta y cinco", *Revista de Economía Argentina*, 1944; and information provided by the Dirección Nacional de Estadísticas y Censos.

After the First World War seasonal immigration disappeared, and the high rate of departures since 1951 corresponds to the last cycle of overseas immigrants, whose assimilation became increasingly difficult.

*This figure refers to arrivals. For net immigration see Table I.

Almost half of the incoming immigrants were Italian, and a third were Spanish. A fifth of the total were Polish, followed numerically by Russians, French, and Germans. Italian immigration maintained its predominance throughout almost the whole period. In the decade following the First World War, there was a notable Polish immigration, which continued during the period of low immigration, becoming then the largest national group up to 1940. Russian immigration was high between the end of the nineteenth century and the beginning of the twentieth, and again in the decade following the First World War. In this same period there are major immigrations from Germany and other Eastern European countries. This inflow included a large proportion of Jews.

TABLE III

Net Immigration by Principal Nationalities. 1857–1958.

Years	Italian	Spanish	Polish	Others	Total
1857–1860	17	21	—	—	100
1861–1870	65	21	—	14	100
1871–1880	44	29	—	27	100
1881–1890	57	21	—	22	100
1891–1900	62	18	—	20	100
1901–1910	45	45	—	10	100
1911–1920	12	68	—	20	100
1921–1930	42	26	13	19	100
1931–1940	33	—	58	9	100
1941–1950	66	29	4	1	100
1951–1958	58	34	—	8	100
1957–1958	46	33	4	17	100

Sources: Alessandro Bunge, "Ochenta y cinco", *Revista de Economía Argentina*, 1944; and information provided by the Dirección Nacional de Estadísticas y Censos.

3. The Demographic Impact of Immigration

In 1869 Argentina had a population of a little more than 1,700,000; in 1960 it had become more than 20,000,000, thus growing almost twelve times in ninety years. Immigration decisively contributed to this extraordinary expansion. The proportion of foreigners to the total population does not accurately indicate the immigrants' contribution to national growth. For example, the proportion of immigrants in the labor force was especially large.

A number of demographers and other social scientists have in the past challenged the common-sense notion that immigration always involves an increase in the receiving population.[4] Malthus maintained that immigration would produce no lasting effect, since the available or potential resources would put an absolute limit on population increase. By different routes other authors have reached the same conclusions as Malthus, and in the United States a "substitution theory" was widely discussed.[5] It is

recognized now that the effects of immigration are quite complex. Most of these hypotheses cannot survive the test of facts, even though they continued to circulate as ideological arguments against immigration. In any case, nobody has contested the essential role of immigration in a sparsely-populated country like Argentina.

An estimate formulated by Mortara suggests the contribution of immigrants and their children to the Argentine population. Table IV indicates that the joint contribution of immigrants and their descendants to the national population exceeds the natural

TABLE IV

Components of Population Growth in Four American Countries. 1841–1940.

Countries	Native natural increase		Immigration		Immigrants' natural increase	
	%		%		%	
All America	. 163.0	70.9	36.0	15.6	31.0	13.5
Brazil .	. 28.6	81.0	3.3	9.4	3.4	9.6
Argentina	. 5.2	41.9	3.6	29.0	3.6	29.0
Canada .	. 8.0	78.4	1.0	9.8	1.2	11.8
United States	. 67.7	59.1	25.0	21.8	21.8	19.0

Summarized from Giorgio Mortara, "Pesquisas Sobre Populações Americanas", ESTUDOS BRASILEIROS DE DEMOGRAFIA, Monografía No. 3, July 1947.

increase of native population. In this sense Argentina represents an extreme case, even in comparison with the United States. With regard to the other Latin American states, it is clear that immigration made a crucial contribution to population growth. During the period 1869-1959, Argentine population grew more than ten times, while the population of another immigrant country like Brazil increased six times, and Chile, where immigration was practically non-existent, needed 110 years for its population to grow less than four times. Mortara has estimated that without immigration the population of Argentina in 1940 would have been 6,100,000 instead of over 13,000,000.[6]

The demographic impact of immigration was increased by the geographic concentration of the foreigners. About ninety per cent of them settled in the Buenos Aires metropolitan area and in the central provinces of the country, a region which includes no more than one-third of the national territory. This concentration was further intensified because most immigrants went to the cities. The urban counties contained a large majority of the foreign population. After 1914 this tendency was reinforced, and in the last census 68 per cent of the immigrants lived in the big cities.

TABLE V

Geographic Distribution of the Foreign-born. 1869–1960.

Years.	Buenos Aires Metropolitan area.*	Provinces of Córdoba, Buenos Aires, Entre Ríos, Mendoza, Santa Fé, La Pampa.	Rest of country.	Total
	%	%	%	%
1869	52	38	10	100
1895	39	52	9	100
1914	42	48	10	100
1947	51	35	14	100
1960	57	27	16	100

Source: Argentine National Census.
*Includes population in the rural sector of the area.

Finally, the proportion of foreigners in certain key sectors of the population was increased by the age and sex composition of European immigration. Over 71 per cent of the immigrants were male, and about 65 per cent were adults between twenty and sixty years of age. This proportion did not change significantly throughout the period of mass immigration.[7] This demographic concentration greatly affected the age and sex composition of the Argentine

TABLE VI

Distribution of the Foreign-born Population by Urban and Rural Counties.**

Counties including cities of population specified in 1947 Census.	1869 %	1895 %	1914 %	1947 %	1960 %
Buenos Aires metropolitan area	52	39	42	51	57
100,000 and more	5	10	12	12	11
50,000–99,000	3	3	3	3	2
2,000–9,999	34	42	39	30	25
Less than 2,000	6	6	4	4	5
Total .	100	100	100	100	100

Source: Argentine National Census.
**The counties were classified on the basis of the size of the major cities they included according to the 1947 Census. Each category of counties also includes a proportion of "rural" population (living in centers of less than 2,000 inhabitants). Such proportion was very small (in 1947) in the first two categories, but it was increasingly larger in the other categories.

population. The most important economic and social consequences were the great expansion of the labor force and an extremely high proportion of foreigners among adult males. The demographic effects of immigration on sex and age composition began to wear off after 1930, but in the last Census (1960) they were still visible. In 1960 most of the immigrants were concentrated in the older age groups. Two-thirds of the foreigners were more than forty years old, and nearly one-third was over sixty.

TABLE VII

Sex Ratio and Age Composition in Argentina. 1869–1960.

	Sex ratio			% 14–64 years old		
Census	Total population	Native-born	Foreign-born	Total population	Native population	Foreign population
1869	106	94	251	56.5	—	—
1895	112	90	173	57.9	48.6	85.0
1914	116	98	171	61.4	50.3	87.4
1947	105	100	138	65.2	61.9	83.7
1960	101	99	110	63.0*	61.3*	75.0*

Source: Argentine Census.
*Estimates on the basis of a sample of the 1960 Census.

4.   Impact on the Economic and Social Structure

The role of immigration in the rapid economic growth of Argentina can hardly be over-emphasized. However, it is very difficult to separate this role from its general context.   Immigration provided the labor needed to occupy the unexploited land and to develop the agricultural production which transformed Argentina from an importing country in 1870 to one of the principal world exporters.   At the same time immigration supplied the manpower to build a railroad system, public works, and housing, and to expand the commercial activities and the service sectors. Finally, it was the immigrant population which provided most of the labor and entrepreneurship in the beginnings of industrial development. But relative political stability and heavy capital investment were needed in order for this role to be carried out.

No less important was the contribution of foreign immigration to modification of the social structure. The system of stratification and many traditional social values were sharply affected by the overwhelming mass of foreign population.   The old creole stock was replaced by a new type which has not yet been clearly defined.

Immigrant participation in economic areas varied a great deal.   Such participation was not only a function of their original skills but also of the kind of socio-economic structure they found in the country and the conditions under which economic expansion occurred.

Most immigrants came from the poorer strata of their native lands.   About 41 per cent were peasants, 23 per cent were unskilled workers, and about 36 per cent had various manual and non-manual skills.   Up to 1890, more than 70 per cent of the immigrants were peasants, but this percentage decreased sharply in following years.   It is known that even those who were originally peasants did not remain in the rural areas. A considerable proportion went to the cities and worked in secondary or tertiary activities.

TABLE VIII

FARM AND NON-FARM OCCUPATIONS OF THE IMMIGRANTS. 1857–1954.

Years			Farm %	Non-Farm %	Total %
1857–1870	.	. .	76	24	100
1871–1890	.	. .	73	27	100
1891–1910	.	. .	48	52	100
1911–1924	.	. .	30	70	100
1925–1939	.	. .	39	61	100
1940–1945	.	. .	20	80	100
1946–1954	.	. .	41	59	100

Sources: Alessandro Bunge, "Ochenta y cinco", *Revista de Economica Argentina*, 1944; and information provided by the Dirección Nacional de Estadísticas y Censos.

The populating of the countryside through rural immigration was limited by the traditional distribution of land ownership and by the methods of the successive governments in subdividing and allocating the remaining public lands. Two facts must be recorded: throughout the history of the country, property tended to be concentrated among a relatively small number of families, with the consequent predominance of latifundium. These procedures caused serious difficulties in the realization of one of the declared aims of massive immigration: the settlement of European population in the deserted or semi-deserted rural areas of the country. This settlement was successful to a certain extent, but

TABLE IX

FOREIGN-BORN PER EVERY 100 PERSONS IN PRIMARY, SECONDARY AND TERTIARY ACTIVITIES. 1895–1947.

Activities				1895	1914	1947
Primary	.	.	.	30	37	18
Secondary	.	.	.	46	53	26
Tertiary	.	.	.	42	30	22
Total occupied population	.			38	47	22

Source: Argentine Census.

it was undoubtedly much smaller than what might have occurred if there had not been a predominance of latifundium.

In the second place, the traditional system of land distribution did not ensure peasant ownership of the land. For the whole massive immigration period, the so-called "colonization" was carried out through the intervention of commercial companies or individuals who took over the subdivision of the land and the organization of the "colonies", making these operations lucrative through what amounted to selfish speculation.

*Cattle ranches.

In many cases, the owners of vastly extensive properties in the more favored areas preferred to exploit their lands by means of renting or similar devices, rather than transferring their property.[8] We should also bear in mind that land exploitation often favored the permanence of large units; this applies not only to cattle breeding but also to extensive farming. Finally, insofar as agricultural and cattle-breeding activities developed, the land became increasingly valuable, thus making it less accessible to immigrants, who continued to arrive in great numbers. Very few immigrants acquired property after 1900. This meant that only a minority of the European peasants could settle in the country on the stable basis of land ownership. A considerable number were able to secure land only by renting, and the majority finally settled in the cities, returned to their own lands, or emigrated to other countries. Moreover, the limitations and conditions under which the immigrant appropriation of land occurred caused a great deal of instability for the peasant and his family. This was particularly true of the renters, for whom this situation meant almost always the last stage of their social ascent, since they never became owners of the land they worked on, and moreover were frequently displaced from one area to another in search of better conditions.[9]

In summary, we can say that, while the tremendous increase in agricultural production was mainly the result of European immigration, such participation rarely developed into ownership. Frequently it was subjected to the conditions established by the title-holders of the land, who either rented it to immigrants or hired them as laborers or managers. In the cattle-breeding sector the immigrants' participation was even lower. The development of this sector began earlier. Because of its nature and traditions, its expansion and modernization was undertaken by the big Argentine landowners. Also, labor was provided by the native-born population, traditionally related to this kind of occupation. The rural creole workers, who did not adapt to agricultural work, either migrated to the cities or gathered in the *estancias*,* devoted to stock breeding.

These circumstances explain the varying participation of foreigners in the different economic activities. The figures given in Table X, although fragmentary, give a clear illustration of the foreigners' participation in the different levels of ownership and control of the primary sectors. Only ten per cent of the landowners, and no more than 22 per cent of the

TABLE X

PROPORTION OF FOREIGNERS IN SOME OCCUPATIONAL
CATEGORIES IN THE PRIMARY SECTOR. 1914.

Occupational categories	Foreigners per every 100 persons in each category
Landed property owners in general* .	10
Owners of cattle-breeding operations .	22
Renters of cattle-breeding operations .	34
Administrators, directors, managers of cattle-breeding operations (including owners and renters) .	44
Administrators, directors, managers of agricultural operations (including owners and renters) .	57

Source: Third National Census.

*Excluding the city of Buenos Aires.

owners of stock-breeding operations, were immigrants. The proportion of the foreign-born approximates the national average in the labor force only in the census category, which lumps together administrators, managers, and renters. In the agricultural enterprises foreigners reach higher proportions than in the national average (but still below the proportion among the owners of commerce or industry).

TABLE XI

PROPORTION OF FOREIGNERS IN SOME OCCUPATIONAL
CATEGORIES IN THE SECONDARY AND TERTIARY SECTORS.
1895–1914.

Occupational and economic category	1895	1914
Owners of industry* . . .	81	66
Owners in commerce** . . .	74	74
Personnel in commerce (workers and white collars)* . .	57	53
Personnel in industry (workers and white collars)* . .	60	50
Liberal professions . . .	53	45
Public administration** . . .	30	18
Persons in artisan and domestic activities**	18	27
Business administration** . . .	63	51
Domestic service workers** . .	25	38

Sources: *Second and Third National Census: special census.
**Second and Third National Census: population census.

The result of the agrarian policy which conditioned foreign immigration was not so much to populate the extensive semi-deserted rural areas as to create an abundant urban labor force and on a lesser scale a rural one, since a minority of the landless immigrants remained in the countryside as salaried peons. The growth of the cities, the emergence of industry, and the resulting transformation of the social structure were consequences of this process, and in turn originated new social conditions affecting the ruling elites. All these circumstances contributed to shaping the geographic and economic distribution of foreigners.

Immigrant participation in certain sectors was preponderant. As we have seen, in the secondary and tertiary sectors foreign participation in the cities was always higher than within the total labor force. The rates included in Table XI indicate the varying proportions of immigrants in some activities. According to the 1895 Census, the conduct of about 80 per cent of industry and trade was in the hands of foreigners. Among salaried personnel the proportion was lower but always higher than in the national average. The native born predominated in artisan activities, other domestic industries, the public bureaucracy, and domestic services.

The data presented in Table XI are too incomplete to offer a basis for systematic observation. Nevertheless, the figures are useful at least to illustrate the orientation of immigration and its distribution in the different strata of the occupational structure. Apparently, in the process of Argentine society's transformation, foreigners were preferentially placed in the emerging strata. Entrepreneurs, workers and managers in strategic areas of industry and commerce were at the root of modernization. They predominated especially in the middle class and the new urban industrial proletariat, both categories belonging to the new economic structure which was replacing traditional society. It was precisely in the older economic activities that the native born continued to predominate, as well as in activities directly related to government operations.

From the economic point of view the recent industrial activities were of only secondary importance. A larger proportion of industry was directly linked with agriculture and stock breeding. This sector, some 40 per cent of the total industrial production, included the industries devoted to perishable goods and the meat-packing plants, which must be considered the only "large scale" industries of that time. The remaining industry was devoted mostly to the production of inexpensive and low-quality consumer goods for the lower strata, while the market for the elite and the upper middle class was mostly supplied by imports. Many of the industrial enterprises were small,[10] and did not represent a key sector in the national economy of the time, even if they supplied two-thirds of the total consumption of the internal market.[11] Nonetheless, the growing number of local industrial enterprises eventually played an essential role in the transformation of Argentine society. The rapid growth of the population and the general economic expansion stimulated the internal market. This resulted in a great increase in the number of industrial and business enterprises and a growth of public services. This expansion not only absorbed immigrant labor but stimulated a crucial change in the social structure: urbanization and the rise of a large middle class. By 1895 the urban population had increased to 37 per cent, and by 1914 the majority of the inhabitants lived in urban centers. As noted earlier, this increase was mostly due to the immigrants, whose proportion was about 50 per cent of the population of all ages in the Buenos Aires metropolitan area and more than one-third in the other large cities.

At the same time, the structure of stratification had been drastically modified. The two-strata system of the mid-nineteenth century was replaced by a much more complex structure, in which the middle layers increased from less than 11 per cent of the population in 1869, to 25 per cent in 1895, and to more than 30 per cent in 1914. Within this emerging middle class the proportion of foreign-born was larger than in the total labor force. This was especially true of industry, commerce, and services.

TABLE XII

PERCENTAGE OF FOREIGN-BORN IN DIFFERENT OCCUPATIONAL STRATA. 1895–1914.

Occupational strata	(a) 1895	(a) 1914	(b) 1960
Middle strata in secondary and tertiary sectors	59	51	16
Middle strata in primary sector	43	45	16
Lower strata in secondary and tertiary sector	39	48	15
Lower strata in primary sector	25	35	15

(a) Computed from an unpublished re-classification of the 1895 and 1914 Argentine Census prepared for the Institute of Sociology of the University of Buenos Aires by Ruth Sautú and Susana Torrado.

(b) Estimates on the basis of a sample of the 1960 Census.

While these estimates are imprecise, they illustrate the importance of foreign immigration in the modernization of the stratification system.

This process, on the other hand, did not only involve the rise of a substantial middle class. It also stimulated the transformation of the lower class by causing the emergence of a modern urban proletariat, predominantly foreign. This process did not affect the occupational structure alone. When we speak of *middle classes* and *urban proletariat*, we are also referring to attitudes, ideologies, aspirations, and self-identifications. The reality of this transition is clearly expressed in the political events of the period corresponding to the appearance of middle-class political parties, and the typical "protest" movements of the rising urban proletariat. But, as we will

indicate later on, the overwhelmingly foreign origin of both the modern middle class and the modern urban workers was itself a basic factor in the political development of the country.

Between 1870 and 1910 a great part of the transition from a predominantly traditional structure to a more advanced pattern was completed, at least in the Buenos Aires metropolitan area and in the provinces of the Littoral region (which included two-thirds of the national population). However, those geographical areas and social groups less affected by foreign immigration tended to maintain archaic traits. The persistence of these internal contradictions had a lasting effect on the subsequent economic and social development of the country. It is true that the landowning elite was not an entirely closed class, even at that time; its origins were fairly recent, and a number of "new" families were able to reach the upper social level. However, regardless of the degree of fluidity within this group, the important fact is that the elite became increasingly concerned with maintaining the economic and social structure favorable to its interests. This meant strictly limiting the process of modernization which the elite itself had initiated. While its attempt to completely control the process was doomed to failure, it managed to maintain a key economic position and continued to orient the economy to the exporting of primary products. For another thing, the existence of a large proportion of the population within the less developed regions and still mostly traditional, involved the problem of its future mobilization and integration into the modern pattern. Both problems were to acquire a dramatic expression after 1930.

The rapid rate of the transition after 1930, especially the expansion of the middle class, made social mobility an important factor in shaping the historical process. A large majority of immigrants belonged to the lower strata of their societies. Table XIII does not give a precise measure of the social composition of the immigrants, but at least it suggests the kind of people who were arriving by the thousands in those years. Only very few immigrants had middle-class backgrounds. As a result, the new Argentine middle class, so heavily recruited from among the immigrants, was mostly of lower-class origin. Between 1895 and 1914 no less than two-thirds of the middle classes were of popular class origin; that is, they were formed by individuals who either had begun their occupational careers as manual workers, or were sons of manual-worker

TABLE XIII

Socio-Occupational Strata of Immigrants, According to Their Occupation Declared at the Moment of Admittance to the Country. 1857-1925.

Socio-occupational categories	1857– 1870	1871– 1899	1900– 1920	1921– 1924	Total: 1857– 1924
Employees in business, industry, services, agriculture; free professionals, technicians; White collar and kindred occupations .	4.4	5.4	8.6	13.4	7.2
Skilled and unskilled workers, day laborers and kindred occupations	95.6	94.6	91.4	86.6	92.1

Source: *Resumen Estadístico del Movimiento Migratorio*, Ministerio de Agricultura. Bunenos Aires, Argentina, 1925.

fathers.[12] Social mobility became a normal pattern in Argentine society (or at least in the central areas), and this trait was accompanied by corresponding attitude changes and ideological expressions. Social mobility must be considered an important factor not only in explaining the process of absorption of the foreign immigrants, but also in explaining essential aspects of the Argentine political and social history in the twentieth century.

5. The Assimilation of the Foreign Population and its Impact on the Culture

The problem that Argentina had to confront between 1870 and 1930 is probably without precedent in other immigration countries. Even the United States, which received the largest share of the great international migrations, was never in a similar situation; the proportion of foreigners in its total population and in the annual migratory stream, although much higher in *absolute* terms, was *relatively* much lower than in Argentina. Moreover, the size of the native-born population was large enough to ensure the possibility of real assimilation; also, the stability of the existing social structure was much stronger, which made it better-equipped to resist the migratory impact. In the United States the maximum proportion of foreign-born population was 14.7 per cent in 1910, and after 1920 it decreased steadily to the present 5.4 per cent. In Argentina immigrants were more than one-fourth of the total population in the last decade of the nineteenth century. This proportion grew to nearly 30 per cent just before the First World War, and it stayed as high as 23 per cent until 1930. In 1960 it was still nearly 13 per cent; that is, a proportion quite similar to the highest ever reached in the United States. But even these figures fail to suggest the immigrants' impact on Argentine

society. As we have seen, the demographic concentration for certain ages and for the male sex, coupled with the regional and urban concentration,

TABLE XIV

Total Population and Percentage of Foreign-born in Argentina and the United States. 1810-1960.

Years	Total population (millions)		Per cent foreign-born in total population	
	United States	Argentina	United States	Argentina
1810	7.2	.4	11.1	*
1850	23.2	1.3	9.5	*
1870	39.8	1.7**	14.1	12.1**
1890	62.9	*	14.6	*
1895	—	4.0	—	*
1900	76.0	*	13.6	*
1910	92.0	*	14.7	*
1914	—	7.9	—	29.9
1920	105.7	8.8	13.2	24.0
1930	122.8	11.7	11.6	23.5
1950	150.7	17.0	6.8	15.8
1960	150.7	20.0	5.4	12.8

Sources: Brinley Thomas (ed.), *Economics of International Migration*. London: MacMillan, 1958, p. 136; Francisco De Aparicio y Horacio Difrieri (eds.), *La Argentina, Suma de Geografía*. Buenos Aires: Peuser, 1961, p. 94; and *Boletines de la Dirección Nacional de Estadísticas y Censos* (various years).
*No date available.
**1869 Census.

increased the proportion of foreigners in the more strategic areas of the country and in most of the important sectors of the population. Immigrants comprised from two-thirds to three-quarters of the total

TABLE XV

Foreign-born Over Twenty Years old (Both Sexes) for Every 100 Persons of the Same Age and Sex. 1869-1947.

Years	Buenos Aires City	Central area. Provinces of Buenos Aires, Córdoba, Entre Ríos, Mendoza, La Pampa	Peripheral area. All other states and territories
1869	67	*	*
1895	74	44	11
1914	72	51	20
1947	37	23	16

Source: Argentine Census.
*No data.

adult population in Buenos Aires City for more than sixty years since 1869. In the remaining provinces of the central area, this proportion remained close to 50 per cent. If we consider only the adult males, we see that for many decades there were in Buenos Aires more than four foreigners for every native-born Argentine, and in the central area the immigrants were considerably more numerous than the natives. We do not have specific rates for the inter-censal years, but we can guess that this proportion must have continued during the early thirties, especially

TABLE XVI

ARGENTINE AND FOREIGN MALES AGED TWENTY YEARS AND
OVER. 1869–1947 (THOUSANDS).

Years	Buenos Aires City		Central provinces of Buenos Aires, Córdoba, Entre Ríos, Mendoza, La Pampa	
	Argentine males	Foreign males	Argentine males	Foreign males
1869	12	48	*	*
1895	42	174	287	309
1914	119	404	557	752
1947	614	433	2,115	747

Source: Argentine Census.
*No data.

before the mass internal migrations from the peripheral regions began to accelerate the Argentinization of the population.

We insist on the sheer size of the proportion because it introduces a factor rarely considered in studies on the assimilation of foreign immigrants. Usually one speaks of assimilation as a concept presupposing a native population with the capacity to assimilate the incoming groups. But how well will the host society be able to maintain its identity if the incoming population is larger than the existing one, and if the absolute size of the latter is very small in the first place ? We suggest that, other things being equal, these two quantitative aspects definitely limit the absorption capacity of the receiving society. There are other, equally important conditions which affect the process: the power structure of the receiving society; the immigrants' position within the structure; their location in the stratification systems of both the native and receiving societies, the differences between immigrant and native cultures, and their relative prestige; the degree of segregation of the immigrant population in relation to the receiving society and to its different sectors and strata; the degree of cultural homogeneity of the immigrants; their solidarity; their attitudes; their level of education; the strength of their original national identifications; the degree of acceptance they find in the new country; and especially the degree of social mobility they experience in the receiving country. Only in the case of a heterogeneous and subordinated immigrant population, characterized by a much lower cultural level than that of the host society and placed under conditions of severe segregation, could a smaller native population limit the impact of immigration on the existing culture and social structure. An illustration of this extreme case could be a large slave population of immigrant origin placed in a society composed of a smaller number of free

individuals. But even in this example the receiving society would eventually change in response to the immigrants' impact. In Argentina conditions were not this extreme. The immigrants were neither nationally nor culturally homogeneous, but there was at least one extremely large national group. The degree of their identification with their country of origin varied, but it was probably fairly low because many immigrants came from backward and traditional cultures. However, they did not regard the receiving country as a superior culture to be imitated. Although many were illiterate, they introduced new skills and new attitudes toward economic activities. Also, the fact of having emigrated involved a rupture with their traditional past. They had been released from that past and were now "mobilized", even if their basic motivation was not to settle permanently in the new country but to get rich, return to the native village, and buy land. In fact, their attempts to fulfill their purposes set them on the path which led them to abandon their traditional mores. And this change was irreversible: unconsciously and unwillingly, the immigrants were the bearers of modernization.[13] On the other hand, they soon gained a better social and economic position than the native born of the lower strata. At the same time, however, they remained practically excluded from positions of economic power, which as we have seen remained firmly in the hands of the elite.

After the deluge of immigration there was still an Argentina; the country did not lose its identity. But the old and new elements had been fused and transformed. A new country emerged, and is still emerging, since the historical process set in motion by the mass nineteenth century immigration cannot be considered complete.

In Argentina the immigration process implied the virtual disappearance (in the areas of immigrant settlement) of the existing native social types and the partial destruction of the social structure which corresponded to them. In their place emerged a new type, still not well-defined, and a new structure.

Among the rural population, which made up its large majority, the typical native had adapted to the occupations and social conditions of the countryside during the colonial epoch. Many of his psychological features were those that characterize the Spaniards. The image of the *gaucho*, who later became a national myth, may illustrate the prevailing values of rural society prior to the impact of immigration. The *gaucho* was a kind of *peón* on horseback. He worked at intervals, never having a permanent occupation or home. His personal life was characterized by freedom. He could move freely in the immense open spaces of the Pampas, which at that time had no limits fixed by wire fences. His work depended only on his ability, on his talent as a horseman and on his courage. These were the values which identified him to himself and to others. There were no habits of regularity, frugality, foresight, or rational calculation in his behavior. On the contrary, these were considered negative characteristics, opposed to the manly ideal. He had no aspiration for social ascent, no special desire to acquire land. Because the *gaucho* sometimes worked as a *peón* in the *estancia*, he has quite often been confused with the ordinary peasant, which he was not. However, there is little doubt that most of his traits were shared by the rural inhabitants who formed a majority of the population. Their relation to the masters of the *estancias* was wholly particularistic, and did not correspond at all to the relationship between a salaried worker and his employer. Insofar as the master displayed some of the traits valued by the *gaucho*, especially personal courage, physical strength, and ability, the latter felt a personal adherence to him, based on sentiments of fidelity, loyalty, and admiration.

The material aspects of the culture were a function of the necessities of a life based on livestock, technically and socially at a primitive level. Agriculture and sedentary work in general were considered inferior; work itself was despised. In the rural areas, and probably in the lower strata in the towns and urban centers as well, the population lacked national identification; their loyalty was mainly local, and it was usually personified in the *caudillo*.* This, of course, was the social basis of the dissolution of the "unitarian state" which occurred soon after Independence.[14]

Thus Argentina in the middle of the nineteenth century, before the beginning of mass overseas immigration, was permeated by traditional values and behavior patterns. Its more modern sectors were found in the urban elites; that is, in a small proportion of its inhabitants sharply contrasting with the rural masses and also with the lower urban strata. The overseas immigrants were the bearers of different attitudes toward agriculture, saving, economic life, and mobility aspirations. Partly because of a different cultural heritage and partly as an effect of displacement, they became a powerful impulse toward modernization. Certainly, even if the majority of the foreigners had little or no education, a consider-

able number of professionals, technicians, and skilled workers did arrive, and they were able to provide most of the specialized personnel for the many new activities required by modernization in all fields. But even the uneducated peasants became innovators. In the Argentine Pampas, for example, they showed a much greater flexibility and creativity than did the local population.[15]

Under the impact of immigration the old cultural patterns practically dissolved. Objects of previously great material value and symbolic meaning, like the horse, lost all importance. Similarly, many aspects of the traditional culture, such as clothes, tools, vehicles, food, housing, furniture, forms of leisure, were totally replaced or profoundly transformed. These changes were mainly due to material necessity, not merely to a wish to emulate. Each immigrant group imprinted its characteristics on the different aspects of the material and non-material culture, and in this way innovation, implicit or explicit, was stamped with the cultural forms imported from Europe.

According to Gori, the immigrant did not easily shed his European culture. On the contrary, "he tried to reaffirm it, especially the Swiss and German, through family training and the schooling of his children. He had staked his sights more on the consulate of his country as an agent of legality than in the formal representatives of Argentine authority, whom he mistrusted, even while being forced to accept".

According to this author and others, the immigrant generally spoke his mother tongue, read newspapers in his native tongue, and maintained organizations to encourage ties with the fatherland. Whenever he could, he chose a wife of his own nationality. Sometimes, in the beginning, the immigrant agricultural colonies chose their own authorities, and quite often geographic isolation made such colonies akin to foreign fortresses in the middle of the nation.[16]

In the cities the isolation and segregation which prevailed in the rural colonies was absent, although there was, particularly in Buenos Aires, some ecological segregation by nationality. The term *colony* was applied to a native group residing in an urban center; this term also referred to settlements of immigrants of any origin throughout the country. They developed separate communities with advanced organizational structure which included newspapers, schools, hospitals, and all kinds of voluntary associations connected with their country of origin.

*Political-military strong man.

In some cases the actions of foreign governments through these associations went farther than the attitudes of the emigrants would have justified. In the case of the Italians and the Spanish the degree of national identification with their country of origin was quite low. Patriotism among the Italians often came *after* emigration, perhaps as an effect of nostalgia, as Sarmiento noted.[17] Moreover, the strongest expressions of national identification with the country of origin came not from the inarticulate masses but from the elites of each national sector. If, as we suggest, the national identification of the largest immigrant sectors was weak, this must be counted as an important factor in the survival of an Argentine national identity.

The prevalence of these voluntary associations is remarkable if we consider the low cultural and economic level of the majority. At first the organizations provided many services which Argentina was unable to offer. Later on, however, education, sanitary facilities, mass communication media, and other services were provided by public and private Argentine institutions, and the need for the foreign national associations was less obvious. Some contemporaries have observed that their underlying purpose was to keep alive the language and traditions of the fatherland.

The associations had other latent functions. For instance, they provided the traditional immigrants with a means of integration into the Argentine society. These functions may account for the fact that the enthusiasm for associations was much higher among the immigrants than among the native born. This fact cannot be explained simply as a consequence of the emigration and of their special situation in a foreign land. Under similar conditions half a century later, the degree of formal and informal participation of Argentine internal migrants was extremely low; in fact, one obstacle to their assimilation was precisely their disorganization upon their arrival in the city.[18]

The remarkable propensity to cooperate and to create voluntary associations among the foreign immigrants was also due to other factors. In the first place, the associations expressed values and attitudes widely different from the anarchic and at the same time "submissive-authoritarian" character predominant among the natives, especially in the rural areas. In the second place, foreign immigration included an important working-class elite, which often had not left their native lands for economic

reasons alone. This elite provided leadership both to the voluntary associations and to the protest movements arising within the new industrial proletariat.

TABLE XVII

VOLUNTARY ASSOCIATIONS BY NATIONALITY OF THE MAJORITY OF THEIR MEMBERSHIP: NUMBER OF AFFILIATES FOR EVERY 1,000 NATIVE-BORN AND FOR EVERY 1,000 FOREIGN-BORN. 1914.

Types of Associations	No. of members for every 1,000 Argentines and for every 1,000 foreign-born living in the area		No. of Associations	
	Buenos Aires City	Rest of the country	Buenos Aires City	Rest of the country
Argentine Associations	104	21	19	153
Foreign Associations:				
—one nationality:	145	151	97	752
—multi-national: (includes workers' centers)	197	14	98	83

Source: Third National Census.

The tremendous challenge to Argentina created by the avalanche of foreigners is reflected in the writings of the decades around the end of the nineteenth and the beginning of the twentieth century. Sarmiento described Argentina as a "republic of foreigners", served by a small number of nationals performing unprofitable and burdensome tasks, such as keeping order, defending the territory, administering justice, and preserving the rights and the special privileges of the immigrants themselves.[19] Even the Italians, who later revealed themselves as the most amenable to assimilation, appeared as a powerful threat to national independence and identity. This was a consequence of their high proportion and concentration, their powerful organizations, and the attitudes of the Italian government, which regarded the Italian immigrants and their descendants as Italian citizens, in keeping with the principle of *Jus Sanguinis*. The problem of foreign schools, the deliberate attempt to create alien national communities, the absence of an Argentine tradition among the immigrants, and their complete political alienation continued to be serious concerns of the Argentine elite for a long time.

The problem was aggravated by certain basic contradictions in the policy followed by the elite in fostering immigration. These contradictions resulted from the difference between the declared and manifest aims of constructing a modern nation, and the limits within which many members of the dominant group wished to restrict the process of modernization. These problems were especially apparent in the political participation of the immigrants.

One of the proclaimed aims of immigration was to provide a stable basis for the functioning of democracy. But it soon became evident that those who were expected to become the new citizens remained totally outside the political life of the country. Indeed, despite the legal facilities for obtaining naturalization (which only required two years' residence and a relatively simple procedure), almost none of the immigrants sought it. There were several reasons for this. The Constitution accorded foreigners the same rights as those of the native-born, except the right to vote and to run for election. Under certain conditions, the foreigner, even without naturalization, could participate in local elections for city administration. In any case, not only economic activities but also all jobs in the civil service of the federal and provincial governments or other public bodies were open to the foreign-born without any requirements for citizenship. Consequently, there was no economic incentive for naturalization. Also, many immigrants were reluctant to lose their foreign national identification, for it gave them *additional* rights, since they were protected also by their respective native governments. In most cases, the immigrant looked down on the native-born as an inferior. Often he simply expected to return to his fatherland as soon as possible after getting rich. This situation caused many heated discussions between Argentines and foreigners, whose point of view was expressed by the booming foreign press. Some foreign sectors requested that naturalization be automatic but not compulsory. That is, foreigners would receive full citizenship rights, without renouncing their previous nationality and without being compelled to accept Argentine citizenship.[20] For certain nationalities and for the more highly educated, the failure to naturalize was certainly an expression of loyalty to the country of origin. But the reasons for the majority of the immigrants, especially Italian and Spanish, were probably different. Their lack of interest in political participation was an expression of the low political culture of the lower-class foreigners who came from countries whose voting was quite restricted and where politics was an activity monopolized by the middle and higher classes.

TABLE XVIII

Naturalized Foreigners for Every 100 Foreigners Residing in Buenos Aires and in the Rest of the Country. 1895–1947.

Regions			1895	1914	1947
Buenos Aires City	.	.	0.2	2.3	9.5
Rest of the Country	.	.	0.1	0.9	7.2

Source: Second, Third and Fourth National Census.

The political elite wanted a genuine functioning of the democracy anticipated in the Constitution, and immigration was stimulated with this in mind. But they found themselves faced with the paradox of a country in which sixty to eighty per cent of the adult male population in the most important areas had no right to vote and was governed by the remaining minority, constituting 20 to 40 per cent. But even these were not the true proportions. Only a minority of the native-born effectively participated in politics, and elections took place amid the general indifference of Argentines and foreigners alike, at least among the popular classes. And the governing elite, whatever its explicit purposes may have been, for a long time resisted the relinquishing of power through elections based on effective universal suffrage. They yielded only when the urban middle and popular classes became endowed with sufficient size and solidity to impose their influence.

When the foreigners created movements that suggested active political participation, the elite became indignant and fearful. It is true that these organizations could not be considered real channels of integration into the national life, since they were found in the context of the so-called Political Centers for Foreigners[21] and not in national political parties. But other attempts by the immigrants at political participation which were not linked to their nationalities were also opposed. This happened in the case of the workers' movements, which were especially vigorous in Buenos Aires since the end of the nineteenth century, and which lacked specific national identification. On the contrary, although the majority of the members were foreigners, they did not possess any unified national character; they were international and cosmopolitan in ideology and composition. These "cosmopolitan" societies and "workers' circles" had a real function in the assimilation of immigrants; they channeled the immigrants' activities into the political life of the country. This participation was not determined by national origin but by location in a given sector or stratum of Argentine society. However, the immigrants' ideologies still could not be readily accepted by the liberal elite. In this sense it was historically impossible for the elites to recognize the latent integrating function of workers' organizations. In fact the ruling group not only did not welcome the immigrants but repressed them through severe laws and systematic police persecution. The elite wanted to populate the desert, but they were not ready to introduce the necessary reforms in the agrarian structure. They wanted to integrate the immigrants into the body politic but did not want to share power with them.

In fact, political participation by the immigrants is only one aspect of this more general problem. We have given some indications of the many problems and internal tensions caused by immigration. What remains to be understood is how, after some sixty years, a relatively integrated and unified nation finally emerged. Systematic research on this subject is not available. Suggestions can be made, but we must recognize that they are speculative.

Perhaps it will be convenient to clarify first the meaning of *assimilation* as the term is used here. We will base our analysis on a preliminary distinction between *individual adjustment, participation, acculturation* and *identification*.[22]

(a) The notion of *adjustment* refers to the manner in which the immigrant performs his roles in the various spheres of activity in which he participates. What is important here is his ability to perform the roles without excessive or unbearable psychological stress.

(b) The concept of *participation* treats assimilation from the standpoint of the receiving society. Here we distinguish between three different dimensions. (i) *Extent* of participation: what roles is the immigrant performing within the social institutions and sectors of the host society; how much is he still connected with his fatherland; what roles is he playing in the social institutions and sectors of the host society, but socially segregated from it. (ii) Another important aspect of participation is the *efficiency* with which the roles are performed. In this case we define *efficiency* from the point of view of the receiving institutions and groups. (iii) Finally, we must take into account the *reception* given by the country to the immigrants. It is important to emphasize that participation may be granted in certain spheres of activities but not in others; indeed, this is usually the case.

(c) By *acculturation* we mean the immigrants' absorption of the cultural patterns of the host society. Such absorption may consist of relatively superficial learning or it may penetrate deeply into the personality. Acculturation is never a one-way process. It affects not only the immigrants but the receiving culture as well.

(d) Finally, an important aspect of assimilation is the degree of *identification* of the foreign-born and their descendants with the new country. To what extent do they lose their previous identification, and acquire a new one; how deep is the new identification, and how does it affect their attitudes and behavior.

These four aspects of assimilation are not necessarily all present in the same group or in the same individual. It is true that in certain spheres of activity adjustment, participation and acculturation will usually be associated, but this does not necessarily include national identification. Given the heterogeneity of the immigrants and the different conditions under which they settled, there should be a variety of situations, according to the different national origins and the educational and socio-economic status of the individuals involved.

In terms of *individual adjustment* there are reasons to believe that massive immigration involved a high cost. The high proportion of "returnees" indicates this. Among the causes were the relative inaccessibility of land ownership and the hardships of life in the rural areas. But in the cities too the adjustment must have been relatively painful. The documents of the period under consideration abound in descriptions of the sufferings, restrictions, and poverty of the immigrants. On the other hand, many acquired a degree of economic and social well-being beyond what they could have expected at home. We know very little about the degree of family organization. It is estimated by some that family organization among the native rural population was not high. If this is true, then immigration helped to establish a pattern of more regular and organized family life among the lower strata.[23]

The *participation* of immigrants varied according to the various spheres of activity. In the economic sphere it was always high. Since immigrant participation in the nation's economic life involved upward social mobility, this must have been a powerful means of integration. Thirty years after the end of mass immigration, in the Buenos Aires area, second generation immigrants were mostly in the middle and higher strata, and together with the foreign born constituted more than three-fourths of the individuals located at these levels.[24] Among the entrepreneurial elite this proportion was even higher: almost 90 per cent at about the same date.[25]

Intermarriage was another essential means of participation and integration into the life of the country. During the period from 1890 to 1910, about 40 per cent of the immigrants married outside their national group, many marrying Argentine women.[26]

The participation of foreigners in the intellectual life of the country was another means of integration. Although of course it was not a means of mass participation, it gave the immigrants an important role among the intellectual elite, and it contributed very much to the national patterns of intellectual and artistic expression. The consequences of this fact are still controversial. Nationalists of the Right as well as the neo-nationalists of the Left feel that the typical cosmopolitism of the Argentine intelligentsia is one of the major obstacles to the rise of an "authentic" national consciousness. Often the blame has been placed on the "oligarchy" and its intellectual establishment.[27] But whatever the evolution of the process, its existence cannot be denied.

TABLE XIX

ARGENTINE AND FOREIGN-BORN HEADS OF FAMILY BY
SOCIO-ECONOMIC STATUS.
BUENOS AIRES METROPOLITAN AREA, 1961.

	Native-born Argentine family heads				
Socio-economic status	Both parents Argentine-born	One parent foreign-born	Both parents foreign-born	Foreign-born family heads	Total population heads of family
Lower (unskilled and skilled manual)	45.6	30.0	33.3	48.2	41.5
Middle (lower middle and upper middle)	49.0	65.6	60.8	49.8	55.4
Upper (lower upper and upper upper)	5.4	4.4	5.9	2.0	4.1
TOTAL	100.0	100.0	100.0	100.0	100.0
	519	262	534	736	2,051

Source: "Stratification and Mobility in Buenos Aires" (Buenos Aires Institute of Sociology unpublished data). Survey based on a random area sample. Socio-economic status is computed on the average of four indicators: occupation, income, education, and standard of living.

As we have seen, the direct political participation of the foreigner was low and frequently inconsistent because of the ambivalent attitudes of the ruling elite. But this was true only of those actually born abroad, not of their children. After 1916 the proportion of second-generation immigrants began to rise among the active politicians. In 1889 their proportion among legislators (deputies and senators) was only 38 per cent, but it had risen to 55 per cent by 1916.[28] The degree of participation of second-generation immigrants reflected the political history of the country. Participation rose with the access to power of the middle class and decreased again when the "oligarchy" returned to power through the military revolution of 1930. After 1945 participation increased again.[29] It is worth noting that the last two constitutional presidents were second-generation Italian immigrants. If we consider the other two sectors of the leading elite—the military and the Church—we will see that the participation of immigrants' descendants is very high. In the last 25 years 77 per cent of the generals and admirals in the Army, Navy, and Air Force and 77 per cent of the bishops were of immigrant origin, mostly sons of foreigners.[30]

One aspect which alarmed the native elite was the immigrants' tendency to segregate themselves in colonies and communities often supported by their respective national governments. At least up to the First World War, Argentina appeared to many observers to be composed of juxtaposed segments, each of which claimed the loyalty of its members. Even in the economic sphere, which was a major field of interaction, the tendency to segregate by nationality appeared to a certain extent. But as time elapsed it became apparent that, below the seemingly chaotic surface of heterogeneous fragments, a sort of unity was being formed. In the first place, for the majority of immigrants ethnic segregation was really limited to certain special sectors of their life. More pervasive segregation occurred only among the higher strata. Moreover, segregation in one area did not affect the adequate fulfillment of universalistic roles within the society as a whole.[31] In fact these segregated structures functioned as intermediaries between the national society and the immigrants. Thus, even while preserving the cultural traditions of their members' homelands, they nonetheless facilitated social integration. In any case a certain degree of survival of native cultural traditions was perfectly compatible with a high degree of integrated participation in other spheres, especially in a society comparatively free from antagonistic ethnic tensions.[32]

Another integrative force was the fact that the immigrants' descendants frequently entered the same voluntary associations as their parents. In this way, such organizations gradually lost their specifically ethnic character. For example, the use of the language of origin in many foreign associations decreased steadily until it almost disappeared, to be replaced by Spanish. It is obvious that the end of immigration in 1930 was a factor in this process.

The participation of immigrants in these organizations varied according to nationality and socioeconomic level. The participation of Italian and Spanish immigrants of the popular classes was less frequent and briefer. Although the large voluntary associations were primarily composed of persons from the lower strata, the proportion of members was probably smaller than for the higher strata. Separate social stratification systems were probably maintained only at the higher class levels. But this segregation was certainly much more limited among the lower strata, and continued to decrease in time.

In addition to the progressive Argentinization of the foreign voluntary associations and the lower formal participation among the working class, there were other factors which favored integration into the national society. In the lower strata the ecological segregation of ethnic groups steadily diminished. In the Buenos Aires area, for example, there was a gradual reduction of the "ghetto" areas occupied by given nationalities. It is important to add that these zones did not have some of the characteristics common to cities in the United States. In some cases in the big cities, for example, certain types of slum, like the *conventillo*,* had a real integrative function for the different nationalities. Obviously the disappearance or drastic reduction of ecological segregation was in many cases due to the replacement of the immigrants by their children.

The process of assimilation should be considered as part of the emergence of new cultural forms and a new human type. This synthesis is the outcome of the interaction of the native and foreign cultures.

This observation brings us to the problem of *acculturation*. Even though we lack scientific studies concerning this process, there is an abundant literature, mostly impressionistic essays, attempting to characterize the society born of massive immigration.[33] The result of mass immigration was not the assimilation of the immigrants into the existing Argentine culture. The outcome was a synthesis that created a new cultural type, which is still not well-defined. In this emerging culture it is possible to recognize the contributions of the different national groups, particularly the Italian and the Spanish. But all of them are substantially modified and submerged in a context which gives them a new meaning. Particularly visible in most of the largest cities is the Italian influence in language, gestures, food, and many customs. The Spanish influence, no less strong, is perhaps less visible because it is more easily confused with creole elements. Some popular products of this fusion, like the *tango*, have great emotional and symbolic importance as expressions of the new Argentine society.

The bearers of this new cultural type are the children of the immigrants and their descendants. They are almost completely acculturated. Italian, Yiddish, Polish, and other Eastern European languages are seldom spoken by second-generation immigrants. Also they would never refer to themselves as belonging to a particular national stock. For example, an Italian immigrant's son would mention when asked that his father was Italian, but nobody would differentiate people on the basis of their ancestry. Instead, Italian language and customs have been adapted to new cultural patterns. The Italians' sons do not speak Italian, but everybody regardless of their national origin understands Italian and would be able to learn to speak it quite easily. This is not only because of its similarity with Spanish (In Spain, Italian is not so easy) but because Italian is so familiar in many ways. Words, idioms, the typical pronunciation of Spanish in Buenos Aires and the central area, as well as manners, inflections, facial expressions, and gestures, all bear the mark of many generations of Italians.

The immigrants' upward social mobility facilitated the acculturation of their children. Often the second generation was assimilated into a different social class, values, style of living and expectations that greatly diverged from those of the previous generation. This is of course a well-known phenomenon in a country of heavy immigration, but the huge proportion of immigrants in Argentina accentuated its consequences.

6. The Argentinization of Argentina and the Surviving Foreign Population

Let us now examine to what extent the process of assimilation was facilitated by the interruption of mass overseas immigration 35 years ago. We may also consider the role of the mass internal migrations in this process.

The Census of 1947 is the only one to give some information on the national origin of the parents. By that time more than one-half of the population was born of native Argentine parents. The rest

*A one or two-floor building with a central courtyard around which the rooms are located. Usually a family lives in each room.

were sons of immigrants or immigrants themselves. The proportion of the foreign element was higher in Buenos Aires. By 1961 only one-quarter of the heads of family were third-generation Argentines on both parents' sides, this proportion increasing to one-third among the adults. One-half of the families living in Buenos Aires included at least one member born abroad.

TABLE XX

NATIONAL OR FOREIGN ORIGIN OF THE POPULATION. 1947-1960.

National origin	Whole country— 1947* (all ages)	Buenos Aires City—1947* (all ages)	Buenos Aires metropolitan area—1961**	
			Heads of family	Population aged 18 and over
	%	%	%	%
Argentine-born from Argentine parents:	53.3	30.9	25.2	33.1
Argentine-born from foreign parents (one or both)	31.1	41.1	39.3	39.3
Foreign-born:	15.6	28.0	35.5	27.6
	100.0	100.0	100.0	100.0

Sources: *1947 Census and **"Stratification and Mobility in Buenos Aires", op. cit.

Thus, the composition of the population is still rather heterogeneous, even taking into account no more than the birth place of the present population and of their parents, and disregarding the origin of grandparents. Only a process of rapid synthesis and a large cultural distance between the first and second generation immigrants can explain the degree of homogeneity apparently achieved. The impact of time on the foreign population was another factor in facilitating the homogeneization. Not only the immigrant group is becoming older, but it is composed of a higher proportion of persons with longer residence in the country.

TABLE XXI

FOREIGN-BORN POPULATION BY AGE GROUPS. 1947.

Age Groups	Buenos Aires metropolitan area	Rest of country
Up to 39 years old . . .	26.2	25.3
40 to 59 years old . . .	51.8	50.1
Over 60 years old . . .	21.2	24.5
Age unknown . . .	0.8	0.1
	100.0	100.0

Source: Fourth Argentine Census.

Some information on the degree of assimilation and identification of the surviving immigrant population may be found in recent surveys. In Table XXIII only the two major immigrant groups were included.

TABLE XXII

PERCENTAGE OF FOREIGN-BORN POPULATION BY NUMBER OF YEARS OF RESIDENCE IN THE COUNTRY. 1947-1961.

Years of Residence	Entire country	Buenos Aires City. 1947*	Buenos Aires metropolitan area 1961**
Up to 9 years .	7.9	6.9	13.9
10–19 years . .	16.5	20.7	17.5
20–29 years . .	25.5	26.7	12.1
Over 30 years .	45.2	41.5	56.5
Unknown .	4.9	4.2	—

Source: *Fourth National Census (unpublished data).
**"Stratification and Mobility in Buenos Aires", op. cit.

Some differences may be noted between Italians and the Spanish, especially between lower and higher socio-economic strata, the former being more easily assimilated than the latter. On the whole, however, these two immigrant groups seem largely assimilated.

TABLE XXIII

SOME INDICATORS OF ACCULTURATION, PARTICIPATION, AND IDENTIFICATION IN ITALIAN AND SPANISH POPULATION AGED 18 YEARS AND OVER. BUENOS AIRES METROPOLITAN AREA, 1961.

Indicators	Socio-economic status:**		
	high	medium	low
Feel closer to Argentina than to home country:			
Italian Immigrants . .	48.6	48.7	46.8
Spanish Immigrants . .	28.9	46.4	51.3
Not affiliated to any foreign association:			
Italian Immigrants . .	88.9	95.7	95.3
Spanish Immigrants . .	75.0	86.3	89.5
Do not wish to return permanently to native land:			
Italian Immigrants . .	94.4	91.7	93.2
Spanish Immigrants . .	83.5	92.7	94.5
Closest friends are Argentinians, or Argentinians and foreigners in same proportion:			
Italian Immigrants . .	100.0	89.5	86.1
Spanish Immigrants . .	78.6	91.7	88.2
No communication with persons in home country:			
Italian Immigrants . .	34.3	46.1	47.6
Spanish Immigrants . .	13.8	40.1	51.0
Never experienced discrimination:			
Italian Immigrants . .	94.3	92.2	94.9
Spanish Immigrants . .	96.6	96.0	93.9
Never or seldom read in native language:			
Italian Immigrants . .	80.0	71.9	88.9
No preference for films, theatre, etc. in own language:			
Italian Immigrants . .	21.4	54.1	49.7
Speak only Spanish or Spanish and own language in the same proportion when at home:			
Italian Immigrants . .	92.9	67.6	39.2
Number of respondents:			
Italian Immigrants . .	20	274	335
Spanish Immigrants . .	33	228	257

Source: data summarized from Francis Korn, "Algunos aspectos de la asimilación de immigrantes en Buenos Aires". Instituto de Sociología, Universidad de Buenos Aires. Unpublished paper based on the "Stratification and Mobility in Buenos Aires" survey, op. cit.
**Composite index of occupation, education, income and consumption level.

Even if they have not lost all emotional ties with their fatherlands, they show an increasing identification with their new country. Practically nobody in these two groups wishes to return to his ancestral land. With the exception of the upper class, one-half of them feel closer to Argentina than to their fatherlands. Only a minority of the Spanish and Italians participate in foreign associations or have predominantly foreign friends. Among the Italians, the use of their native language seems confined to their homes.

Argentina has been rather successful in achieving a high degree of cultural homogeneity and national identification, as well as in capturing the loyalty of immigrants. However, many Argentine writers have challenged this suggestion. Such doubts have been expressed not only when the country was submerged in the flood of foreign immigration, but also in recent years. One prominent Argentine historian has described the present society as a "hybrid mass, formed by creole and foreign elements coexisting without predominance by either".[34] In other Argentinians we find a nostalgia for the homogeneous creole society. This attitude is typical not only of Right wing nationals but also of liberal intellectuals like Erro, Borges, or Mallea.

The political instability since 1930, the economic stagnation of the last fifteen years, and especially the

fragmentation of many groups and institutions have been imputed to the lack of real community feeling. However, Argentina was stable and economically prosperous when the degree of cultural homogeneity was much lower and the threat to national identity far more serious. The present troubles have other causes, even if they are in part an expression of the painful process of national integration. In fact, one of the consequences of the great internal migrations was precisely to halt the segregation of the old creole population and to facilitate its fusion with the descendants of immigrant stock.

Perhaps doubts and fears could simply be dispelled or confirmed by empirical evidence alone, even if such evidence were actually available. The contrasting interpretations may be caused by divergent expectations of the degree and kind of cultural homogeneity and national consciousness that can be achieved in Argentina. If one takes into account the risks involved in the incorporation of such a mass of foreigners in so short a time, then the present situation can be viewed with optimism. But if this same situation is measured by the yardstick of a country with a longer historical tradition of homogeneous culture, then of course there is less cause for optimism. The problem is primarily one of time, and this is a limit which even the most efficient assimilation cannot possibly overcome.

NOTES

[1] The other countries which received the largest share of inter-continental immigration were Canada (8.7 per cent), Brazil (7.4 per cent), Australia (5.0 per cent), New Zealand (1.0 per cent), and South Africa (1.3 per cent). The United States, Argentina, and the above-mentioned countries account for some 90 per cent of the total immigration of the period. See, Julius Isaac, *Economics of Migration*. New York: Oxford University Press, 1947, p. 62.

[2] Gino Germani, "Inquiry into the Social Effects of Urbanization in a Working-class Sector of Greater Buenos Aires". In Philip Hauser (ed.), *Urbanization in Latin America*. Paris: UNESCO, 1961.

[3] José Luis Romero, *Las ideas políticas en Argentina*. Mexico: Fondo de Cultura Económica, 1956, p. 176; and Domingo F. Sarmiento, *Condición del Extranjero en América*. Buenos Aires: A. B. Sarmiento, 1900, *Obras Completas*, Volume V, pp. xxxvi and p. 73 and *passim*.

[4] Julius Isaac, *op. cit.*, chap. VI.

[5] Joseph J. Spengler, "Effects Produced in Receiving Countries by Pre-1939 Immigration". In Brinley Thomas (ed.), *Economics of International Migration*. London: Macmillan, 1958, p. 22 ff.

[6] Giorgio Mortara, "Pesquisas Sobre Populaçoes Americanas". *Estudos Brasileiros de Demografía*, Monografia No. 3. Rio de Janeiro: Fundação Getulio Vargas, 1947.

[7] Walter F. Willcox (ed.), *International Migrations*. New York: National Bureau of Economic Research, 1929, Vol. 1, p. 540.

[8] The diffusion of the system had many causes, but the interests of the big landowners, coupled with the nearly complete lack of official support for a real colonization, are the basic factors. Other complementary causes have also been mentioned. At the beginning the rent was generally low and some immigrants, even if they had the required capital, were therefore more inclined to rent. Given the high market demand, the immigrant was induced to produce as much as possible and preferred to rent large areas of land rather than buy smaller ones. This must be related to the immigrants' basic aim to get rich and return to the homeland. At the same time, the landowner found it much more convenient to rent than to sell, since the price of the land was rapidly increasing. Also, many landowners preferred cattle breeding to agriculture, and the renting system allowed them to convert from one to the other while at the same time improving the condition of the land and benefiting from its increasing value. One of the most negative aspects of the renting system was the duration of the contracts, mostly less than three years. This caused a kind of "nomad agriculture", and a very high instability of the peasant, with all its economic and social consequences. On this problem see Manuel Bejarano, "La Política Colonizadora en la Provincia de Buenos Aires", Instituto de Sociología y Centro de Historia Social, Universidad de Buenos Aires, 1962, especially paragraph two. Also see Mark Jefferson, *The Peopling of Argentine Pampas*. New York: American Geographic Society, 1926, pp. 114-5 and 141 ff. The classic book on the high concentration of land ownership is Jacinto Oddone's *La Burguesía Terrateniente Argentina*. Buenos Aires (no publisher indicated): 1930.

[9] Gastón Gori, *El Pan Nuestro*. Buenos Aires: Raigal, 1958, p. 84.

[10] In 1913 only one-half of the industrial enterprises could be considered "factory industries"; these enterprises concentrated some 60 per cent of the capital, 80 per cent of the production, and approximately 65 per cent of the workers. The average number of workers per plant was 8.4; in 1947 it had risen to 14.7. See Adolfo Dorfman, *Evolución Industrial Argentina*. Buenos Aires: Losada, 1942, pp. 16-17. See also Gino Germani, *Estructura Social de la Argentina*. Buenos Aires: Raigal, 1955, p. 130.

[11] Adolfo Dorfman, *op. cit.*, pp. 21-2.

[12] Gino Germani, "La Movilidad Social en la Argentina", Appendix to Spanish translation of Reinhard Bendix and Seymour M. Lipset, *La Movilidad Social en la Sociedad Industrial*. Buenos Aires: Eudeba, 1964.

[13] Domingo F. Sarmiento, *op. cit.*, pp. 229-30, 64 ff., and *passim*.

[14] The literature on the *gaucho* is very extensive; for evaluation and synthesis, see Ezequiel Martínez Estrada, *Muerte y Transfiguración de Martín Fierro*. Mexico: Fondo de Cultura Económica, 1948, v. I, pp. 237-92; see also, for contrasts with the immigrants, Gastón Gori, *op. cit.*, and Gastón Gori, *La Pampa sin Gaucho*. Buenos Aires: Raigal, 1952.

[15] Domingo F. Sarmiento, *op. cit.*, pp. 64 ff.

[16] Gastón Gori, *La Pampa Sin Gaucho, op. cit.*

[17] Domingo F. Sarmiento, *op. cit.*, p. 76. Sarmiento calls this attitude "retrospective patriotism".

[18] Gino Germani, "Inquiry into the Social Effects of Urbanization", *op. cit.*

[19] Domingo F. Sarmiento, *op. cit.*, p. 101.

[20] Domingo F. Sarmiento, *op. cit.*, pp. 301 ff., 328 ff., and *passim*.

[21] Gastón Gori, *La Pampa Sin Gaucho, op. cit.*

[22] Some parts of the following typology have been summarized from Gino Germani, "The Assimilation of Immigrants in Urban Settings". In Philip Hauser (ed.), *Handbook of Urban Studies*. Paris: UNESCO, forthcoming. The typology follows the theoretical suggestions of S. N. Eisenstadt in his *Absorption of Immigrants*. London: Routledge and Kegan Paul, 1954, chapter 1.

[23] In 1942 this difference was still observed. Cf. the remarks by Carl C. Taylor, *Rural Life in Argentina*. Baton Rouge: Louisiana State University Press, 1948, chapter 13.

[24] The average socio-economic status of the native Argentines whose parents were both natives was lower than that of second-generation immigrants. The average relative position of the foreigner was lower than that of the native, but slightly higher than that of the native internal migrants. Here the emigration to the city was another important factor in determining the socio-economic status. Cf. Gino Germani, Blanca Ferrari, and Malvina Segre, "Características Sociales de la Población de Buenos Aires", Instituto de Sociología, Universidad de Buenos Aires, 1965 (unpublished manuscript).

[25] José Luis de Imaz, *Los que Mandan*. Buenos Aires: Eudeba, 1964, p. 136-138 (Tables 72 and 73).

[26] Franco Savorgnan, "Homogamia en los Immigrantes en Buenos Aires", *Boletín del Instituto Etnico Nacional*, 1957.

[27] Especially by the ideologues of the "national Left". Cf. Juan José Hernández Arregui, *Imperialismo y Cultura*. Buenos Aires: Amerindia, 1957 and *La Formación de la Conciencia Nacional*. Buenos Aires: 1960.

[28] Darío Cantón and Mabel Arruñada, "Orígenes Sociales de los Legisladores", Instituto de Sociología, Universidad de Buenos Aires, 1960, unpublished paper.

[29] José L. de Imaz, *op. cit.*, p. 9.

[30] José L. de Imaz, *op. cit.*, p. 60 and p. 175. In the Armed Forces the high officers of Italian origin accounted for one-fourth of the total, 35 per cent were of Spanish origin, while the remaining 16 per cent were of French or Anglo-Saxon (including German) descent. Among the bishops, the Italian influence was higher: one-half of them were sons of Italian peasants.

[31] Cf. S. N. Eisenstadt, *op. cit.*, chapter 1.

[32] In Argentina there is some anti-semitism. However, its degree and diffusion are not higher than in other Western countries, like the United States or France. Some episodes which have received international attention are an expression of the complex political situation, but not of a widespread or intense racial prejudice. In a survey it was found that about 22 per cent of the family heads in a random sample of the Buenos Aires metropolitan area gave anti-Jewish answers (when asked specifically about Jews). For similar questions, the verbal attitudes reported in studies in West Germany, France, and the United States indicated a similar or smaller proportion of prejudiced answers. Cf. Gino Germani, "Antisemitismo Ideológico y Antisemitismo Tradicional", *Comentarios*, 1962, no. 34. In any case, it is well-known that the prejudice against Italians or the Spanish is much lower. In the same survey the anti-Italian answers were 4.4 per cent and the anti-Spanish 3.5 per cent. These reactions were obtained from respondents of all national origins and all social classes. The attitudes of native Argentinians classified by socio-economic status (see Table A) showed the usual correlation between low education (and socio-economic level) and prejudice.

TABLE A

Attitudes toward Immigrants by Native-born Family Heads. Percentage of Respondents who would "Exclude" the Different National or Ethnic Groups. Buenos Aires metropolitan area, 1961.

National and ethnic groups "excluded"	Low socio-economic status	Middle socio-economic status	High socio-economic status
Italians	12	3	1
Spanish	9	2	0
Jews	34	22	14
North Americans	24	13	5
English	18	10	3
Polish	17	10	7
Rumanians	15	8	7

The hostility against Italians and Spanish was the lowest and very small at all socio-economic levels. The anti-North American and anti-English attitudes indicated more of an ideological orientation than an ethnic prejudice. There was strong evidence that negative reactions regarding the Jews and other lower-class eastern Europeans were more frequently an expression of "traditionalism" than of ideological anti-semitism. Cf. Gino Germani, "Antisemitismo Ideológico y Antisemitismo Tradicional", *Comentarios*, 1962, no. 34; and Francis Korn, "Algunos Aspectos de la Asimilación de Immigrantes en Buenos Aires", Instituto de Sociología, Universidad de Buenos Aires (unpublished paper based on the same survey).

[33] Among Argentine writers, the most important are Ezequiel Martínez Estrada, Jorge Luis Borges, José Luis Romero, Carlos Alberto Erro, Eduardo Mallea, and Raúl Scalabrini Ortíz.

[34] José Luis Romero, *Argentina. Imágenes y Perspectivas*. Buenos Aires: Raigal, 1956, p. 62.

JULIAN PITT-RIVERS

Race, Color, and Class in Central America and the Andes

AMONG ITS many *fiestas*, the Hispanic world celebrates one with the name of "El día de la raza" (which is what is called Columbus Day in the United States). Why it should be so called remains something of an enigma. It was inaugurated in Spain in 1917 to encourage friendship with Latin America, but its name has been changed there to "El día de la Hispanidad"—in the cause, more suitable to present times, of extolling Spanish culture rather than Spanish genes. The old name still remains, however, in Mexico and in other countries. The *fiesta* might, more consequentially, have been called "The Day of Race Relations" rather than of "The Race," for it celebrates the day on which they may be said to have commenced.

For the Spaniards, the celebration evokes the age, long since eclipsed, when they conquered half the world; it pays tribute to the egregious stamina of their ancestors. But Mexicans tend to think it refers to the Aztec race; the Monumento a la Raza in Mexico City is composed of a pyramid surmounted by an Aztec eagle.[1] In other countries, some people think it refers to the Spanish race, but it seldom evokes for anyone the name of Columbus, whose race remains a matter of dispute to this day.

Quite apart from the mysteries surrounding The Day of the Race, the concept of *race* itself is unclear in Latin America. My concern here is not with what anthropologists mean by *race*, but only with what the people of Latin America think the word means when they encounter it in their daily speech. By minimal definition, it refers to a group of people who are felt to be somehow similar in their essential nature. El Día de la Raza is above all a patriotic *fiesta;* it expresses national unity, the common nature of the whole nation. As such, it is certainly worth celebrating, especially in countries where racial differences

542

pose such grave moral and social problems on other days of the year. It is in keeping with this interpretation that the *fiesta* should be a comparatively modern innovation coinciding with the growth of national and social consciousness.

The word *race* is, of course, also used to mark differences of ethnic identity within the nation. Sometimes awareness of any implication of heredity is so slight that a man can think of himself as belonging to a race different from that of his parents. The word clearly owes little to physical anthropology but refers, however it may be defined, to the ways in which people are classified in daily life. What are called race relations are, in fact, always questions of social structure.

Ethnic classification is the end product of the most elusive social processes that endow not only words but feelings and perceptions with a special significance. The varied definitions of *race* have no more in common than the fact that they say something about the essential and indelible nature of people. Hence, for all its ambiguities, the notion of race possesses a prime claim upon the solidarities that bind men into social and political alliance.

Approaches to the study of race relations have varied considerably. Certain theories constructed out of the commonplaces of the traditional popular idiom attribute culture to "blood." Moral qualities, like psychological characteristics and intellectual aptitudes, are thought to derive from heredity, since the "blood" is what is inherited. The social order depends, by implication, upon genetic transmission, since the capacities and the character that fit people for a particular status are acquired by birth.

This view leads to the conclusion that social status should be hereditary and derive from the nature of persons. The system works well enough because the totality of a person's descent is not only hard to know in a genetically homogeneous population, but also quite easily falsified. Birth produces the expectation of excellence. Recognized excellence demonstrates the presence of distinguished forebears who may not have previously been claimed. "Blood will out!" In operation the system confirms its premises. Thanks to its flexibility, the facts can be made to fit; the reality of social mobility can be reconciled with a belief in the determinism of birth.[2]

Where descent can be inferred from appearance, such a theory finds itself constricted. Plebian origins do not "show"; colored origins do. Putative descent can no longer be invoked to vali-

543

date the reality established by the social process, but the real ancestors come to light in the phenotype. "Bad blood" explains moral and intellectual defects, but in those who show visible signs of having it, these can be expected in advance. Moral qualities are no longer inferred from status; rather, status is accorded on the basis of physical qualities that can be seen, and these, then, determine the nature of persons. Birth decides not merely opportunity but fate. In a homogeneous society the possession of a prestigious ancestor entitles a man to claim status. Once blood is a matter of ethnic distinction, however, its purity becomes the subject of concern. The attribution of an impure ancestor destroys status. Blood exchanges a positive for a negative significance. Preoccupations with "purity of descent" take on a racial connotation and bring an adverse value to miscegenation (a word which by the unhappy fortuity of its spelling becomes misconstrued today to imply that racial prejudices have a scientific background). The result is a color bar, prohibiting social mobility and enforcing ethnic endogamy.[3]

When blood is considered the determinant of culture, racial differences between peoples can be used to explain all else, even military and political fortunes. Purity of blood becomes the key to national success. The most distinguished literary expression of such ideas is that of Gobineau. By zeal and industry rather than by any great originality of mind, he succeeded in elevating the social prejudices of a petty noble of the mid-nineteenth century to the status of a philosophy of history. If Gobineau committed what Claude Lévi-Strauss has called the "original sin" of anthropology,[4] later anthropologists have committed other less spectacular sins in their attempts to grapple with the problems of race relations—or, more often, they have sinned by default in not attempting to grapple with them at all.

The "diffusionist" theory offered such an evasion. Viewing race relations in terms of culture contact, this theory concentrated upon establishing the origin of the cultural traits of different peoples to the neglect of their present social function. The preoccupation with the transmission of culture between different ethnic groups, rather than with reciprocal modes of behavior, left this branch of anthropology with little to say about the problems of race relations. This is particularly important in Latin America, where in the past a great many anthropologists have devoted their labors to the discovery of the cultures of pre-Hispanic times on the assumption

544

that they have been preserved among the Indians of the present. This archaeological orientation has meant that, until recently, in spite of the quantity of professional work done in Latin America, few accounts have been concerned with race relations as such. Concentrating on the passage of cultural traits rather than on the social structure through which these traits passed, the anthropologists tended to deal with only one side of the ethnic division and touched only incidentally its relationship to the other.

The Marxist interpretation of race relations has been of the greatest importance in stressing their economic aspects and in giving them a dynamic dimension. It has clarified in particular the stages of colonial development. But if the proponents of the "acculturation theory" have neglected the society within which acculturation took place, the Marxist sociologists have tended to neglect the significance of culture by treating race relations simply as a special instance of class relations carried over into a colonial setting.

The same reproach cannot be leveled at the American urban sociologists whose awareness of the factor of culture and whose feeling for its nuances have brought a high level of excellence to their ethnography. But, as Professor Everett Hughes pointed out a dozen years ago (and it is still true), they have been inclined to conduct their analysis within the framework of their own values and reformist desires. For want of a comparative field of reference, they have tended to overlook the wider significance of their data.

Studies of race relations by political thinkers have seldom given sufficient weight to the course of feeling that lies behind political events or to the dynamics of a changing consciousness and the formation of fresh solidarities. Politics has been called the science of the possible. Time and again it has turned out to be, where racial issues were concerned, the science of what was once possible but is so no longer.

A study that straddles the frontiers of established disciplines requires consideration from such varied viewpoints. It must above all achieve a synthesis of the cultural and the social aspects. The detail of the ethnography must be integrated in an overview of race relations in space and time. The preliminary condition of such an enterprise is a clear description of the systems of ethnic classification at the local level and a recognition of their social sig-

545

nificance. Charles Wagley was making this point when he coined the phrase "social race."[5] He went on to point to the importance of knowing how the terminology varies, for this matter is filled with confusion. Not only do the words used vary from area to area and from class to class, but the conceptions to which they correspond also change, and the criteria on which the system of classification is based vary in relevance. It is difficult to say what is an Indian,[6] but it is scarcely easier to say what is a Negro.

Terminological inconsistencies complicate from the outset discussion of race relations in Latin America. Indeed, there is not even agreement as to whether or not a "problem" of race relations exists in Latin America. The nationals of these countries often deny the existence of racial discrimination. They claim from this fact a virtue that makes them, despite their supposed economic and technological underdevelopment, the moral superiors of their northern neighbor, whose "inhumanity" toward colored people they deplore. Moreover, this opinion is held not only by Latin Americans themselves, but by outside observers, the most eminent of whom is Professor Arnold Toynbee, who speaks of the Latin American's freedom from race prejudice.[7]

This point of view, in many cases a way of expressing criticism of the United States, is also held by many patriotic American citizens, including especially some who are "colored" and whose testimony, if firsthand, might be thought to suffice.[8] Nevertheless, it is not by any means held universally and is sometimes regarded as a myth. Certain critics, both national and foreign, maintain that race is as important in Latin as in North America, once it is admitted that in addition to differences in the form discrimination takes, there is a major difference: The race that is penalized is the Indian rather than the Negro. Neither of these points of view appears correct.[9] Both are confused as to the nature of the question. Yet by examining the observations upon which they are based and how they have come to hold sway, one can understand better the role ethnic distinctiveness plays in ordering the society of Latin America.

"Segregation" as it is found in the United States does not exist in Latin America. "Color" in the North American sense is not the basis of a classification into two statuses to which differential rights attach. Segregated schools, public facilities, transport, or restaurants do not exist in Latin America. The Negro is not formally distinguished at any point. While many institutions are devoted specifically to the Indians, the definition of Indian in this regard is not based on physical criteria. Moreover, neither color nor phenotype has sufficed in the past to debar men from prominence in the national life, as the long list of Negroid or Indian-looking men of eminence in Latin American history shows.[10]

Intermarriage is not regarded with horror. Among the upper classes and in many places among the population generally, it is, however, considered denigrating to marry someone much darker than oneself. This is so, for example, in Barranquilla, Colombia, where the greater part of the population is more or less Negroid. The idea of physical contact with darker races is nowhere considered shocking, nor is it regarded as polluting by the whites. Dark-skinned people are thought to be more sensual and therefore more desirable sexually. This is not the expression of a neurotic fear of sexual insufficiency but an accepted and openly stated commonplace. Pale-skinned people of both sexes are thought to be more frigid and proud, and less warmhearted. Mistresses tend, consequently, to be more swarthy than wives, whose pale skin indicates social superiority.

The immense majority of the population from Mexico to Bolivia are well aware of their mixed ancestry. "A touch of the tarbrush" can, therefore, never mean total social disqualification. "We are all half-castes," Mexicans commonly remark, pointing to their forearm to show the color of their skin. Still, they sometimes go on to stress that only a small percentage of their blood is Indian. National unity demands that to be truly Mexican they must have some Indian blood, but social aspirations require that they should not have too much. Color is a matter of degree, not the basis of a division into black and white.

In consequence, physical characteristics cannot be said to be socially insignificant; their significance is only different. Physical traits never account for more than part of the image that individuals present. These images are perceived in terms of what they can be contrasted with; there is no color problem where the population is homogeneous in color, whatever that color may be. Social distinctions must then be made according to other criteria. From one place to another, in greater or lesser degree, physical traits are qualified by cultural and economic indicators in order to produce that total image which accords a social identity.

Arnulfo Arias, a former president of Panamá known for his "racist" policy, is credited with the proposal to exterminate the

547

Negroes. In a country whose capital city is predominantly Negro, he nevertheless retained sufficient popularity to be a close runner-up in the presidential elections of 1964. This is no longer curious when one realizes that the term *Negro* refers only to the population of Jamaican origins. Imported for the construction of the canal, these people have retained their English tongue and their Protestant faith. Language and religion are the significant qualifiers of color in the definition of *Negro* in Panamá.

In Barranquilla, Colombia, color is qualified by other social factors, and the term *Negro* confined to the slum-dwellers of the city. In the modern housing developments where no one is to be seen who would not qualify as a Negro in the United States, one may be told: "Only white people live here." The definition of *Negro* varies from place to place and, of course, from class to class. A man may be defined as Negro in one place, but simply as *moreno, trigueño, canela,* or even white in another. A man who would be considered Negro in the United States might, by traveling to Mexico, become *moreno* or *prieto,* then *canela* or *trigueño* in Panamá, and end up in Barranquilla white. The definition of *Indian* presents a comparable problem once the word no longer refers to a member of an Indian community. Different places and classes use different criteria.

Skin color is merely one of the indices among physical traits that contribute to a person's total image. It is not necessarily more significant than hair type or shape of eye. The relative evaluation of different physical traits varies. The Reichel-Dolmatoffs record of a village in Northern Colombia:

Distinctions are made mainly according to the nature of the hair and of the eyes and to a certain degree according to stature. Skin color, the shape of the lips or nose, or other similar traits are hardly taken into account. In this way, a person with predominantly Negroid features, but with long and wavy hair is often considered a "Spaniard." On the other hand, an individual with predominantly Caucasoid features and a light skin, but with straight black hair, slightly oblique eyes and of small stature, is considered an "Indian."[11]

The social structure is divided, primarily according to place of residence, into two segments—Spanish and Indian. This dichotomy, while employing a strictness which the Reichel-Dolmatoffs regard as exceptional in Colombia, allows no place for the category "Negro."

The system of classification makes what it will of the objective

548

reality of the phenotype. The forces of the social structure utilize the raw material of phenotypical distinctions, building out of it the social statuses into which people are classified.

It has sometimes been said that the difference between Anglo and Latin America is that in the former anyone who has a drop of Negro blood is a Negro, whereas in the latter anyone who has white blood is a white.[12] The first statement is approximately true, but the second is emphatically not so. The concept of "blood" is fundamentally different in the two and has, in the past, varied from one century to another.

In Latin America, a person with non-white physical traits may be classed as white socially. A trace of European physique is, however, quite insufficient in itself to class a person as white. Although Indians with pale skin and European traits or gray hair may be found sporadically throughout Latin America, they are considered to be no less Indian on this account. In any market in the Andes one or two can usually be seen, and the *indio gringo* ("fair-skinned" or "blond" Indian) is a recognized type in parts of northern Peru. There is nothing anomalous in this description. "Indian" is not, in the first place, a physical type but a social status. The Indian is distinguished not by genetic inheritance but by birth in, and therefore membership of, an Indian community and by possession of that community's culture. This is all that is needed for the definition of an Indian, though Indians normally look "Indian." The word *Indian* has, therefore, come to mean "of Indian descent"; it is used of persons who no longer occupy Indian status, but whose physical resemblance to the Indians implies descent from them. Since Indians are the "lowest" or least "civilized" element of the population, the word in this sense means "low class." It can also be used to mean "savage," or "uncivilized," or "bad" in a purely figurative way—equivalent, say, to that of *canaille* in French. *Negro*, on the other hand, denotes a physical type that commonly carries with it the general implication of low class, but culture is usually quite subsidiary to the definition.[13]

Racial status in the United States, defined in terms of "blood" and identified purely by physical appearance, divides the population into two halves within which two parallel systems of class differentiation are recognized. In Latin America, appearance is merely one indicator of social position. It is never sufficient in itself to determine how an individual should be classed. The dis-

549

crimination imposed on the basis of "color" in the United States has sometimes been called a "caste" system and has been contrasted with class systems. This distinction is impossible in Latin America where color is an ingredient of total social position, not the criterion for distinguishing two racial "castes." A policy of segregation on the basis of color would, therefore, be not merely repugnant to Latin Americans but literally impossible.

Even in Panamá where the bulk of the urban population is Negro and the "oligarchy," as the traditional upper class is called, entirely European, the notion of segregation is repulsive. A member of the Panamanian upper class concluded a bitter criticism of discrimination in the United States with the remark: "After all, it's a matter of luck whether one is born black or white." It remained to be added, of course, that in Panamá it is nevertheless bad luck to be born black and good luck to be born white.

At the time of the race riots in Oxford, Mississippi, Hector Velarde, a distinguished critic, took the occasion to deplore racial discrimination in the United States in an article in a Peruvian newspaper. Why can the North Americans not learn from us the virtue of racial tolerance? he asked. He went on to illustrate his argument with the usage of the word *negrita* as a term of affection. *Negrita de mi alma* was an expression used toward a sweetheart, he said. Indeed he did not exaggerate, for *negrita* and *negra* are both forms of address that imply a certain intimacy or informality (as a diminutive the former carries the implication of a potential sexual interest the latter lacks). Velarde did not mention the Indians (who are very much more numerous in Peru than the Negroes). If he had, it would not have helped his thesis since *Indian* is never used in an equivalent fashion, though *cholo* ("civilized Indian") and *zambo* ("half-caste") are both used as terms of affection among comrades.[14]

The implication of racial equality that he drew from his examples invites precision. Such terms do not find their way into such a context because they are flattering in formal usage, but precisely because they are not. Intimacy is opposed to respect; because these terms are disrespectful, they are used to establish or stress a relationship in which no respect is due. The word *nigger* is used in this way among Negroes in the United States, but only among Negroes. Color has, in fact, the same kind of class connotation in the Negro community as in Latin America: Pale-skinned means upper class. Hence *nigger,* in this context dark-skinned or lower

550

class, implies a relationship that is free of the obligation of mutual respect. Velarde's example, consequently, shows that color is an indicator of class, not a criterion of caste.

Those who find no racial discrimination in Latin America take the United States as their model. They point out, correctly, that there is no color bar and that race riots do not occur. (Indian risings are a matter they do not consider.) On the other hand, those who do find racial discrimination in Latin America are concerned with the fact that there exist high degrees of social differentiation that are habitually associated with physical traits and frequently expressed in the idiom of "race." They justify their view by the racial overtones given to social distinctions. In Latin America, these critics are commonly persons of left-wing sympathy who see racial discrimination as a bulwark of class distinction and, evading all nuances, they equate the two. Taking more easily to the emotive aspects of Marxism than to its dialectic, these would-be Marxists end by finding themselves as far from reality as those colonial legislators who once attempted so vainly to control the legal status of individuals on the basis of their descent. Because there is no color bar but rather a color scale that contributes only partially to the definition of status, they are pushed to an implied definition of race that is worthy of Gobineau. They speak of "racial hypocrisy" to explain why certain people claim a "racial" status to which their phenotype would not entitle them if "race" were really a matter of genes. This "false race-consciousness" is false only by the standards of a theory that would obliterate the historical evolution of the past four hundred years. History may validate these theorists if the Chinese interpretation of Marxist-Leninism acquires authority, and the class struggle, transposed to the international plane, becomes a matter of race.

The contrary opinion is usually held by persons of right-wing views. They regard class distinctions as either unobjectionable, insignificant, or at least inevitable. Once they can cite examples of people of upper-class status who show marked traces of non-European descent, they are satisfied that there is no racial discrimination in their country. (This conviction accords with the liberality of their nature and the official creed of their nation.) They are content that there is no problem if there is no "discrimination" as in the United States.

551

In the first case, the distinctiveness of class and color must be denied; in the second, the association between the two. The first theory ignores the individual instance; only the statistical aspect counts. The exception is evaded lest it disprove the rule. The second theory takes as significant only the chosen individual instance, overlooking the existence of a statistical norm. Indeed, no one is boycotted on account of his phenotype if his class standing is secured by the other criteria that define high status. In such a case, infrequent as it may be in Panamá, color may properly be said to be a matter of luck in the sense that it is a contingency that carries little of the weight of social definition. Economic power, culture, and community are what count.

The disapproval that Latin American visitors to the United States feel of the segregation they find there is not unconnected with the disrespectful attitude they are likely to inspire as Spanish speakers. They know that as Hispanics they are judged socially inferior in many places. Visitors from the United States, on the other hand, are often highly critical of the treatment the Indians of Latin America receive. This strikes them as much more reprehensible than the treatment of the Negroes in their own country, who have indeed much greater opportunities to improve their economic position and who, as domestic servants, are treated with more courtesy and consideration by their employers than the Indians of Latin America—a fact not unconnected with the shortage of domestic servants in the United States. Moreover, the treatment of Indians appears all the less justifiable to these visitors because Indians are not the object of discrimination throughout the greater part of North America.

Thus, comfortably blinkered by the assumptions of their own culture, each nation sees the mite in the other's eye.

In the United States one does sometimes find strong sentiments of hostility toward Indians in areas surrounding their communities; the same is sometimes true in Latin America of the Negroes (however they happen to be defined there). If Indians are not generally subject to discrimination in the United States nor Negroes in Latin America, it is in the first place due to their numerical weakness. In both countries, they pose local, not national, problems. There is roughly one Indian to fifty Negroes in the United States; in Latin America, the inverse disproportion would be greater even if one were to include only those

552

recognized as Negro. Such a comparison can be taken no further than this, however, since the nature of social distinctions is different in the two lands.

The Indian's predicament in Latin America can be likened to that of the Negro in the United States in only one way: Both provide a major national problem at the present time. There the resemblance stops. Not only is the nature of race relations fundamentally different in the societies that evolved from the English and Spanish colonies, but Indians and Negroes are different in their physical appearance and cultural origins. They are different above all in their place within the structure of the two societies, and have been so from the very beginning of colonial times. The Indians were the original inhabitants of the land; their incorporation or their refusal to be incorporated into colonial society hinged on the existence of Indian communities with a separate culture and a separate identity. The Negroes came in servile status and were marketed as chattel to the industrialized producers of sugar and metals. Cut off from their fellows, they soon lost their language and their original culture and became an integral part of colonial society.[15]

The Negro's status was within colonial society. The Indian's was not. To the extent that the Indian abandoned his Indian community and changed his culture, he lost his Indian identity. While the status of Negro refers to phenotype and attaches to individuals, Indian status refers to culture and attaches to a collectivity. One might speak of individual versus collective status, with all that these imply in terms of social structure. Consequently, while phenotypical differences are irrelevant to the definition of the Indian—hence the *indio gringo*—they have importance in according an individual status once he becomes "civilized." They establish a presumption as to descent, and this is an ingredient of class status. Paradoxically, the genetic background is important only in social distinctions between persons who are recognized as belonging to the same "non-Indian" race; not in the distinction between them and the Indians. "Race" is a matter of culture and community, not of genes, though class is connected with genes.

The problems of race relations in North America and Latin America are, therefore, fundamentally different. One concerns the assimilation of all ethnic groups into a single society; the other, the status distinction between persons who have been assimilated for hundreds of years but who are still distinguished socially by their appearance. The two are comparable only at the highest level of abstraction. One may wonder, therefore, whether the word *caste*, which is so often used in reference to the status distinction between Indians and *mestizos* (or *ladinos*) in Latin American society is not something of a misnomer. It carries quite different implications in Latin as opposed to North America. It would appear that it comes into the sociological literature about Latin America on the basis of several different and all equally false assumptions which will be dealt with elsewhere.

While the value of color is somewhat similar within the Negro community of the United States and the Hispanic section of Latin America, the Negro community is separated by a *caste* distinction from a socially superior element defined by phenotype; the Hispanic population of Latin America is distinguished by language and customs, beliefs and values and habitat from an element it regards as inferior, which does not participate in the same social system and, for the most part, far from wishing to be integrated into it, desires only to be rid of the *mestizos* physically. For this reason, the aims of Indian rebellions are the opposite of the aims of race riots. The former would like to separate once and for all the two ethnic elements; the latter are inspired by the resentment at the existence of a separation. Indians rebel to drive the intruders out of the countryside; Negroes riot in towns when they are not accorded full civic privileges.

The ethnic statuses of modern Latin America vary in number from the simple division into Indian and *mestizo* found in Mexico north of the Isthmus to the four tiers of highland Peru which include *cholos* and *blancos*: (*indio, cholo, mestizo, blanco*). These "social races" have much in common with the class distinctions of stratified societies. Woodrow Borah has even maintained that the ethnic distinction in Mexico is no more in essence than a matter of social class. This view raises a further problem in those areas where a regional ethnic consciousness emerges, for example among the Tlascalans, Isthmus Zapotecs, and the wealthy, educated Indians of Quetzaltenango in Guatemala.

Admitting that the class structure of Latin America carries ethnic overtones, how is this structure affected by class differences being thought about largely in the idiom of "race"? Such a view implies that classes are different in their essential nature. If the

554

concept of "social race" teaches us to think about race in terms of social structure, we should also have a concept of "ethnic class" to remind us that class systems no longer function in the same way once class has phenotypical associations. Processes of selection come into operation that cannot exist in a homogeneous population however it is stratified.

This observation leads to a conclusion that does not altogether accord with that of Professor Wagley[16] who states: "At least, theoretically, it is only a question of time until such populations may be entirely classed as mestizo by social race and social differentiation will be entirely in terms of socioeconomic classes."[17]

In terms of his thesis continued racial intermixture produces in Latin America, unlike North America, a blurring of the distinctions among different "social races." This would be true enough, if time could be trusted to produce phenotypical homogeneity, but it ceases to be so once one introduces the notion of selection into the theory. The absence of a bar on intermarriage does not necessarily produce homogeneity.

Distinctions of status are not always exhibited in the same ways. The castes of India are held apart by prohibitions on physical contact and commensality, and by endogamy. Feudal Europe accorded no importance to the first two and little to the third. The division of labor implied by any social distinction can bring people into either direct co-operation or segregation, depending upon the range of their ties and the basis of their "complementarity." If their status difference is assured in one way, it may prove indifferent to any other basis of distinction. For this reason the intimacy to which servants were admitted by their masters was greater in an earlier age when social distinctions were more clear-cut.

Physical differences can never be obliterated, but whether they, rather than cultural or social differences, are regarded as significant is a matter each social system decides for itself. It is for this reason that the value accorded to physical appearance varies so greatly from place to place and class to class in Latin America. But the significance of phenotype also varies greatly according to context. Political or commercial alliances are not the same as alliances through marriage. Their products are of a different order. Profits are colorless, children are not. Hence, phenotype may not matter in commercial dealings, but it is never more important than in marriage.

555

In Latin America today the grandchildren of a rich man who looks Indian or Negroid always appear much more European than he is himself. Color is an ingredient, not a determinant of class. It can, therefore, be traded for the other ingredients. It is not something that can be altered in the individual's life, but it is something that can be put right in the next generation. For this reason, the wives of the well-to-do tend to look more European than their husbands. In the lower classes, paler children are sometimes favored at the expense of their more swarthy siblings; their potential for social mobility is greater.

Individual motivations are ordered to produce conformity with an ideal image of ethnic class. This tends to reinforce the original image. Moreover, demographical factors reinforce this conformity in other ways—through the immigration of Europeans into Latin America and the existence of a pool of unassimilated Indians on the land. Indians are constantly abandoning their Indian identity and becoming integrated into the nation. This process is not unconnected with the current flight to the cities, for you lose Indian status once you settle in the city.[18] The result is a continual influx of persons of mainly Indian physique into the proletariat. At the same time, the immigration of Europeans into these countries has been very considerable in the last two decades, and these Europeans have almost all been absorbed into the upper classes. For demographic reasons, the correlation between class and color is increasing rather than diminishing.

Moreover, the significance of this correlation is also increasing under modern conditions. (It would be rash to say that it will go on increasing in the future, for the structure itself may well change to offset this effect.) The expansion of the open society at the expense of the local community changes the criteria whereby people are defined socially. Where known descent establishes status, color may carry little of the weight of social definition, but the descent must be known. It must be known whose child you are if you are to inherit the status of your father. If you have exchanged your local community for the big city, your descent becomes a matter of conjecture; you can no longer be respected because of your birth despite your Indian features. If you look Indian, it will be concluded that you were born of Indian parents. Thus, in the open society, appearance takes over the function of descent in allocating social status. In a world in flux, the fact that appearance cannot be dissimulated recommends

556

it above all other indicators. Clothing, speech, and culture are losing force as indicators of status in the context of expanding cities, but color is becoming ever more crucial.

Although these same conditions might create an increase in social mobility that would tend to reduce the phenotypical correlation of class, it appears that the opposite is happening today. If the classification into social races is losing its precision, the ethnic aspect of class is coming to have increased importance. The social structure is changing and with it the criteria of social classification. Under modern industrial conditions, much of Latin America is moving from the systems of social race that flourished in the communities of yesterday to a system of ethnic class adapted to the requirements of the open society of tomorrow.

REFERENCES

1. There is also a celebration on that day in front of the memorial to Columbus.

2. Sociologists have recently asserted that social mobility is as great in the traditional societies of Europe as in the U. S., which pays homage to the ideal of social mobility. The anomaly is quite superficial: Nobody has ever acted in accordance with an ideal notion of this type. It provides not a rule of conduct but only a basis for validating an achieved position. It is as easy to claim to be a self-made man as to claim not to be. The former claim appears to be as often untrue in the contemporary U. S. as the latter was in Victorian England.

3. The desire of the European aristocracy to maintain endogamy required a man to be able to quarter his arms and thereby prove his noble descent in both lines for four generations. Class status was treated as if it were a matter of race, as the term *breeding* implied. But, in the absence of any phenotypical indications, the margins of doubt were very great, and genealogists were entrusted with the task, performed in simpler societies by the memories of the elders, of bringing history into line with present social relations. Only in Renaissance Spain, because of the Moorish and Jewish populations of the Peninsula, did purity of blood relate to any ethnic distinction. This distinction was a social and religious one rather than a matter of phenotype. In fact, the differences in color among the different religious communities appear to have been negligible. The Moslems were mainly of Berber stock and, as such, very similar to the Iberians, if somewhat darker than the descendants of the Visigoths. Contrary to what is often imagined, there was no "color problem" in ancient Spain.

4. Claude Lévi-Strauss, *Race et Histoire* (Paris, 1952), p. 5.

557

5. Charles Wagley, "On the Concept of Social Race in the Americas", *Actas del 33 Congreso Internacional de Americanistas* (San José, 1959). Reprinted in Dwight B. Heath and Richard N. Adams, eds., *Contemporary Cultures and Societies of Latin America* (New York, 1965).

6. Woodrow Borah, "Race and Class in Mexico," *Pacific Historical Review*, Vol. 23, No. 4 (November, 1954); Julian Pitt-Rivers, "Who Are the Indians," *Encounter* (September, 1965).

7. "In Latin America happily this racial distinction is not important and this is very much to Latin America's credit." Arnold Toynbee, *The Economy of the Western Hemisphere* (Oxford, 1962), p. 4. "Here is a country [Mexico] whose population is racially diversified yet is socially and culturally united. . . . I can only hope that the Latin American and Islamic freedom from race prejudice is the 'wave of the future.'" Arnold Toynbee, "The Racial Solution," *Encounter* (September, 1965), p. 31.

8. For example, Robert S. Browne, *Race Relations in International Affairs* (Washington, 1961), p. 22: "South and Central America have in some places developed veritable interracial societies." The qualification is vital.

9. Juan Comas reviews some of the more scholarly versions of the two views in "Relaciones inter-raciales en America Latina, 1940-60," *Cuadernos del Instituto de Historia, serie antropologica,* No. 12 (Mexico, 1961).

10. Paez, Morelos, and Alamán looked Negroid; Porfirio Díaz, Juarez, and Melgarejo looked Indian. This can be verified from contemporary evidence. In modern popular literature and schoolbooks they are sometimes quite literally "whitewashed."

11. G. and A. Reichel-Dolmatoff, *The People of Aritama* (Chicago, 1961), p. 138.

12. See, for example, Albert Sireau, *Terre d'angoisse et d'espérance* (Paris, 1959), p. 22.

13. The situation in Panamá, referred to above, is exceptional. It derives from the influx of a large number of persons of different language and culture. Some slight difference in style of speech is attributed to Negroes in certain regions.

14. The same is true in Ecuador. N. E. Whitten, *Class, Kinship and Power in an Ecuadorian Town* (Stanford, 1965), p. 91.

15. This loss of language and culture does not hold for parts of the West Indies and Brazil. Aguirre Beltran maintains that elements of African culture have survived in Mexico. This is true in the case of certain details of material culture and musical style, though it might be more exact to call these Caribbean rather than African. In any case, they have long since ceased to be recognized as such. See, Aguirre Beltran, *Gonzalo: La Poblacion Negra de Mexico, 1519-1810* (Mexico, 1946), p. 96.

16. If I disagree with Professor Wagley ultimately with regard to the prospects

558

of the future (about which wise anthropologists refrain from speculating), I do not wish to obscure my debt to Professor Wagley's thinking on this subject nor to deny homage to his admirable essay. But I would not write about this subject at all if I did not think there remains something more to be said.

17. Wagley, "On the Concept of Social Race in the Americas," p. 540.

18. Only exceptionally, as in the Isthmus of Tehuantepec or Quetzaltenango, can a man become integrated while retaining an Indian (or is it a pseudo-Indian?) identity. Then region replaces community as the defining unit.

559

BEYOND POVERTY :
THE NEGRO AND THE MULATTO
IN BRAZIL *

by Florestan FERNANDES

1. Introduction :

The most impressive aspect of the racial situation in Brazil appears under the trenchant denial of the existence of any " color " or " racial " problem. Racial prejudice and discrimination, as racial segregation, are seen as a sort of sin and as dishonorable behavior. Thus, we have two different levels of reality perception and of action connected with " color " and " race " : first, overt, in which racial equality and racial democracy are supposed and proclaimed ; second, covert, in which collateral functions perform through, below and beyond the social stratification.

This overlay is not exclusive to race relations. It appears in other levels of social life. In the case of race relations it emerges as a clear product from the prevailing racial ideology and racial utopia, both built during slavery by the white-dominant stratum — the rural and urban masters. Slavery was not in conflict with the Portuguese law and cultural tradition. The Roman law offered to the crown ordinances the elements with which it would be possible to classify the " Indians " or the " Africans " as *things*, as moveable property, and establish the social transmission of social position through the mother (according to the principle *partus sequitur ventrem*), deny to the slave any human condition (*servus personam non habet*, etc...) On

---

* This paper was first presented, in a condensed version, at the seminars on *Minorities in Latin America and the United States*, (The College of the Finger Lakes, Corning, New York, December 5, 1969).

the other hand, slavery was practiced on a small scale in Lisbon, and was attempted in Açores, Madeira, Cabo Verde and São Tome, pioneering the modern plantation system. But slavery was in conflict with religion and the mores created by the Catholic conception of the world. This conflict, of a moral nature, did not give to the slave, in general, a better condition and more human treatment, as Frank Tannebaum believed. It only brought about a tendency to disguise things, separating the permissive from the real being.

Nevertheless, Brazil has a good intellectual tradition of penetrating, realistic, and unmasking objective knowledge of the racial situation. First of all, the conservative pride had given rise to very clear distinctions (as usually happened with the masters and some aristocratic white families arrogantly self-affirmative on matters of racial inequality and race differences). Second, some outstanding figures, leaders of the ideals of national emancipation or of abolitionism, as Jose Bonifacio de Andrade e Silva, Luiz Gama, Perdigao Malheiros, Joaquim Nabuco, Antonio Bento, etc., tried to point out the nature of the white behavior and value-orientations, connected with the Negroes and the Mulattos. Third, the " negro movements " after the First World War (especially in Sao Paulo and Rio de Janeiro during the 20's, 30's and 40's), as well as intellectual Negro conferences on race relations, have contributed to a new realistic perception and explanation of the complex Brazilian racial situation.

The findings of modern sociological, anthropological, or psychological investigations (Samuel Lowrie ; Roger Bastide and Florestan Fernandes ; L. A. Costa Pinto ; Oracy Megueira ; A. Guerreiro Ramos ; Octavio Ianni, Fernando Henrique Cardoso and Renato Jardim Moreira ; Thales de Azevedo ; Charles Wagley, Marvin Harris, Henry W. Hutchinson and Ben Zimmerman ; René Ribeiro ; Joao Baptista Borges Pereira ; Virginia Leone Bicudo ; Aniela Ginsberg ; Carolina Martuscelli Bori ; Dante Moreira Leite ; etc.), have confirmed and deepened the evidence discovered by earlier writers. In the present discussion, I will limit myself to three special topics : the roots of competitive social order in Brazil ; some objective evidences of racial inequality and its sociological meaning ; the Brazilian pattern of racial prejudice and discrimination [1].

2. The Roots of Competitive Social Order in Brazil :

As occurred in all modern countries in which slavery was connected with colonial exploitation and the plantation system, the Brazilian society faced great difficulties in spreading and integrating the competitive social order.

----

1. Cf. *L'Esclavage au Brésil*. Paris, Librairie de Guillaumin et Cⁱᵉ, 1881 ; *Le Brésil en 1884*, Faro & Lino, Editeurs, Rio de Janeiro, 1884.

Literally speaking, this social order emerged with the rupture of the old colonial system, but its evolution was more an urban phenomenon, until the last quarter of the nineteenth century. Slavery and the relative importance of the freedmen as a source of an earning social category were a great obstacle to the differentation and universalization of the competitive social order. The reason is very well known. As Louis Couty pointed out, the devaluation and the degradation of work produced by slavery impeded or obstructed the constitution of a wage-earning class in urban as in rural areas and the emergence of a small farmer sector. Because of this, until the middle of the nineteenth century the market economy didn't give rise to a typical modern organisation, in a capitalistic sense, of work and of economic relations. Only in a few cities competition performed some basic constructive functions and could integrate the roles or the positions of some social agents (the landlords or planters, as suppliers of tropical products ; the agents of export-import business ; native and foreign merchants and traders ; some bankers of financial agents ; the professionals, teachers and bureaucrats ; the few manufacturers and factory workers ; the technicians, artisans and skilled workers, etc.).

With the interruption of the slave traffic and the emancipationist laws this sector began to enlarge and to grow. In the last quarter of the nineteenth century, the crisis of the slavery system — which attained a structural and irreversible trend at the decade of sixty — reached its climax. Then the modernization of the urban sector became a strong and autonomous social force, operating simultaneously through the economic and political levels. This was an historical point of inflexion, in which the disintegration of the master-slave social order and the integration of the competitive social order appeared as concomitant social phenomena [2].

In this large context, the situation of the Negroes and the Mulattos was affected in three different directions. Until this period, as slaves or as freedmen, they have had a strong and untouchable position in the structure of economy. As soon as the entire structure of the system of production began to change, this position was menaced on two fronts. The international market supplied the country with immigrants who came from Europe and looked for the richer and developing areas, to work as wageearning class, rural and urban, or as traders, merchants, shopkeepers or manufacturers. On the other side, white traditional families started to move from

---

2. As a large frame of reference : F. FERNANDES, *A Integração do Negro na Sociedade de Classes*, São Paulo, Dominus Editôra — Editôra da Universidade de São Paulo, 1965, vol. 1, cap. 1 ; R. BASTIDE e F. FERNANDES, *Brancos e Negros em São Paulo*, São Paulo, Companhia Editôra Nacional, 2ª edição, 1959, caps. I-II ; O. IANNI, " *O Progresso Econômico e o Trabalhador Livre* ", *in* S. Buarque de Holanda, História Geral da Civilização Brasileira : *O Brasil monárquico*, Vol. III, São Paulo, 1964, Difusão Europeia do Livro, pp. 297-319 ; C. PRADO Junior, *História Econômica do Brasil*. São Paulo, Editôra Brasiliense, 2ª ed., 1949, cap. 19.

the interior to the great cities, and the poor or dependent people [3] arose as a growing wage-earning sector.   In the North and Northeast, the relative economic stagnation of plantation economy stimulated two correlative processes — the sale of the surplus slave labor to the coffee plantations of São Paulo, Rio de Janeiro and Minas Gerais ; and the consolidation of the positions of the Negro or Mulatto freedmen as agents of free labor (unskilled or skilled, especially in the growing urban economy).   In the rapidly developing regions of coffee plantations (but in particular in São Paulo), the newcomers, foreigners or nationals, absorbed the best economic opportunities, even in the rural areas, accelerating the crisis of slavery and converting the Negroes and Mulattos, predominantly, into a marginal sector of the population and into a subproletariat.   In the areas of the South, in which the foreign colonization was combined with small farmers or those in which the cattle ranch predominated, controlled by powerful traditional families, the Negroes and the Mulattos were also out of competition for the new opportunities, monopolized by the Europeans, or remained in disguised dependent or marginal positions [4].

Thus, as a general conclusion : the victim of slavery was also victimized by the crisis of the slave system of production.   The social revolution of the competitive social order started and finished as a *white revolution*. Because of this, white supremacy was never menaced by abolitionism.   On the contrary, it was only reorganized in other terms, in which competition had a terrible consequence — the exclusion, partially or totally, of the ex-agent of slave labor and of the freedmen from the vital flux of economic growth and social development.

At the zero point of their inclusion in a new social order, therefore, the Negro and the Mulatto had several choices, all spoliatory and deplorable. First, the return to the regions of their origins (or of their ascendants), that is, to some rural area of the North-east or a stagnant and backward community of the interior of São Paulo, Minas Gerais or Rio de Janeiro.   This solution implied a submersion into a natural economy of subsistence.   Second, the permanence as a rural laborer, in general changing from the old master to a new employer.   This solution, as the ex-slave didn't have the institutions

---

3. In general, a racial mixed sector of population, in the South phenotypically and socially " white ".   The process occurred simultaneously in the cities and in the rural areas.

4. With reference to the Northeast and the emergence of a free labor market, the considerations are based on an unpublished study of Barbara Trosco, on the freedman in Bahia.   With reference to São Paulo. Rio grande do Sul, Paraná e Santa Catarina : cf. R. BASTIDE, e F. FERNANDES, *Brancos e Negros em São Paulo, loc. cit.*, F. FERNANDES, *A Integração do Negro na Sociedade de Classes, loc. cit.* ; F. HENRIQUE CARDOSO, *Capitalismo e Escravidas no Brasil Meridional*. São Paulo, Difusão Europeia do Livro, 1962 ; O. IANNI, *As Metamorfoses do Esclavo*, São Paulo, Difusão Europeia do Livro, 1962 ; O. IANNI, *Racar e Classes no Brasil*, Rio de Janeiro, Editôra Civilização Brasileira, 1966 ; F. Henrique CARDOSO e O. IANNI, *Côr e Mobilidade Social em Florianópolis*, Sao Paulo, Companhia Editora Nacional.

and the cultural traditions of the immigrants, and had, on the other hand, to compete with them in terms of low payment [5], implied a permanent incapacity to use domestic cooperation, the resultant techniques of thrift and social mobility as a mechanism of accumulation of capital and of competition. Third, the concentration in a big city, like São Paulo, and the conglomeration in the slums. This solution implied permanent or temporary unemployment for the man, parasitism and over-burdening for the woman and general anomie for all. Life in the city rarely was equivalent of sharing the opportunities of the city. Three succeeding generations have known what social disorganization could mean as a style of life. Fourth, the flight to little cities, in which the semi-skilled, skilled or artisan could protect himself from the competition with the whites, foreigners or nationals, and start a new life. This solution implied a voluntary acceptance of disadvantageous positions with no hopes in regard to the future. It had the same meaning that the absorption of freedmen, in the North-east, acquired during the period of disintegration of slavery. The destiny of the agents, then, was a function of the stagnation or progress of the selected community, a matter of blind chance.

From this perspective, it is clear that the problems of the Brazilian Negroes or Mulattos is, above all, a problem created by the incapacity of the national society to develop rapidly a growing capitalistic economy, able to absorb the ex-slaves and the freedmen in the labor market. Because of this, they were expelled to the periphery of the competitive social order or to semi-colonial and colonial structures inherited from the past. These semi-colonial or colonial structures performed important functions in the maintenance of the rural economy, especially where the plantations, cattle ranches or the villages were (or are) dependent on semi-capitalistic forms of work [6].

One could argue that, in this aspect, the ex-slaves and the freedmen underwent the destiny common to all " poor people " in Brazil. The destitution of the slaves and the elimination of the freedmen by the effects of competition with the free European immigrants would explain sociologically that process. Nevertheless, as Caio Prado Jr. has pointed out [7], slavery didn't prepare its human agent to become a free worker, even as unskilled or semi-skilled laborers. Behind the social structure of the master-slave social order, the " slave " and the " Negro " were two parallel elements. When the " slave " was eliminated by social change, the " Negro " became a racial residuum. He lost the social condition which he acquired under slavery and was expelled, as " Negro ", downward to the bottom of the " poor people, " at the exact moment in which some of its sectors were sharing the

5. On the low wages of the rural free labor, see E. Viottida da Costa, *Da Senzala à Colonia*, São Paulo, Difusão Europeia do Livro, 1966.

6. See bibliography in note 4.

7. C. Prado Junior, *Formação do Brasil Contemporâneo Colônia*. Sao Paulo, Livraria Martins Editora, 1942, pp. 341-342.

opportunities opened by free work and the constitution of a wage-earning class. Thus, the Negro was victimized by his position and by his racial condition. He started, by his own means, the process by which he could be metamorphosed from " Negro " to a new social being [8]. But, when he was trying to impose upon himself and upon the indifferent whites the " Second Abolition ", the attempt was refused and condemned, as a manifestation of " racism " [9]. In other words, he was denied a self-affirmation as " Negro " in spite of his social marginality as such.

3. Evidence of Racial Inequality and its Sociological Meaning :

If the description given above is correct, the changes in social structure that have occurred in Brazilian society from the abolition of slavery until now, have had no profound effects (or very slight effects) on the racial concentration of wealth, social prestige and power. The lack of objective indicators do no permit a complete verification of this conclusion. The last census (in 1960) has excluded the racial aspects of the Brazilian population. Nevertheless, the census of 1950 offered some useful information.

As is well known, the percentage of the different racial stocks (or color categories) varies in each physiographic region of the country (cf. Table I). In consequence, the degree of concentration of each racial stock (or color category)in the different regions varies with clear intensity (cf. Table II).

Nevertheless, the two basic indicators — occupational position and level of schooling — which we could use through the census data, reveal a basic trend of monopoly of the best opportunities by the whites. We have selected the position of employer and the completed educational levels in some representative states and in the country as the best indicator accessible They involve roles, values and cultural traditions expressive in terms of white evaluations of prestige, control of power and upward social mobility.

The basic sociological evidence of the data is not negative, considering that slavery was ended only sixty-two years ago (with reference to the census of 1950), the total negligence of the human problems of the " poor people " in general and of the destitute population of slave origin, the lack of value orientations and of experience with the economic, social and cultural requisites of the developing competitive social order predominant among negroes and mulattos, the indifference or disguised opposition of whites to a democratic sharing of economic or educational opportunities with both

---

8. Cf. O. Ianni, *As Metamorfoses do Esclavo, op. cit.* ; F. Fernandes, *A Integração do Negro na Sociedade de Classes, op. cit.*, vol. I, cap. I e vol. II, cap. 5.

9. Cf. R. Bastide e F. Fernandes, *Brancos e Negros em São Paulo, op. cit.*, cap. 5 ; F. Fernandes, *A Integração do Negro na Sociedade de Classes, op. cit.*, vol. II, cap. 4.

sectors of Brazilian population, etc., the census data shows an improvement of the situation by the effort of these color groups to take the possible advantages of freedom and progress. Most of the issues, naturally, are connected with the gradual acquisition of new value orientations and cultural traditions, the importance of negroes and mulattos as economic agents (as labor force or as predominantly small entrepreneurs), and the discovery and use of educational opportunities as a ladder to social integration and upward mobility. The importance of these aspects is greater than could be realized at first glance, because of the cumulative effects of the economic, social or cultural process involved in the future of new generations.

Nevertheless, the progress has been too moderate and deceptive. In reality, the Negroes and the Mulattos were projected into the strata of the poorest people, which doesn't share (or shares very little) the trends of economic development and sociocultural change. Even in the regions in which the Negroes and the Mulattos constitute the majority of the population, as in the Northeast and in the East (in which they constitute, conjointly, 53.7 % and 47.3 %, respectively, of the region ; and in which they are more concentrated — 72.8 % in the Northeast and 95.5 % in the East, by color group) they have an extremely poor participation in the position of employers and in the best educational opportunities. In terms of the states selected, the range of inequality relating to the employers' positions gives to whites a striking supremacy (they share these positions in a proportion of 3, 4, 5 and even 6 or 8 times to one of the Negroes.) The same occurs in relation to the Mulattos, instead of their being in a better situation than the Negroes (the whites share the employers' positions, on the average, in a proportion which oscillates between 2, 3 or 4 times more than the Mulattos, excepting the case of Rio de Janeiro). The same trends are reproduced in the sharing of educational opportunities, especially at the levels of the secondary shcools and the universities, in some states, in a shocking manner. (See Tables III and IV). The comparison of the data furnished by these tables with that of Table V shows that the exclusion of the Negroes and the Mulattos from the best economic and educational opportunities follows the same general pattern, in the eight selected states. The predominance of Mulattos, considered alone, or of Negroes and Mulattos, considered together, makes only a slight difference even in the more " mixed " and more racially " democratic " states.

The meaning of this data is evident. The racial structure of Brazilian society, until now, favors the monopoly of wealth, prestige and power by the whites. The white supremacy is a reality in the present, almost in the same way it was in the past. The organization of society impels the Negro and the Mulatto to poverty, unemployment or underemployment, and to the " Negro's job ".

4. The Brazilian Pattern of Racial Prejudice and Discrimination :

Only now are Brazilian social scientists trying to discover the real explanation of this deplorable situation. As Costa Pinto has pointed out, the basic explicative factor is inherent in the persistence of some deep-rooted attitudes and racial orientations of the whites, to treat the Negroes and the Mulattos as subalterns (then to subalternize them). These attitudes and racial orientations are predominant among the upper and middle white classes ; but they appear also in the lower classes and even in the rural areas, especially in the South.

For many Brazilians, these attitudes and racial orientations are products of " external influence ", a negative contribution of immigrants and of the modern mass media of communication. They were and are considered an " imported cancer " [10], to be extirpated by law and formal control. However, the various researches made by Oracy Nogueira ; Roger Bastide and F. Fernandes ; L. A. Costa Pinto ; Octavio Ianni, Fernando Henrique Cardoso, and Renato Jardim Moreira have shown that the described attitudes and racial orientations are an inherited cultural pattern, widespread in Brazilian society as much as slavery was in the past.

Thus, at the core of the Brazilian racial problem is the persistence of an asymmetrical pattern of race relations, built to regulate the contact and the social ordination between " master ", " slave " and " freedman ". As happened in the South of the United States, this type of asymmetrical race relation involves a sort of ritualization of racial behavior [11]. The master's domination and the slave's or freedman's subordination are part of the same ritual, by which emotions and feelings could be put under control and masked. In Brazil, this type of ritualization had the same functions, reinforced by Catholic pressure to preserve, in some apparent sense, the Christian way of life of masters, slaves and freedmen.

Racial prejudice was inherent in the asymmetrical pattern of race relations, because it was a necessary element in basing the slave-master, or freedman-white relations in the " natural inferiority " of the Negroes and in the efficient performance of slavery and subjugation of the slaves and freedmen. At the same time, the discrimination was inherent in the slave-master social order, in which the proper manner of behavior, the clothing, the language, the occupations, obligations and rights of the slave and the freedman were rigidly prescribed [12]. The persistence of the two elements

---

10. See especially R. BASTIDE e F. FERNANDES, *Brancos e Negros em São Paulo, op. cit.*, cap. V.

11. Cf. B. Wilbur DOYLE, *The Etiquette of Race Relations in the South. A Study in Social Control*, Chicago, Illinois, The University of Chicago Press, 1937 (and especially the preface of Robert E. Park, pp. XI-XXIV).

12. Cf. especially R. BASTIDE e F. FERNANDES, *Brancos e Negros em São Paulo, op. cit.*, cap. 2.

after the disintegration of slavery is explained by the fact that the class system had not destroyed all structures of the *ancien regime,* especially the structures of race relations [13].

It is necessary, nevertheless, to take into account that this result is not only part of a process of cultural lag. Under dependent capitalism, the class system is unable to perform all the destructive or constructive functions it has had in the developed capitalistic countries [14]. Two processes run together — the modernization of the archaic, and the archaization of the modern, as a normal factor of structural integration and of evolution of the society. In reality, as soon as the Negro and the Mulatto were put predominantly outside of economic, social and political reconstruction, they became a marginal partner.

The crisis of the asymmetrical pattern of race relation started even before the Abolition. However, as the Negro and the Mulatto had lost their importance as historical social agent, they suffered the static effect of their new social position. Only now, thanks to internal migrations, the economic progress produced by national integration of society, and the weak upward social mobility, they acquired conditions to cope with white supremacy, predominantly in a disguised and accomodative way.

In spite of some active resistance of Whites, not to these phenomena, but to some outstanding upward-mobile Negro and Mulatto personalities, this long period of starvation contributed to maintain the ritualistic freezing of racial relations. The Negro and the Mulatto, as individuals, but especially as a color minority, are not free to use aggressive competition against Whites, and to explore social conflict to fight against racial inequality. In this context, it is very clear that the price of race tolerance and race accomodation is paid for by the Negro and the Mulatto.

For these reasons, color is not an important element in racial perception and racial consciousness of the world by the White. He has never been menaced, up until now, by the disintegration of slavery and by competition or conflict with Negroes and Mulattos. The White only perceives and is conscious of the Negro or of the Mulatto when he faces a concrete, unexpected situation [15], or when his attention is directed to questions related to the " color problem. "

For the same reasons, the " Brazilian racial dilemma " is also complicated. Not so much because the Whites, Negroes and Mulattos play the expected roles of disguising or denying the " color prejudice " and " color discrimi-

---

13. See especially F. FERNANDES, *A Integração do Negro na Sociedade de Classes, op. cit.,* vol. II, cap. 6.

14. Cf. especially F. FERNANDES, *Sociedade de Classes e Subdesenvolvimento,* Rio de Janeiro, Zahar Editores, 1968, cap. 1.

15. Because of this, some techniques, applied by North American psychologists, social psychologists, anthropologists or sociologists in the personal study of perception of race, race differences or race identifications are inefficient in the study of the Brazilian situation.

nation ", but because the only way open to the change of the racial situation depends on gradual, very slow, and irregular prosperity of Negroes and Mulattos. Under this aspect, it is out of the question that prejudice and discrimination, in the forms that they assume in Brazil, contribute more to maintain the asymmetric pattern of race relations, than to eliminate it.

This means that, sociologically considered, color prejudice and discrimination are a structural and dynamic source of the " perpetuation of the past in the present ". The Whites do not victimize the Negroes and the Mulattos consciously and willfully. The normal and indirect effects of the functions of color prejudice and discrimination do that, without racial tensions and social unrest. Because they restrict the economic, educational, social and political opportunities of the Negro and the Mulatto, maintaining them " out of the system " or at the margin and on the periphery of the competitive social order, color prejudice and discrimination impedes the existence and the emergence of a racial democracy in Brazil.

5. Conclusions :

This general discussion was oriented by some basic assumptions. Considered sociologically, *the structural element of the Brazilian racial situation* has two distinctive dimensions. One, which is specifically social. It is connected with the impossibility, faced by underdeveloped capitalistic and class societies of Latin America, of creating a competitive social order able to absorb the different sectors of population, even partially, in the occupational and social strata of the system of production. The other, which is, by its nature, the " *color problem* ", a complex heritage of the past, continuously reinforced by the trends assumed by inequality under dependent capitalism, and preserved through the conjoint manifestation of prejudiced attitudes and discriminatory behavior on the basis of " color. "

These two elements work together, in such a manner that they produce cumulative effects dynamically adverse to the change of the racial structure of society, inherited from the past. The social order is changing and, with it, the patterns of race relations. Nevertheless, the relative position of color groups tend to be stable or to change very slightly.

It is beyond question that the most important factor, on the average, is the structure of a class society under dependent capitalism. The static effect of the extreme concentration of wealth, power and social prestige impedes or restricts severely even the upward social mobility and integration to the competitive social order of white racial stocks. The figures given by numbers and proportions of Whites who attained employers' positions (or who monopolize the best educational opportunities) are striking. A comparison with the Japanese suggests that, among the Whites, there prevails a definite trend to maintain and perhaps strengthen either economic and political privileges or social inequities, at the expense of all color and poor groups, including the " white poor people ".

However, the static effects are clearly stronger when we consider the Negroes and the Mulattos.   Instead of the relative advantages of the Mulattos with regard to the Negroes, they also share the economic, social, and political inequities of Brazilian society in a very hard way (if we compare the percentages on color composition and concentration of population with the distribution of employers' positions and the best educational opportunities).   Some could argue that " passing " — so easily, especially in the regions in which the Mulattos constitute the majority or a large part of the population — would explain these adverse figures.   But in reality, this argument has no sociological meaning.   Each color group, sociologically understood, embraces people who consider themselves and who are accepted under a given color category.   On the other side, our research with Bastide has shown that the overlapping or crossing, in terms of color lines, is more complicated than had been presumed.   As some " light " Mulattos try to " pass for white ", others refuse to do that and even prefer to classify themselves as " Negroes. "   This was a surprising result.   Indeed, what counts, suggests a dramatic situation which cannot be denied or hidden.

The economic, social and cultural condition of the Negroes is the most terrible aspect of the entire picture, given by the census data.   At the 1950 census, the Negroes comprised almost 14 million (11 % of the total population), but they shared less than 20,000 opportunities as employers (0.9 %), predominantly at modest levels, and only 6,794 (0.6 %) and 448 (0.2 %) had completed, respectively, courses in secondary schools and universities.   A situation like that involves more than social inequality and insidious poverty. It presupposes that the individuals affected are not included, as a racial stock, in the existing social order, as if they were not human beings or normal citizens.

BIBLIOGRAPHY

Azvedo (J. Lucio de), *Epocas de Portugal Econômico*, Lisboa, Livraria Clássica Editôra, 1928.

Azevedo (T.), *Les Élites de Couleur dans une Ville Brésilienne*, Paris, Unesco, 1953 ; *Ensaios de Antropologia Social*, Salvador, Universidade da Bahia, 1959.

Banton (M.), *Race Relations*, New York, Basic Books, 1967 (ch. xi).

Bastide (R.), *Sociologie du Brésil*, Paris, Centre de Documentation Universitaire, s. d.

Bastide (R.) e van den Berghe (P.), « Stereotypes, Norms and Interracial Behavior in Sao Paulo, Brazil », *American Sociological Review*, 22, 1957, pp. 689-694.

Berghe (P. van den), *Race and Racism*, New York, John Wiley & Sons, 1967, (ch. iii).

Bicudo (V. L.), « Attitudes dos Alunos de Grupos Escolares em Relação com a Côr de Seus Colegas », *in* Unesco-Anhembí, *Relações entre Negros e Brancos em São Paulo*, São Paulo, Editora Anhembí Ltda., 1955, pp. 227-310 ; « Atitudes Raciais de Pretos e Mulatos em São Paulo », *Sociologia*, São Paulo, IX-3, 1947, pp. 195-219.

Costa Pinto (L. A.), *O Negro no Rio de Janeiro*, Relações Raciais numa Sociedade em Mudança, São Paulo, Companhia Editôra Nacional, 1953.

Eduardo (O. C.), *The Negro in Northern Brazil*, A Study in Acculturation, Washington University of Washington Press, 1948.

Fernandes (F.), « Aspectos da Questão Racial », *O Tempo e o Modo*, Lisboa, 1967, pp. 36-49, « The Weight of the Past », *Daedalus*, Cambridge, Mass., Spring, 1967, pp. 560-579.

Freyre (G.), *Casa Grande & Senzala*, Roi de Janeiro, Livraria José Olympio Editôra, 9a edição, 1959 (2 vols.) ; *Sobrados e Mucambos*, Rio de Janeiro, Livraria José Olympio Editôra, 2ª edição, 1951 (3 vols.).

Ginsberg (A. M.), « Pesquisas sobre as Atitudes de um Grupo de Escolares de São Paulo em Relação com as Crianças de Côr », Unesco-Anhembí, *Relações entre Negros e Brancos em São Paulo*, São Paulo, Editora Anhembí Ltda., 1955, pp. 311-361.

Harris (M.), *Town and Country in Brazil*, New York, Columbia University Press, 1956 (pp. 112-124), Patterns of Race in the Americas, New York, Walker & Co., 1964.

Ianni (O.), *Raças e Classes no Brasil*, Rio de Janeiro, Editôra Civilização Brasileira, 1966.

Leite (D. M.), « Preconceito Racial e Patriotismo em Seis Livros Didáticos Brasileiros », *in Boletim de Psicologia*, No. 3, São Paulo, Faculdade de Filosofia, Ciências e Letras da Universidade de São Paulo, 1950, pp. 206-301.

Lobo (H.) e Aloisi (I.), *O Negro na Vida Social Brasileira*, São Paulo, S. E. Panorama Ltda., 1941.

Lowrie (S. H.), « O Elemento Negro na População de São Paulo », *Revista do Arquivo Municipal*, São Paulo, IV-XLVIII, 1938 ; « Origem da População da Cidade de São Paulo e Diferenciação das Classes Sociais », *Revista do Arquivo Municipal*, São Paulo, IV-XLIII, 1938.

Martuscelli (C.), « Uma Pesquisa sobre Aceitação de Grupos « Raciais » e Grupos Regionais », *in Boletim de Psicologia*, No. 3, São Paulo, Faculdade de Filosofia, Ciências e Letras da Universidade de São Paulo, 1950, pp. 53-73.

Moreira (R. J.), « Brancos em Bailes de Negros », *Anhembi*, São Paulo, VI-71-XXIV, 1956, pp. 274-288.

Nogueira (O.), « Atitudes Desfavoráveis de Alguns Anunciantes de São Paulo em Relação aos Empregados de Côr », *Sociologia*, São Paulo, IV-4, 1942, pp. 328-358 ; « Preconceito de Marca e Preconceito Racial de Origem », *Anais do XXXI Congresso de Americanistas*, São Paulo, Editôra Anhembí Ltda., 1955, vol. I, pp. 409-434 ; « Relações Raciais no Município de Itapetininga », Unesco-Anhembí, *Relações entre Negros e Brancos em São Paulo*, São Paulo, Editôra Anhembí Ltda., 1955, pp. 311-361.

Perdigão Malheiros (A. M.), *A Escravidão no Brasil*, Rio de Janeiro, Tipografia Nacional, 1866 (3 vols.).

Pereira (J. B.) Borges, *Côr, Profissão e Mobilidade*, O Negro na Rádio de São Paulo, São Paulo, Livraria Pioneira Editôra, 1967.

Pierson (D.), *Brancos e Pretos na Bahia*, São Paulo, Companhia Editôra Nacional, 1945.

Ribeiro (R.), *Religião e Relações Raciais*, Rio de Janeiro, Ministério de Educação e Cultura, 1956.

Santana (E. T.), *Relações entre Pretos e Brancos em São Paulo*. Preconceito de Côr, Sao Paulo, Edicao do Antar, 1951.

WAGLEY (C.), com a colaboração de HUTCHINSON (H.), HARRIS (M.), ZIMMERMAN (B.), *Races et Classes dans le Brésil Rural*, Paris, Unesco, s. d.

WAGLEY (C.) e HARRIS (M.), *Minorities in the New World*, New York, Columbia University Press, 1964.

WILLEMS (E.), « Race Attitudes in Brazil », *The American Journal of Sociology*, LIV-5 1949, pp. 402-408.

TABLE I.

Brazilian Population : Physiographic Regions and Color (1950) *.

Physiographic Regions	Color Groups					Total
	Whites	Negroes	Mulattos	Yellows**	N° declaration	
North.	577,329	90,061	1,171,352	1,446	4,467	1,844,655
	31 %	5 %	63.5 %	0.07 %	0.2 %	100 %
Northeast	5,753,697	1,374,899	5,339,729	216	25,936	12,494,477
	46 %	11 %	42.7 %	0.002 %	0.2 %	100 %
East	9,978,386	2,959,423	6,007,294	5,967	41,937	18,893,007
	52.8 %	15.6 %	31.7 %	0.03 %	0.2 %	100 %
South.	14,836,496	1,093,887	696,956	316,641	31,313	16,975,293
	87 %	6.5 %	4 %	2 %	0.2 %	100 %
Central-West.	981,753	174,387	571,411	4,812	4,602	1,736,965
	56.5 %	10 %	32.3 %	0.3 %	0.3 %	100 %
BRAZIL	32,027,661	5,692,657	13,786,742	329,082	108,255	51,944,397
	61.6 %	11 %	26,6 %	0.6 %	0.2 %	100 %

* Census data Instituto Brasileiro de Geografia e Estatistica — Conselho Naçional de Estatistica, *Recenseamento Geral do Brasil*, Rio de Janeiro, Serviço Grafico do I.B.G.E., 1956 (Volume I, p. 5).
** Asiatics, predominantly Japanese.

TABLE II.

Brazilian Population : Percentage Distribution by Color Groups, According to the Physiographic Regions * (1950).

Regions	Whites	Negroes	Mulattos	Yellows
North.	1.8 %	1.6 %	8.5 %	0.4 %
Northeast	17.9 %	24.1 %	38.7 %	0.06 %
East.	30.8 %	52.0 %	43.5 %	1.8 %
South.	46.3 %	19.2 %	5.1 %	96.2 %
Central-West	3.06 %	3.1 %	4.0 %	1.5 %
BRAZIL	100 %	100 %	100 %	100 %

* Omitted the cases without declaration of color.

TABLE III.

Employers by Color Groups — Brazil and Selected States (1950) *.

States	Number			
	Whites	Negroes	Mulatto	Asiatic *
Para.	5,089	208	3,132	88
Pernambuco	21,121	904	5,836	17
Bahia	28,178	5,295	20,837	10
Minas Gerais...........	85,084	3,910	15,949	107
Rio de Janeiro..........	46,477	447	1,283	64
Sao Paulo..............	146,145	2,561	1,396	9,179
Rio Grande do Sul........	49,008	429	576	16
Mato Grosso............	5,171	401	1,330	94
BRAZIL	519,197	19,460	78,448	11,018

States	Percentage in Each Color Group			
	Whites	Negroes	Mulattos	Asiatics **
Para.	5.4	0.9	1.4	34.2
Pernambuco	4.0	0.7	1.2	34.6
Bahia	6.8	1.6	2.8	15.6
Minas Gerais	6.4	1.0	2.5	14.6
Rio de Janeiro..........	8.2	0.3	0.8	12.5
Sao Paulo..............	5.1	0.8	1.2	10.1
Rio Grande do Sul........	4.2	0.5	0.7	8.8
Mato Grosso............	6.6	2.3	2.5	8.9
BRAZIL	5.1	0.9	1.8	10.2

* Census data. Omitted the cases without declaration of position (excepting Para, in which these cases were included).
** The Asiatics are nearly all Japanese.

TABLE IV.

Educational Levels Completed by Negroes and Mulattos — Brazil and Selected States (1950) *.

States Negro Mulatto	Educational Levels Completed					
	Primary		Secondary		University	
	Number	% of total **	Number	% of total **	Number	% of total **
Para						
Negroes	1,599	2.2	85	0.6	10	0.5
Mulattos.	27.536	39,4	2.371	19.2	180	9.5
Pernambuco						
Negroes	5,899	3.3	192	0.5	7	0.5
Mulattos.	42,669	24.2	2,889	8.0	189	3.6
Bahia						
Negroes	17,732	8.3	666	2.1	88	1.5
Mulattos.	78,742	37.1	44,772	15.2	578	10.1
Minas Gerais						
Negroes	36,805	5.4	471	0.4	44	0.2
Mulattos.	103,082	15.3	4,757	4.6	459	2.8
Rio de Janeiro						
Negroes	44,541	5.8	2,035	0.8	112	0.2
Mulattos.	104,315	13.7	9,895	4.1	725	1.6
Sao Paulo						
Negroes	76,652	4.3	1,879	0.6	95	0.2
Mulattos.	31,585	1.8	1,659	0.5	170	0.4
Rio Grande do Sul						
Negroes	10.091	1.9	310	0.4	14	0.1
Mulattos.	11,702	2.2	775	1.0	74	0.6
Mato Grosso						
Negroes	2,543	5.3	59	0.8	3	0.2
Mulattos.	12,911	27.0	1,148	16.2	89	8.0
BRAZIL						
Negroes	228,890	4.2	6,794	0.6	448	0.2
Mulattos.	551,410	10.2	41,410	4.2	3,568	2.2

* Census data omitted in the case without declaration of color and grades (excepting Para, in which only the cases without declaration of grades was excepted).
** Total number of persons who have completed the specified level of education for each state.

TABLE V.

Population by Color in the eight Selected States (1950) *.

STATES	COLOR GROUPS					Total
	Whites	Negroes	Mulattos	Yellows	Not Declared	
North						
Para	325,281	59,744	734,574	875	2,799	1,123,273
	28.96	5.32	65.39	0.08	0.25	100
Northeast						
Pernambuco.	1,685,028	316,122	1,386,255	83	7,697	3,395,185
	49.63	9.31	40.83	0.00	0.22	100
East						
Bahia................	1,428,685	926,075	2,467,108	156	12,551	4,834,575
	29.55	19.16	51.03	0.00	0.26	100
Minas Gerais..........	4,509,575	1,122,940	2,069,037	2,257	13,983	7,717,792
	58.43	14.55	26.81	0.03	0.18	100
Rio de Janeiro g. b......	1,660,834	292,524	415,935	1,032	7,126	2,377,451
	69.86	12.30	17.50	0.04	0.30	100
South						
Sao Paulo.	7,823,111	727,789	292,669	276,851	14,003	9,134,423
	85.64	7.96	3.21	3.03	0.16	100
Rio Grande do Sul......	3,712,239	217,520	226,174	495	8,393	4,164,821
	89.14	5.22	5.43	0.01	0.20	100
Central-West						
Mato Grosso..........	278,378	51,089	187,365	3,649	1,563	522,044
	53.32	9.79	35.89	0.70	0.30	100

* Information compiled from " Estudos Demograficos No. 145 " (elaborado por Remulo Coelho), Laboratorio de Estatistica do Instituto Brasileiro de Geografia e Estatistica — Conselho Nacional de Estatistica, Rio de Janeiro, 1955.

ROGER   BASTIDE

The Present Status of Afro-American Research in Latin America°

ALTHOUGH ENTIRE aspects of African civilization have been preserved in Latin America so clearly that no concept of "reinterpretation" is needed to discover them, it is much more difficult to do Afro-American research in South America than in North America. This is partly because miscegenation continues to occur, creating considerable ambiguity with regard to the terms "Negro" and "mulatto": Marvin Harris found no less than 492 different categories of racial identification in Brazil.[1] And how can one establish a science if its very object cannot be clearly defined? Does the term "Afro-American" include all ethnic categories where there is black blood? If not, at what point shall we limit the group we study? One must not dismiss this as a nominal difficulty, for those who claim that there is no black problem in Latin America lean heavily on this ambiguity.

Furthermore, where one cannot speak of a single ethnic identity, one cannot speak of a cultural identity either, for cultural identity will tend to shift from constituent nationality groups to the nation as a whole. In the cultural domain, in other words, the concept of syncretism corresponds to the physical concept of miscegenation. Although it might be difficult to distinguish 492 different categories, there is clearly a continuum of categories of syncretisms in Brazil, ranging from the world of the *candomblés* (where Africa is the dominant influence) to the world of peasant folklore (where Portugal dominates). I will not play this little game. But I understand why Latin American Africanology stresses syncretism as if it were the fundamental problem, and why it cannot go beyond a mechanical concept of syncretism as a simple tally sheet of cultural traits of different racial origin—a concept long obsolete in contemporary anthropology.

The second difficulty follows. If syncretism is the basic phenomenon, and if cultural identity shifts from blacks and mulattos to the nation as a whole, one will find African cultural traits in whites as well as European cultural traits in the descendants of Africans. Gilberto Freyre stressed that, as a result of this cultural transfer from blacks to whites through the black wet-nurse and the colored mistress, one now finds as much of Africa in one race as in the other.[2] One can understand that these conditions of interracial cultural mobility present difficulties for the researcher. When asked why he didn't publish a book on Brazil, Herskovits

° Central America and most of the Antilles belong to Latin America. Contemporary anthropology, however, tends to single out one special area—the Caribbean—which it enlarges constantly so that today it includes Colombia, Equador, and the Guianas. This means that my article can deal only with the rest of South America, a problem since, with the exception of Brazil, we have at our disposal only a few studies on Afro-Americans from these countries, and many of them are old, as are those on Argentina.

93

answered that he would first have to do some research in Portugal, so that he would not mistake the origins of cultural traits he had patiently inventoried among blacks. Perhaps these difficulties explain why, in Brazil, after a brilliant period of research and publication ranging from the end of World War I to the beginning of World War II, interest in Afro-American studies abruptly ceased, and is being resumed only now.

At the beginning of World War II, these studies were characterized, first, by the radical separation of disciplines. In all of Latin America, the black was the object of historical studies based on archive documents and conducted, with a few exceptions, such as the work of Gilberto Freyre, according to the traditional methods of classical history, those which call for descriptions of events in their chronological order. On the other hand, sociology was almost nonexistent, and the ideology of "racial democracy" which took its place prevented all objective research into the nature of the relationships between the descendants of masters and slaves.

These studies were characterized, secondly, by a lack of research continuity and a consequent failure to accumulate knowledge. After having gathered a great deal of new data in the field, each scientist simply repeated the same facts from one book to another as if he had forever depleted his area of interest, instead of continuing to explore, year after year, to fill in the gaps.

Finally, the theories used to systematize the observations were exogenous. Instead of springing from the data, they were imposed from the outside, borrowed first from Europe, then from the United States, as were, for example, the theories of Levy-Bruhl's prelogical mentality and Arthur Ramos' Freudian psychoanalysis. Afro-Brazilian descriptions were like simple illustrations of reference systems born elsewhere; often, furthermore, they were behind the times in terms of the evolution of the science. Nevertheless, at the time there was a great fervor for Afro-American research in Brazil (although interest did not develop until later in other Latin American countries from Uruguay to Colombia and Venezuela). It was as if Brazil, in the wake of "modernist" literary movements which had sought to discover Brazilian originality and break the umbilical cord to Europe, suddenly became aware of the value of cultural traits which had come from Africa. From 1934 to 1938, important Congresses, at Récife, at Bahia, and in the State of Minas, gathered writers and scientists to lay the foundations for a distinctive Africanology and to find channels of communication among the opposing disciplines represented, ranging from history to folklore, from mythology to psychiatric epidemiology.

But there was already opposition to this first attempt at defining Afro-American research. Black values were stressed, but this was done by whites for the benefit of whites. Certain critics, such as Sergio Buarque de Holanda, denounced the racism of these works which, by emphasizing what was different and exotic about the Negro, placed him in a kind of cultural ghetto, so as not to have to deal with his fundamental problems—those of integration and improvement in his social, educational, and professional status. The Afro-Brazilian civilization was treated as a source of aesthetic enjoyment for whites, who remained outsiders, and manipulated in order to create a cultural nationalism which might compensate blacks for the whites' simultaneous push to maintain the country's colonial economy. Blacks, however, were beginning to become aware of their marginal positions and of the insidious racism of such Afro-Brazilian research. At the end of this period, this awareness took on a political aspect (*A Frente Negra*) not subject to our analysis. The current resurfaced after the Second World War, but this time with a political nature strong enough to rescue cultural matters from analysis by white Africanists.

The transition from the work of these congresses to the present type of Afro-Brazilian research is marked by Herskovits' visit to Bahia, and the research on racial relations in Brazil funded by UNESCO. Herskovits broke in a definitive way with the old interpretations, which placed trance at the center of the *candomblé* and saw it as a pathological phenomenon. By proclaiming that trance was an institutional phenomenon, Herskovits opened new roads by detaching research from old bases which had not left it free to innovate. He suggested to Brazilian scientists some completely neglected fields of analysis which should be approached, like the social organization and economic intra-structures of Afro-Brazilian cults. In short, he gave new life to Afro-Brazilian research.[3] At the same time, he trained a new generation of researchers and assigned them to new geographical areas of study: Ruy Coelho to Honduras, for example, and Octavio da Costa Eduardo to Maranhao. To René Ribeiro, who was working in Récife, which was already under study, he suggested new approaches. If I may mention myself, I made an analogous effort with my students in São Paulo to open new explorations which seemed more promising to me than the old ones.[4] René Ribeiro's work proves that this renewal has been fruitful (although Octavio da Costa Eduardo and Ruy Coelho have abandoned the field of Afro-American research). The change, however, does not constitute a total break with the old methods, in that the theories through which the researcher observes and explores the facts are always exogenous conceptual systems applied to new groupings—based, in this case, on the functionalism brought from the United States by Herskovits. And no one can deny that this functionalism has made possible important breakthroughs: the discovery of the dual system of adaptation in Afro-Brazilian cults in relation to their own members and to the black society; and of the ways blacks achieve balance, catharsis, and resolution of tensions and consequent social integration into their environment. On the other hand, Herskovits risked locking Afro-Brazilian data into an international system of explanation which, like all international systems, will one day be rejected as a distortion of reality (North American functionalism is now under criticism for this reason by both structuralists and Marxists). Few years will pass in Brazil before blacks become aware of their need to create an Afro-Brazilian science themselves, based on their own experience, and to reject calls for exogenous theories which falsify the true significance of phenomena—calls for what the black sociologist Guerreiro Ramos has so appropriately called "consular sociology."

In 1950-1951, at the request of UNESCO, Alfred Metraux organized a group of research projects on racial relations in Brazil. They were directed in the north and center of the country by Charles Wagley, Thales de Azevedo, and Luis A. Costa Pinto in collaboration with H. W. Hutchinson, Marvin Harris and Ben Zimmerman; in the state of São Paulo, where successful industrialization posed problems of social relations in new terms, by Florestan Fernandes and myself in collaboration with sociologist Oracy Nogueira, psychologists Virginia Leone Bicudo and Aniela Meyer Ginsborg, and the leaders of black associations of São Paulo. This research has resulted in a series of publications;[5] it is sufficient here to note the lesson their work offers in terms of the rejuvenation of methods and theories. The northern group affected only a partial revolution; it moved from cultural anthropology to social anthropology, but remained, even when dealing with history, within the realm of an Anglo-Saxon-type anthropology in which the synchronic outweighed the diachronic. The southern group, on the other hand, started a total revolution: the transition from anthropology to sociology as the only discipline capable of elucidating, in depth, the Afro-Brazilian data. Its particular brand of sociology was imbued with history, put together not by the old methods of factual analysis, but by a new method inspired by Marxism—the dialectic. This is why, in the North, once the research requested by UNESCO was accomplished, interest diminished and research stopped, whereas in the South, a new school appeared, contested but still successful, which I will call the São Paulo School, with Florestan Fernandes, Fernando Henrique Cardoso and Octavio Ianni.

UNESCO's contribution did not end with this research. After the war was over, black intellectuals who had become aware of their problems recreated their old Defense Associations, but now the socialist humanist inspiration prevailed over the old reversed racist inspiration and they were of a predominantly political nature. They also created new groups, such as the Experimental Black Theater of Abdias do Nascimento, in order to rejuvenate their strategies of change with new ideologies and practices. They felt confirmed in their claims by the first results of the UNESCO research. This research revealed, first, that interpreting the Brazilian racial situation in terms of the North American racial situation, as suggested by Pierson in *Negroes in Brazil* (1942), obscured the true meaning of that situation, for, although alienation, dependence, and discrimination take forms different and less manifest in Brazil than in the United States, they are nevertheless just as operative.[6] In the second place, the group in the south criticized certain stereotypes such as the idea that Brazil has the distinction of not having any prejudices, illuminated myths such as that concerning social democracy, and elucidated ideologies such as that regarding the progressive whitening of the population.

In an article criticizing all the theories proposed from the time of Nina Rodrigues and Gilberto Freyre to the present, Guerreiro Ramos initiated black discussion of blacks; he rejects, as equally distorted by ethnocentrism, all prior white discussion, whether delivered by foreigners, whom he sees as incapable of decoding the Brazilian message, or by nationals, who, he says, falsify the facts by trying to fit them into conceptual systems from abroad.[7]

One more Afro-Brazilian Study Congress was organized, much like the prewar congresses, but by blacks, although interested whites were invited to attend. It took place in Rio, in 1950, in a climate of optimism inspired by the UNESCO research. One has only to compare the texts published by this congress with those from previous congresses to perceive the almost complete change in approach affected between 1945 and 1955.[8]

The change was not a total one, however, for empirical descriptions continued to be widespread in all of South America after the Second World War, especially in the area of folklore. A National Commission on Folklore in Rio de Janeiro, and federal commissions in each Brazilian state gather facts on folklore, disseminate them in specialized, more or less short-lived journals (of which there are several—in Rio, in the south, and in São Paulo) and maintain folklore by presenting large musical or choreographic demonstrations. Of course we are talking about Brazilian folklore, but, since blacks play an important part in the folklore, they are very important in the overall scheme. We shall not deal with this abundant literature here. We do not scorn it, however. On the contrary, a theory cannot decode a cultural or sociological message unless facts have been gathered with objectivity, scientific honesty, and patience, then inventoried as completely as possible. This empirical research on folklore is not of interest here, however, precisely because it does not offer decoding rules and hence it does not contribute to our "knowledge" of the Afro-American. The research remains, in fact, somewhere between aesthetics and science—between ideology (research draws attention to the originality of the Brazilian culture at a time when urbanization and industrialization are "debrazilianizing" it) and praxis (by fossilizing folklore, research kills it while trying to save it, tearing it away from the spontaneity of life, which is unceasing becoming). Although this study deals with new theoretical approaches, not with strictly empirical research, this folklorization of black culture in Latin America constitutes a sociological fact which can become, in and of itself, an object of science. It seemed so important to me on a recent research trip in Brazil, that I plan to dedicate an entire chapter to it in my next book.[9]

Cultural Anthropology

When one is dealing with cultural traits transferred from Africa to the New World, empirical research invariably leads to comparative research. The comparative method was used from the start, of course, by such specialists in Afro-Brazilian religions as Nina Rodrigues and Arthur Ramos, but only by means of books. Due to lack of funding and interest, researchers could compare data from their field observations in Brazil only with published descriptions of African religions much too general for effective comparison. Finally, Pierre Verger, by constantly moving between the city of Salvador (Bahia) and the old Slave Coast (Togo, Dahomey, Nigeria), established a comparative method based on double field research on cultural, mythical and ritualistic traits.[10] His book on this research is illustrated with magnificent mirror photographs on facing pages, showing, for example, the same ceremony as interpreted in Africa and in Brazil. The work had a slight bomb-shell effect, since Brazilian specialists had tended, more and more, to insist upon acculturation, syncretism, and change, and thus to describe the *candomblé* as more Brazilian than African. Verger demonstrated irrefutably that Afro-Brazilian religion was a continuation of African religion whose extraordinary faithfulness extended even to the most minute details of the ceremonials—including sequence, duration, and even, here and there, the manipulations of the sacred as it was lived and spoken.

But precisely because the Afro-Brazilian religion was rooted in African thought, though undoubtedly in a mutilated form, a new vision was possible, different from that of the old researchers who, even when their descriptions were empirically exact, gave the impression that Afro-Brazilian religion was a system of superstitions rather than a coherent philosophy of man's fate and the cosmos. My first encounter with the world of the *candomblés*, in 1944, led me to write that there was an "extremely rich and subtle philosophy" behind this religion, which, though different from our own, was as valid intellectually as that of Plato or Spinoza. I persuaded young researchers to explore these new paths, promising them many discoveries. I myself made a first attempt at describing this philosophy with relation to African epistemology and the structure of the logical processes of African thought.[11] Clearly, however, even if I entered the *candomblé* as a member and not just as an observer, the law of the secret's maturation, which dominates any initiatory religion, would still keep me too much of an outsider to do more than introduce a certain black vision of the world. Only a priest of the cult, high up in the hierarchy, could provide the kind of text I hoped for. Thus I attach great importance to the work of Deoscoredes M. dos Santos, *West African Sacred Art and Ritual in Brazil* (1967), and of his wife, Juana Elbein dos Santos, *Le Nagô et la Mort* (1972) and to the works they collaborated on, such as *Esù Bara Léroye*. Unfortunately, even now these texts, which reveal all the richness of esoteric Afro-Brazilian thought, are available only in mimeographed form and in relatively short supply; they are unable to find Brazilian publishers, as if the white society, willing as it is to accept the *candomblé* as folklore or artistic spectacle, feels its intellectual security threatened by the competition, on an equal basis, of a philosophy other than its own—a philosophy I shall call *négritude*, meaning true *négritude*, not that *négritude* which is nothing more than a political ideology.[12]

Nonetheless, cultural anthropology must not become hypnotized by the world of the *candomblé*, or by its fidelity to an ancestral culture. Afro-Brazilian religions are living religions which, in order to survive, have adapted to the new socio-economic structures of Brazil and other metamorphoses, giving birth to new forms—first *macumba*, and above all, *Umbanda spiritualism*. For approximately half a century, the analysis and interpretation of the new religions which have been appearing and multiplying everywhere in the world has been gaining importance in anthropology. A whole series of categories has been suggested for classifying and understanding them: prophetism, millenarianism, nativism, vitalism, religious movements of oppressed people, and salvationistic religions. Earlier, however, we denounced the easy method which consists of applying exogenous reference systems to original facts, and, as Rainer Flasche points out, none of the suggested categories can be applied to *macumba* or *Umbanda*.[13] Hence the interest of his study for comparison with similar religious movements.

Curiously, despite the fact that *Umbanda spiritualism* has millions of followers, and poses a problem for the missionary activities of the Catholic Church so great that it produces almost daily polemics in the newspapers, it has, to my knowledge, given rise to only one scientific publication in Brazil, the excellent work of Procopio de Camargo,[14] though it has aroused impassioned interest abroad (among such scholars as Flasche, H. H. Figge, E. Pressel, Mombelli, and myself).[15] I am not interested, here, in enumerating the various interpretations of this religion and its functions in the society as a whole—interpretations which are contradictory and range from those which see the religion as one of black protest to those which see it as a religion of national integration. Paradoxical as it may seem, we believe that these interpretations, are all true, for *Umbanda* is the meeting place of racial groups—whites, Indian half-breeds, blacks, European migrants, even Japanese—each of which plays a unique part. What interests us here is the diversity of approaches and perspectives through which these phenomena are grasped and judged: the sociological approach (To what extent does spiritualism reflect the transition from folklore to urban society?); the psychological approach (To what extent do the phenomena of possession or dissociation of the personality constitute defense mechanisms against the stresses of urban society?); the political approach (To what extent is *Umbanda* a revolutionary alternative or the expression of a black counterworld?); the phenomenological approach (What is the nature of African religiosity as it is expressed in *Umbanda* and to what extent is it identical with that expressed in Brazilian peasant Catholicism?); and what I call the Weberian approach because it attempts to define what Max Weber called the "social ethic" of the religion and to observe the effects of this living ethic on social facts.

Of course, whether one takes a diachronic or a synchronic perspective, there are other approaches. From a diachronic point of view, black culture in Brazil appears, not as a frozen culture, but as a dynamic one, capable of constant innovations and original creations, each of which removes it a little further from Africa, but is nonetheless authentically Negro. This could lead either to a theory of discontinuous continuity—the only one, in my opinion, which takes into account Afro-American blackness—or to an undoubtedly interesting analysis of the Afro-Brazilian imagination in the process of constructing an "other society," although following Steger's expression, the utopia here is built on the past rather than oriented toward the future. From a synchronic perspective, one could study *Umbanda* by means of the structuralist theory: *Umbanda* offers a structure for the integration of contradictory elements, because it reflects and unites all the contradictions of a society in transition—a society economically, ethnically, and racially heterogeneous, and searching for its identity, an identity which must turn out to include oppositions in dialectical relationships to each other.

Although *Umbanda* is the most original of the "new" religions springing up in South America, it is not the only one. Batuque of the Para, born from the encounter of African *vodun* and of Amerindian *pagelance,* was studied by Seth and Ruth Leacock using life histories and case analyses with an eye to the motivations and psychology of its members,[16] but it is only of local interest. More important is the cult of *Maria Lionza* in Venezuela, of Indian origin, which is becoming more and more Africanized through contact with national and immigrant (Cuban) blacks and has given rise, in the past few years, to interesting descriptions and sociological reflections by Angelina Pollak-Eltz.[17] Clearly, a comparison of all these Afro-Latin-American religious innovations, perhaps including the rural messianic phenomena in South America (although blacks have a very secondary role there, if any)[18] could contribute to our knowledge of what a "new religion" is.

History

Is it not possible that the history of blacks in Latin America might be enriched by using the methods and orientation of cultural anthropology, by applying the perspectives we have just enumerated to the past, for example? This idea inspired one of Acosta Saignes' recent books on Venezuela, which, though concerned with events, particularly slave revolts, aims above all to reconstitute black *culture* as it existed under slavery: work techniques, diet, methods of healing the sick, matrimonial and sexual relationships, etc.[19] This could be related to an earlier work by Gilberto Freyre, *Maîtres et Esclaves,* which related descriptions of social history and the slave's everyday life more to the ecology and geography of the big planta-tion than to classical cultural anthropology. It could also be related to certain current attempts by black intellectuals, both in Anglo-Saxon America and in Latin America, to provide themselves with an ethnohistory separate from that which whites write for them. We would then have a continuum extending from the culture of the slavery system as a whole, at least in Portuguese countries (G. Freyre), through the culture of the slave under this system (Acosta Saignes), to ethnohistory as a foundation on which the American Negro can build his racial identity.

Social Anthropology

I would like to return now to the São Paulo School which arose from the new orientation resulting from the UNESCO inquiry. Although Florestan Fernandes, Henrique Cardoso and O. Ianni[20] differ from one another in the handling of method and the use of Marxist dialectics, this discussion will confine itself to what is common among them.

The first notion they emphasize is that of "totality." Contrary to what happens in cultural anthropology, facts are always considered on a macroscopic level, in all their historical-sociological and structural-functional aspects, and in terms of their connection and reciprocity. The black can be understood only in terms of his in-teractions with whites within a certain mode of organizing productive labor. The functionalists, of course, also give special status to the notion of "whole" or of system. One cannot, however, as the functionalists believe, arrive at the concrete from purely empirical research, for what defines the concrete is the pattern of affinities among empirical relationships, a pattern not defined by simple experience, but arrived at by the reasoning process. Furthermore, whereas functionalist theorists can understand social change only as a malfunction of the system, the São Paulo school authors see it as part of a continuum because they hold that social systems are not closed, but open, engaged in a process of dynamic evolution guided by human praxis. The dynamic aspects of the system of racial relations constituted the basis for the research of the São Paulo team in the states of Santa Catarina, the Parana, and the Rio Grande do Sul. The idea of "totality" is expanded to the point where what happens in Brazil can be understood only in terms of what happens in the rest of the world, and where the evolution and ultimate suppression of slavery are seen as mere manifestations of a broad dialectical movement from commercial and protected capitalism toward industrial and competitive capitalism.

The second major notion of the São Paulo school is that of praxis or human creativity. Since what interests our authors is flux and motion, their approach to the problems of blacks in Brazil is essentially historical. What distinguishes their ap-proach from the classical historical one, or even from a historical approach emphasizing economic determinism, is that they attempt to observe history "in the making," step by step. The important thing, in other words, is not so much the historical situation itself, but the way various social participants perceive it. Their awareness alone gives meaning to things and guides their activity; indeed, "dialec-tics," as I understand it, is basically nothing more than this incessant exchange between creative man and the weight of socio-economic determinisms. Still another element removes this approach from that of linear, classical history: although events move from a *before* toward an *after*, our authors use the *after* to elucidate the *before*. When slavery was at its height, the ideology of the masters permeated the whole system and obscured its internal contradictions; when the system ceased to function satisfactorily, however, the crisis enabled observers to measure its uniqueness and to understand the meaning of the facts. The importance ascribed by our three authors to crises and internal conflicts is fundamental to their commitment since praxis is clearly favored by periods of competition. Florestan Fernandes, for example, defended the transition from accommodation to conflict, pointing out that conflict presents a chance for democratization of racial relations, whereas accommodation leads to the passive capitulation of blacks to whites.

In my opinion, the great value of this dialectical approach has been to debunk a good deal of data previously considered empirically established. These authors have shown that certain notions once held as factual—"racial democracy" in Latin America, the "progressive whitening or Aryanization" of the Brazilian population through the mixing of blood and of values,[21] and even the "luso-tropicalism" which Gilberto Freyre presents as a new "science" and not as a philosophy or aesthetic vision of colonization[22]—are nothing more than ideologies or myths evolving further with each crisis. They reveal that such notions are based on re-elaborations of a mental logic designed to insure the continuity, despite historical disruptions, of the social domination of one race by another. "Racial democracy," according to Ianni, is linked to the "metamorphosis" of the "slave" into the "Negro" and the "mulatto," a metamorphosis which began at the time of the emancipation crisis and marked the transition from slavery to the suppression of servile labor. "Luso-tropicalism" began with the contemporary crisis in which Brazil is being transformed from a traditional and very rural country to an urbanized and industrialized one.

There are, however, gaps in this approach. It entirely omits any study of black culture. If black culture were mentioned, even in parentheses, this would not be very grave, for the expert has every right to limit the object of his studies (despite his contradictory wish to study concrete "totalities"). More often than not, however, these authors deny black culture. They state, for example, that the Latin American world was so shaped by and for the white man, that the black man never had any say in how he should live, preserve his cultural heritage, or exert a creative cultural influence; and that the black, lacking the tools to create a coherent image of himself, is forced to understand himself in terms of the counterimage which the white man has of him. I agree that blacks remained on the fringe of historical events and the social processes of the industrial revolution. But does one have the right to carry this general observation of social anthropology into the area of culture?[23] I also agree that black culture is controlled by the white man, used by him for his own profit, and manipulated by the governing class; J. B. Borges Pereira's little pioneering book on the Negro, broadcast on São Paulo radio, proves it well, (see note 20), and the "folkorization" imposed by whites on Afro-Brazilian culture is a case in point. If, however, Afro-Brazilian culture can be manipulated, it must exist. And it is unfortunate that the São Paulo School did not try to integrate it into its own anthropological perspective. I tried to do this myself a few years ago by studying African religions in Brazil from the perspective of social anthropology rather than of cultural anthropology—by studying them, that is, in terms of their dialectical ties to the transformation of economic and social infra-structures.

Toward a New Vision of Afro-Latin-American Cultures

Three main conclusions can be drawn from this paper. First, even if empirical research dominates in terms of quantity, only theoretical research can draw the meaning of things, revealing what is hidden in the evidence. Secondly, during the last two or three decades, profound changes have occurred in the fields people choose to study; we have moved, for example, from a genetic cultural anthropology engaged in researching origins, to a structural-functionalist cultural anthropology. However, and this is my third conclusion, researchers too often used foreign theories, emanating from Europe or the United States, rather than theories based on their own analyses, thereby running the risk of neglecting the most original aspects of Afro-Latin-American data. The only exceptions to this rule were Guerreiro Ramos' affirmation of a black sociology based on the black Brazilian's awareness of himself and of his fate, and Deoscoredes dos Santos' revelation of an original cosmology and psychology, based on oral traditions transmitted from one generation to another by the priests of the candomblés.

Except in the immediate prewar period dominated by Arthur Ramos and giving rise to three Congresses on Afro-Brazilian Studies,[24] and the immediate post-war period (when UNESCO revolutionized the preoccupations of researchers), scholars interested in blacks have not been very numerous in Brazil. They are even less numerous in other South American countries. This is because, until very recently, Afro-Brazilian research was limited to members of the university community; except in the realm of folklore, with its contests and prizes, no other institution actively supported it. Thus, the only incentive for participating in such research has been the publication of a thesis. However, since Janio Quadros' short-lived Presidency of Brazil, and especially since the army assumed power, Brazilian politics has become a politics of reconciliation and solidarity with the new African states. This policy can bear fruit only if the government values Brazil's black people and their cultural contributions. A whole series of research institutions has sprung from this change. Previously, the only one was the Joaquim Nabuco Institute of Récife; although it was set up to encourage economic and social development of the northeast, thanks to Freyre and Ribeiro, it made an important contribution to Afro-Brazilian research. Among the new institutions are the Center for Afro-Oriental Studies—first affiliated with the University of Bahia but now under the authority of the Ministry of Foreign Affairs—with its journal *Afro-Asia*, which has published important articles by people like Vivaldo da Costa Lima and Rolf Reichert; and the Centers for African Studies at the Universities of Rio de Janeiro and of São Paulo, with their post-graduate courses and seminars. During my recent trip I observed with great satisfaction that well-prepared young researchers in Afro-Brazilian affairs were getting ready to relieve the old researchers. Funding for future research projects, however, is still a problem; one can only seek money from foundations which have more general goals, such as the *Fundacao de Amparo á Pesquisa do Estado de São Paulo*.

At present, it is difficult to foresee the future direction of Afro-Latin-American studies or to predict what kind of position the black intellectuals gathering in the universities will occupy. Clearly, however, social anthropology will be the springboard for tomorrow's research because it has shown that the Afro-Brazilian can only be understood within the network which ties him to the society as a whole, and thus that Brazilian society must be studied as a pluralistic one from now on, rather than as a series of individual segments, including a very separate black segment. But to analyze the pluralistic society, future researchers must overstep social anthropology by including cultural anthropology, for it is cultural values which mediate among individuals and among social groups, and constitute the basis for the interaction networks and the semantic fields which give social groups their meaning. Fortunately for Brazil, these researchers must also discover new concepts, ones which will enable Brazil to free herself from old categories, such as those of "caste" and "social class," which, though still useful, have now almost depleted their heuristic fruitfulness. I shall limit myself to one example, the one I have studied in most depth. One cannot understand Afro-Brazilian religions in isolation from other religions which fulfill analogous functions within the same social strata, such as folk Catholicism or the Pentacostal movement. One must lump them all together on the market of beliefs and look at them through an economic model, in isolation from other forms of power.[25] Seen from this point of view, Afro-Brazilian religions are a manifestation of the search for a power effective against the forms of power monopolized by the whites, and thus are best seen in terms of a political model.

I could make analogous statements concerning other areas, such as black folklore or the structure of the black family. The important thing is to find new methods of analysis which can elucidate phenomena which have thus far been slighted because they were dealt with only in terms of limited perspectives, and of categories dating from the beginning of the twentieth century. Then it will become clear that black culture is not, as it appears, frozen into a system of defense mechanisms too rigid for change, but a living culture, capable of constant creation, keeping in step with the rhythms of change in the global society, of which it is not a marginal but a dialectical element.

REFERENCES

1. Marvin Harris, "Referential Ambiguity in the Calculus of Brazilian Racial Identity," *Afro-American Anthropology*, ed. Norman E. Whitten, Jr. and J. F. Szwed (New York: The Free Press, 1970), pp. 75-86.

2. Gilberto Freyre, *Casa Grande e Senzala* (Rio de Janeiro: J. Olympio, 5th ed., 1946).

3. Melville J. Herkovits, *Pesquisas Etnologicas na Bahia* (Bahia: Publicaçõe de Museu da Bahia, 1943).

4. Roger Bastide, *Metodologia Afro-Brasileira*, I, *O metodo liquistico* (São Paulo: Revista do Arquivo Municipal da São Paulo, 1939); II, *O metodo psicanalitico* (idem, 1943); III, *Estudos Afro-brasileiros* (idem, 1944).

5. UNESCO-Anhembi, *Relacoès raciais entre Negros e Brancos em São Paulo* (São Paulo: Anhembi, 1955); L. A. da Costa Pinto, *O negro ao Rio de Janeiro* (Rio de Janeiro: Companhia Editora Nacional, 1953); C. Wagley, ed., *Races et Classes dans le Brésil rural* (UNESCO); Thales de Azevedo, *Les élites de couleur dans une ville brésilienne* (UNESCO, 1953); Réne Ribeiro, *Religião e Relacões raciais* (Rio de Janeiro: Ministerion de Educação e Cultura, 1956).

6. In this article we are not going to deal with Van den Berghe and his dichotomy between the two racial situations, paternalistic and competitive, since—although we have brought Van den Berghe into the study of racial relations in Brazil in terms of stereotypes, norms and interracial behavior in São Paulo (*American Sociological Review*, 22, No. 6 [1957])—Van den Berghe's work evolves outside South America. The Brazilian example would be relevant to show that the two derived types belong to one and the same transformation group.

7. Guerreiro Ramos, "O problema do negro na sociologia brasileira," *Cadernos do Noso Tempo*, 2 (1954), pp. 207-215.

8. Abdias do Nascimento, ed., *O Negro Rebelde* (Rio de Janeiro: Ed. G. R. D., 1968).

9. *The African Religions in Brazil During the Industrial Era* (Paris: Flammarion, forthcoming).

10. Pierre Verger, *Notes sur les cultes des Orisa et Vodun à Bahia, la Baie de tous les Saints au Brésil et à l'ancienne Côte des esclaves en Afrique* (Dakar: IFAN, 1957).

11. The book in which I called young researchers to a new approach to the world of the *candomblé* appeared, in Portuguese, under the title of *Imagenes do Nordeste misto en branco e preto* (Rio de Janeiro: 1945). The book where I present the Afro-Brazilian conception of man and the cosmos appeared in French under the title of *Le Candomblé de Bahia, rite nagô* (The Hague: Mouton, 1958).

12. Blackness, as a political ideology, is the black's answer to the white's challenge. However, precisely because it is, the "answer" is determined *a priori* by the structure of the challenge; in other words, it is "colonized" by the way the white man has put the terms which serve as its stimulus. On the other hand, true blackness does not encumber itself with polemics, it is an existential affirmation.

13. Rainer Flasche, *Geschichteund Typologie afrikanisches Religiosität in Brasilien* (Marburg an der Lahn: Marburger Studien zur Afrika und Asien Kunde, 1973).

14. Candido Procopio de Camargo, *Aspectos sociologicos del espiritismo en São Paulo* (Friburg: Feres, 1961).

15. R. Bastide, *Religions Africaines au Brésil* (Paris: Presses Universitaires, 1960), Ch. IV; Hanns-Albert Steger, "Revolutionäre Hintergründe der Kreolischen Synkretismus," *Int. Jahrbuch für Religionsoziologie* (Koln: Bd. VI, 1970); L. Weingertner, *Umbanda-Synkretische Kulte in Brasilien* (Erlander: Evangelical Lutheran Mission, 1969); Savino Mombelli, *Umbanda, Fede e Civiltà*, 9-10 (1971); Rainer Flasche, *op. cit.*; Esther Pressel, "Umbanda in São Paulo: Religious Innovation in a Developing Society," *Religion, Altered States of Consciousness and Social Change*, ed. E. Bourguignon (Columbus, Ohio: Ohio State University Press, 1973), pp. 264-318; Horst H. Figge, *Geisterkuit, Besessenheit, und Magie in der Umbanda Religion Bresiliens* (München: Alber Freiburg, 1973).

16. Seth and Ruth Leacock, *Spirits of the Deep* (New York: American Museum of Natural History, 1971).

17. Angelina Pollak-Eltz, *Cultos Afroamericanos* (Caracas: Univ. Catol. Andres Bello, 1972).

18. As those studied by Maria-Isaura P. de Queiroz, for example, in *Images messianiques du Brésil* (Cuernavaca, Mexico: *Sondeos*, No. 87, 1973).

19. Miguel Acosta Saignes, *Vida de los esclavos negros en Venezuela* (Caracas: Hesperides, 1967).

20. Florestan Fernandes, *A integração do negro à sociedade de classes* (São Paulo: Thesis, 1964); *O Negro no mundo dos brancos* (São Paulo: Difusão Européia do Livro, 1973); Fernando Henrique Cardoso, *Capitalismo e Escravidão* (São Paulo: Difusão Européia do Livro, 1962); Oactavio Ianni, *As metamorfoses do escravo* (São Paulo: Difusão Européia do Livro, 1962). The last comer to Afro-Brazilian research in São Paulo, Joao Bastista Borges Pereira, can be linked to this São Paulo School, even though his early Marxism has been abandoned—*Côr, professão e mobilidade* (São Paulo: Bibl. Pioneira, 1967).

21. We are speaking of Latin America in general, because Mexican sociologists have taken up, for the Indian, what the São Paulo School had already established for the black, through similar analyses, showing, for example, that the Indian does not define himself "culturally" but rather by dialectical opposition to the *Ladino*, while the progressive *ladinization* of the Indian was more a myth to hide the genocide of the Indian than an effort to move him toward modern civilization.

22. G. Freyre, *O mundo que o português criou* (Rio de Janeiro: J. Olympio, 1940); *Aventura e rotina* (Lisboa: Livros do Brasil): G. Freyre's luso-tropicalism is not of direct concern to this article since he wishes to define a science of the adaptation of the white man to tropical life, but it is of indirect concern insofar as the idea of racial democracy is a part of the Portuguese mentality.

23. The problem is discussed, in part, in the book edited by Jürgen Gräbener, *Klassengesellschaft und Rassismus*, dedicated to the problem of Negro marginalism (Düsseldorf: Bertelsmann Universitätsverlag, 1971); See the texts by F. Fernandes and R. Bastide.

24. We should add the magnificent collection of data from the Mission Mario de Andrade in the northeast and in Amazonia, funded by the São Paulo Prefecture. This data was published after the death of Mario Andrade, through the care of one of his disciples, Oneyda Alvarenga, in the collections of the Municipal Record Library of São Paulo. The loss of Mario de Andrade unfortunately deprived us of the interpretation which could have been given to these facts.

25. Jean Ziegler, *Le Pouvoir africain* (Paris: Ed. du Seuil, 1971).

AFRICAN CULTURE IN BRAZILIAN ART

ABDIAS DO NASCIMENTO

State University of New York at Buffalo

It would not be possible to understand the relationship between African culture and the development of the Arts in
Brazil, or to establish the influences resulting from it without
mentioning first, however briefly, the necessary historical
data. Levi-Strauss (1952: 97) once said that "the way to progress is laden with adventures, ruptures, and scandals." We
should start, then, by examining the greatest scandal, the one
never surpassed in the history of humans: the enslavement of the
Black Africans.

In Brazil, it is slavery that defines the quality, the extensive-
ness, and the intensity of the physical and spiritual relationship
between the sons of three continents that met there; confront-
ing each other in the epic of building a new country, with its
own characteristics, both in the formation of its people and in
the specificity of its spirit—that is to say, a culture and civilization in its own right.

The starting point was the "discovery" of Brazil by the Portuguese in 1500. The immediate exploitation of the new land
progressed with the simultaneous appearance of the Black
Race and its fertilizing of Brazilian soil with tears, blood, and
the martyrdom of slavery. Around 1530, the Africans, who
had landed in chains, had already started playing their new
role of "labor force"; by 1535, the slave trade to Brazil was
already a regular and organized business, which would very
rapidly increase to enormous proportions. As the first productive activity of the Portuguese colony, sugar mills and sugar

JOURNAL OF BLACK STUDIES, Vol. 8 No. 4, June 1978

cane plantations spread along the northeastern coast; more specifically, along the states of Bahia and Pernambuco. By 1587 Bahia had 47 sugar cane mills, a fact which clearly illustrates the speed with which the sugar industry developed.

Among the intricate connections and implications of this speedily assembled draft, factors of social and historical character meet with religious, cultural, psychological, literary, folkloric, linguistic, and other dimensions, and become the necessary tools for the grasp of the artistic dynamics involved.

The population of the newborn country was estimated (Filho, 1946: 45) in 1600 as follows:

Indians	35,000
Whites	10,000
Africans and the descendants	20,000

For centuries slavery in Brazil was regarded as an institution which was benign and human in character, and was considered philanthropic. But Portuguese colonialism always resorted to very specific modes of behavior in order to conceal its fundamental violence and cruelty. World consciousness must still have a lively memory of the mystifications by means of which colonialist Portugal attempted to hide its racist nature under the guise of legislation for Angola, Mozambique, and Guinea named *Indigenato, Provincias de Alem-Mar,* and other demagogic artifices.

In Brazil, from the very beginning, the enslaved Africans denied the official version of their docility in the regimen to which they were forcibly subjected, as well as the allegations regarding the Black man's natural aptitude for slave-work. The slaves resorted to a variety of forms of protest against their condition, including suicide, crime, escape, insurrection, and revolt. The most tragic form assumed as a rejection of slave life was the *banzo.* The African suffered something like a pathetic paralysis of will and energy, and with increasing despair, died slowly.

Physical punishment, deformation of the body, tortures that sometimes would kill a slave, also bear witness against any invocation of leniency favorable to slavery in Brazil. In that part of the world it was invested with the same supreme iniquity existent whenever and wherever slavery may have existed. Nabuco, a white congressman who lived in the time of slavery and fought against it, energetically expressed his disapproval of the country in the following terms:

> the lie spread abroad allows the Government to avoid taking an attitude within the country and to leave the slaves abandoned to their own fate [1949: 102].

What does Nabuco mean by: "their own fate"? The African was subjected to a condition of "peca da costa," the status of an object, a sheer muscular force devoid of humanity, thus a nonentity deprived of history, culture or religion. But in reality, in spite of the denials of the system, African cultures arrived in Brazilian territory. They were very diversified; those stronger than others, or more flexible, adapted themselves better for their survival, permanence, and development. Those whose cultural structures survived, are the following, according to a classification by Ramos:

(a) Sudanese cultures: represented mostly by the Yoruba peoples from Nigeria, the Geges from Dahomey, the Fanti and Ashanti from the Gold Coast, and some other smaller groups.

(b) Guineo-Sudanese cultures, islamized, originating mainly from the Peuhl, Mandingas, and Haussas, from Northern Nigeria.

(c) Bantu cultures, represented by the Angola-Congo tribal groups, and by those from the area called *Contra-Costa* (1946: 279).

It is obvious that the African bearers of those cultures and their descendants were in no condition to contribute to the new country's culture all that they could have, under a different set of circumstances. Permanent victims of violence, their institutions disintegrated as a result of the rape to which they were submitted. However, in spite of so many denials, and of the many forms of violation and distortion which they suffered, the Africans kept on developing their cultural trajectory.

Rodrigues, a criminologist and psychiatrist who lived in Bahia and died in 1906, is considered to be the pioneer of Black Brazilian studies. In his book *Os Africanos no Brasil* (The Africans in Brazil), he makes use of the theories of the European Lang to characterize the African as a savage. On the level of psychology, Rodrigues says:

> he showed an obscure consciousness; from a social perspective, he maintained totemic conceptions [1945: 279].

These concepts, whose scientific facade barely covers an imperialist ideology, are not only characteristic of past times. To this date, statements to the same effect, or equivalent, are to be commonly found. Laytano, for instance, the author of an official publication of the Brazilian Government, states that:

> The Negro's entrance in Brazil was simultaneous with the country's discovery. He knew slavery, cultivated it, and entertained it as a political system. Slavery was practiced in Africa proper. *The Africans themselves transplanted it* to America [1971: 2].

Aggression, human disrespect, falsification of history, have become normal to a great extent. Valladares, ex-member of the *Conselho Federal de Cultura* (Federal Council on Culture), and a participant of the first and second Festivals of Black Arts holding key decision-making positions, also holds that: "The Whites did not hunt the Blacks in Africa, but they *peacefully* bought them from the Black tyrants (my emphasis; 1966: 4). He adds further that "it is no surprise that a better understanding and analysis of Africa is not to be found among Africans." This is because:

> On what concerns the historical dimension, there seems to exist a certain feeling of inferiority that is African. Thus it is not possible to present a historical text running parallel to that of Western Countries.

In the first place, with regard to the subject of feelings of inferiority, such people reveal their own feelings of superiority; and afterward, they remain silent about the true conditions in which about 50,000,000 Africans were criminally enslaved by Western weapons which the Europeans also used to violate and rob the land, to threaten, corrupt, and buy off tribal chiefs, to appropriate the mineral wealth, and to promote the theft of artistic treasuries. Europeans built fortresses along the coast and inside the African territory; they also built a wall of silence around African history, so that they could later offer a convenient vision of this "mysterious and unknown continent."

The metaphysical conceptions, the philosophical ideas, the structure of African's religions, rituals, and liturgies, never received respect or consideration as values constituting the identity of a national spirit. And while despising the culture, the Europeans reinforced the racial rejection. All the goals of thought, science, public and private institutions stand as proof of such a conclusion. Once again we will quote Rodrigues, because of his great prestige but despite the opposition of such scholars as Ramos (1957: 142-144) who denies the scientific value of Rodrigues' work about Black people. Thus Rodrigues says:

> As far as science is concerned, this inferiority [of the Black race] is nothing but a phenomenon of a perfectly natural order ... which explains to this date the reason why the Negroes were not able to establish themselves as a civilized people.

111

And as a consequence, "The Black Race in Brazil will always stand at the base of our inferiority as a people" (Rodrigues, 1945: 24-28). However, those agents of "our inferiority" were the ones who bore, alone, the responsibility of building our country; of waging a struggle without respite to reconquer freedom itself. In many instances, they attempted to conquer the independence of the country, as in the case of the *Conjura dos Alfaiates* (Conspiracy of the Tailors), smothered in Salvador, Bahia in 1798: the four African descendants, Luiz Gonzaga das Virgens, Lucas Dantas de Amorim Torres, Joao de Deus Nascimento, Manuel Faustino Santos Lira, involved in the rebellion, were arrested, condemned, and on the eighth of November 1799, were the only convicted conspirators to be hung in public. Afterwards their bodies were torn in four pieces, which were then exposed in the streets, and their sons declared damned forever (Andrade, 1971). Like these, many blacks and mulattos (half breeds) sacrificed themselves fighting slavery and the tyranny of the Portuguese.

One century before this incident, Brazilian history had registered another important event: the so-called *Republica dos Palmares*—the Republic of Palmares—a true African state organized in the forests of the state of Alagoas by runaway slaves. From 1630 to 1697, the "Black Troy" resisted 27 attacks launched by the Portuguese and the Dutch, who dominated for some time the state of Pernambuco. Palmares at one time held about 30,000 people including men, women, and children; they kept a perfect political and social organization functioning, as well as a system of production, a religious life, and a vigorous military system of defense. Palmares represents the first heroic and desperate outcry of the Africans against the disintegration of their culture in the lands in the New World.

For almost two centuries, the planting of sugar cane and the processing of sugar demanded a concentration of slaves in the northeastern region, although there were Africans all over the national territory. The discovery of gold and diamonds in the state of Minas Gerais displaced the African focal point further to the south. With the downfall in the productivity of the mines and the beginning of the coffee cycle, located mainly in the states of Rio de Janeiro and Sao Paulo, the necessity for a labor force once more changed the main direction of the slave market.

The demographic census of 1798 revealed that the population of Brazil was formed of (Azevedo, 1973: 67):

Whites	1,010,000
Civilized Indians	250,000
Slaves	1,582,000
Free Blacks	406,000

It is almost impossible to estimate the exact number of slaves who entered the country. Not only on account of the absence of correct statistics, but mainly because of the regrettable *Circular No. 29,* of May 13, 1891, issued by the Minister of Finance, Rui Barbosa, who ordered the destruction by fire of all historical documents and files related to the slave trade and slavery. Such estimates therefore lack reliability. There is an estimate which seems to me to be smaller than reasonable, which suggests that 4,000,000 Africans were imported and distributed according to the following approximate proportion: 38% for Rio de Janeiro, from where they were redistributed to Minas and Goias; 25% for Bahia; 13% were destined to Pernambuco; 12% to Sao Paulo; 7% to Maranhao, and 5% to the State of Para.

Based on the facts, Fernandes wrote that:

All of those who have read Gilberto Freyre know of the double interaction which established itself in both directions. However, at no time did those reciprocal influences [between masters and slaves] change the sense of social progress. The Black remained forever condemned to a world that did not organize itself to treat him as a human being and as an "equal" [1972: 15].

In this new phase of Black studies the emphasis moved from the classification of savage, inferior, to a eulogy of the virtues of mixed-breeding (the rape of the Black woman by the White master producing that which is called *mulatto, pardo, mestico,* and so forth) and the simultaneous operation of transculturation. The scientific base of the racial ideology in Brazil was formed this way, and it came to be known as *racial democracy.* A strange democracy indeed that only allowed the Black the right to become white, inside and outside. The passwords of this "imperialism of whiteness" became *assimilation, acculturation*; but in the depths of the theory, the belief in the inferiority of the Blacks persisted, untouched. Another sociologist, Oliveira Viana, exposes the situation frankly:

> [T]he quantum of Aryan blood is increasing rapidly among our people. Well, this increase will fatally act on the anthropological type of our mixed breed, in the sense of molding them to the white man's type [Ramos, 1957: 138].

Before this, Silvio Romero expressed an identical opinion: "we will not constitute a nation of mulattos; for the white form keeps obtaining and will obtain" (Ramos, 1957: 129).

We should not forget that with the exception of a few, in general the scientists who approached this issue did so in accordance with criteria imported from abroad, because the country had a formal independence, but its mentality and culture remained colonized. The points of reference and spiritual gravitation were still in the metropolis, that is, in Europe. And from there, judgments and ideas such as this one, from de Lapouge, arrived in Brazil. These fell upon the Aryanizing aspirations of the Brazilians as a true curse: "Le Bresil... constituera sans doute d'ici un siecle un imense etat negre, a moins qu'il ne retourne, et c'est probable, a la barbarie" (Lapouge, 1896: 187).

As it is, rationalizing the prejudice existent in our country eradicates neither the subliminal prejudice nor the one expressed in the form of open or covert discrimination. We should consequently understand *racial democracy* as a metaphor for racism, Brazilian style: a racism which is not formally institutionalized as racism is in the United States or in South Africa—it matters little, since the result is the same. Brazilian immigratory policies expose this reality in a rather crude manner, and there is little doubt that it is founded in a racist base. The decree of June 28, 1890, barely two years after the abolition of slavery in the country, dictates

> free entry by persons healthy and able to work—except natives of Asia and Africa, who can be admitted only by authorization of the National Congress, and in accordance with the stipulated conditions [Skidmore, 1974: 137].

As Gillian has shown: "Brazil's 'official' solution to 'the problem' is miscegenation, and exhorts *whites running away from independent African* nations to choose Brazil" (my emphasis; 1975: 24).

Expressions, such as "Brazil has attained a very high degree of acculturation," or "the common denominator of acculturation," are frequent, and supposedly portray the perfect assimilation of the colored population in the standards of a prosperous society. A sample of integration of blacks in the national prosperity can be taken from the City of Rio de Janeiro:

> That is where residential segregation reaches its peak. It is enough to visit the ghettos of the "favelas" (shantytowns). The *O Estado de Sao Paulo* special supplement of April 13, 1960 published the following data for 1950: *Population of Rio*: Whites 1,660,834; Blacks and Mulattos 708,459. *Population of the Shantytowns*: Whites 55,436; Blacks and Mulattos 113,218. This means that for each three inhabitants of Rio one is black or mulatto. For each white "favelado" there are two blacks or mulattos living in the shantytowns. If we consider the fact that

according to present statistics blacks made up one third of the
Rio population, while in the "favelas" their number is 100%
higher, we have before our eyes the hateful segregation in
housing when it comes to the colored population [Nascimento,
1968b: 33].

Out of evil intent or naivete people will say, "But the blacks
live in the favelas because they choose to do so, or because they
have no money, but never for reasons of race." Thus we reach
the class/race labyrinth. Again I will refer to Fernandes:

> In spite of the extreme concentration of income and social
> prestige, which leads to an occupational structure precariously
> "democratic" [or balance] in the state of Sao Paulo, whites
> enjoy positions of greater advantage in a significantly higher
> proportion than their part in the composition of the population
> as a whole would allow [1972: 147].

This situation holds true for the rest of the country. The state
of Bahia can help clarify the issue. There Blacks and Mulattos
are the majority according to the 1950 census. The total population is 4,822,024, distributed in the following manner: Whites
1,428,685 (30%); Blacks and Mulattos 3,393,183 (70%); Asiatic
156 (0.003%). Occupational situation: employees: Whites
23.01%, Blacks and Mulattos 76.98%; employers: Whites
51.87%, Blacks and Mulattos 48.11%; education: Whites, elementary school 54.46%, high school 82.56%, university
88.21%; Blacks and Mulattos, elementary 45.52%, high school
17.43%, university 11.64% (Fernandes, 1972: 60).

It is not the task of this brief account to present a detailed
analysis of the aspects mentioned above. This would require
more space than is available to me at this time. The numbers,
however, are eloquent and speak for themselves. In spite of
these limitations I believe I have touched, if only lightly, upon
the surface of a social cancer. To reinforce this, there follow
some numbers and statistics referring to the national level.
Again from the 1950 census, we have: population of the
country: 51,944,397; with the following ethnic distribution:

Whites 32,027,661 (61.6%), Blacks and Mulattos 19,479,399 (37.6%), Asiatic 329,082 (0.6%), race not declared 108,255 (0.2%); employers: Whites 82.66%, Blacks and Mulattos 15.58%, Asiatic 0.7%; education: White, elementary school 90.2%, high school 96.3%, university 97.8%; Blacks and Mulattos, elementary 6.1%, high school 1.1%, university 0.6% (Fernandes, 1972: 57, 59).

These figures, however, require some explanation.

(1) In a country where the population is conditioned by a concern for being white, if the declaration of color or racial group is left to each interviewed individual then obviously a great part of the black and Mulatto population will declare itself white. It would be correct to estimate that at least 50% of the population of Brazil belongs to the Black race, at least phenotypically.

(2) The percentage of Blacks and Mulattos falling within the employer category refers only to very modest businesses or enterprises, with no significance in the context of the country's economy.

Another observation: the more recent demographic censuses in Brazil no longer provide information about color or race, apparently in compliance with the constitutional article which declares all Brazilians equal before the law. In practice, the absence of Black and Mulattos from the demographic censuses is on a par with that measure already mentioned above, which ruled that all documentation referring to the slave trade and to slavery in general was to be burned, so that the "black stain" would be erased from Brazilian history. To that end, "white magic," or "judicial magic" was resorted to.

CANDOMBLE: THE SOURCE OF ARTS

The Candomble is the name given in Bahia to the Cult of the Orixas. It refers mainly to the religion of the Yoruba-speaking peoples brought from Nigeria, but also encompasses the variations of other cultural groups such as the Angola-Congo. It has played an important and revolutionary role in Brazil, where the Catholic Church has for centuries maintained a position of power as the official state religion. Attacked by the Catholic priests, persecuted by the police, the Candomble temples—*terreiros*—had to be hidden in woods, hillsides, and all sorts of places of difficult access and visibility for the enemies. The religion, however, remains the deepest source from which flows the inspiration and the basic lines of Black creativity. Through the Candomble, predominantly, the Africans and their descendants have exercised a powerful influence in all aspects of Brazilian art: music, dance, visual arts, literature—including poetry, the novel, and theatre. Place of worship, point of social convergence, and cultural citadel, the Candomble provided the Black with a means for resisting and for "guarding in his heart, safe from the deluge and the ice" (Mourao, 1957: 26) and within the light of Xango's fire, that physical and spiritual vital force with which Mother Africa had branded him: her indelible stamps of love and identity.

We mentioned above the Republic of Palmares, whose organizers along with their last chief, Zumbi, were predominantly Bantu Blacks. In the Candomble the Sudanese cultures assume the leading role. In the structure of the "pegi" (a sort of chapel inside the terreiro) the architecture reveals an African tenor. Also drawings and representations of ritual objects, paintings of symbols of the cult, can be found on their walls. These were the first manifestations of continuity of the mythopoetic civilizations:

> The mythic-poetic adventure is concomitant with our existence while at the same time much older. Part of the subject and part of the object, it is capable of inducing and being reflected. Our reason is poetic as well as forged—an instrument to detect our prospective visions [Nascimento, 1974: 22].

The first sculptures were also born inside the terreiros; they were of religious inspiration, but the intolerance of whites and of the official religion insisted on calling them "idols" or "fetishes." However, they were nothing but the pure representation of the artist/priest, giving his perspective of certain characteristics of the deities. These were taken by surprise in a gesture or posture, a symbol or a color, a form or a space.

Under the criteria of the scientific antecedents mentioned above, Black artistic production was often considered as a document of "pathological minds," in which case it would be requested by psychiatrists and mental institutions; in other instances such sculptures, symbols, and ritual objects bore testimony to the "criminal nature" of the authors, and ended up in the police museums. This phenomenon is exemplified in the Nina Rodrigues Institute, In Bahia, or the Museum of the Police in Rio de Janeiro.

Rodrigues, whose work has already been mentioned here, was also the author of some observations of critical nature about a sculpture representing the double ax symbol of Xango. He turns to the support of the theories of Richer and Charcot about the *demon in art* (Rodrigues, 1945) and establishes connections that neither the form nor the meaning of Xango authorized. It is important to point out this attitude within criminology, as it repeats itself in the work of Fernando Ortiz, from Cuba, who started his extensive studies on the Afro-Cuban cultures following the same direction. The critic of the Xango sculpture was, in reality, incompetent. Rodrigues proceeds to denounce the "lack of ability of the artist," qualifying the "improper" proportion between the arms and legs of the figurine as a deformity and a joke. He wrote these observations before Modigliani, Picasso, and other modern artists appropriated those distortions as fundamental qualities in the exercise of creative liberty.

A decree of October 20, 1621 forbade the activity of Africans and their descendant in the crafts of gold—another repression of their artistic tendencies. The Catholic Church, which to be sure ran lucrative farms with the work of slaves owned by some religious orders and institutions, in keeping with its part in the social structure of control, also offered very few opportunities to Black and Mulattos for the development of their artistic aptitudes. As can be anticipated, all paintings and sculptures had to be reduced to the Catholic orientation and sense. The eighteenth century was marked by intense artistic activity in the main centers of the country. In the city of Rio de Janeiro a slave named Sebastiao reveals qualities worthy of respect in the several churches he decorated with oil paintings. In this same city Valentim de Fonseca e Silva (1750-1813), born in Minas Gerais, developed prolific and diversified artistic work, sculpting in wood and working with cast iron and gold. He is known as Mestre Valentim as he gathered around himself a group who worked under his influence. The Black painter Aseas dos Santos was born in Bahia in 1865, while at the turn of the century Francisco Chagas produced sculptures. At a later date, Manuel Querino drew, painted, and collected in books the mores, religions, and arts of his brothers. Manuel Cunha was born a slave, studied art in Lisbon, and returned to Brazil where he bought his freedom and became a well-known painter before his death in 1809. Still in Rio de Janeiro, other names deserve to be mentioned: Martinho Pereira, who worked in silver, and Joao Manso Pereira, who knew Greek and Hebrew, worked in iron and steel, fabricated porcelain, varnish and lacquer, as well as experimented in chemistry.

During the colonial period, the most remarkable artist was the mulatto Antonio Francisco Lisboa (1730-1814); son of a Portuguese father and an African mother, he was born in Sabara, in the state of Minas Gerais, and when he reached the age of 40 fell ill with leprosy. The disease devoured his fingers and hands: hence his nickname of *Aleijadinho*—The Little

Cripple. A church architect, he was the powerful sculptor of the twelve prophets, executed in soapstone, in Congonhas do Campo. He painted mulatto saints and angels in ceilings and walls of the churches of Minas Gerais, and he represented the genial explosion of the baroque in Brazil. But, underlying the European form of his woodcuts, figures, and images, a definite African ferment reveals itself; he created forms involving magic, and burning passion.

Estevao Silva, a black painter who died in Rio de Janeiro in 1801, became famous through a painting about slavery called "Charity." A native of Paraiba, the mulatto Pedro Americo (1843-1905), painted historical scenes in grandiose dimensions. From the end of the nineteenth century to the present, black themes of black characters were used by many painters among whom can be named Candido Portinari, Lazar Segal, Cicero Dias, Di Cavalcanti, Noemia, Teruz, Djanira, Ivan Serpa (deceased), Caribe (painter and sculptor), Mario Cravo (sculptor), E. Bianco, and many other white artists. Among the Blacks and Mulattos of our time are: Dias Junior, Heitor dos Prazeros (deceased), Barros, O mulato, Santa Rosa (deceased) who innovated the design of theatrical sets in the Brazilian scene; Sebastiao Januario, Yara Rosa (painter and tapestry maker), Celestino, Jose de Dome, Cleoo, Jose Heitor (sculptor), Agenor (sculptor), Otavio Araujo, Yeda Maria, Manoel Bonfim, Rubem Valentim, Agnaldo Manoel dos Santos (1926-1962) who died prematurely and was a sculptor of exceptional talent, a keeper and follower of the traditional African sculpture to which he contributed with powerful and original plastic solutions. Agnaldo, winner of the international grand prize for sculpture of the I World Festival for Black Art of Dakar, 1966, produced a work of intense and intimate cultural compromise with Africa. This African authenticity brought him recognition as one of the greatest contemporary Brazilian artists.

When I founded the Museum of Black Art in Rio de Janeiro in 1968, I proposed the following:

> a pedogogic action and reflection destined to valuing Black
> art and the Black artist, as a process of ethnic and aesthetic
> integration, re-evaluating simultaneously the primitive sources
> and its fecundating power in the artistic manifestation of the
> Brazilian people. . . . A relevant feature of the Museum of
> Black Art is its implicit sociologic-pragmatic content, which
> makes it an instrument for the transformation of attitudes and
> for social harmonizing, aiming at an urgent humanization
> regarding the blacks, falsely free and supported in our society,
> but in reality unarmed and unprepared for the competition.
> Blacks are not the only poor, but they are the only ones who
> were slaves [Nascimento, 1968a: 62].

The purpose was not the organization of a static heritage, just
for collecting and keeping, but to create a dynamic organ for
the systematic study of the Afro-Brazilian arts. Also, it was
necessary to try to influence a qualitative change to overcome
the tendency toward "folklorization" of artistic creation
whenever it referred to African culture.

At the end of 1968 this artistic direction led me to assume
my own experience as a painter. I did not aim in my painting
either a folkloristic transcription or the commercial spontaneity of primitivism. In a real sense my paintings emerge
from a projection of Afro-Brazilian symbols and myths,
mainly those which express religious emotion. However, they
do not seek in it an orthodox ritual art. The artist, as a member
of a certain culture, is essentially the prophet of a language
which is his own and it is through this medium that he maintains a dialogue with the world and with his fellow man,
modeling the problems of his time. It is therefore within this
concept of freedom that my work is to be defined. My art does
not conform to systems or norms, and if it occupies the world
of symbols and images it is to use them, to discover them, and
to intensify their archetypal or pristine meaning. That is, the
use of myth as an instrument of effective knowledge—the
language of art—paralleled to rational knowledge—the language of science. For us the emotion caused by the sacred is
at the same time the aesthetic emotion. As a result painting
reaches a level beyond the mere visual-aesthetic perception.

Technical skill, as a principal goal, almost always over-shadows deep emotion and initial purity. I try to make my art penetrate deeply the culture and the historical experience of the Black man. And this retrospective journey to the cosmo-gonic fiat should not be interpreted as an "incestuous contemplation of ancestral residues." To understand art as a process of struggle—spiritual and intellectual struggle of mankind—is to understand that artistic creativity has to be freed from routine ritual, from dogma. Black art, with its inherent freedom, rises against the methods and norms of Western art not so much to negate them but to impede their criteria from prevailing in our work. After four hundred years of Black Diaspora, of violence, and pressure from Western culture, the moment has arrived to redeem the mythic-poetry meaning of the ancient Black African civilizations. In seeking such objectives my art distinguishes between those symbols and myths which exist only in tradition—the dead symbols—from those that signify dynamic forces. Rather than visualizing a return we focus on the defense of the integrity and continuity of the Black vital flow; its elementary, vital, and cosmic sources so different from the technological mechanization of the white Western world. The symbols which are alive establish the foundations of a culture and form the base for the aesthetic emotion. My painting is born out of fantasy yet is not illusion or a gratuitous act: the myth here is the instrument used to reveal and uncover the historical experience of the Black people. While reaching for the roots of images and symbols, we are creating an art truly culturally meaningful, as opposed to the production of a Black art which manifests itself only at the level of folklore, of which the Blackness lies only in the epidermic color (Nascimento, 1974: 5).

THE DRAMATIC DANCES

Part of our memories as descendants of Africans is given back to us through the dramatic dances and the folkloric music, the anonymous tales, the games, the rhythm, the poetry that the slaves brought with them, religious dance, warrior dance, dance for its own sake. An Angolan wedding dance—*Quizomba*—contributed a great deal to the batuque and the Brazilian samba. From religious dances originated the secular steps of the *Aluja, Jarre,* and *Jequede.* The Angola-Congo Batuque projected a basic influence in the creation of Brazilian dance; from it comes, for instance, the *embigada (semba)* literally, "the meeting of the belly-buttons," that many take as the origin of the name Samba. The music and choreography of Samba take different forms and names according to the region; in Rio de Janeiro, Samba presents the gliding step. There were old forms such as the *lundu* and *bahiano.* The ones to be found today are rich and various: *tambor da crioula,* from Maranhao; *tambor,* from Paaui; *bambelo,* from Rio Grande do Norte; *samba de roda,* Bahia; *jongo,* from the states of Rio de Janeiro and Sao Paulo; *samba* and *partido alto,* from the city of Rio de Janeiro; *samba lenco,* Sao Paulo; *caxambu,* from the states of Rio de Janeiro and Minas Gerais. In the samba schools of Rio de Janeiro can be found the creative force of this kind of popular music in a permanent state; it is from those centers that samba radiates, influencing the whole country.

The trajectory of samba has been full of accidents. Dance faced resistance, opposition, and even persecution similar to that exercised against the cultural expressions brought from Africa. Dr. Melo Morais wrote against the "black men and women dressed in feathers, *growling* african chants and making *barbarous* noise with their rude instruments" (my emphasis; Rodrigues, 1945: 283) in the streets of Bahia on the eve of the feast of Reisado (January 6). Meanwhile, the *Jornal de Noticias* of the same city, on the 12th of February 1901, regretted the Africanization of the carnival, asking at the same time for police intervention to stop those *batuques* that spread through the streets, "singing the traditional samba,

for all of this is incompatible with our state of civilization"
(Rodrigues, 1945: 255).

Even from the top of the pulpits the priests condemned the
batuques as immoral. However, for security reasons, the
batuques found a defender in the person of the Count of
Arcos; in the beginning of the nineteenth century, this high
representative of the administration expressed the following
views:

> Batuques as seen by the Government have one meaning, while
> viewed by the people of Bahia they have a very different one. . . .
> The Government looks at the batuques as an insensitive and
> mechanical act forcing the blacks every eight days to renew
> their ideas of reciprocal hostility, which have been natural to
> them since birth, but which, however, begin to be effaced little
> by little through their common disgrace. These ideas can be
> considered the most powerful guarantee of security for the big
> cities of Brazil. Well, then, to forbid the only act of disunity
> among the blacks is the same as the Government promoting
> indirectly, unity among them, a possibility I can only view as
> embodying terrible consequences [Rodrigues, 1945].

It would not be a mistake to interpret the support to the
Congos and *Mozambiques,* as well as other types of dramatic
dances realized annually and on fixed dates, as nothing more
than other links in the same chain of strategy exposed by the
Count of Arcos: the division, the stimulation of the tribal
fights among the Blacks as a form of security for the whites.
The church patronized and surveilled the realization of several
festivities. Fraternities for the "savage Blacks", for "crioulos"
and for "mulattos" were created for this purpose, and such
organizations had, by imposition, white treasurers. (Bastide,
1953). In the Congos, the dramatic situation shows the prince
destined to die in sacrifice for his people dominated by the
armies of the Ginga Queen. The dramatic dance, *Bumba-meu-
Boi,* considered by many as the most interesting and original
creation of our folklore, seems to be of European origin. But

it presents Black-African magical characteristics and Black influence in the configuration of the theatrical part *(auto)* as well as in the roles of the dramatic action itself. These became so strong and dominant as to transform the dance in a "violent satire" (Almeida,n.d.: 43). The perpetuation of the memory of the heroic feats of the Republic of Palmares can be found in the *auto dramatico* Quilombos, in the state of Alagoas. The folkloric unconscious registered the refrain, "play Black, White doesn't come here" that the palmarinos would sing, dizzied in their freedom.

Several dramatic dances in Brazil present the episode of death and resurrection of the protagonist. For me, these are ancient projections of African beliefs, the Egyptian myth of Osiris brought to Brazil through a long spiritual journey, in time and space, and incorporation to the Yoruba spiritual foundations.

The African arts were integrated, joining dance, music, and chants to the dramatic episodes, the poetry, the painting (in the masks), the clothes and ornaments. In a presentation of the *Congos* in Bahia around 1760, there were 80 masks (Andrade, n.d.). Shawls, bracelets, earrings of Nigerian procedure; turbans or *rodilhas* of maometan origin; beads and *balangandans* coming from Angola and Congo—all of those elements blended in Brazil to form the aesthetics of the Black woman in her typical *Bahiana* attire. The making of the clothes and ornaments typical of Bahia, a tradition which has persisted since colonial times, is to this day the center of one of the most active handcrafts complex in that state.

Our folklore shows figures connected to the historical situation of the African slave, Pai Joao, corresponding to the American "Uncle Tom," the old black man, defeated and resigned, a dramatic symbol of imposed domestication; in his stories about Africa and slavery, we can barely perceive the revolt or protest which sprouts in small ironies. The Negrinho do Pastoreio is another celebration of martyrdom, showing this time the sacrifice of Black children under the brutality of the white master. The Mae Preta (Black Mother), another martyr, cannot hide under the auro of easy sentimentality with which Brazilian tradition involves her, the inhuman sexual violation that victimized the enslavened African woman. Ironically, this criminal action against the Black woman is used to show that, since the Portuguese man "mixed" with her, he showed no racism—in perfect accordance with the official versions. In a woman's congress that took place in Rio de Janeiro in July 2, 1975, the Black women issued an important document, in which they say:

> The fate of the Black woman in the American continent, like that of all her brothers of the same race, has been, since her arrival, to be a thing, an object, an instrument of production or sexual reproduction. So the Black Brazilian woman received a cruel inheritance: to be not only the object of production [as the Black man also was], but more still, to be an object of pleasure for the colonizers. The fruit of this cowardly inter-breeding is that which is now acclaimed and proclaimed as "the only national product that should not be exported: the Brazilian mulatto woman." But if the quality of this "product" is said to be high, the treatment she receives is extremely degrading dirty, and disrespectful.

MUSIC

The Africans also brought several musical instruments, some of which persisted and are in use among us today, such as the drums—*atabaques,* of several styles and sizes—the *ganza,* the *adja, agogo, urucungo, gongue;* those instruments added to the dramatic dances and to the folkloric music, generated an excitement which seduced and fascinated the composers of classical music.

The Black Father Jose Mauricio (1767-1830), however, did not get his inspiration from these sources. His musical formation was European. He sang, played the harpsichord and the viola, and also wrote religious music. He was the Master of the Royal Chapel under D. Joao VI, and a musician of rare talent within his sphere. In contrast, in the eighteenth century the mulatto poet Caldas Barbosa sang modinhas and wrote lundus. Joaquim Manoel, another mulatto, expressed his talent as a guitar and cavaquinho player in the Rio de Janeiro of 1822. Many others would contribute with various tonalities and degrees of the Black character to the beginnings of Brazilian music: Marcelo Tupinamba, Chiquinha Gonzaga, Eduardo Souto, Paulinho Sacramento. More recently we can name: the mulatto Franciso Braga, conductor and composer; the Black Paulo Silva, teacher of fugue and counterpoint at the National School of Music; Lorenzo Fernandes, who wrote *Batuque* and *Jongo;* Luciano Gallet, Ernani Braga, Camargo Guarnieri, Frutuoso Viana, Francisco Mignone, Barroso Neto, Heckel Tavares, Jose Siqueira, all of whom produced works showing the Black influence in their structure, theme or other formal element.

Other important Black names also appear, in the present as in the recent past of Brazilian music and dance: Ismael Silva, Heitor dos Prazeres (deceased), Ataulfo Alves (deceased), Dorival Caymmi, Ze Queti, Gilberto Gil, Jorge Ben, Caetano Veloso, Paulinho da Viola, Milton Nascimento. A special reference should be made to honor Mercedes Batista, a choreographer and dancer of great talent, for her efforts toward the development of Black values in Brazilian dance, within high artistic standards and preserving its genuine roots. The same applies to Abigail Moura, recently deceased, who was a conductor and composer and created the Afro-Brazilian Orchestra.

The suffering of the Black emerged stylized in his lyrical flow and added unknown dimension to his dramatic impulse. The mark of his sensitivity manifests itself in the totality of folkloric creation, in the choreography, as well as in the singing, verse, stories, colors, and rhythmn. The Black is present in all modes of creativity. Still during slavery times, some Blacks united in a sort of collective labor organization—the *canto*. Those Blacks were known as *Negros de ganho*. In the canto they pursued handicrafts and other types of activities: they carried *cadeirinhas,* loads, vine barrels, pianos, all kinds of heavy burdens; they swept the streets, they were cobblers, ironsmiths, tailors. Each canto had its own elected leader, the *capitao* (captain). Those workers also created their own work songs. The meaning of some of those outgrew the limits of simple musical support to heavy labor. An example can be found in the songs of the piano movers: the song was not destined to alleviate the weight of the cargo, but to keep the musical instrument in tune. From Angola came the *Capoeira,* originally a system of martial arts, and which in Brazil integrated dance forms, of which it now represents one of the most beautiful expressions at the sound of the exquisite *berimbau.*

The *Casa Grande,* where the white master lived with his family, also suffered in African "invasion": mores, superstitions, *orixas,* herbal pharmacy and medicine, food and cookery, even the way of walking, talking, and the African politeness left a deep mark. The contact with those transformed forever the white families themselves, and competing with European influnce, the presence of Africa is now totally visible in the descendents of those who were once the masters. These seductive powers touched all, even men of religion, such as those once arrested, together with *babalaos* (the priests of the African religions) and worshipers of the Xangos, in one of the frequent police raids in Recife (Ribeiro, n.d.). African spirituality offers an approach to life and nature that speaks directly and clearly to the world of feelings inside all of us. In Pernambuco, the African cults are known as Xangos, whereas in Bahia, as we have already seen, they are called Candombles. More to the south, the predominately Bantu rituals, blended with the presence of the Indian and the white influence mainly the Kardecist spiritism, as well as the Christian religious forms—resulted in the *Umbanda,* which is today a true religious force. In Rio de Janeiro, the name *Macumba* is used for the Afro-Brazilian rituals, and in Rio Grande do Sul those are known as *Batuques*.

LITERATURE

Under the impact of the difficulties of communication, among themselves and with the whites, the Blacks created words, altered the phonetics, the morphology, and the syntax, transforming as a result the structure of the Portuguese language. In a study about the persistence of the Yoruba language in Bahia, Nigerian Ebun Omowunmi Ogunsanya considers that: "More in depth scientific research needs to be undertaken to show the influence of Yoruba language on the Brazilian language" [Ogunsanya, 1971: 66]. As it happens, some blacks revealed themselves both aggressive and competent in the improvisation of poetic *desafios*. The Northeast has kept the names of famous improvisers—repentistas, Black or Mulatto: Inacio da Catingueira, Azulao, Manuel Preto, Teodoro Pereira, Chica Barbosa, and many others. The relationships between Blacks and Whites was a common theme in those poetic tournaments.

cantor branco	*white singer*
Moleque de venta chata	Flat nosed little boy,
de boca de cururu,	of cururu toad mouth,
antes de treze de maio	before the 13th of May
eu nao sei o que eras tu	I don't know what you were
O branco e da cor da prata	White is the color of silver
O negro e da cor do urubu	Black is the color of vultures.

cantor negro	*Black singer*
Quando as casas de negocio	When the houses of business
fazem sua transacao	engage in their transactions
o papel branco e lustroso	the white paper is shiny
nao vale nem um tostao,	but it is not worth a penny,
escreve-se em tinta preta	one writes with black ink
fica valendo um milhao	and it becomes worth a million

Gregorio de Matos, in the seventeenth century, introduced Black motifs in his poetry. The strong Black presence leaves marks and traces, injects vitality and color, spreads poetry and drama in Brazilian literature. However, the possibility of becoming a literary producer in a formal sense was closed to Blacks. In the first two centuries after the discovery of Brazil, their participation was only possible in the anonymous form of folklore, specifically as narrators, recalling the *arokin* or *akpalo* from Nigeria. It was a contribution within the perspective of oral tradition: tales, divination, verses, sayings, word-puzzles, and satires. Jose Basilio da Gama (1741-1795), a mulatto from Minas Gerais, wrote epic poetry and similarly some Blacks and mulattos, in spite of the existing restrictions, managed to ascend to the highest levels of poetic creativity of their time: Caldas Barbosa, Jose da Natividade, Antonio Goncalves Dias (born in 1823), a mulatto from Maranhao who wrote lyrical poetry intensely permeated by pantheism; Castro Alves (1847-1871), the Condor of Bahia, who raised in flight in defense of the slaves in his poem *Vozes da Africa*—"Voices of Africa," *Navio Negreiro*—"Slave Ship," *Poema dos Escravos*—"Poem of the Slaves," burning pieces of tragic beauty, describing the horrors of the slave trade and of slavery; Luiz da Gama, another implacable voice who was, himself, a slave. Born in Bahia (1830-1882), when he was 10-years-old, his father, a Portuguese aristocrat, sold him; he was sent to Sao Paulo, there he became a freeman and achieved a position as a journalist, lawyer, and spokesman, dedicating himself totally to the cause of the liberation of his race. He wrote the satire, *A Bodorrada,* to ridicule the presumptions of certain "mock-whites." His mother, Luiza Mahin, a liberated Black woman, became famous as one of the leaders of the slave rebellions in Bahia during the period 1820-1835. The Black Cruz e Souza (1809-1861) was a very unique personality, unrivaled in Brazilian literature. Born in Florianopolis, State of Santa Catarina, he lived in Rio de Janeiro a life of deadly pain. He suffered shame and persecution, but left immortal poetic works: *Farois, Evocacoes,* and *Ultimos Sonetos*

(Lighthouses, Evocations, and Last Sonnets). In prose, he left *O Emparedado* ("The Walled-In Man"), a moving testimony to his existential adventure. A symbolic poet he is placed by critics side by side with Baudelaire and Mallarme. According to Bastide (1973: 77), the "Black Swan" "changed his racial protest into aesthetic revolt, his ethnic isolation into the isolation of the poet, the barrier of color into the barrier of the philistines against the pure artist." Cruz e Souza aspired to penetrate the night "until a new and unknown visual interpretation of the black color shone forth." More recently, other Black and mulatto voices emerged in poetry: Lino Guedes (deceased) from Sao Paulo; Omar Barbosa from Espirito Santo; Solano Trindade from Pernambuco, who died in Sao Paulo (1974) where he lived and directed the *Teatro Popular Brasileiro;* Jorge de Lima (deceased), the well-known author of the poem *Essa Negra Fulo;* Raimundo Souza Dantas from Sergipe, a novelist; Fernando Goes, critic and chronicler in Sao Paulo; Deoscoredes M. dos Santos (Didi), a priest at the terreiro Axe Opo Afonja (Salvador, Bahia) who collected the "Nago Tales"; Sebastiao Rodrigues Alves from Espirito Santo, unrelenting militant of black culture, who published a study entitled "Ecology of the Afro-Brazilian Group"; Romeu Crusoe, mulatto from Northeast, who wrote *A Maldicao de Cannan* ("The Curse of Canaan"), a novel which deals with the racial situation in his home region; Eduardo de Oliverira from Sao Paulo, author of *Gestas Liricas da Ne gritude;* Ironides Rodrigues, a dramatic author who wrote *A Estetica da Negritude,* still unpublished. Guerreiro Ramos, a mulatto from Bahia, is a very imporant name in the formation of Brazilian sociology; he brings into focus the aesthetic alienation of the country, where the black color suffers discrimination and is equated to ideas of "evil" and "ugliness." He expresses thus a vital concept.

> Black beauty is not, prechance, a cerebral creation of those whom circumstance gave a black skin, a mode of rationali-

zation or self-justification, but an eternal value, worthy even if never discovered [Ramos, 1957: 195].

It would take too much space to enumerate the totality of those writers who were influenced by the black culture, but I cannot leave without mentioning the name of Antonio Olinto. In his novel, *A Casa da Agua* ("The Water House"), he paints a vast picture of the life and mores of the descendants of slaves who returned to Africa; the action follows three generations, in Brazil, Nigeria, and Dahomey. Gerardo Mello Mourao, "damned poet" of Ceara, Carlos Drummond De Andrade, Manoel Bendeira (deceased), Cassiano Richardo, also eulogized Blackness through their poetic work. Another Black man who, facing untold difficulties and problems of survival, left some of the most important novels of our literature was Lima Barreto, born in Rio de Janeiro. Mario de Andrade, a mulatto from Sao Paulo, had a leading role in the Brazilian intelligentsia, especially in the famous *Modern Art Week* which took place in Sao Paulo in 1922. There came to the surface pioneering and timid references to the importance of African and Black cualtures in the development of the arts. Jorge Amado, from Bahia, is the Brazilian writer whose work has been translated into a greater number of foreign languages. His numerous books almost always portray aspects of the daily, as well as the religious, life of the Blacks in Bahia. A vast gallery of Black and mulatto characters are the agents of his story-telling. It is regrettable, though, that the glorification of mixed breeding, as manifested in his books, serves the purpose of reinforcing the theory of the "whitening" of our people.

I have already had the occasion in *Open Letter* (Nascimento, 1966) to manifest my rejection of the aggressive purpose of assimilation and aculturation. It coincides with the pronouncement of Amilcar Cabral when he states, that "colonial domination has tried to create theories which, in fact, are only gross formulations of racism." And he adds: "This, for example, is the case with the so-called theory of progressive *assimilation* of native populations, which turns out to be only a more or less violent attempt to deny the culture of the people in question" (Cabral, 1973: 40). Among us there are many instances of Blacks and mulattos so deeply marked by this assimilation that they manifest self-hatred and try to exercise their Blackness through self-flagellation. This is so, for instance, with the ethnographer Edison Carneiro, a mulatto from Bahia, when he declares: "the work of that which we call "civilization in Brazil" has been precisely this destruction of Black and Indian cultures" (80 *Anos de Abolicao,* 1968: 58). He proceeds to complete his reasoning: "the rupture of the ties with Africa, even by means of frequently brutal processes, seems to me a *valid acquisition* of the Brazilian people." (my emphasis; 80 *Anos de Abolicao,* 1968: 60).

THEATER AND FILM

The foundation for an authentic Brazilian theater can be traced to the dramatic dances, the popular "autos," the Afro-Brazilian ritual, and to historical characters and facts, such as *Palmares* and its last chief, the heroic Zumbi; to the revolts of the Males (Haussas) in Bahia, as well as to the *Revolt of the Tailors.* The legend of Chico-Rei, who arrived in Brazil as a slave after having been king in Africa, is very demonstrative of this tradition. He managed to free his entire tribe, bought a gold mine, and built a state within the state in Mina Gerais in the eighteenth century. In the dramatic literature of the colonial period the Black appear only incidentally in funny, picturesque, or decorative roles. The rule on our stages was paint a white actor Black, when the role demanded a dramatic emphasis. Even so we can quote some plays where the Black is an important character or the dramatic issue: Joaquim Manoel de Macedo (1849) *The Blind; Calabor* by Agrario de Menezes; *O Escravocrata* (The Enslaver) and *O Liberato* (The Liberated) by Arthur Azevedo; and *O Mulato* (The Mulatto) by

Aluisio Azevedo; *O demonio familiar* (The Familiar Demon); and *Mae* (Mother) by Jose de Alencar. Martins Pena used the presence of the Black on stage more as a picturesque element. However, we stand before an almost total vacuum in so far as Blacks are concerned in this area, as there are other works of the period where nothing relevant can be mentioned.

I thus felt compelled by these circumstances to start the *Teatro Experimental do Negro* (TEN)—Black Experimental Theater—which I founded in 1944 in Rio de Janeiro with a small group of friends. I have had the opportunity to write about TEN before:

> Before 1944, when I made a reality of the *Teatro Experimental do Negro* (Black Experimental Theater), known as the TEN, in Rio de Janeiro, other thoughts developed, as a result of which the original project became much more profound and complex. I asked myself: What could there be, besides the ornamental color bar, that justified the absence of the Black on the Brazilian stage? Could the theory of their inability to play serious roles, their lack of artistic responsibility, be true? Was it that they were considered capable of playing only the picturesque "black-boy" or the folkloric characters? Could there be deeper implications, a basic difference of artistic conception or theatrical expression—perhaps a white aesthetic and a black aesthetic, produced by the conditioning of segregation and conflicting interests? There must have been something underlying that objective abnormality that existed back in the year 1944. Because to speak of genuine theater—the fruit of man's imagination and creative power—is to speak of plunging into the roots of life. And Brazilian life had exluded the Black from its vital center only out of blindness or the deformation of reality. Thus we must go back in history to decipher the contradictions that face us and perhaps to find the illumination for the path that the Black theater in Brazil must follow [Nascimento, 1967: 36].

After further consideration, I continued:

> A Black theater in Brazil would by necessity have to begin from a knowledge of the historical reality which would condition its

revolutionary mission. With this in mind, the TEN took as its fundamental aim the task of redeeming in Brazil the values of Afro-Brazilian culture, so much denied and degraded by the pressure of white European culture; what was proposed was the social elevation of the Blacks by means of education, culture, and art. We would have to work urgently on two fronts: to promote the denunciation of the mistakes and alienation purveyed by the studies of the Afro-Brazilian and to see that the Black became aware of the objective situation in which he found himself. It was basic to the task we forget the spirtual slavery in which the Black was kept before, as well as after, May 13, 1888, when he was theoretically freed from slavery. Theoretically, because the very same economic and social structure was maintained, and the freed Black reaped no economic, social, or cultural dividend. The first task of TEN was to make literate its first participants—recruited from among workers, maids, slum-dwellers without any definite occupation, humble civil servants—and to offer them a new attitude, a criterion of their worth which would also make them see and perceive the position they occupied as Afro-Brazilian in the national context [1967: 40].

The TEN sponsored the First Congress of the Brazilian Black in Rio de Janeiro, 1950, and promoted a contest among painters around the theme *Black Christ* in 1955. From 1944 to 1968 when TEN ceased to exist as a formal institution, it exercised its influence in aiding the transformation of the situation in Brazilian theater, opening the way for the inclusion of Black actors and actresses, such as Ruth de Sousa, Claudiano Filho, Lea Garcia, Jose Maria Monteiro, Haroldo Costa, and dozens of others. Some are now integrated as professionals in television, cinema, and theater. TEN stimulated the emergence of plays with Black heroes, produced some of them, and published part of this dramaturgy in an anthology entitled *Dramas para Negros e Prologo para Brancos* (Dramas for Blacks and Prologue for Whites). This book includes: *O Castigo de Oxala* by Romeu Crusoe, *Auto da Noiva* by Rosario Fusco, *O Filho Prodigo* by Lucio Cardoso, *Aruanda* by Joaquim Riberiro, *O Emparedado* by Tasso da Silveira, *Filhos de Santo* by Jose de Morais Pinho, *Sortilegio* (Black Mystery) by Abdias do Nascimento, *O Anjo Negro* by Nelson Rodrigues, and *Alem do Rio* (Medea) by Agostinho Olavo. This anthology is now available in English translation, but lamentably there seems to be little or no interest in publishing this landmark work.

A great actor that TEN uncovered was Aguinaldo Camargo who lost his life in a car accident. About him Ramos wrote:

> A fabulous man with an incoercible vocation for grandeur, one of the most complex spirtual organisms ever born in Brazil. A creature of great elevation who was refused recognition by a mediocre and narrow-minded environment [1966: 104].

The TEN waged an inflexible war against any form, overt or subtle, that under the label of folklore, paternalism, or even anthropological and ethnological science, aimed at the reduction of Black values to the level of primitive, naive, or magical. The process of Black theater in Brazil is only at the beginning of a fertile road within the artistic creations of the country.

And what would be the position of Blacks in Brazilian cinema? This may be the area where they are least visible, even with the existence of a fabulous actor such as Grande Otelo, who has played in films for over thirty years. The typical, laughable Black character has been part of many comedies and musicals of no importance or relevance. There are some films worth mentioning though, among them: "Amei um bicheiro." (1951) by Jorge Ilehi; "Moleque Tiao" (1941); Jose Carlos Burle's "Tambem somos irmaos" (1947) where Otelo plays with Aguinaldo Camargo; "Rio 40 Graus" and "Rio Zona Norte" (1957) by Nelson Pereira dos Santos; "Sinha Moca" (1953) by Tom Paine.

Marcel Camus, a Frenchman, directed the most famous film with a Black cast, and taking place mostly in a *favela* of Rio de Janeiro, "Black Orpheus" (1958). It was awarded the Grand Prix in Cannes. In reality, however, this film is nothing more than a commercial exploitation of the misery of the hills of Rio, transfigured through the Carnival into a place of joy, songs, and love, where the rhythm, the colours, the sound of the drums, and the chorus of guitar exist to bring those people happiness. "Assalto ao trem pagador" (1962) by Roberto Farias is a film which shows that the "favelado" steals because he lives in extreme poverty.

From the artistic and cultural point of view, the most valid attempt to film the Blacks is due to Glauber Rocha in "Barravento" (1961). Full of beautiful and strong images of Black life, and without resorting to easy schemes, this film touches the theme of class struggle and the traditional Black cultures in Bahia. "Ganga Zumba" (1963) by Carlos Diegues places itself within a perspective of Black history—whereas in any other film the Black is seen from outside, in accordance with the white point of view. It deals with the life of Zumbi as an adolescent slave before assuming his position as chief in Palmares. "Macunaima" (1969) by Joaquim Pedro de Andrade means, according to Joao Carlos Rodrigues:

> the great allegory about the destiny of Blacks in Brazilian society, where at a certain point the hero, black and ugly (Gran de Otelo), through a magical trick becomes white and handsome (Paulo Jose).

The intolerance of the Catholic Church toward the Afro-Brazilian beliefs is portrayed in "O Pagador de Promessas" by Anselmo Duarte. Some of the more important Black actors and actresses in Brazilian movie-making are Lea Garcia, Ruth de Sousa, Pitanga, Milton Goncalves, Jorge Coutinho, Adalberto, Zeni Pereira, Luiza Maranhao and Zozimo Bulbul. However, there is not a single Black film director in Brazil.

REFERENCES

ALMEIDA, R. (n.d.) "Le folklore Negro au Bresil." La Contribution de L'Afrique a la civilisation Bresilienne.

ANDRADE, J. (1971) "Quatro Tiradentes Baianos." Realidade (November).

ANDRADE, M. (n.d.) Dancas Dramaticas do Brasil. Sao Paulo: Martins Editora.

AZEVEDO, T. de (1973) "Os groups Negro-Africanos." Historia da cultura Brasileira. Rio de Janeiro: Conselho Federal de Cultura Ministerio da Educacao e Cultura.

BASTIDE, R. (1973) Estudos Afro-Brasileiros. Sao Paulo: Editora Perspectiva.

——— (1953) Relacoes Racias entre Negros e Brancos em Sao Paulo. Anhembi (Volume XI).

CABRAL, A. (1973) Return to the Source. New York: Monthly Review.

——— 80 Anos de Abolicao. (1968) Rio de Janeiro: Cadernos Brasileiros.

FERNANDES, F. (1972) O Negro no Mundo dos Brancos. Sao Paulo: Difusao Europeia do Livro.

FILHO, L. V. (1946) O Negro na Bahia. Rio de Janeiro: Jose Olimpo Editora.

GILLIAN, A. (1975) Language Attitudes, Ethnicity and Class in Sao Paulo and Salvador de Bahia. New York: Union Graduate School. (unpublished)

LAPOUGE, G. V. de (1896) Les Selections Sociales. Paris.

LAYTANO, D. de (1971) Origens do Folcore Brasileiro. Rio de Janeiro: Ministerio de Educacao e Cultura—Campanha de Defesa do Folcore Brasileiro, Cadernos de Folcore No. 7.

LEVI-STRAUSS, C. (1952) Race et Histoire. Paris: UNESCO.

MOURAO, G. M. (1957) in Sortilegio (Black Mystery) play by Abdias do Nascimento. Rio de Janeiro: Program of Municipal Theatre, (August).

NABUCO, J. (1959) O Abolicionismo. Sao Paulo: Instituto Progresso Editorial.

NASCIMENTO, A. do (1974) Cultural Revolution and the Future of Pan-Africa Culture. Dar Es-Salaam, Sixth Pan-African Congress, speech delivered June 23, 1974.

——— (1968a) "Interview on the Museum of Black Art." Jornal do Brasil. Caderno.

——— (1968b) O Negro Revoltado. Rio de Janeiro: GRD.

——— (1967) "The Negro Theater in Brazil." African Forum (Spring).

OGUNSANYA, E. O. (1971) Residual Yoruba-Portuguese Bilingualism. Harvard University. (unpublished)

RAMOS, A. (1946) As cultures Negras no Novo Mundo. Sao Paulo: Companhia Editora Nacional.

RAMOS, G. (1966) "Um Heroi da Negritude." Teatro Experimental do Negro-Testemunhos.

——— (1957) Introducao Critica a Sociologia Brasileira. Rio de Janeiro: Editorial Andes.

RIBEIRO, R. (n.d.) Religiao e Relacoes Raciais. Rio de Janeiro: Ministerio de Educacao e Cultura.

RODRIGUES, N. (1945) Os Africanos no Brasil. Sao Paulo: Companhia Editora Nacional.

SKIDMORE, T. (1974) Black into White: Race and Nationality in Brazilian Thought. London: Oxford Univ. Press.

VALLADARES, C. do Prado (1966) "A deFasagem Africana on Cronica do I Festival Mundial de Artes Negros." Cadernos Brasileiros (July-August).

Abdias do Nascimento is Professor of Puerto Rican Studies and Adjunct Professor of Black Studies, State University of New York at Buffalo. He is a major voice in the Pan-African movement, having organized the Afro-Brazilian movement for national expression. His publications are numerous, including Racial Democracy in Brazil, *his latest book. A veritable man of letters and the arts, Professor Nascimento is among the most outstanding artists of the contemporary Black world.*

A Comparative Study of the Assimilation of the Chinese in New York City and Lima, Peru

BERNARD WONG

University of Wisconsin, Rock County Campus

This paper is concerned with the various causative factors for the differences in assimilation of the Chinese in Lima, Peru, and in New York City.[1] Assimilation is a process whereby immigrants discard the culture traits of their land of origin and acquire the culture of their host country through intermarriage, participation in the institutions of the host society on primary group levels, internalization of the values of the larger society and adoption of their behaviors and attitudes (Gordon 1964; Park and Burges 1921; Gould and Kolb 1964). Generally speaking, the Chinese in Lima are more assimilated than their counterparts in New York.

Chinese in Lima are quite willing to adopt Peruvian speech behavior and to learn the Peruvian way of social interaction. Chinese in New York City, however, tend to adhere to Chinese traditions. In Lima, Chinese readily enter the cliques, clubs and institutions of Peruvian society. The Chinese community in New York is 'closed,' with few participating in the institutions of the larger society. Moreover, unlike New York, where Chinese rarely wed members of the host society, intermarriage between the Chinese and Peruvians is frequent. The offspring of Chinese–Peruvian marriages speak Spanish, interact with Peruvians, identify with that country and are completely assimilated into it (Vasquez 1970; Kwong 1958). In present-day Lima, there is no exclusively Chinese neighborhood. The so-called 'Chinatown' in Lima is not a residential area but a place with a high concentration of Chinese businesses. All of the 'To-San' (more than 90,000 in 1975)[2], which includes all native-born Chinese,

[1] The fieldwork data of this paper were obtained from field research in Lima, Peru (1971) and in New York City (1972–73). I would like to express my gratitude to the Ibero-American Studies Program of the University of Wisconsin at Madison, the Ford Foundation and the National Science Foundation for their financial support of my fieldwork, and also to my colleagues Gregory Guildin, Robert Griffin and to Dr. James W. Loewen for their valuable criticism of the manuscript.

[2] This is a rough estimate given me by my informants. It is almost impossible to obtain official statistics on this matter since the native-born Chinese and the offspring of Chinese–Peruvian parentage are subsumed under the category of Peruvians in the census data, which have no information about the ethnic parentage of their citizens.

offspring of Chinese/non-Chinese marriages and 98 percent of all the alien-born Chinese in Lima (15,000 in 1975)[3] do not live in the Chinatown area. They dwell among Peruvians in different residential neighborhoods depending on their economic situations. New York's Chinatown, in contrast, is both a commercial and a residential area for the Chinese. According to the Consolidated Chinese Benevolent Association, about 100,000 Chinese lived in New York City as of 1976, 50 percent of them in the Chinatown area.

These two Chinese communities offer an excellent opportunity for a comparative analysis of assimilation, for they share many sociocultural characteristics but differ in their rates of assimilation. First, most members of both communities emigrated from the same region in China—i.e., Kwangtung Province (Coolidge 1909; Seward 1881; Stewart 1951; Ho 1959; Kwong 1958; Wong 1971)—and speak a similar dialect. Second, the original migration movement of the Chinese to the Americas was drawn by the economic needs of the host countries and propelled by poverty and overpopulation in the home country (Coolidge 1909; Seward 1881; Ho 1969; Wong 1971). The migrants were initially recruited by the host countries as laborers. Third, both communities have existed for about the same length of time, approximately 130 years. Chinese began to settle in the two cities in the mid-1870s and lived under the constraints of an urban environment (Wu 1958; Wong 1974; Ho 1969). The purpose of this paper is to describe and analyze the causal factors for the different assimilation patterns of the Chinese in the two communities.

THEORETICAL ORIENTATION

In selecting a theoretical framework for the analysis of the assimilation of the Chinese in the Americas, many models and theories are clearly inappropriate. One example is the 'natural history' model which assumes that assimilation is a natural and inevitable outcome of race contact marked by stages of competition, conflict, accommodation and integration (Park 1926: 196). Despite the long years of settlement, automatic assimilation has not taken place as a consequence of race contact in the Chinese community of New York.

Another group of theories to be excluded in the present study is that advocated by Walter G. Beach (1934) and Stephen Thompson (1974). These authors believe that the barriers to minority assimilation lie in the minority group and their old-world culture. The assumption is that certain ethnic groups and cultures are ethnocentric and are antiassimilative (Beach 1934). The Chinese both in Lima and in New York came from old, conservative and stationary social organizations with a similar system of customs, and the great majority came from the lower social stratum in the

[3] This figure was given me by the Nationalist Chinese Embassy in Lima in 1971.

rural areas of southern China. The early immigrants in these two communities were laborers. Initially both groups had similar ethnic organizations such as mutual aid associations, family or clan associations, hometown and dialect associations. However, as time passed, the Lima Chinese lost interest in these organizations (Wong 1971). The Chinese in New York, on the other hand, still adhere to the traditional associations and coordinate much of their social life around them (Wong 1974). The number of Chinese associations in Lima is declining because of nonparticipation; the number of those in New York has recently multiplied (Wong 1974). Thus in one case the Chinese immigrants gravitate into their traditional associations and in the other abandon their traditional associations and are drawn into the mainstream of Peruvian life. Hence the barriers to assimilation cannot lie in the ethnic group nor in the cultural background per se. Ethnic group attitudes toward the larger society and their anti-assimilation organization are likely to be defense mechanisms, created by the larger society (see Amyot 1960).

The assumption that physical traits are barriers to assimilation (Gordon 1964; Lee 1960; Myrdal 1944) cannot apply in the case of the Chinese in the two communities. Both groups possess physical traits distinguishable from the majority groups of the host societies, so that physical distinctions in themselves do not explain the differential rates of assimilation.

It is equally difficult to accept the concept of 'adaptive capacity' (Wagley and Harris 1958) in this regard. Both groups migrated from the same region and possess similar adaptive potential, yet the Lima Chinese are highly assimilated into the host society (Vasquez 1970; Thompson 1974), while the New York Chinese are highly conservative and non-assimilative. Therefore it would be futile to concentrate on the socio-cultural background, physical traits, or adaptive potential of the Chinese in order to explain the differential assimilation, since these are all identical in both communities.

A framework that could be useful for the analysis is a comparative study of the macroenvironmental variables of the larger society that can act as stimulating as well as constraining factors for assimilation of ethnic groups. For instance, the syncretistic and pluralistic attitudes of the larger society and its acceptance of ethnicity, as pointed out by Sharot (1972), facilitate the assimilation of Jews. Sharot also argued that an ethnic group's assimilative process would accelerate when members of an ethnic group were not disposed to enter a peculiar structural niche. Other authors (Broom and Kitsuse 1955; Crissmen 1967; Yuan 1963; Lee 1960) point out that the larger society could present obstacles to assimilation by limiting political participation, by passing anti-ethnic legislation and by restricting economic participation. Those obstacles could engender an ethnic-centered, defensive political strategy and a selective group participation on the part of an ethnic group. The approach of the present study is to concentrate on those structural factors of the larger societies that define the nature of inter-ethnic contact, determine the mode of adaptive responses and influence the use or nonuse of ethnic identity.

THE MACROENVIRONMENTAL FACTORS OF ASSIMILATION: A COMPARISON

Based on participation and observation during fieldwork in New York and Lima, as well as on available written sources, the author has tentatively identified three macroenvironmental factors that seem to be responsible for the differential rates of assimilation in these two similar ethnic groups. These factors are: political–legal, social and economic.

Political and Legal Factors. Anti-ethnic legislation and unfavorable immigration policies frequently discourage assimilation of an ethnic group (Broom and Kitsuse 1955: 47; Sharot 1974). An examination of the Chinese immigration policies of Peru and the United States reveals the impact of the legal structure and its policies on Chinese assimilation. The immigration policies of both countries in respect to the Chinese fluctuate from time to time depending on economic conditions and international politics (Kung 1962; Kwong 1959; Ho 1967; Stewart 1951). Both countries have had periods of relaxation as well as restriction on Chinese immigration, but the U.S. immigration policies toward the Chinese until recently were more drastic, restrictive and discriminatory than those of Peru. One of these is the infamous 'Chinese Exclusion Law,' enacted in 1884 specifically to prohibit the Chinese from entering the United States.

Before the passage of the Exclusion Law anti-Chinese legislation already existed, especially in California. In 1854 the state Supreme Court of California ruled that the Chinese should not be allowed to testify in the courts. This legal discrimination resulted in many crimes—such as assault, robbery and even murder—being committed against the Chinese by the white population that could and did go unpunished so long as no white person was willing to witness on behalf of the Chinese (Sandmeyer 1939; C. T. Wu 1972: 13; S. Y. Wu 1954). Learning from such experiences, the Chinese soon organized various protective societies and mutual aid associations. One of their major functions was to informally mediate disputes brought forward by the Chinese. This tradition of solving disputes still persists in the present-day New York Chinatown. During the course of my fieldwork, I saw many cases involving Chinese, as well as non-Chinese, brought to the Consolidated Chinese Benevolent Association, and the majority of the disputants proclaimed their satisfaction with its mediation service.

Blatant discrimination in the late nineteenth century created a feeling of rejection among the Chinese. Many immigrants felt and still feel that the United States had no intention of accepting and assimilating the Chinese; the legislation of 1878 specifically denied naturalization to all alien-born Chinese.[4] Although they could be admitted legally as permanent residents according to that law, they could not become naturalized and obtain citizenship (Wu 1972: 11–13; Lee 1960: 420; Kung 1962). This 1878 legislation was finally repealed in 1943, but the psychological damage was done. Even those who had the right and privilege to become naturalized did not always take the necessary steps to acquire their citizenship. This was true in the 1940s and is still true among many older immigrants in New York's Chinatown, who have developed emotional and attitudinal resistance toward the larger society and mistrust it. A common remark among many of these older immigrants is: 'We should not expect too much from the U.S. This is not our true home. This is a country for the white persons.'

Since the passing of the 'Chinese Exclusion Law' in 1882, there have been other discriminatory immigration policies against the Chinese. For instance, the Fiftieth Congress passed the Scott Act (1888) which stated that Chinese laborers who left the United States should not be permitted to return and that all certificates of identity issued to Chinese laborers who had left the country for temporary visits abroad should be declared null and void (Kung 1962). As a consequence, many Chinese laborers who had left with such certificates in their possession could not return. Although the Chinese Exclusion Act was repealed in 1943, subsequent immigration laws relating to the admission of the Chinese were discriminatory. The Quota Act of 1943 limited the number of Chinese to be admitted to the United States to 105 a year. Persons with one parent of Chinese ancestry and the other of British, German, Mexican or any other origin were considered to be Chinese and were included in the annual allotment (Lee 1960; Kung 1962), making the Chinese the only group in the world whose ancestry was more pertinent than their place of birth. Chinese born anywhere in the world were designated as Chinese and were to be included in the quota of 105. On the other hand, a quota of 65,000 a year was extended to Great Britain, although half of that was never used (Chin 1971; S. Y. Wu 1954; Kung 1962; Lee 1960).

Unfavorable legislation continued to be enacted and implemented until very recently. In 1965, the National Origin Quota Act was abolished, and a preferential system was set up to determine the admissibility of immigrants from all over the world (Wong 1974). With the passage of this more equitable immigration law, the United States ended almost a century of discriminatory immigration policies against the Chinese.

[4] Actually, naturalization laws in 1790 had already stated that only 'free white persons' could be naturalized (see Wu 1972: 14). The laws of 1878 specifically denied citizenship to the Chinese.

During the eighty-three years of legal discrimination, the Chinese had internalized their feelings of mistrust and insecurity, which were inculcated in the second- and third-generation Chinese Americans.

Discriminatory immigration policies were compounded by discriminatory immigration procedures applied to the Chinese upon their entry into the United States. In the 1900s there were fourteen ports from which the Chinese could enter the country. In each of these there were temporary housing quarters for all Chinese awaiting the required inspection. While other nationalities were cleared the same day, a Chinese had to wait up to four weeks for an inquiry, during which time no visitors were allowed. As 'all Chinese looked alike' to their American hosts, a detailed examination including height, limbs and head measurements was given. Distances between the mouth and nose were measured by the Bertillon system, used traditionally by French prisons to identify their inmates. Stringent admission procedures and various anti-Chinese laws induced elements of fear and discouraged any initiative toward assimilation.

As a reaction to the legal discrimination, the Chinese looked back toward their motherland. They gradually developed an attitude or orientation which the sociologists labeled 'sojourner' (Siu 1952: 34–44). Although making a living in the United States, the immigrants had no incentive to improve their lot since they knew that this was not their home (C. T. Wu 1971: 16). They considered the United States a temporary place to work and to accumulate savings so that they could eventually go home to live a leisurely life. Nurturing such an attitude, they became impervious to many 'short-term' injustices and inconveniences; they never complained to the government about illegal practices. Throughout the years, agents of the Immigration and Naturalization Service frequently searched the premises of households in Chinatown without warrants, causing major disruptions of business; often no illegal aliens were apprehended. Though such a practice is a violation of civil rights (the Fourth and Fifth Amendments), Chinese residents did not protest.

The long years of legal discrimination also brought about other consequences. Most of the Chinese in Chinatown were afraid to ask for welfare assistance or even for social security benefits. Instead they relied on their ethnic associations. It is true that these associations filled many emotional needs and provided welfare and legal services for the older immigrants. But in doing so, they further segregated the residents of Chinatown from the larger society. Although much of the anti-Chinese legislation has been abolished in recent years and many bills have been enacted for the civil liberties of minorities, the older Chinese still have not forgotten the discriminatory experiences. 'Now that things have improved,' says an informant, 'we are satisfied. It's good enough. Don't ask for too much!' In claiming that they are still disliked and suspected by the government, some Chinese cite the statement made by the F.B.I. Chief J. Edgar Hoover to the Congress about the possible existence of spies among the Chinese. C. T. Wu describes the fear and uneasiness of the older immigrants:

Aware of the frightening oppression in the past and the tragic experience of the American Japanese in World War II, many Chinese, especially in the older generation, are extremely cautious in expressing their views regarding anything concerning communists. Many leaders of the Chinese community in this country are rather reluctant about freely uttering their opinions. In other words, the Chinese today are still politically living in fear (C. T. Wu 1971: 9).

The anti-Chinese legislation also created a sense of common fate and destiny which served to strengthen ethnic solidarity among the Chinese. For the well-being of its residents, New York's Chinatown began to organize many protective associations. In 1890, the first Chinese society incorporated under the Societies Act of New York State came into existence: the Chinese Consolidated Benevolent Association (CCBA), then known as the Chinese Charitable and Benevolent Association of New York. Its stated goals were to improve living conditions, to care for the sick and distressed, to give pecuniary assistance and advice to reputable and deserving Chinese in New York City and generally to aid and succor all worthy Chinese in need (Bylaws of the CCBA). The CCBA is composed of fifty-nine family name and mutual aid societies and is still an important organization in Chinatown. Trade associations, such as the laundry and restaurant associations that guard the interests of the Chinese in those lines of work, are important as well.

Despite the Chinese Exclusion Law of 1884, poverty and overpopulation in China brought continued, but illegal, immigration. After 1884, there were three routes by which Chinese immigrants were smuggled into the United States (Wu. 1958)—Canadian, Mexican and West Indian. Lacking legal residence status and any ability to use the English language, the illegal entrants crowded into the various Chinatowns. Illegal immigrants used adaptive strategies such as seeking employment from other Chinese, believing that, so long as they stayed in a Chinatown, they were in less danger of being exposed to the immigration officials. Members of the community were expected to protect their countrymen, and outsiders were distrusted because they commanded political and economic power capable of destroying the general well-being of the Chinese, especially if he were an illegal entrant. The 'they' and 'we' feelings were highly demarcated: 'they' are to be held in suspicion; 'we' are to be trusted. Thus the anti-Chinese legislation that created fear among the Chinese also created a sense of common fate and identity.

The legal structure of the United States posed other impediments to the assimilation of the Chinese through its implementation of the miscegenation laws which prevented Chinese Americans from marrying white

Americans. Not until 1967, when the Supreme Court ruled that states could not outlaw marriages between whites and nonwhites, was this barrier to assimilation overturned. Because of the long years of miscegenation laws in different states, there were extremely few interracial marriages and so fewer children born. Although there has been no legal prohibition against such marriages in New York City, an endogamous pattern of marriage is very much the rule in the Chinese community. Knowing the existence of the miscegenation laws in many states and sensing the resistance of the general public to interracial unions between Chinese and whites, many Chinese Americans in New York believe that they should not enter into such marriages, thereby avoiding hostile situations that might cause hardship to other members of the group. By abstaining from interracial unions, the Chinese hope to avoid and eliminate conflict with the larger society's desire to maintain racial homogeneity (Lee 1960: 251). The endogamous pattern of marriage resulting from legal and social pressures was indeed a stumbling block for assimilation (Lee 1960; Kung 1962; Wagley and Harris 1958; Blalock 1967). Authors like Mitchison (1961) and Lyman (1968) eloquently demonstrated that second and third generations of mixed marriages are the facilitators of assimilation. In the present-day Chinese population, there are fewer than 500 descendants of Chinese/white marriages. The ratio between mixed-blood and pure-blood Chinese is 500 to 100,000, or one to 200. The United States' immigration and miscegenation policies have created barriers against assimilation.

In comparison, the immigration policies of Peru toward Chinese immigrants have been relatively equitable. Peru's initial immigration law relating to the Chinese is known as 'La Ley del Chino' and was designed to attract immigrants (Ho 1967). The number of Chinese immigrants during the period 1849 to 1874 is a matter of controversy. Some estimate 160,000 (Kwong 1958), others 100,000 (Ho 1967). Although at times there was mistreatment of and discriminatory legislation against the Chinese, those situations were soon corrected. For instance, Chinese immigrants in the 1860s were subjected to harsh conditions of servitude imposed by some unscrupulous employers (Stewart 1951: 55–76), conditions so abhorrent that they aroused national and international protests (Stewart 1951; Kcomt 1970; Ho 1959, 1967), and the Peruvian government was forced to take protective measures in favor of the immigrants. On 26 July 1874, to help correct abuses, China and Peru drew up the treaty called 'Tratato de Paz, Navegacion y Amistad' to encourage Chinese trading activities in Peru and promote the migration of laborers into the mines and into the building of railroads (Ho 1967; Kcomt 1970).

Discriminatory legislation enacted in 1909 imposed a heavy tax on any Chinese immigrants. This law was passed on 14 May, and lasted only until 17 August when the intervention of a Chinese diplomat brought about its nullification and the Chinese continued to migrate freely to Peru with no legal restrictions until 1923. Between 1923 and 1944, there were restrictive regulations on Chinese emigration and reentry. Again after the Second World War the Chinese experienced no hardship in their immigration movement. Although in 1958 Peruvian government legislation created new immigration policies, it did not specifically discriminate against any ethnic group. In fact the quota for Chinese immigrants is 150, which is similar to that of other groups and, in substance, has no effect on the Chinese community. First, because of economic and political instability in the past two decades, there were fewer Chinese wishing to emigrate to Peru. Second, the constant rumors and speculation that the Peruvian government favored socialism discouraged many Chinese businessmen, and some of them have already left the country for economic opportunities in Brazil, Bolivia, Canada and other capitalistic countries. The increase of government control and regulation and the rigid allotment in recent years of a dollar quota for businessmen hardly serve as attractions for newcomers. Third, the diplomatic recognition given to the People's Republic of China by the Peruvian government has created uneasiness among the Chinese in Lima, once the headquarters of the Kuomintang in Latin America.

All things considered, there are far fewer discriminatory immigration policies against the Chinese in Peru than in the United States. Moreover, the Chinese have enjoyed at least periodic protection by the government in Peru and consequently many Chinese have chosen to settle there. Because there is no drastic policy against their immigration, there is no organized smuggling route for the Chinese to enter Peru illegally and no need for a Chinatown to house illegal immigrants.

Peruvian law did not forbid interracial marriage. There is no prevailing racist attitude against intermarriage between the Chinese and non-Chinese in Peru, so the number of interracial marriages is quite large. The number of children born of such marriages is estimated by my informants to be more than 180,000. Half that number is in Lima, with the ratio between Chinese mestizos and the full-blooded Chinese at 90,000 to 15,000, or six to one.

Social Factors—Compadrazgo as an Integrating Mechanism. An important structural factor facilitating assimilation is the presence or absence of powerful inter-ethnic social institutions. The social institution most conducive to assimilation of the Chinese in Lima is *compadrazgo—* godparenthood[5] (Mintz and Wolf 1950). Godparenthood exists in the

[5] Some Chinese–Mississippians and Chinese–Filipinos use 'godparents' as a means of connecting to the host society (see Loewen 1971; Amyot 1960). The differences between the use of godparenthood in Lima and in other overseas Chinese communities lie in the extensive and unique usage, the social ramifications and the heavy impact on assimilation brought about by such an institution.

United States as a ritual arrangement, without the social ramifications of its counterpart in Latin America. Ninety percent of the Chinese in Lima are baptized as Catholics. The reasons for such a large number of Catholics are many: Peru is a Catholic country, and the church is the only legitimate authority for performing marriages, so it is convenient if both partners are Catholic. Any Chinese who wants to marry officially has to be baptized, and many of my informants were baptized only shortly before being married. Another advantage is that *compadrazgo* brings influential Peruvian *padrinos* (godfathers). Normally, *compadrazgo* does not stress the godfather–godson relationship but rather that between the godfather and the father of the initiate (Mintz and Wolf 1950). In Lima, Peruvian godfathers of the Chinese always act as protectors and givers of favors for their Chinese godsons. Since such a relationship is obviously advantageous, many Chinese are not hesitant about acquiring many godfathers. The more affluent Chinese have at least three or more godfathers obtained from, say, baptism, marriage or inauguration of a new business, with the concomitant economic advantages of having an influential Peruvian *padrino*. The *padrinos* are bridges between the community and Peruvian society in both an economic and cultural sense. Economically, connections and assistance can be obtained from the Peruvian government through them. Culturally, in order to deal with their Peruvian patrons, the Chinese have had to familiarize themselves with the customs and social institutions of the larger society. Most important, the *compadrazgo* system conveys to the Chinese that they are acceptable in the larger society and that they can interact even with the middle or upper classes of Peruvian society. In short, the system induces a sense of allegiance on the part of the Chinese and encourages their participation in the civic, political and religious activities of the larger society.

The Chinese in New York, on the other hand, are deprived of the opportunity to acquire a white godfather through their churches. Unlike their counterparts in Peru, they are not obliged to be Catholics or Christians; there are no legal requirements for conversion before one can marry officially. Indeed, there are few Catholics or Protestants in the Chinese population because of the relatively stringent requirements before an adult Chinese can be admitted to membership in a Christian church. Also, most of the Christian churches in Chinatown hire Chinese ministers who can speak Chinese to organize religious and social activities. The Chinese in Lima come into contact with the larger society through the Catholic church, while the Chinese in New York are isolated from the larger society because of the presence of churches within the confines of Chinatown. Since most of the ministers and priests in Chinatown are from Taiwan and Hong Kong, they tend to emphasize the preservation of Chinese culture and thus become further stumbling blocks to assimilation.

Such parallels can also be found among other ethnic groups in the United States. For instance, Tavuchis (1963) noted that the pastors and religious elite actually delayed the assimilation of Norwegian immigrants into the larger society by emphasizing a Norwegian school for the children of the immigrants and by discouraging Norwegian contact with 'unreligious' outsiders.

Accordingly, the powerful Catholic church and its *compadrazgo* system in Lima made an immense difference in the process of assimilation of the Chinese in Peru. *Compadrazgo*, in addition to mediating between the Chinese and Peruvians, serves as a symbol of acceptance of the ethnic Chinese by Peruvian society and thus creates favorable conditions for participation of an ethnic group in the larger society.[6] Mention should also be made of other social factors which permit the successful working of the integrating mechanism of *compadrazgo* in Lima: the pluralistic nature of the economy and the population components in Peru. In its economic sector, there is no one racial group dominating the entire economy of Peru. In its population, the whites are numerically a minority group. As we have seen, white and nonwhite intermarriages have been common from colonial times and their offspring are numerous (Vasques 1960). The Peruvians are used to cooperating with people of many different cultures in the economic and social spheres. There is no desire to maintain a superior race or the homogeneity of a ruling racial group. Their racial attitudes are tolerant and their economic and social structures are pluralistic. These social conditions facilitate the successful operation of the integrating mechanisms of *compadrazgo*.

Economic Opportunity. Economic opportunity is another aspect of the environmental structure of the larger society that has played an important role, affecting the assimilation of an ethnic group in a variety of ways. In the first place, economic success and its accompanying upward mobility can provide incentives for assimilation (Fellow 1972; Befu 1965), but restricted economic opportunity may induce ethnic groups to use economic adaptive strategies, such as the formation of ethnic niches, which may deter assimilation (Barth *et al.* 1969). Again, if there is limited access to economic opportunity and lack of protection, ethnic group members may resort to the formation of closed ethnic associations and neighborhoods for protection and thus isolate themselves from the larger society (Wong 1974). Finally, ethnic groups may use their ethnicity as a resource for socioeconomic activities and thus perpetuate the ethnic boundary (Bennett 1969; Lyman and Douglas 1973).

In a comparative study of two Japanese communities in California, Befu (1965) found that, although they were originally identical in their

[6] The significant effect of religion in the larger society on assimilation is noted by students of ethnic groups elsewhere—e.g., Elkins 1968, Sharot 1974.

151

geographical place of origin, social and economic background, time of migration to the United States, skills possessed and future aspirations, one community is highly acculturated and the other unacculturated. The major factor responsible for this difference, according to Befu, has been the availability of opportunities for economic improvement. Where opportunities for Japanese upward mobility had been restricted, the Japanese were unacculturated; where such opportunities had been available, the opposite was true.

Similar parallels are seen in the two Chinese communities under study. Since the Chinese in Lima have more economic access and mobility, they are able to move up socially in Peruvian society and gain entrance to affluent neighborhoods and prestigious clubs and associations. Because it is possible to attain high economic success and social prestige, the Chinese in Lima have an incentive to assimilate. In the case of the Chinese in New York, it has been relatively difficult for most Chinese to achieve upward mobility. Many of them find it difficult to leave their ghetto and mingle with the white middle class in a wealthy neighborhood. This fact is recognized by many social scientists in the United States (Julian 1973; Graham and Gurr 1969; Yin 1973). For instance, sociologist Joseph Julian says: 'Achieving the promise of American equality has been natural if your ancestors were Protestant Englishmen; somewhat less easy if they were Protestant non-Englishmen, Catholics, or Jews; very difficult if they were Japanese or Chinese' (Julian 1973: 264).

Specific economic adaptive strategies selected by an ethnic group can affect its assimilation. The Chinese in New York are a case in point. The economic structure of the larger society poses many constraints to most of the minority. The highly capitalistic and competitive nature of the economy makes the successful participation of the small businessman a difficult matter. Certainly, the big corporations and the various business conglomerates have command of many resources and often possess competitive advantages over minority-group businessmen who have neither 'big money' nor political backing. What follows is a typical complaint of the Chinese businessman in New York:

Even without any economic and legal discrimination, it is already difficult for us to succeed in business. The competition is keen in this country, especially in New York City which has the 'best hands' and 'best brains' in all trades. Besides, you need 'big money' to succeed. Where can we get a substantial amount of capital? Our savings from small businesses are limited. The banks often discriminate against us. We are not second-class citizens, we are third-class minorities. It is harder for the Chinese than for the Puerto Ricans and blacks to get business loans because we have no political backing (Informant, 1972).

Historically, economic opportunities for the Chinese to participate in American life are few and limited, as we shall see. Restrictive and discriminative economic policies have made the Chinese resort to adaptive strategies that call for ethnic solidarity and the maintenance of their ethnic boundary. Numerous social scientists (Barth *et al.* 1969) have found that the presence or absence of certain adaptive strategies could be instrumental in the maintenance or loss of ethnic identity. In the case of the Chinese, economic discrimination led to the creation of an ethnic niche, which includes: population concentration for self-protection and for mutual aid; occupational specialization in businesses that are not in conflict with white enterprises; and the establishment of interlocking protective and mutual aid associations. Strong community organization and a closely knit economic niche, which are the defense mechanisms for the survival of the Chinese in New York, reinforce their ethnic boundary and make assimilation difficult.

Concentration of the Chinese population into the Lower East Side of Manhattan began in the 1870s, and geographic concentration can be viewed as a strategy related to their general economic adaptation. Historically, the Chinese migration movement to the United States was initiated in the 1850s, with California as the original destination. The majority of the early immigrants were laborers working on the railroads and in the mines. According to the census statistics, more than 80 percent of the Chinese in the United States were living in the Pacific states, especially in California (U.S. Census of Population 1880; C. T. Wu 1958: 12). Only after the 1850s did the exodus from California take place. The completion of the Central Pacific Railway in 1869 and the closing of many mining companies in the period immediately following brought many Chinese, as well as white, laborers to California to look for employment. According to various authors (Sandmeyers 1939; C. T. Wu 1958; Lee 1960; Lyman 1961), economic competition precipitated the anti-Chinese campaign and the passage of the Exclusion Law in 1884. Anti-Chinese sentiment was so strong that many white employers were afraid to employ Chinese laborers, who were often viewed by white laborers as potential rivals for employment, since they worked harder and were willing to accept lower wages (C. T. Wu 1958). The resentment of the whites was deeply felt by the Chinese. Because of the anti-Chinese sentiment in California, the alternatives for the Chinese were to stay in California, return to China or leave California for other states. Continuous poverty and instability in nineteenth-century China ruled out the possibility of returning there. Although some did stay in California, many pursued a new adaptive strategy: geographical dispersion, concentration in the major metropolitan areas and occupational adaptation.

In its embryonic stage, Chinatown in New York had only 500 inhabitants in 1873 (*The New York Times* 1873: 26 July); by 1900 there were 6,321 (U.S. Census of Population 1960). The drastic increase of the population in such a short time was due mainly to the exodus of the Chinese from the

West Coast. In changing their place of residence, they also changed their occupation. To avoid competition with white laborers, the Chinese sought to find new niches that would not put them in direct competition with whites. After 1890, they gradually disengaged themselves from industries such as mining and started to enter enterprises like hand laundries, personal service and restaurants (C. T. Wu 1958). The washing of clothes was considered by most of the white pioneers to be women's work, and they were loath to participate in such a 'demeaning' occupation. Domestic service and cooking were also menial jobs with very few white contenders. In the case of Chinese restaurants, the required ethnic expertise was not possessed by whites.

Throughout the years, limited economic opportunities made it difficult for the Chinese to diversify their economic pursuits. Since Chinese immigrants were denied naturalization and since many states required citizenship as a prerequisite for employment, the Chinese were excluded from many professions. In fact, before 1940 New York State prohibited Chinese immigrants from participating in more than twenty-six specific occupations, which included attorney, physician, bank director, chauffeur, dentist, embalmer, guide, liquor, pawnbroker, pilot, plumber, horse track employee, veterinarian, watchman, architect, CPA, engineer, realtor, registered nurse, teacher, and others (Konvitz 1946: 1920–211).

In the past two decades, employment opportunities for the Chinese have been broadened,[7] yet discrimination in employment still exists. With the exception of scientific and technical fields, the Chinese still experience restriction everywhere. For instance, Chinese blue-collar workers in New York find it difficult to obtain employment from the larger society since many of the vacancies are handled by labor unions, which exclude Chinese from membership. The Chinese immigrants who became permanent residents of the United States were not allowed civil service employment for more than a hundred years, and this restriction was declared unconstitutional by the Supreme Court only in 1976. Given adequate time, the situation may change, since the government is now interested in implementing the Equal Opportunity and Affirmative Action programs and in assisting minorities to achieve economic betterment.

[7] Only after the Second World War did some states begin employing more Chinese in the professions. In 1940, there were 1,028 Chinese professionals out of a labor force of 36,454. The number of Chinese professionals, according to the U.S. census of 1960, increased to 3,425 in 1950 (the total Chinese labor force was 48,389). The major factors for the increase were the demand for engineers and scientists during the Second World War (Kung 1962: 181), the presence of stranded Chinese professionals as a consequence of civil war, and the subsequent communist takeover in China (Lee 1960: 271). A significant increase of Chinese in the professions came about only after the enactment of federal and state legislation removing racial restrictions in the past twenty years. Only in 1956 did the General Electric Company begin to recruit Chinese in New York City. Equitable employment opportunity has become available to the Chinese only recently, especially after the Civil Rights legislation of 1964. Understandably, it is difficult to correct a century of discriminatory employment practices in a short time.

The present economic picture, however, has not greatly changed. Chinese restaurants and laundries remain today the most important businesses in the Chinese community of New York. The reasons for continuous concentration in the ethnic niche are: lack of capital to participate in any capital-intensive enterprise; a desire to avoid competition with laborers in the labor market and to be self-sufficient; the ease of attracting clientele to a Chinese restaurant because Americans like Chinese food, and the difficulty for Chinese, especially those who lack English, to find jobs in the larger society where they confront subtle discrimination. In order to protect their ethnic niche, the Chinese have manipulated friendship, kinship and patron–client relationships to form protective and mutual aid associations, many of which interlock. Thus limited economic opportunity has driven the Chinese into Chinatown and united them to protect a common interest.

There are about 1,700 Chinese restaurants in New York City engaging approximately 35,000 Chinese. Next in economic importance are the laundries; in 1960, there were 2,700 of them in New York City. This number dwindled to about 1,000 in 1975, with fewer than 5,000 Chinese in the laundry business. Technological improvements, invention of wash-and-wear fabrics and the use of home washers and dryers were the principal reasons for the decline. Garment factories, together with restaurants and laundries, are called 'the three trades of the Chinese' by the residents of the community. There are about 300 Chinese garment factories which specialize in sportswear and skirts and contract for materials and patterns from manufacturers who are mostly Jewish–Americans. The garment factories in Chinatown are similar to the sweatshops of the early days, and the income for seamstresses is meager. The total labor pool in the Chinatown garment factories is approximately 16,000.

Other businesses in present-day Chinatown are gift shops, grocery stores and meat and poultry stores. Only in the past two decades did some Chinese begin to work in the institutions of higher learning, and some in the scientific and engineering fields. In the 1920s, many Chinese–Americans with college degrees had to be content with their humble ethnic businesses in Chinatown. In the 1930s it was not uncommon to find college graduates with advanced degrees from major universities manning Chinese grocery or novelty stores (Leong 1936; Lee 1960; Kung 1962; Wong 1974). Even in the 1940s, there were Chinese–American professional men returning to China in order to utilize the knowledge and techniques they had acquired in the United States.[8] In other words, the economic opportunities offered to Chinese immigrants and Chinese–Americans, citizens or not, have been very limited. The current statistics on Chinese employed

[8] Between 1935 and 1944, there were only 190 Chinese scholars employed by American universities or colleges (Chinese Institute et al. 1954: 58).

in universities and research institutions in the New York area are far from impressive: there are fewer than a dozen Chinese professors, with engineers faring a little better. However, most of the four hundred Chinese engineers in the New York area are not connected with the Chinese community. The majority of them are stranded students or recent graduates who obtained a visa adjustment through their employment. Thus they differ greatly from other Chinese in the community who came over as immigrants solely with the intention of achieving economic betterment and making their home in the States.

On the whole, economic opportunities for the Chinese in New York still lie in ethnic businesses zealously guarded by their various trade associations. The Chinese Hand Laundry Association and the Chinese–American Restaurant Association are important and influential organizations in New York City. An interesting incident arose when a weekly newspaper suggested that some Chinese restaurants substituted dog meat for pork. The Chinese American Restaurant Association immediately initiated a million-dollar lawsuit against the newspaper for defamation. Later, the newspaper retracted its statement and apologized, and the association withdrew its suit. Most of the overall community organizations, such as the Chinese Chamber of Commerce and the Consolidated Chinese Benevolent Association, are watchful in respect to the well-being of the ethnic niche. The fostering of the ethnic niche and the concentrated activities within it, the establishment of ethnic associations and the use of collective resources for self-protection have the effect of isolating the community from the larger society.

The employment practices in New York's Chinatown are such that they do not provide intimate contact between members of the community and outsiders. Almost all Chinese firms there hire only Chinese because it is more profitable. Knowing that there are limited employment opportunities outside Chinatown for the Chinese, many Chinese employers pay minimal wages. In the case of illegal immigrants, employers are not hesitant to pay them miserably. The practice of employing immigrants, legal and illegal, can thus increase the profits of employers. In the environment of the Chinese firms, employers encourage traditional festivals and customs, and Chinese social etiquette is observed. Thus the Chinese are further isolated in their workplaces, assuring employers of a cheap labor pool which of course enhances profits.

A recent economic adaptation of the New York Chinese is the use of ethnicity to create new jobs for themselves. Many young Chinese, especially second- and third-generation Chinese–Americans, are aware that they have been discriminated against in the past and are anxious to do battle against racism. To this end ethnic consciousness must be raised, and ethnic solidarity maintained in the community. Hence deliberate efforts have been made to educate the Chinese in their civil rights and to initiate collective bargaining with the city on matters relating to the general welfare of the Chinese community. Individually, many young Chinese use their minority status to apply for jobs that give special preference, under federal government pressure (e.g., Equal Opportunity and Affirmative Action Program), to minority group members. The short-term effect of using ethnicity to gain special advantages is the accentuation of the 'we' and 'they' rationale. This demarcation may not necessarily produce hostility, but it does discourage identification with the larger society.[9]

Limited economic opportunity retards assimilation in other ways. For instance, without large-scale financial success, few Chinese can afford to move to desirable white neighborhoods and gain entrance to the voluntary associations of the larger society. Without economic success, it is more difficult for the Chinese minority in New York to participate in the civic and political institutions of the larger society.

The Chinese in Lima, on the other hand, have no exclusively Chinese neighborhoods nor ethnic niches. Economic opportunity there is relatively open, so that their adaptive strategies in Lima differ from those in New York in many respects. There is a nonexclusive attitude in the economy, so that the businesses that the Chinese engage in vary with the demands of the socioeconomic environment. This flexible mode of adaptation is also reflected in the selection of sites for businesses. There is practically no restriction on business locations and so no need to concentrate all Chinese activities in one area. The so-called Chinatown in Lima is not a residential area but is composed of two short streets occupied by Chinese firms, mostly owned by those who have businesses elsewhere as well.

Historically, the Chinese first went to Peru as laborers. During the early period of migration (1849–1909) they worked principally on plantations, in the processing of guano beds, in the mines and on the railroads (Levin 1960; Kwong 1957; Ho 1959; Wong 1971; Stewart 1951). After 1909, Chinese businessmen, professionals and relatives of Chinese residents started to migrate to Lima. The immigration policy of 1909 particularly favored the Chinese merchants because the Peruvian middle class believed that the participation of Chinese merchants in commercial activities would contribute to the economic welfare of the country. Many former Chinese laborers, after fulfilling their contracts, either returned to China or turned to commerce. The majority of them started small business units such as *bodegas*, grocery shops, furniture and repair stores providing for the daily needs of Peruvians. Beginning in 1910, the Chinese expanded their eco-

---

[9] I believe that such a demarcation effect is likely to be temporary if the Chinese are able to achieve their 'American dream' and are to be treated as bona-fide Americans by the larger society.

nomic sphere, becoming shopkeepers instead of laborers. Migration of Chinese traders, merchants and professionals in subsequent periods further diversified their economic pursuits in Peru.

By the mid-1920s, there were numerous small factories and shops operated by Chinese entrepreneurs. The Second World War gave enormous impetus to commercial and industrial activities in Peru; demand raised the potential value of Peru's resources (Chaplin 1967). Chinese merchants gained great advantage during this period because the Japanese were almost eliminated as competitors (Kwong 1959). Furthermore, North Americans, Europeans and rich Peruvians were more interested in the industrial and export sectors and tended to leave a vacuum in the commercial sector which was filled rapidly by the Chinese. This simple economic picture makes clear the general position of the Chinese which is still the same today in Peru. According to the census of 1940, 70 percent of the alien-born Chinese engaged in commerce. Professionals comprised their second largest occupation (11.6 percent), leaving 8 percent in agriculture and 6 percent in industry. Today, few alien-born Chinese work the land. The majority of them are still in commerce but, because of the competition of Europeans and North Americans, Chinese control of the Peruvian commercial sector is said to be relegated to second place (Kwon 1959).

There is no legal or social discrimination against the Chinese in employment. The second- and third-generation Chinese mestizos, or native-born Chinese–Peruvians, tend to be professionals—architects, accountants, doctors, engineers, professors and civil servants. The first-generation Chinese are free to pursue their economic interests according to their capabilities. Their lines of business today are diversified and include: *abarrotes* (food stuffs), export, import, retail and wholesale businesses of all kinds, shoe and leather factories, clothing, hardware, furniture, meat stores, fruit stores, vegetable stores, electrical appliances, construction, real estate, travel agencies, theaters, hotels, printing shops, *chifas* (restaurants). It is estimated that the alien-born Chinese control 40 percent of the *abarrote* business (including export, import, retail and wholesale) of Peru and 25 percent of the leather industries in the country. The restaurants are lucrative and there are many alien-born Chinese entrepreneurs who have made a fortune in them. It should be emphasized that there is no 'Chinatown-type' economy. The Chinese do not have to organize protective societies for their respective trades. Because of the relative flexibility here, they can change their occupation or enter a new business quite easily.

The alien-born Chinese–Peruvians are constantly shifting occupations and are quick to seize economic opportunity. They were among the first to utilize the abandoned airport site in Lima for the construction of tourist restaurants with Chinese and Japanese gardens. After the war, they were the first to start textile and fish meal factories. In the past twenty years, some of them recognized opportunities for maximizing profits in the real estate business and became landlords; many modern apartment buildings were constructed by alien-born Chinese for middle-class Peruvians. The alien-born Chinese also opened many entertainment facilities, first-class nightclubs and movie houses to cater to the needs of the affluent Peruvians. The travel and tourist boom attracted the attention of some entrepreneurs who were quick to respond to the economic opportunity by building hotels. Recently, because of the influx of rural Peruvians to Lima, the slum areas have become increasingly crowded and Chinese entrepreneurs have built low-cost movie houses which, because of low operational cost and great demand, have become high-profit enterprises.

Another interesting adaptation is the use of Peruvian employees in almost all the Chinese concerns. Most of the Chinese in Lima are employers, since it is relatively easy to start a small business in a developing economy with a low capital investment. The Chinese then employ Peruvians because they speak Spanish and are willing to accept low wages. The hiring of Peruvian employees, inspired by the ever-present profit motive, has meant that there is more opportunity for interaction between Chinese and Peruvians, with many fewer of the 'in-group' cliques that predominate in New York's Chinese firms.

Because of the open economic opportunity structure in Peru, the Chinese saw no need to form ethnic niches or to concentrate in a Chinatown for mutual protection. As a consequence, the associational structure in the Chinese community in Lima is weak. There are no secret societies or tongs, and only one family-name association. Although there are the Sociedad Beneficencia de China and the restaurant trade association, they are mainly concerned with social or recreational activities. In fact, the Chinese restaurant trade association was still in its organizing stage during my fieldwork in Lima in 1971. In other words, there are no closely knit community organizations because their existence is not deemed necessary by the opportunity structure (Glade 1967). Similarly, there is no exclusively Chinese neighborhood in Lima since the Chinese can travel freely and have high economic mobility. Formerly, the Chinese lived in places near their stores. With the improvement of their economic position, many have moved out of the business districts to different residential areas according to their economic status, many in exclusive sections of Lima such as Miraflores, San Isidro and Monterricos.

The lack of a Chinese neighborhood also brings beneficial effects for assimilation. As noted by William Skinner (1960), it is far easier for a foreign family to be assimilated if it is surrounded by indigenous neighbors rather than by compatriots. That is, the relatively open economic structure facilitates the assimilation of the Chinese in three principal ways: the nonexistence of exclusive neighborhoods; the absence of a closely knit ethnic niche; and the frequent contacts or interaction between the Chinese and Peruvians either in the business environment or in their neighborhoods. Befu (1965), Broom and Kitsuse (1955) and a host of other authors (Loewen 1971; Sharot 1974; Lee 1960) make a similar argument: the economic opportunity offered by the larger society affects positively the character of inter-ethnic participation and rate of assimilation.

SUMMARY

A comparative study of assimilation like the present one has shown that the structural or environmental factors in the larger society are principally responsible for the differential rates of assimilation. Historically, the United States has been racist in its treatment of nearly all immigrants. Eastern and Southern Europeans were judged inferior along ethnic/racist lines (Gordon 1964), let alone those with more pronounced physical characteristics such as blacks, Latins or Asians. The legal structure erected in the United States, which includes the historical anti-ethnic legislation, discriminatory immigration policies and racist miscegenation laws, reflects the attitudes and perceptions of the host society. The long years of unfair policies and discriminatory practices implemented against the Chinese produced feelings of rejection among them. In Lima, by contrast, the Hispanic cultural tradition does not emphasize racial differences. Although therere is a subtle racism in Lima, there is no miscegenation law, and children born of marriages between Chinese and Peruvians become important factors in the assimilation of the Chinese.

The social institutional factor—the existence or absence of powerful bridging mechanisms—affects the differential rates of assimilation. In particular, the Chinese in Lima benefit from the social institution of the *compadrazgo* system which acts as a powerful integrator in the assimilation of the Chinese into Peruvian society. In the case of the New York Chinese, there is no equivalent system. The economic factor and the accompanying discrimination in the United States, which led to the formation of a tightly knit ethnic niche among the New York Chinese, make assimilation difficult. In Lima, the relatively open economic structure permits the Chinese to achieve upward social mobility and facilitates their assimilation into Peruvian society.

The various social institutions are not direct transplants of old-world traditions. They are adaptive responses to particular social and cultural forces from the larger society. The secret societies and other associations, even the phenomenon of Chinatown itself, are adaptive responses. Differently put, the cohesiveness and the interlocking of associations in the Chinese community of New York are a function of economic, social and legal discrimination by the larger society.

Ethnographically, it is simply not true, as held by some authors (Mallory 1956; Felix 1966), that the overseas Chinese can never be assimilated. Nor is it correct to assume that the major deterrent to their assimilation originated in their homeland (Beach 1934) or from their physical appearance (Gordon 1964; Lee 1960). The present study finds that the two groups of Chinese came from similar social, economic and cultural backgrounds, yet the Lima Chinese are assimilated and the New York Chinese are not. The fundamental cause of this difference emanates from the larger society.

Methodologically, the causal factors of assimilation should not be determined solely on the basis of a single case study. In order to ascertain the specific factors of assimilation, two or more comparative case studies should be undertaken. One can control for the cultural backgrounds of the ethnic groups and concentrate on exploring the variables in the host cultures that determine the differential rates of assimilation. This study followed such an approach, which has the advantage of not presuming, a priori, that ethnic boundary maintenance is necessarily a matter of personal or ethnic group choice. Such an approach provides ample opportunity to focus attention on an ethnic group's adaptive responses brought about by the larger society. These responses are keys to the understanding of many ethnic groups' assimilation in the sense that they determine the mode of inter-ethnic interaction, the existence or non-existence of ethnic niches, the presence or absence of ethnic neighborhoods and the formation of ethnic associations.

REFERENCES

Amyot, Jacques (1960) *The Chinese Community of Manila*. Chicago: Research-Series Monograph, No. 2, Philippine Study Program, University of Chicago.

Barth, Fredrik (1969) *Ethnic Groups and Boundaries*. London: George Allen and Unwin.

Beach, Walter G. (1934) 'Some Considerations in Regard to Race Segregation in California,' *Sociology and Social Research*, XVIII (March), 340–50.

Befu, Harumi (1965) 'Contrastive Acculturation of California Japanese,' *Human Organization*, 24, 209–16.

Bennett, John W. (1971) *Northern Plainsmen*. Chicago: Aldine Publishing Co.

Blalock, Hubert (1967) *Toward a Theory of Minority Group Relations*. New York: Wiley.

Broom, Leonard and John Kitsuse (1955) 'The Validation of Acculturation: A Condition of Ethnic Assimilation,' *American Anthropologist*, LVII (48), 44–48.

Chang, Stephen (1970) *The Chinese Around the World*. Mountain View, CA: World Chinese Publishing Association.

Chaplin, David (1971) *The Peruvian Industrial Labor Force*. New Jersey: Princeton University Press.

Chen, T. (1923) *Chinese Migration with Special Reference to Labor Conditions*. United States Bureau of Labor Statistics, No. 340.

Chinese Institute *et al.* (1954) *A Survey of Chinese Students in American Universities and Colleges in the Past Hundred Years*. New York: National Tsing Hua University Research Fellowship Fund and Chinese Institute in America.

Chu, Y. K. (1975) *History of the Chinese People in America*. New York: The China Times.

Coolidge, Mary Roberts (1909) *Chinese Immigration*. New York: Arno Press and *The New York Times*.

Crissman, Lawrence (1967) 'The Segmentary Structure of Urban Overseas Chinese Communities,' *Man*, 2: 185–204.

De Vos, George *et al.* (1975) *Ethnic Identity: Cultural Communities and Change*. Palo Alto: Mayfield Publishing Co.

Dirección Nacional de Estadísticas (1944) *Censo Nacional de Población y Occupación*.

Eisenstadt, S. N. (1954) *The Absorption of Immigrants*. London: Routledge and Kegan Paul.

Elkins, Stanley M. (1968) *Slavery*. Chicago: University of Chicago Press.

Fellows, Donald K. (1972) *A Mosaic of America's Ethnic Minorities*. New York: John Wiley:

Fried, Morton, ed. (1958) *Colloquium on Overseas Chinese*. New York: Institute of Pacific Relations.

Geertz, Clifford, ed. (1963) 'The Integrative Revolution,' *Old Societies and New States*. New York: Free Press, 105–57.

Glade, William (1967) 'Approaches to a Theory of Entrepreneurial Formation,' *Exploration in Entrepreneurial History*, 4 (3), 234–59.

Gordon, Milton (1964) *Assimilation in American Life*. New York: Oxford University Press.

Graham, Hugh Davies and Ted Robert Gurr (1969) *Violence in America: Historical and Comparative Perspectives. A Report to the National Commission on the Causes and Prevention of Violence*. Washington, DC: U.S. Government Printing Office, Vol. 2.

Ho Ming Chung (1959) *Overseas Chinese Enterprises in South America*. Taipei: Chung Kuo Chiu Chin She Hui.

Instituto Nacional de Plantificación (1964) *Sexto Censo Nacional de Población*.

Julian, Joseph (1973) *Social Problems*. Englewood Cliffs, NJ: Prentice-Hall, Inc.

Kcomt, Eduardo (1970) 'A Special Report on the Chinese Community of Lima— Submitted to Banco de Lima' (manuscript).

Konvitz, Milton G. (1946) *The Alien and the Asiatic in American Law*. Ithaca, NY: Cornell University Press.

Kung, S. W. (1962) *Chinese in American Life*. Seattle: University of Washington Press.

Kwong, Alice Jo (1958) 'The Chinese in Peru,' in Morton Fried, ed, *Colloquium on Overseas Chinese*. New York: Institute of Pacific Relations, 41–48.

Lee, Rose (1958) 'The Hua-Ch'iao in the United States of America,' in Morton Fried, ed., *Colloquium on Overseas Chinese*. New York: Institute of Pacific Relations.

Lee, Rose (1960) *The Chinese in the United States of America*. Hong Kong: Hong Kong University Press.

Leong, Gor Yun (1956) *Chinatown Inside Out*. New York: Burrows Mussey.

Levin, Jonathan (1960) *The Export Economy*. Cambridge, MA: Harvard University Press.

Loewen, James W. (1967) *The Mississippi Chinese*. Cambridge, MA: Harvard University Press.

Lyman, Stanford M. (1961) 'The Structure of Chinese Society in Nineteenth-Century America,' Ph.D. dissertation; Berkeley: Library Photographic Services, University of California.

Lyman, Stanford M. (1968) 'Contrast in the Community Organization of Chinese and Japanese in North America,' *The Canadian Review of Sociology and Anthropology*, 5 (2), 51–67.

Lyman, Stanford and William Douglas (1973) 'Ethnicity: Strategies of Collective and Individual Impression Management,' *Social Research*, 40 (2), 345–65.

Mallory, Walter H. (1956) 'Chinese Minorities in Southeast Asia,' *Foreign Affairs*, 34 (2), 258–70.

Miller, Stuart C. (1969) *The Unwelcome Immigrant*. Berkeley: University of California Press.

Mintz, Sidney and Eric R. Wolf (1950) 'An Analysis of Ritual Co-Parenthood (Compadrazgo),' *Southwestern Journal of Anthropology* 6, 341–68.

Mitchison, Lois (1961) *The Overseas Chinese*. London: The Bodley Head.

Myrdal, Gunnar (1944) *The American Dilemma*. New York: Harper Brothers.

Nagata, Judith (1974) 'What is a Malay? Situational Selection of Ethnic Identity in a Global Society,' *American Ethnologist*, 1 (2), 331–49.

The New York Times (1873) 26 July.

Overseas Chinese Economy Yearbooks (1969, 1970, 1971, 1972, 1973) Taipei: Overseas Chinese Economy Yearbook Editorial Committee.

Park, R. E. (1926) 'Behind Our Masks,' *Survey Graphic*, 56, 135–39.

Ross, Peter (1974) *They and We*. New York: Random House.

Sandmeyer, Elmer Clarence (1939) *The Anti-Chinese Movement in California*. Urbana: The University of Illinois Press.

Schwartz, Shepard (1951) 'Mate Selection Among New York City's Chinese Males, 1931–1938,' *American Journal of Sociology*, LVI (6), 562–68.

Seward, George (1881) *Chinese Immigration*. New York: Charles Scribner's Sons.

Sharto, Stephen (1974) 'Minority Situation and Religious Acculturation,' *Comparative Studies in Society and History*, 16 (3) June, 329–54.

Siu, Paul C. (1952) 'The Sojourner,' *American Journal of Sociology*, 58, 34–44.

Skinner, William (1960) 'Change and Persistence in Chinese Culture Overseas,' *Journal of the South Seas Society*, XIV, 80–100.

Stewart, Watt (1951) *Chinese Bondage in Peru*. Durham, NC: Duke University Press.

Tavuchis, Nicholas (1963) *Pastors and Immigrants: The Role of Religious Elite in the Absorption of Norwegian Immigrants*. The Hague: Martinus Nijhoft.

Thompson, Stephen (1974) 'Survival of Ethnicity in the Japanese Community of Lima, Peru,' *Urban Anthropology*, 3 (2), 243–61.

U.S. Census of Population (1880, 1950, 1960, 1970).

Vasquez, Mario (1970) 'Immigration and Mestizaje in Nineteenth-Century Peru,' in Magnus Morner, ed., *Race and Class in Latin America*. New York: Columbia University Press, 73–99.

Wagley, Charles and Marvin Harris (1968) *Minorities in the New World*. New York: Columbia University Press.

Wong, Bernard (1971) 'Fieldwork Report—Chinese in Lima,' submitted to Ibero-American Studies Program, University of Wisconsin, Madison (manuscript).

Wong, Bernard (1972) 'Social Stratification in the Chinese Community of Lima' (manuscript).

Wong, Bernard (1974) 'Patronage, Brokerage, Entrepreneurship and the Chinese Community of New York,' Ph.D. dissertation; Madison: University of Wisconsin.

Wong, Bernard (1976) 'Adaptive Strategies and the Chinese Community of New York,' *Urban Life* (April), 33–52.

Wu, Cheng-tu (1958) 'Chinese and Chinatown in New York City,' Ph.D. dissertation; Ann Arbor: University Microfilms.

Wu, Cheng-tu (1971) 'Third Class Minority,' *Bridge Magazine*, 1 (2), 14–19.

Wu, Cheng-tu (1972) *Chink!* New York: The World Publishing Co.

Wu, S. Y. (1954) *One Hundred Years of Chinese in the United States and Canada*. Hong Kong: S. Y. Wu.

Yin, Robert K., ed. (1973) *Race, Creed, Color or National Origin*. Itasca, IL: F. E. Peacock Publishers, Inc.

Yuan, D. Y. (1963) 'Voluntary Segregation: A Study of New Chinatown,' *Phylon*, XXIV (3), 225–68.

Ethnicity, Secret Societies, and Associations: the Japanese in Brazil

TAKASHI MAEYAMA

Shinshu University

INTRODUCTION

The Japanese in Brazil may be called "an associational people in an unorganizational society." More than fifty years ago, Oliveira Vianna, a pioneer in Brazilian social sciences, remarked: "The institutions of social solidarity are extremely scanty among our people. Here men live, as a rule, isolated either within the large estates or within their family circles. . . . The non-solidarity is complete. We cannot discover any trace of association among the neighbors for the sake of common utility" (Vianna 1920: 169–70).

This thesis has been widely accepted by modern sociologists and anthropologists. Charles Wagley, for example, maintained that: 'The predominance of kinship in ordering social life explains the relative absence in Brazil of such voluntary associations as parent-teacher groups, garden clubs, civic clubs, and the like. People give greater value to kinship relations than to relations based upon common interest or even occupation" (Wagley 1964: 188).

Although there are few such studies based on fieldwork in the urban situations voluntary associations seem to be significantly weak in both rural and urban Brazil (Smith 1954:497; Hutchinson 1966:18; Maybury-Lewis 1968:161; and many others). The Japanese in Brazil on the other hand seem to have a mania for associations. "Two Japanese make an association, and three found a newspaper," as a Japanese saying in Brazil goes. Interestingly enough, the Japanese do not appear to be culturally an associational people.[1]

I wish to thank Professor William L. Rowe (Department of Anthropology, University of Minnesota) for many valuable suggestions and criticism. Acknowledgement is also made of research support from the National Science Foundation Grant #GS-671, "Acculturation in a Complex Society," John B. Cornell and Robert J. Smith, Principal Investigators.

[1] Of course I do not deny the importance of voluntary associations in modern Japan. My contention here is that the Japanese tend to give stronger emphasis to vertical linkage than associational ties. Edward Norbeck for example, discussed some aspects of voluntary associ-

If Chie Nakane is correct: "Without either 'frame' or 'vertical links', it seems to be almost impossible for the Japanese to form a functional group. In fact, in Japan it is very difficult to form and maintain the sort of voluntary association found so often in western societies, in that it does not have the basis of frame or existing *vertical personal relations"* (Nakane 1970: 59–60; emphasis added). Thus the over-inflated voluntary associations among the Japanese in Brazil do not seem to have derived primarily either from Brazilian or Japanese models, although both cultures doubtlessly played crucial roles in shaping their patterns. These associations may not be accounted for as something brought from their home country or something found in and learned from their host society; neither the continuity of the Japanese culture nor the acculturative process with the group satisfactorily explains the phenomenon. We can better account for these associations if we look at them as strategical devices for organizing social action in the particular situations encountered in Brazil. In this paper I shall try to interpret the emergence of *the association-oriented structure* within the Japanese ethnic group in Brazil in terms of the particular situations of the group.

IMMIGRATION AND INITIAL ADAPTIVE STRATEGIES

The Japanese ethnic group in Brazil has been there for some seventy years. It involves approximately 700,000 individuals, mostly concentrated in two neighboring states, São Paulo and Paraná, in southern Brazil. The bulk of the Japanese immigrants arrived in the 1920s and 1930s. Some 94.3 percent of them started their lives in Brazil in agriculture and more than 90 percent came as *colonos,* that is, as contract laborers to the coffee plantations. During the 1930s, only 8 percent of the residents in the state of São Paulo were in urban areas. Urbanization was however very rapid during the following decades, and the census that the Japanese minority group conducted in 1958 revealed the fact that 44.9 percent of them had been urbanized by that date (Suzuki 1969: 36). It is estimated today (1978) that about 65 percent of them are urban and that three-fourths of them were born in Brazil.

Unlike the Brazilians, they had at first relatively few kinship ties, chiefly because of their emigration pattern. Tatsuo Honda's model of the basic migration pattern in modern Japan is quite accurate: an average couple until the late 1950s used to have five children: one died before coming of

ations in Japan (1961, 1962, 1967) when he wrote of the importance of "common-interest" or "communal" associations in a rural community there. Although they need more theoretical and empirical examination, these rural organizations may be, I think, better considered as subsystems of the community than voluntary associations. Norbeck admits that these "common-interest associations find far greater development in its rural areas" (1962: 81). Ronald Dore, in examining similar aspect in an urban setting, concludes that "the Japanese are not great 'joiners' " (1958: 422).

age; two daughters went out of their household when they married; and two sons married a wife from outside. One couple stayed home as successors to their parents' household, and the other went to the city. Thus the total number of farmers' households in Japan remained unchanged for about ninety years after the Meiji Restoration of 1868 (Honda 1952: 59). This means that migrants were separated from their siblings and parents. Migration on the total household level was extremely rare. Because strong practices of primogeniture and ancestor worship prevailed, the eldest son usually became successor of the household, daughters married without sharing the inheritance, and the younger sons, single or married, while still young, migrated to the city and sometimes abroad. Kinship and primogeniture played a crucial role in separating young emigrants from their close relatives.

Unlike the Japanese immigration to Hawaii, the United States mainland, and Peru, migration in family units was the rule. The Brazilian immigration policy was primarily responsible for this basic difference. Experience throughout the long history of European immigration had taught Brazilian plantation masters that young isolated individuals would not stay long on the plantations. In order to obtain more stable contract laborers, therefore, the Brazilian immigration laws were established, requiring immigrants to come in family units which included at least three economically active members (twelve to fifty years of age).

In adapting to this Brazilian policy, many artificial family compositions were created by using the widely practiced traditional Japanese custom of adoption (*yōshi*). Young couples most commonly adopted the husband's or wife's younger siblings, cousins, nephews, or nieces, and, if these were not available, non-relatives as well. In adopting non-relatives, neighbors and previously known individuals were preferred, but strangers were also acceptable in many cases. Many young people married at emigration. Some married only in name, divorcing or separating as soon as possible after arrival. These artificially formed families, including those formed through adoption of relatives, are called *kōsei kazoku* (literally, constructed family) or *tsure kazoku* (family with companions). Whether or not real kin ties were used to construct these artificial families, I prefer to use the term "feigned family" even though many of these families in fact functioned effectively as a sort of extended family. The practice of feigned family was particularly strong among the earliest immigrants of the 1908–23 period. Although it also had various negative effects, particularly for the junior adopted members, the feigned family system was successful enough for them at least to reach Brazil.

The immigrants' experiences in the first stage of immigration were essentially bound up with those of other Japanese migrants. They cultivated very strong feelings of "co-migranthood," which usually took a form of informal fictive kinship, thus filling the gap caused by their being uprooted. These informal fictive kinship ties were gradually fostered and shaped by shared experiences during the "middle passage" of two to three months on the same ship, of common regionality and dialect, and of first alien experiences on the same plantations (for details, see Maeyama 1972).

Once in Brazil, a binary opposition of the Brazilians and the Japanese became increasingly important to them. The Brazilians—white, mulatto, and black indiscriminately—were called *gaijin* (literally, foreigner, generally used in Japan to refer to Caucasians), in contradistinction to *nipponjin* (Japanese). This conceptual opposition is precisely a "we-they" distinction. Because of the relative absence of other Asian peoples and Amerindians, this *gaijin-nipponjin* contrast has not caused any major classificatory confusion. In this way being Japanese became for them far more important than it had been in Japan. Upon arrival in multiracial Brazil, the immigrants became for the first time essentially "Japanese." Thus ethnicity was functional for cultivating overall identity, whereas informal fictive kinship ties were functional for forming small solidary groups within the ethnic framework.

Formal organizations were insignificant on the plantations. Interpersonal relations were extremely limited under the control of the plantation administrators. The immigrants worked six days a week from bell to bell, from sunrise to sunset. On Sundays they worked on their small free plots, granted them by the plantations for the cultivation of subsistence crops or for earning extra money. Because their initial idea was to return home as soon as possible with considerable savings from plantation work, and because social control on the plantations was very strong, formal organizations did not develop readily.

Major problems were usually discussed at informal meetings held by family heads on Saturday nights and rainy days (Handa 1970: 44, passim). Discontent, grievances, and protests were frequently channeled through the quasi-official Japanese emigration agencies and the consulate-general in São Paulo or in Ribeirão Preto but these institutions tended to suppress the immigrants rather than to improve conditions. The most common solution of their problems came in the form of collective or individual runaways. Even individual runaways were usually supported by all or many of the Japanese immigrants on the same plantation. Although organization and interaction were highly restricted, they created an explicit group identification of co-migranthood and informal fictive kinship throughout their plantation life, which later enabled them to form a local ethnic community.

COMMUNITY-ORIENTED STRUCTURE

The Japanese immigrants became independent farmers relatively quickly.

Although contracts with the coffee planters were normally for one or two years, most of the Japanese tried to leave the large plantations as quickly as possible because plantation wages were too low for them to save money. An average Japanese family did not stay under the planters' direct control more than a few years. This was made possible by the fact that the most intensive Japanese immigration occurred when the Brazilian coffee economy was declining, and consequently very cheap land and cheap labor were easily available to the immigrants. Thus they gradually changed their plans from the initial short-term project of saving money by selling their labor to a long-term project of acquiring cheap land and labor in order to secure enough capital to return home wealthy. Throughout the pre-World War II period, more than 90 percent of the immigrants remained in the rural areas, either as contract laborers on the coffee plantations or as independent or semi-independent small farmers (small landowners, share-croppers, contractors, and tenant farmers), usually gathered in small Japanese local communities.

Once they had become independent or semi-independent farmers, they settled together in *shokuminchi* (literally, colony, but it means in practice a "Japanese local community" in Brazil, and it will be used in this sense hereafter). There they established such formal organizations as *nihonjin-kai* (Japanese association,), *seinen-dan* or *seinen-kai* (youth association), *shojo-kai* (girls' association), agricultural cooperatives, and the like. All these formal organizations and other informal groups were integrated into a single structure of a Japanese local community, which was formally represented by a *nihonjin-kai* (hereafter Japanese association). In the thirties and forties the Japanese local communities numbered several hundred throughout Brazil, most of them concentrated in the state of São Paulo.

In founding a Japanese local community, informal fictive kinship ties, co-migranthood, and ethnicity were crucial. Interpersonal networks were maintained primarily through fictive kinship ties, co-migranthood, friendship, and neighborhood. But a Japanese local community was usually a face-to-face community in its strict sense, so that the internal integration was strong and everyone interacted to some extent with every other member. Compared to its counterpart in Japan, it was heterogeneous because of (1) a relative lack of kinship and affinity ties, (2) the use of different dialects, (3) the lack of a common origin of community and region in their home country, and (4) diverse occupational backgrounds.

In integrating these heterogeneous people into the single structure of a corporate community, ethnicity was an effective common denominator and was almost always a sufficient criterion for accepting new members. Although class stratification became increasingly crystallized, it did little to reduce unity based on ethnicity. In the pre-World War II period Japanese local communities in rural Brazil were ethnically oriented, but rarely class-oriented. Ethnicity also played an important role in structuring the external as well as the internal systems of the community. Internally it kept the various components together, and externally it provided a basis for classifying people in two distinct categories: *nipponjin* (Japanese) and *gaijin* (all others).

This ethnic integration and identity were dramatized and ritualized in emperor worship, organized by the executive staff of a Japanese association (Maeyama 1972). Because they practiced few rituals of ancestor worship among them, emperor worship was almost the only ritual, except for funeral rites, observed by the Japanese in prewar Brazil. The local community provided the arena, and emperor worship the content for the ethnic identity required for defining themselves and identification for organizing their everyday actions in an alien situational context.

These communities were controlled through strict norms and sanctions made "sacred" by means of the ritual practices of emperor worship. No Japanese living in the territory with which the community was concerned was able voluntarily to escape involvement in the community. No Brazilians of non-Japanese origin were considered for membership in the Japanese associations, except in rare cases when local power figures became honorary members. The number of Japanese immigrants who held Brazilian citizenship was insignificant. Living in the territory and being a Japanese meant being a member of the association or facing rejection and the violation of "natural law." Anyone who rejected membership was expected to disappear from the territory. The same was true for those who were rejected for membership or removed from the membership list for some reason. Normally physical coercion was not used against them, but they became socially invisible and were referred to as "non-Japanese." Frequently a statement in the name of the association was published in a Japanese newspaper, declaring simply that an individual was no longer a member of the Japanese association or that he was no longer a "Japanese"; in this way he became effectively ostracized. But usually it was not difficult for him to join, if he would, another Japanese association in another territory. As for the Brazilians living among them in the same territory, they were also socially invisible, at least with respect to the Japanese community. For example, it was very common for them to refer to a Japanese living some distance away as "my next-door neighbor" or "my closest neighbor," ignoring a number of Brazilians living between them. In sum, the Japanese local communities or the Japanese associations were not "voluntary associations," but rather were "compulsory associations" in Weber's sense (1947: 151).

We must admit, however, that the Japanese associations did include significant voluntary factors. To some extent, all the Japanese came to Brazil by choice, chose where and with whom they settled, and voluntarily joined a local community, although largely within the structural/functional frameworks. Nobody could join solely by birth, but everyone became involved in it on the basis of the single specific criterion of being Japanese. The Japanese local community in prewar rural Brazil was by definition a community, but not a common-interest association in the strict sense.

It was not rare, however, for them to form common-interest associations, such as *tanomoshi-kō* (a sort of rotating credit association), and, although to a much lesser extent, religious groups. These were not normally formal subsystems of the community; they were to a great extent voluntary associations. But it was also true that the recruitment of members was highly selective and that leaving a group once having joined it was difficult. These associations were not common, at least in the pre-World War II period.

All Japanese local communities were symbolically connected with Japan as a nation through the Japanese consulate-general in São Paulo and through the quasi-religious practices of emperor worship. There was no well-integrated organization established by immigrants themselves above the local level. A quasi-official agricultural cooperative (*Burajiru Takushoku Kumiai* or *Buratac* as abbreviated), a quasi-official emigration company (*Kaigai Kōgyō Kabushiki Gaisha*, or K.K.K. as abbreviated), and the consulate-general in São Paulo functioned effectively in integrating as well as controlling all the Japanese communities in Brazil. The immigrants looked upon these three agencies as paternalistic protectors and as representative authorities sent by the Japanese nation. These agencies indeed acted authoritatively and frequently paternalistically toward the immigrants. They were called collectively *go-sanke*, which literally means "the three royal families," once used in feudal Japan to mean the three hereditary superintendent *daimyō* or feudal lords of the Tokugawa shogunate belonging to the Tokugawa lineage. *Go-sanke* is the specific word designating these royal counselor families of the Tokugawa reign. The Brazilian *go-sanke* of the 1930s, like their counterparts in feudal Japan, ruled the Japanese minority group in Brazil. In local understanding, these "three royal families" of the Japanese "colony" were official institutions of the "colonial" administration provided by the Japanese Imperial Government rather than an overall structure originating with the immigrants themselves. These *go-sanke* were *royal* and sacred for the immigrants because they were directly and symbolically connected with the Japanese Emperor, the central object of their emperor worship.

The Japanese group was most commonly called, among themselves, *zaihaku dōhō* (compatriot residents in Brazil), *zairyū-min* (foreign residents), or *hōjin shakai* (the society of the Japanese nationals). It was symbolically an aggregate of the temporary Japanese residents in Brazil

171

rather than an integrated community. Each of the local communities was symbolically connected with Japan through the consulate-general rather than with their own overall system or through this system with Japan. The Japanese colony in the 1920s and 1930s was, as it were, a *tobichi* (detached territory; exclave), a supplementary part of the Japanese nation. The immigrants formed a single structure *because of Japan,* but not because of themselves.

They identified themselves as *dōhō* (compatriots, but it also means brothers) and *hōjin* (literally the nationals, but it is in practice applied only to Japanese nationals, with the connotation of "we-Japanese"). These terms were for use among themselves. *Dōhō* and *hōjin* tended to be used more frequently when the conceptual opposition between Brazilians and Japanese was implicit, whereas the term *nipponjin* (Japanese) was used when the opposition was explicitly in mind. Functionally, the concepts of *dōhō* and *hōjin* were used for enforcement of internal integration and identification, whereas that of *nipponjin* was for classification, in contradistinction to *gaijin.* Some of the most common usages of these terms are: *zen Burajiru hōjin yakyū taikai* (Pan-Brazil Japanese nationals baseball tournament); *Zempaku Hōjin Taiiku Kyōkai* (Pan-Brazil Japanese Nationals Athletic Association); *hōjin shokumin jigyō* (colonization activities by Japanese nationals); *hōjin menka* (cotton [produced by] Japanese nationals); *zaihaku nijūman dōhō* (two hundred thousand we-Japanese resident in Brazil); *"Ta-jinshu to no kekkon wa waga nipponjin no minzoku-teki jisatsu de aru"* (Intermarriage with other races is for us, the Japanese, ethnosuicide); and so on. Very frequently they called themselves "children of the Emperor." These terms characterized their ethnic identity throughout Brazil.

It is understandable that no significant leaders beyond the local community level emerged among the immigrants. All the responsible staffs were administrators officially and quasi-officially sent from Japan by the government or by its "appendages." Local-level leaders with immigrant background rarely became influential leaders on the level of *hōjin shakai* (the society of the Japanese nationals) or the Japanese colony as a whole. Only minor exceptions are found, usually among those who worked for Japanese newspapers. Relations between local-level leaders (immigrants) and the administrators of *go-sanke* (the three royal families) were almost identical to those between community representatives and officials sent by the central government within the Japanese domain.

In short, the Japanese immigrants in the pre-World War II period did not form a well-organized society under their own leadership; ethnicity, dramatized and ritualized in emperor worship, played a very important role for them in reformulating their identity; and a sort of overall group structure was constructed, half imposed from without, with relation to Japanese political power. The orientation was primarily toward Japan, with a certain consistency between the social and symbolic structures.[2]

RADICAL CHANGES AND SECRET SOCIETIES

This portrait of the Japanese minority group changed radically when faced with two changes that occurred in two different political domains outside the group. One was Brazilian nationalism, the other Japan's involvement in World War II. Brazilian nationalism was responsible for radical change within the Japanese group structure because of its political power over the minority group, and World War II because of the group's social and symbolic attachment to Japan (Brazil and the immigrants themselves hardly became involved directly in the war). It is noteworthy that two *external* factors were particularly significant in transforming the group structure.

The "revolution" of 1930 led by Getúlio Vargas may be understood as the results of a populist coalition between the urban middle classes, including the national industrialists, and the urban working class. After "coffee begot industry" in the late nineteenth century, part of the traditional ruling class *(latifundista-exportador)* and the commercial bourgeoisie became the national industrialists. Other sectors of the urban middle classes grew partly because of a special policy of *"estado cartorial"* (Hélio Jaguaribe's terminology: see Jaguaribe 1969: 395) under the overwhelming domination of the *latifundista* oligarchy. The traditional oligarchy retreated one step further when it faced the coffee crisis caused by the world panic of 1929. The emerging urban middle classes, who were greatly dependent on the oligarchy, were not strong enough to lead the nation. The populist leader Vargas, by successfully manipulating the military, managed to form a coalition of various sectors and rose to national power in place of the oligarchy. In order to crystallize a vital dynamic force for leading the nation and for national development, dictator Vargas sought to centralize and nationalize political power, and, as a result, promoted a strong cohesive nationalism and also a radical assimilationist policy for foreign immigrants. Two anti-Japanese movements in prewar Brazil (1923–24, 1933–34) were among the manifestations of this long-standing Brazilian nationalism. After a new coup, Vargas established the *Estado Novo* (New State) and issued a new constitution in 1937. When the new immigration laws and the assimilationist policy came into force, it was the Japanese group that experienced the greatest psychological and social difficulties because of its short history in Brazil (three-fourths of all the Japanese immigrants at this time had arrived in Brazil within a decade before the adoption of the new

---

[2] By symbol I mean stored subjective meanings. It is conceptually very close to culture (cf. Geertz 1957: 422).

policy) and because of the cultural distance that separated them from the host society.

Education led by aliens and taught in foreign languages became strictly suppressed in 1938. Aliens were not allowed to operate any schools in rural areas; no classes except the teaching of language itself were permitted in foreign languages; and even foreign language classes were limited to children above the age of fourteen. Almost all the Japanese schools, numbering about six hundred at the time, suddenly ceased to operate, although some of them continued to function clandestinely. Newspapers in foreign languages were placed under strict censorship by the government in 1940, were required to have half their space written in Portuguese after 1941, and finally were entirely suppressed later in the same year. In 1940 the Japanese group had four major newspapers in Japanese published daily in São Paulo State, with a total daily circulation of more than fifty thousand. When half their pages were required to be in Portuguese, two of them dropped out immediately; after foreign language newspapers were entirely suppressed, only one managed to circulate in Portuguese, although it lasted only a few months and its circulation was reduced to one-tenth. After Pearl Harbor at the end of the same year, Japanese immigrants were no longer permitted to publish any newspapers, even in Portuguese. Thus they lost all of their own mass media. They called this period the "Dark Age." Brazil severed diplomatic relations with Japan in January 1942. Thereafter the Japanese in Brazil lost all freedom to travel in the country, the meeting of more than three Japanese was strictly prohibited, and they were not allowed even to talk in Japanese outside their homes. In this way Brazilian nationalism, coupled with World War II, brought about the restructuring of the social and symbolic systems of the group.

Japan's involvement in World War II produced a sudden and abrupt change in the group's structure. After the severance of diplomatic relations between the two nations, all official and quasi-official organizations and their administrators suddenly disappeared. All of them returned home by an exchange ship. In this way the immigrants lost their social structure overnight primarily because of the nature of the prewar structure described above.

It was not until these radical changes had taken place that numerous ultranationalistic secret societies were formed among the Japanese in Brazil. Most of them tried socially and symbolically to reorganize underground the suddenly disintegrated Japanese local communities, and some of them, for example *Shindō Remmei* (The League of the Way of the Subjects), were intended to unite all resident Japanese into a single structure with an ultranationalistic symbolic system.

One of the principal planks of *Shindō Remmei* was described as follows: "Shindō Remmei's major mission was to re-integrate the Japanese organizations destroyed by the war in order to get the Japanese in Brazil back to the real Japanese through emperor worship and the system organized by Shindō Remmei" (cited in Handa 1970: 673).

The war and Japan's defeat brought to the immigrants not only the stigma of destruction in their home country but also the sudden loss of their own social and symbolic structures. They actually lost a way of thinking and were at a loss to know how to define themselves, how to organize their lives and to interact with others. They no longer knew "where and how to live or where to return." They had either to seek some new basis for their thinking and behavior or reestablish their lost structures on the basis of the old well-known value system. The appearance of the secret societies was one response to this internal difficulty. If revivalistic movements are defined as "emphasizing the institution of customs, values, and even aspects of nature which are thought to have been in the mazeway of previous generations but are not now present" (Wallace 1956: 267), then these secret societies were characteristically revivalistic, though the old institutions had been actually experienced by the same generation until a few years before.

Thus the Japanese suddenly lost their social structure, but the symbolic structure could not change overnight, and an apparent inconsistency emerged between the two structures. Oppression does not necessarily result immediately in internal crisis. Many Japanese schools operated underground. Home education was invoked to replace formal school education. Formal organizations disappeared, but informal interactions and channels of communications continued to operate. It was called an age of *kunan* (distress) but not of *kommei* (confusion or disorder); the latter was applied only to the period after Japan's defeat in war. Their symbolic structure suffered an internal crisis only after *Shinkoku Nippon* (The Divine Nation Japan) was defeated. The defeat, once recognized, meant that "the Divine Nation Japan," sanctified by thousands of years of history and governed and protected by the Emperor, had been defeated by a *gaijin's* profane nation; the Emperor's sacred reign was replaced by subjugation under a *gaijin,* General MacArthur; and so on. The ritualistic basis of emperor worship that had made their social and symbolic system alive was seriously undermined. Numerous rumors spread through the Japanese local communities throughout Brazil. For example, one rumor held that "the Japanese Empress had now become General MacArthur's concubine." This rumor, certainly uncommon and probably absent in Japan, in many ways contributed enormously to the activation of the conflict.

In accord with this internal difficulty, many of the informal, loosely structured, clandestine gatherings were transformed into more formal, though still clandestine, "ritualistic" organizations or secret societies and were subject to very strict norms and rules. A covenant of blood was often made when a group was founded or accepted new members. Formalization of the groups came very quickly. Some of the representative groups were: *Shindō Remmei* (The League of The Way of The Subjects), *Aikoku Seinen-dan* (Patriotic Youth Association), *Aidō Jissen Remmei* (The League for Promotion of The Way of Love), *Zaihaku Zaigō Gunjin-kai* (The Association of Reservists in Brazil), and the like. *Kōdōsha,* the predecessor of *Shindō Remmei,* started as a small group in February 1944, and changed its name to *Shindō Remmei* in May 1945, that is, before the end of the war, but its extraordinarily swift expansion and systematization came only after Japan's defeat in September of the same year. These groups were all radically nationalistic and frequently fanatic. To maintain a consistent symbolism and point of view before and after the war was for them imperative. It was logical and even rational for them to reject uncondi-tionally the "ambiguous" information offered by the *gaijin's* newspapers and other mass media about the "victory of a *gaijin's* nation," that is, the United States. Because of the overflowing "ambiguous" news, they became increasingly fanatic and in many respects millenarian.[3] All the news offered by *gaijin* was "tricky" and "cheating." Americans were trying surrepti-tiously to change "Japan's glorious victory" into their own victory. *"Kōhō"* (official news) had to come directly from the Emperor to them. News might or might not be reasonable and reliable until the real *kōhō* arrived, available only through direct radio communication with Japan. All the well-equipped short-wave radios belonging to members of the victory group informed them only of "the glorious victory of Japan." Other information offered by different radios was simply ignored, rejected, and forgotten. Static, very common during the period in question in Brazil especially when one tried to catch any foreign voice, was interpreted by the "specialists" in terms of their millenial dreams. Some more cool-headed Japanese, who were doubtful and tried in vain to hear, catching only meaningless noises from the radio informing *Shindō Remmei* members, about Japan's glorious victory, were always told that only "real" Japanese with the right *nippon seishin* (Japanese spirit) could hear the messages. And only these *dai shōri* (great victory) rumors circulated. Japan's victory, and later a complete silence on Japan's defeat, became an imperative norm for this group. This

---

[3] I do not intend here to describe extensively the millenarian character of this group. Only a short summary of its millenarian ideas is given here: Japan as *shinkoku* (The Divine Nation) and the Emperor are sacred, therefore the United States as a *gaijin's* profane nation is by no means able to defeat Japan; the "rumors" about the victory of the United States are false and the reverse is the truth; Japan enjoyed a glorious victory and consequently the world is to be governed by the Emperor's sacred reign; the Japanese in Brazil will have a special new role in governing of the world by virtue of their profound experiences with tropical agriculture and enterprises; the Emperor's ships will come to the Brazilian shore to meet the Japanese (not all of them, only their group) to take them to their mission in tropical Asia for the new ordering of the world. Many of them actually left their lands and homes, coming to the shore ready to embark on the ships that never arrived. This idea grew out of the psychological and physical sufferings they experienced in an enemy country throughout the war.

was the rule. Any violation was to be punished sometimes through terrorism. Within a short period of time fifteen Japanese and one Brazilian were killed, and eleven seriously wounded (Handa 1970: 663) by the *tokkō-tai* (special mission corps, a term used for *kamikaze tokkō-tai* during the last war in Japan). The corps was organized mostly by *Shindō Remmei* to carry out *tenchū* (divine punishment).

These secret societies did not try to be voluntary, but were compulsory for their members and in the application of their norms. They claimed that all the traditional Japanese values were still alive and that they were offering to the "lost Japanese" or "non-Japanese" the way of returning to the status of real Japanese and to the beliefs they needed for reintegration. Thus *Shindō Remmei*, notorious among the Brazilians at the time, once gained, it is said, about 90 percent of all the Japanese residents in Brazil as its members. The faction of the *kachi-gumi* (victory group) immediately after the end of the war was made up of these clandestine networks of secret societies, headed by the "overall system" of *Shindō Remmei*. This was a response, based on the old value system, to the difficulties brought about by such drastic change. It was an effort to return to the community-oriented structure destroyed by the change brought about in large part by factors external to the group.

FACTIONALISM AND THE RISE OF AN ASSOCIATION-ORIENTED STRUCTURE

Stimulated by the activities of the secret societies, an opposing faction was quickly organized. Most of the ideology and behavior manifested by the followers of the secret societies were largely anachronistic in the eyes of the intellectual and acculturated Japanese as well as of the Brazilians. These "anachronistic," "fanatic", and *"gammei na"* (bigoted or obstinate) activities were understood by the other faction of the Japanese as a crucial factor, in augmenting their cultural crisis and in leading to the rise of anti-Japanese movements noted among the Brazilians twice before the war. They viewed these events as threatening the socio-economic future in Brazil. Thus the formation of formal and informal organizations among the "intellectuals" and the "acculturated" was essentially factional and, at least at the very beginning, in opposition to the secret societies of the victory group.

Thus the two factions of the Japanese community became clearly crystallized: the *kachi-gumi* (victory group), sometimes called the *kyōkō-ha* (tough faction), and the *make-gumi* (defeat group), frequently called the *ninshiki-ha* (enlightened faction). More specifically, the victory group called themselves *kyōkō* (the tough) and the opposition simply *haisen* (the defeatists). The defeat group, on the other hand, called themselves the *ninshiki-ha* (enlightened faction) and the opposition group *kachi-gumi* (victory group) or *fanaticos* (fanatics, in Portuguese).

177

The defeat group sought to restructure their society and culture primarily through *ninshiki undō* (the movement for enlightenment) among the opposing group members. The immediate objective of this movement was to persuade the victory group to realize the fact that Japan had been defeated. Most of their efforts failed, and many of their leaders were killed. Despite the failure of the immediate aim, this movement made it possible for them to develop their own leaders beyond the local level and to stabilize a number of formal organizations. Also through promoting these activities they set up new norms and the world view that their country was not Japan but Brazil; that they were not *dekasegi imin* (migrant laborers) living only temporarily in Brazil but *colonia-jin* (a term of Portuguese-Japanese mixture meaning "colony men") and *nikkei-jin* (people of Japanese origin) who were a normal and legitimate part of the Brazilian nation and were to die there; that their descendants would be Brazilian, not Japanese. Through this factional struggle they gained a revised ethnic identity. They are now *nikkei-jin,* and their ethnic community on the national level is now called *nikkei colonia* (a Portuguese-Japanese term meaning "the colony of Japanese origin"). In this way they finally came to distinguish themselves from the Japanese in Japan. They are now Japanese *in origin.* It is noteworthy that they have neither lost their ethnic identity nor become Brazilians. The *colonia* is a part of, and has a loyalty to, Brazil, in contrast to that *shokuminchi* (colony in Japanese) which was a part of, and had a loyalty to, Japan. This was the other response, based on new values to the same drastic change.

In March 1947, after the Brazilian government had suppressed the terrorism of the secret societies (177 leaders of the victory group were put in jail and isolated on Anchieta Island in the Atlantic Ocean), the leaders of the other faction organized *Nihon Sensai Dōhō Kyūen Kai* or *Comité de Socorro às Vítimas de Guerra do Japão* (Committee for the Relief of the War Victims in Japan, hereafter simply *Kyūen Kai)* to send money and subsistence items to their home country and to help brothers in difficulty. In practice, however, this was an effort to put an end to factionalism and reorganize all the Japanese into an integrated structure. "Help Japan!" was a strategic device invented by the new leaders for its own sake. They were no longer factional, because they were now concerned with benefits for the Japanese in Brazil as a whole (cf. Firth 1957: 222).

The committee of *Kyūen Kai,* after three years of activity, became the *Kyōryoku Kai* (Cooperating Committee) for participating in preparations for the fourth centennial festival of the foundation of the city of São Paulo. This time the organization formally represented the Japanese community as a whole, in response to an official request made by the local government of São Paulo. The former *Kyūen Kai* had claimed to represent the Japanese minority group in Brazil for the home country. This new committee did the same for the host country. This was a great advance in understanding, because it was the first time the immigrants had seem themselves as representatives to the Brazilian government. They had achieved legitimacy (Swartz *et al,* 1966: 10) in this respect in the country they live in. In 1955, as soon as the objective of the committee had been accomplished, it transformed itself again into another (this time more permanent) organization, namely, the *Sociedade Paulista de Cultura Japonesa* (São Paulo Society of Japanese Culture). This *Sociedade* functioned as the headquarters of all the Japanese local communities in Brazil. In 1970 it quietly changed its name to the *Sociedade Brasileira de Cultura Japonesa* (Brazilian Society of Japanese Culture), which occasioned little public attention because in fact it signified no change; it had already been the de facto Brazilian headquarters. Thus an overall ethnic structure was finally established by the immigrants themselves.

Factionalism contributed greatly to the reorganization of the immigrants into a wider structure beyond local ethnic communities. The same was true of the victory group. The "anachronistic" activities of the secret societies encouraged the development of various leaders and organizations. Although the principal leaders of the victory group suspended their activities, and although the immediate organizations of the secret societies were suppressed by the Brazilian government, the secondary leaders and informal networks were still alive. These informal networks inherited from the secret societies provided an excellent channel for the propagation of Japanese religions. The leaders of the former secret societies became propagators of the "real" Japanese religions, which provided the lost immigrants with the "real meanings" of Japanese values and symbols and the way to become "real Japanese." Thus many of the secret societies were in effect transformed into various Japanese religious associations. In religion they found a base for their revised ethnic identity and for organizing their actions. *Seichō-no-Ie* is a typical religious organization of this sort (Maeyama 1967, especially pp. 260–80).

Research conducted by Izumi and Saito in 1952–53 revealed the fact that the victory group included 85.5 percent of the Japanese in the south, where 96.4 percent of the Japanese in Brazil were located, at the time of their research (Izumi 1957: 82). They found no defeat group members among the *Seichō-no-Ie* followers (ibid.: 108). This ethno-religious organization grew rapidly during the fifties and sixties. In the forties it had only a few thousand adherents; but by 1956 it had 6,459 followers and 235 associations, and in 1966 it claimed to have 15,630 followers and 553 associations throughout Brazil. At the time of my research in 1966–67, they were almost 100 percent Japanese.[4] The central staff was composed almost entirely of

[4] In the 1970s, the situation is quite different because of the radical change in the sect policy toward the Brazilians adopted in 1966.

locally converted preachers and they were all openly proud of being former adherents of the victory group. A single example illustrates the way this "Japanese religion" has grown. Mr S.E., legal president of *Seichō-no-Ie* in Brazil from 1952 until the end of my research in 1967, had been president of two of the most influential organizations of the victory group. These were *Nippaku Sangyō Shinkō Kai* (its official name in Portuguese was *Clube Bandeirante*), which had promoted their politico-economic activities, and *Zenpaku Seinen Remmei* (Pan-Brazilian Youth League) which had organized local youth associations into a unified federation within the framework of the victory group. The first supported Ademar de Barros, a populist political leader in São Paulo, and the second promoted various sorts of tournaments of such Japanese national sports as judo, *sumō* (Japanese wrestling), baseball, and others. *Seichō-no-Ie* practices various rituals. The following is a typical example of one of the collective prayers recited at every meeting:

His Majesty the Emperor, thank you, thank you, thank you: Her Majesty the Empress, thank you, thank you, thank you: Our president Professor Taniguchi, thank you, thank you, thank you: Madame Teruko, thank you, thank you, thank you: Our ancestors, thank you, thank you, thank you: All the human beings, all the things in the world, thank you, thank you, thank you: Mr. President of Brazil, the Brazilian People, thank you, thank you, thank you.[5]

In this ethno-religious association, Japanese values in general, ethnicity ritualized in emperor worship, and the traditions of Japanese folk religions are vital in creating their group identification.

Today the victory group no longer forms a clear-cut faction, although most of the interpersonal networks of the immigrants have been formed on the basis of their old factional linkages. New generations do not know nor care about this continuity. Some of the Japanese voluntary associations in Brazil, especially the ethno-religious organizations, still retain the strong impact of factionalism, but they no longer maintain any integrated overall structure of their own. They have been absorbed into the structure of the former defeat group, at least on the level of local compulsory associations and on the level of the Japanese minority group as a whole. No ex-victory group leaders are found today among the top leaders of the Japanese-Brazilian community.

Today in São Paulo, as well as in other cities in southern Brazil where considerable numbers of the Japanese are found, there are numerous voluntary associations—Japanese associations, occupational unions and cooperatives, religious associations, sports clubs, hobby and literary clubs, nisei recreational associations, various types of rotating credit associations, provincial associations (*kenjin kai*), women's associations, and the like,

[5] Taniguchi is the founder of the sect and Teruko is his wife. This English version is my translation from the original Japanese.

mostly within the Japanese ethnic framework. Despite their names, commonly indicating one or two major objectives, most of them are multifunctional, providing stages for multiplex interpersonal networks (Gluckman 1955: 19) among a part, but usually not all, of the members. A given individual may belong to several associations, but is likely to be intensively involved in only one of them. I call the latter "focal association." This intensive involvement in a particular focal association, but not in others, emerges from personal inclinations and social networks more than from the unique nature or expressed objectives of the association. In his focal association, he finds community-like multifunctional networks, and in his other peripheral associations he finds more uniplex relationships. In practice, however, this description varies with the social status of the individual.

Although the major functions of these associations differ widely, they may and do provide community-like multifunctions for those who are looking for a focal association. As focal associations they provide places for the members to seek friends, mating partners, recreation, social solidarity, all sorts of information, norms of the urban way of life, and so on. In this way they function as a socializing mechanism fitting the immigrants for the Brazilian way of life, as an adaptive device to urbanism and industrialism for "peasants in the cities," as an instrument of the minority endogamy for the youth, as a source of interpersonal networks for everyone, as a training ground (as well as a tool for manipulating people) for political leaders, and so on. All these help members to acquire and reinforce group identification, customs, and culture.

Contrary to the prewar rural situation, native-born adults are now important components of subgroups in the Japanese community. Direct participation of the Japanese born in Brazil in the immigrant-controlled Japanese and other associations is relatively weak. In rural areas the Brazil-born Japanese are usually integrated into compulsory associations of the local Japanese community and the youth associations which are subsystems of them. In the cities the Brazil-born Japanese, especially the youth, tend to form independent associations. Some of them are in one form or another incorporated into immigrant-oriented associations. Even in these cases some maintain only loose connections with them, and others engage in separate activities within a single framework. A good portion of the nisei associations in the metropolitan São Paulo region formed, in 1966–67, a league that was formally integrated into the overall organization of the *Sociedade Brasileira de Cultura Japonesa,* with headquarters in the building of the *Sociedade.* They maintained, however, almost entirely separate activities and did not necessarily consider their organization a subsystem of the Sociedade. Only occasionally did they hold combined meetings. Many others were independent. Class-oriented associations became increasingly common among the nisei associations. This is not the case among the immigrants, although ego-centered networks are highly class-oriented. In all cases ethnicity is of utmost importance.

The Japanese in Brazil are for the most part of the middle class. Broadly speaking, Brazil-born Japanese show a striking cleavage between the new and old middle classes in forming associational organizations. The new middle class identifies itself symbolically with Brazilian culture, and the old with Japanese culture (Maeyama 1970). These class-oriented associations operate within the ethnic framework, though there are some ethnically mixed associations. It is not uncommon for us to find, though their numbers are usually insignificant, some marginal members of non-Japanese origin in Japanese-oriented associations, as well as to find some marginal Japanese members in Brazilian-oriented associations. Politically these associations among the Japanese in Brazil send their ethnic representatives, directly or indirectly, to the Brazilian local and national governments. But significantly enough, they rarely exhibit any collective political attitudes, except that of supporting governmental decisions.

DISCUSSION

As Max Weber put it, the study of associations lies in the gap between "the politically organized or recognized powers" such as the State and "the natural community of the family" (Weber 1940: 1). There are some alternative forms of interpersonal relationships beyond the family and below the State: "unbounded" social networks such as kin ties, friendship, neighborhood, and other forms of individual choice (Barnes 1954: 43–44); informal but "bounded" groups; formal groups such as voluntary associations, race, class, and the like.

From the studies of overseas Chinese, Freedman suggests that "the formal associations fail to emerge when the solidarities to which they are devoted are otherwise expressed" (1960: 44). This seems to be the case among the Brazilians because of their strong kinship ties (cf. Wagley 1964: 188) and their patron-client relationships; it is also the case among the Japanese in Japan because of their "vertical ties" (Nakane 1970: 59–60). Among the Japanese in urban Brazil today, voluntary associations are clearly of the utmost importance among the many varying forms of cohesion and solidarity. In comparison with the Brazilians, kinship ties have been relatively weak. In comparison with the Japanese in Japan, "the vertical ties" were weaker at least in the early years of the immigrants' history. These facts have contributed indirectly to the emergence of the voluntary associations. They contributed *directly* to the strenthening of such ties as ethnicity, informal fictive kinship, co-migranthood, and local community. These new patterns in turn provided a basis for the rise of secret societies and the later ethnoreligious associations, as well as for other forms of voluntary associations.

Freedman also suggests that "when immigrants are thrown down in a strange setting where they must make their social life among themselves, they are likely to divide into units which express the solidarity of homeland ties" (1960: 43). This point does not appear to be the case among the Japanese in Brazil. Although culture provided them with forms, the Japanese immigrants used them rather to create new ties that were not necessarily direct products of their homeland ties. Even ethnicity in terms of "Japaneseness" does not seem to be one of the homeland ties so far as the Japanese immigrants are concerned. Upon arrival in Brazil, they became Japanese and identified themselves as such in their everyday life. Natives of uniracial Japan do not normally identify themselves as "Japanese" in their everyday life. Thrown into a multi-ethnic situation in Brazil, and in need of establishing a mutual solidarity with ethnic friends facing a minority situation, they began for the first time, to identify themselves as Japanese, giving a new meaning and new interpretation to their ethnicity. In creating new ties and identity, the social and political factors of the host society have also been crucial. Thus ethnicity, social relationships, and organizations among the Japanese in Brazil may be accounted for more in terms of the particular situations they confronted in Brazil than in terms of a continuity of Japanese ties and culture.

Kinship and vertical ties are continuously increasing and are no longer weak. These ties are certainly microcosmically undermining associational groupings, but voluntary associations as a whole are continuously increasing in number and in membership. Once a pattern is set, it tends to continue. Weakness of kinship ties may contribute to the strengthening of associational ties, but increasing kinship ties do not necessarily weaken associational bonds. Kinship and vertical ties effectively persist within the framework of formal associations.

Among the Japanese in Brazil, voluntary associations do not appear to diminish the importance of kinship roles, as Little maintains they do in an African case (Little 1965: 144). As Wallerstein suggests, voluntary associations represent "an effective mechanism of crossing kin barriers and creating national groups" (1964: 330–31). But the Japanese in Brazil represent a case where kinship ties are effectively used to obtain other ties and to create associational groupings. Another suggestion made by Little is analytically important, that is, that voluntary associations help to redefine tribal affiliation, operating as a means whereby people may identify themselves with another tribe (1965: 144). The case of the Japanese in Brazil illustrates the fact that voluntary associations are an effective means whereby members may enforce their identification with an original ethnicity. And within the framework of ethnic voluntary associations members also seek information, linkages, and interactions with peoples of ethnically different categories. Associations as organizations are socially and symbolically ethnic, but their activities involve mechanism to acquire external contacts with and information of the wider settings. Associations provide a setting for the creation of an identity beyond kinship frameworks and other small units like peer groups, but normally not one beyond ethnicity. Associations are also important as a means for ethnic endogamy. In this way kinship and associations, both the result of and the mechanism for achieving endogamy, operate to enforce, rather than undermine, ethnic solidarity.

The study of change in associational forms is important as Freedman (1960) and Rowe (1973: 243) suggest. The point is probably not change from primary to associational ties. We must take into account primary ties within the framework of formal associations and regard associations as mechanisms to enforce primary ties as well as to create channels of contact beyond primary and ethnic frameworks.

Firth maintains that factionalism functions as a training ground for more orthodox political activities (Firth 1957: 294). The Japanese case in Brazil shows that it functions also to create and train nonpolitical leaders and to develop symbolic and social systems that include norms, world view, and formal organizations, in the face of social change. After the loss of their traditional structure, we have seen the emergence of secret societies and factionalism, the rise of new leaders and voluntary associations, and also the restructuring of symbols and social systems. For all these changes, external factors as well as internal developments have been crucial, as they have been in colonial systems. Because their old systems symbolically and structurally constituted an exclave (*tobichi*) of the Japanese nation, Japan's involvement and defeat in World War II profoundly affected the Japanese colony in Brazil. Because of their minority status, changes in the Brazilian sociopolitical structures and policy have played decisive roles in transforming the group structure.

The factors that were external to the group, at least in part, gave them the chance to transform their community-oriented structure into an association-oriented structure. The secret societies and factionalism constitute a transitional period in this particular respect, representing the collective efforts to return to their old community-oriented structure. The two factions, governed by distinct orientations based on either a new or an old value system, tried to impose a compulsory system on all the Japanese in Brazil. When they failed to do so, the association-oriented structure emerged.

REFERENCES

Barnes, J. A., 1954. "Class and Committee in a Norwegian Island Parish," *Human Relations,* 7, 39–58.

Comissão de Recenseamento da Colonia Japonesa, 1964. *The Japanese Immigrant in Brazil.* 2 vols. Tokyo: The University of Tokyo Press.

Dore, Ronald P., 1958. *City Life in Japan.* Berkeley & Los Angeles: University of California Press.

Firth, Raymond, 1957, "Factions in Indian and Overseas Indian Societies," *British Journal of Sociology,* 8, 291–95.

Freedman, Maurice, 1960, "Immigrants and Associations: Chinese in Nineteenth-Century Singapore," *Comparative Studies in Society and History,* 3, 25–48.

Geertz, Clifford, 1957, "Ethos, World-View and the Analysis of Sacred Symbols," *The Antioch Review,* 17, 421–37.

Gluckman, Max, 1955. *The Judicial Process among the Barotse of Northern Rhodesia.* Manchester: Manchester University Press.

Handa, Tomoo, 1970. *Imin no Seikatsu no Rekishi.* São Paulo: Centro de Estudos Nipo-Brasileiros.

Honda, Tatsuo, 1952. "Nihon Jinkō Mondai no Shiteki Kaiseki," in *Nōson Jinkō Mondai Kenkyū,* Vol. II, Nōson Jinkō Mondai Kenkyū Kai ed. Tokyo: Nōrin Tōkei Kyōkai.

Hutchinson, Bertram, 1966. "The Patron-Dependent Relationship in Brazil," *Sociologia Ruralis,* 6, 3–30.

Izumi, Seiichi, 1957, "Burajiru no Nikkei Colonia," in *Imin,* Seiichi Izumi ed. Tokyo: Kokon Shoin, pp. 9–127.

Jaguaribe, Hélio, 1969. *Economic & Political Development: A Theoretical Approach and A Brazilian Case Study.* Cambridge, MA: Harvard University Press.

Little, Kenneth, 1965. *West African Urbanization.* Cambridge: The Cambridge University Press.

Maeyama, Takashi, 1967. *O Imigrante e A Religião: Estudo de Uma Seita Religiosa Japonesa em São Paulo.* São Paulo: Escola de Sociologia e Política de São Paulo, unpublished M.A. thesis.

―――, 1970. *Religion, Kinship, and the Middle Classes of the Japanese in Urban Brazil.* Paper presented to the 69th Annual Meeting of the American Anthropological Association, San Diego, CA.

―――, 1972. "Ancestor, Emperor, and Immigrant: Religion and Group Identification of the Japanese in Rural Brazil," *Journal of Inter-American Studies and World Affairs,* 14:2, 151–82.

Maybury-Lewis, David H. P., 1968. "Growth and Change in Brazil Since 1930," in *Portugal and Brazil in Transition,* R.S. Sayers, ed. Minneapolis: University of Minnesota Press, pp. 159–73.

Nakane, Chie, 1970. *Japanese Society.* Berkeley & Los Angeles: University of California Press.

Norbeck, Edward, 1961. "Postwar Cultural Change and Continuity in Northeastern Japan," *American Anthropologist,* 63, 297–321.

―――, 1962. "Common-interest Associations in Rural Japan," in *Japanese Culture,* R. J. Smith & R. K. Beardsley, eds. Viking Fund Publications in Anthropology. No. 34, pp. 73–85.

―――, 1967. "Association and Democracy in Japan," in *Social Change in Modern Japan,* Ronald Dore, ed. Princeton: Princeton University Press. pp. 185–200.

Rowe, William L., 1973. "Caste, Kinship, and Association in Urban India," in *Urban Anthropology,* Aidan Southall, ed. N.York & London: Oxford University Press, pp. 211–49.

Smith, T. Lynn, 1954. *Brazil: People and Institutions,* 2nd ed. Baton Rouge; Louisiana State University Press.

Suzuki, Teiiti, 1969. *The Japanese Immigrant in Brazil: Narrative Part.* Tokyo: University of Tokyo Press.

Swartz, Marc J., V. W. Turner, & A. Tuden, eds., 1966. *Political Anthropology,* Chicago: Aldine.

Vianna, Oliveira, 1920. *Populações Meridionaes do Brazil,* vol.I. São Paulo: Edicão da "Revista do Brazil."

Wagley, Charles, 1964. "Luso-Brazilian Kinship Patterns: The Persistence of a Cultural Tradition," in *Politics of Change in Latin America,* J. Maier & R. W. Weatherhead, eds. New York: F. A. Praeger. pp. 174–89.

Wallace, Anthony F. C., 1956. "Revitalization Movements," *American Anthropologist,* 58, 264–81.

Wallerstein, Immanuel, 1964. "Voluntary Associations," in *Political Parties and National Integration in Tropical Africa,* J. S. Coleman and C. G. Rosberg, Jr., eds. Berkeley & Los Angeles: University of California Press, pp. 318–39.

Weber, Max, 1940. *Max Weber's Proposal for Sociological Study of Voluntary Associations.* Translated for private use by E. C. Hughes from: Max Weber, 1911. "Geschaftsbericht," in *Verhandlungen des Ersten Deutschen Soziologentages vom 1922 Oktober, 1910 in Frankfurt a.M.,* Tübingen, pp. 52–60.

———, 1947. *The Theory of Social and Economic Organization.* New York: The Free Press.

Willems, Emilio & Hiroshi Saito, 1947. "Shindō-Renmei: Um Problema de Aculturação," *Sociologia,* 9, pp. 133–52.

RESEARCH IN THE POLITICAL ECONOMY
OF AFRO-LATIN AMERICA*

Pierre-Michel Fontaine
University of California, Los Angeles

Ideally, the study of the political economy of Afro-Latin America should be part and parcel of that of the political economy of Latin America as a whole.[1] Unfortunately, true to the tendency toward fragmentation and specialization in the human as well as in the physical sciences, that has not generally been the case. The problem has been made worse by the low salience of the nonwhite races in the Americas, due to their low socioeconomic and political status.[2] It is further compounded by the ambiguity and evasiveness of the Latin American racial ideology, especially in its Brazilian form, which leads both local and foreign observers and social scientists to conclude first that there is no racial problem (though such a position is no longer seriously held by scholars) and then that race is irrelevant to the study of the region's political economy.[3]

This is, to some extent, a problem of the sociology of knowledge. It is a reflection of the structure and distribution of knowledge in the Americas, which is in turn a reflection of the structure and distribution of wealth, power, and status in the region. To put it more directly, this situation reflects the fact that Afro-Latin Americans, for reasons of their low wealth, status, and power, have had little input into the shaping and development of the study of the political economy of Latin America (Bryce-LaPorte 1979). The consequences of this situation for Brazil and the need to remedy it were long ago pointed out by the Brazilian sociologist Guerreiro Ramos (1954).

*This article was written as part of the work done in preparation for the Symposium on the Political Economy of the Black World held at the UCLA Center for Afro-American Studies on 10–12 May 1979, with the support of the National Endowment for the Humanities. It also developed in the context of a research project on career mobility of Afro-Brazilians supported by the UCLA Committee on International and Comparative Studies (Ford Foundation), UCLA Institute of American Cultures, and the Center for Afro-American Studies. Summer research support was provided by the UCLA Faculty Development Program. I am grateful for all these contributions. I also wish to thank Michael Mitchell for important advice and suggestions; Zé Maria Nunes Pereira for letting me use the library of the Centro de Estudos Afro-Asiático (Rio de Janeiro); Clotilde Blake for valuable research assistance; and the three anonymous reviewers from the LARR. None of these persons or institutions is responsible, however, for any errors in this article.

111

The term political economy, as used here, can be understood in two ways. In a broad sense, it refers to the study of economic and political forces, behaviors, and institutions. This is really a loose definition, the idea being to exclude ethnological, folklore, philosophical, and literary studies. The purpose is to focus attention on the role and position of Afro-Latin Americans in the process of production, distribution, exchange, control, and consumption of goods and services, in relations of power and influence, and relations of social stratification and class interaction.

In a stricter sense, political economy is used in its classical connotation, especially the Marxian version. Octavio Ianni (1978, pp. 3–50), using the significant work of Karl Marx, among others, has shown the crucial connection between mercantilism, the slave trade, plantation slavery (and other forms of New World forced labor), and the birth and ascendency of industrial capitalism in Europe, especially in England. Slavery and its consequences are, of course, central to an understanding of Afro-Latin America. The virtue of a political economy approach, strictly conceived, is to place the phenomenon under study within the totality of world social relations, focusing on the social relations of production, without neglecting those of distribution and consumption. Such an approach is at once materialist and historical; above all, it "assumes the centrality of economics and the power inherent in control of production and exchange" (Léons and Rothstein 1979, pp. xvi–xxxii). With respect to the racial question, a central issue in Afro-Latin American studies, this approach further assumes that, in the words of a leader of the Unified Black Movement against Racial Discrimination in São Paulo, "What determines the continuity of racism are economic relations and relations of production" (Cardoso 1979, p. 37).

This essay attempts to accommodate both definitions of political economy. It is, therefore, concerned with the relations of Afro-Latin Americans to modes of production (slavery, capitalism, socialism), economic institutions (the plantation, transnational corporations), economic development models, transnational relations, political systems, institutions, behavior, group and class relations (including class struggle), social mobility, and political mobilization. It does not exclude discussions of culture, religion, or folklore; they, too, may exhibit dimensions of protest and struggle (Carvalho-Neto 1978, Fernandes 1966, Warren 1965), though Ianni (1970, p. 75) has warned us that this has not been proved conclusively as far as the content of the black religions is concerned.

With this somewhat eclectic frame of reference as a guide, one finds that standard texts on economics, politics, political economy, or even sometimes sociology tend to ignore the African presence and its

112

implications, in spite of millions of blacks, *morenos* (browns), mulattoes and *zambos* (mixtures of blacks and Indians) in Latin America. For instance, Charles W. Anderson's (1967) widely adopted study of the political economy of change in Latin America does not mention the problem of race. Yet the same Anderson, a few years later (1970), presented a very able critical survey of the use of race and class as explanatory forces in the study of Latin American politics. He correctly pointed out that there had been widespread use of these two variables by students of Latin American politics. But apart from repeated references in these studies to such pseudo-racial, and probably racist, concepts as "Hispanic cultural heritage," "hot blood," or "hot temper," the primary and almost exclusive racial reference has been to the "unassimilated" Indians, especially in Mexico, Guatemala, and Ecuador. Some of the classic works in this area have been by George Blanksten (1951), Roland H. Ebel (1964), and Kalman H. Silvert (1954, 1961).

In the early years of the study of Latin American politics, the "political pathologist" Russell Fitzgibbon (1950) diagnosed "the presence of unassimilated Indian populations" as a cause of the "pathology of democracy in Latin America." What was missing in all of this, though —and this is a problem that Anderson seemed not to have noticed at all —was an acknowledgment of the presence of Africans in Latin American societies. One finds this blindness to the black presence even in country studies. For instance, Colombia was estimated to have by 1970 a population of only 25 percent whites, the rest being made up of *mestizos* (42 percent), mulattoes (20 percent), blacks (8 percent), and Indians (5 percent) (Smith 1970). Yet, one of the most well-known books on Colombian politics devotes roughly five pages out of 452 to a small section entitled, "Population: Racial Composition and Demographic Trends" (Dix 1967); only two of these five pages mention the black or the Indian, and the issue is not raised again throughout the book.

Similarly, a relatively recent volume on authoritarianism in Brazil (Stepan 1973) never mentions the Afro-Brazilian population in spite of its vast size and the fundamentally authoritarian nature of its relationship with the white and quasi-white population. In fact, the author of one of the essays was, in the early years of his intellectual career, one of the most perceptive students of black-white relations in Brazil (Cardoso 1960, 1962, 1965, 1969), and another is the author of an influential book on the pervasive impact of the African presence on Brazilian philosophical and social thought (Skidmore 1974). Another volume devoted to the study of the Latin American masses failed to pay even lip service to the blacks of the region (Horowitz 1970).

Here and there, however, some efforts have been made. For in-

113

stance, in a modest book on Latin American politics, Martin C. Needler (1976, pp. 16–22) offered a brief discussion of the relationship between race, class, and political development. In a subsequent book, Needler (1968, pp. 98–116) included a chapter entitled "Social Structure, 'Race', and Politics," in which he attempted a macroanalytical study of the correlations between racial/ethnic types of societies ("European," "mulatto," "mestizo," and "Indian") on the one hand, and GNP per capita, life expectancy at birth, income distribution, electoral participation, and political stability on the other. Similarly, in his influential study of revolutionary politics and working class in Cuba, sociologist Maurice Zeitlin (1967) includes a chapter on "Race Relations and Politics," in which he seeks to relate race to life chances, prerevolutionary attitudes toward the Revolution, and other variables. More recently, W. Raymond Duncan (1976, pp. 84–92, 119) engaged in a brief and superficial discussion of "ethnicity" in what he calls the "missing nations of Latin America," by which he means those cultural groups which are not coterminous with sovereign states. It is an extension of Needler's framework.

The situation is even worse in the case of straightforward economic studies; no published work is known to this author, at least for Brazil. This is especially surprising for the post-1964 period in Brazil, for which a considerable body of work on income distribution has been produced, both by Brazilian and American scholars. One explanation might be that economists of the neoclassical persuasion have a greater need than other social scientists for demographic and survey data, which have been practically nonexistent since the 1950 census. However, at least one of the post-1964 studies of income distribution used the 1.27 percent subsample of the 1969 census that was published (Langoni 1973), and that sample (and the unpublished bulk as well) did contain racial data (Silva 1978, pp. 93–94). The only effort on Brazil by an economist, known to this author, is the attempt by Eduardo Matarazzo Suplicy of the Getúlio Vargas Foundation in São Paulo to determine the racial distribution of the student body there in 1974. Needless to say, the black representation he found was less than 1 percent. This study does not appear to have been published.

Anthropologists and historians have shown greater interest in the study of Afro-Latin America. The former, for obvious reasons, have been fond of studies of ethnic and racial groups, especially of the traditional kind or in traditional society. Anthropologist Melville Herskovits (1930, 1943a, 1943b, 1966), although not working from a political economy perspective, devoted much time to the study of the black experience in Africa, North America, Latin America, and the West Indies. Although his mechanical search for African survivals has been properly criticized, he at least clearly understood the term "Afro-American" in the larger sense that included all the Americas (1945, 1948, 1960). Of more relevance to this discussion is the work of another anthropologist, Norman E. Whitten, Jr., who has done some promising studies in the political economy of Afro-Latin America by examining the interface between the international and national political/economic systems and black community power structures in Northwest Ecuador and Southwest Colombia (1969a, 1969b, 1974). Specifically, he shows how international demand for the agricultural and mineral products of the area brought an influx of nonblack Ecuadorians, Colombians, Europeans, and North Americans, with the result that the local social system, which he had earlier diagnosed as "successfully adapting . . . to new and expanding economic, social, and political orders" (1965, p. 1), is now being disrupted, producing economic growth, but also racial conflicts and "black disenfranchisement." A similar correlation between economic growth and hardening of racial cleavages was found by Pitt-Rivers (1967) in a study of Central America and the Andean region.

Aside from this work, however, the anthropologists' contribution to the study of Afro-Latin America has not generally been in the realm of international political economy.[4] In fact, Bastide (1974) considers it to have been a partial revolution when the UNESCO team in the North and Northeast of Brazil (see below) moved the study of race relations in the area from the familiar level of cultural anthropology to the more promising one of social anthropology.

The historians' concern has been generally with slavery, the slave trade, the abolition of slavery, and the effect of the "peculiar institution" on relations between the races. It might be argued that not enough historical work on postabolition Afro-Latin America has been done that was not directly related to slavery or its end. Yet, slavery, as the principal form of social labor and production of the classical plantation system, and its abolition are crucial to our understanding of the foundations of the political economy of the black world. Luckily, a good bit of the historical work has been comparative.

Inspired by the Brazilian historical sociologist (or sociological historian) Gilberto Freyre (1945), who had written effusively about the favorable status of blacks in Brazil, in both slavery and freedom, as compared to the United States, Tannenbaum (1946) launched the comparative study of New World slavery. He attributed the allegedly greater degree of racial "tolerance" in Brazil and Spanish America, as compared to the British Caribbean and the United States, to the supposedly more humane experience of slavery in the former; there, law and customs recognized and protected the humanity and legal personality of the

115

slave, whereas in North America the slave was mere chattel property. Tannenbaum explains this difference in terms of the longer tradition of Iberian contact with Africa, the early development of a legal system to regulate slavery even in the homeland, and the moderating influence of the Catholic Church.

These arguments were taken up, among others, by Stanley Elkins (1959) who used them as the foundation for his comparative study of slavery, though he emphasized that the difference was more in the acceptance of the moral personality of the slave than in their actual physical treatment. Clearly, some of the differences and contrasts allegedly discovered were rather abstract and "idealistic," as pointed out by Eugene Genovese (1969a, 1969b), or even without serious practical implications, as argued by David Brion Davis (1966). Although critical of Tannenbaum, Genovese acknowledged the contribution made by him and by Freyre to the development of the comparative study of slavery.

Davis sharply challenged Tannenbaum's thesis on the grounds that: (a) he erroneously assumed that North American law, unlike Latin America's, rejected the slave as a moral personality; (b) he overlooked the fact that Iberian Americans perceived the slave as both chattel and a human being with a soul; and (c) he viewed Latin American slavery in static terms, as if the humane laws of the late eighteenth and nineteenth centuries had been in existence and uniformly enforced during the whole period of slavery in the region. Davis reached two major conclusions: (1) competitive capitalism, which admittedly was more characteristic of North America than of Latin America, correlated better and more consistently than other variables with the harshness of slavery; and (2) since the intensity of capitalism tended to vary in time and place in *both* regions, the differences between these regions were no more significant than the differences in time and place within each and even within individual countries (1966, pp. 224–87). However, even he took a little too seriously the idea propagated by Freyre and Tannenbaum, among others, that somehow "Latin Americans (had) avoid(ed) the tragic hatreds, the malignant fears, and the unjust discriminations that followed the abolition of slavery in North America."

In his seminal study, Eric Williams (1944) had long established the connection between slavery and the rise of British commercial capitalism, which, with monopoly, developed into industrial capitalism; the latter in turn destroyed both slavery and the power of commercial capitalism (1966, p. 210). Williams quoted the French historian Gaston-Martin on "the essential importance of the slave trade: on its success or failure depended the progress or ruin of all the others."[5] He also showed that the highly cruel plantation systems in Saint Domingue (Haiti) in the

116

late eighteenth century and Cuba in the mid-nineteenth century corresponded with the integration of these economies into the world market, and the relatively closed economies of Cuba and Trinidad in the late eighteenth century coincided with relatively mild systems of slavery (1957, p. 54).

This connection between capitalism and slavery has been taken up by Ianni (1978, pp. 3–50) in an exploration of the paradox of the Europeans' simultaneous implantation of free labor in Europe and forced labor in the Americas. The key to the paradox is the process of primitive accumulation. Ianni offers an analysis of the evolution of the relations between forced labor and mode of production. It is, in fact, a reformulation, in more orthodox Marxist terms, of the Williams argument. Slavery and other forms of forced labor were imposed by European mercantilism on the so-called New World as a means to exploit its resources. In order to secure the production of increasing quantities of mineral and agricultural goods, commercial capital had to attach the workers to the mines and the land, because, given the "free" availability of land, free workers would soon have appropriated these resources for their own use. Karl Marx had already pointed to the availability of cheap land and the scarcity of manpower in Europe as causes of the choice of slavery as a mode of production. The slave trade became the method of primitive accumulation for such cities as Liverpool, for example.

As this process developed, however, the focus shifted gradually from exchange to production as the source of accumulation; as a result, commercial capital was eventually supplanted by industrial capital. Thus, while mercantilism created slavery, the primitive accumulation generated by the latter brought about the transformation of mercantilism into capitalism with, of course, the help of the state and of state corporations. Thus, the slave became the foundation of the free laborer. Eventually, the apparent paradox of forced labor and free labor became a structural contradiction, especially as it was internalized in the New World itself, as a result of the independence of the American colonies. Slavery became incompatible with developing capitalism in as much as it tended to create absolute surplus-value, whereas capitalism tends to generate relative surplus-value (Ianni 1970, p. 47). In other words, as it turned into an obstacle to the further growth of industrial capitalism, slavery had to be abolished.

In another chapter, Ianni (1970, pp. 51–80) discusses what he calls the social reproduction of the races by the extant system of social relations. He sees the sense of alienation of the blacks and mulattoes in Latin America and the Caribbean as being most frequently expressed in their religious values and practices. But he later cautions that it has not

117

been demonstrated that the content of Afro-Latin American and Afro-Caribbean religions "corresponds effectively to a counterculture or a counterideology" (1978, p. 75).

The theme of culture is further explored in a UNESCO-sponsored book edited by the Cuban historian of slavery, Manuel Moreno Fraginals (1977). This volume symbolizes a considerable evolution in UNESCO's approach to Afro-Latin American studies from its strong disappointment in the results of the research that it sponsored in Brazil in the early 1950s, because it had failed to support the myth of racial democracy, to its decision to appoint a Marxist Cuban historian to lead a series of studies on the African presence in Latin America.[6] This volume should also be seen in the context of growing institutional interest in the field of Afro-Latin American studies. For example, the First Congress of Black Culture in the Americas was held in Cali, Colombia, in August 1977 under the leadership of Manuel Zapata Olivella and the Center of Afro-Colombian Studies, and the publication of the proceedings of the Congress has been assumed by the Organization of American States. A Second Congress was scheduled for 1979 in Panama, but because of lack of enthusiasm on the part of that country's government it was rescheduled for 1980 in São Paulo, Brazil.[7] In the same vein the American Anthropological Association sponsored recently a survey of its contributions to Afro-American ethnohistory in Latin America and the Caribbean, under the direction of Norman E. Whitten, Jr.

Of course, not all of these studies fall within the scope of this article; similarly, not all of the essays in the Moreno Fraginals book are of interest here. Of special significance, apart from the chapter by Moreno Fraginals himself, are those by Ianni ("Organización social y alienación," pp. 53–76), René Dépestre ("Saludo y despedida a la negritud," pp. 337–62), and Sidney W. Mintz ("Africa en América Latina; una reflección desprevenida," pp. 378–97). After reviewing the positions of those who claim that African culture pervades all the former slave societies; of those who maintain that African culture has been reelaborated and modified by the experience of slavery; and of those who insist that the African and slave cultures have been superseded by one imposed by the dominant capitalist structures and relations of our times, Ianni attempts, not too successfully, to take an intermediate stance. In his effort to reconcile these differing points of view, he argues that, as the _x-slaves became the "blacks" and the "mulattoes," what is African or black about their culture is what is continuously reproduced by "the relations of interdependence, alienation, and antagonism characteristic of capitalism" (p. 58).

118

Moreno Fraginals argues that a process of "deculturation," though not a total one, characterized the experience of slavery in the Americas. The mechanisms of this deculturation are found in the ethnic diversity of the slaves, the age at which they were brought from Africa (15 to 20 years), the imbalance of the sexes (a disproportionate male-female ratio), the dietary practices, the clothing practices, and the lodging facilities, most of which were determined primarily, and in some cases exclusively, by the requirements of production. Thus, the necessities of the production process, including work itself, generated deculturation and alienation. For Moreno Fraginals, therefore, one cannot study Africanity in Latin America outside the context of the class struggle and the role of the black African in the New World as producer of surplus value, both during and after slavery. He concludes by claiming that the Cuban Revolution performed the "miracle" of eliminating racial prejudice by breaking the capitalist economic and class structures. As a consequence, he suggests, "the elements of the subordinated culture . . . have passed into national folklore or are disappearing because the reason that brought them about no longer exists . . . the subordinate culture loses its reason for being" (1977, p. 33). To many blacks this may sound very much like another kind of deculturation, another version of the traditional Latin American attitude toward black cultural manifestations. It is precisely this problem that separates so many black scholars from the Cuban Revolution, a point to which I shall return later.

Dépestre approaches the issue at the level of ideology. He sees negritude as a form of maroon ideology, one that serves some limited psychological and political purposes, but is inadequate to the task of liberation from capitalist domination and imperialism. Thus, he rejects it in favor of an ideology of "Americanism" that would unite the region's various ethnic and racial elements. In the intellectual realm, he proposes an Americanology *a secas* (dry), without prefix, whether Afro, Indo, or Euro (p. 341).

Mintz starts with a discussion of the relationship between capitalism and slavery along the Marxist lines taken by Ianni, but, unlike Moreno Fraginals, he does not speak of deculturation. Instead, he affirms that the Afro-Latin Americans were not "the passive and unconscious object of external processes, but at least, and on the contrary, active agents of their own transformation" (p. 392). Still, he maintains that Afro-Latin culture can only be understood adequately in the specific social and cultural systems in which the various Afro-Latin groups are found. He warns that the concept of the marginalization of the

119

Afro-Latin people must not blind the student to the realization of the profound integration of these people into the bottom positions of the existing economic systems.

These essays raise and explore some of the important issues in the political economy of Afro-Latin American culture, but the book as a whole cannot be said to be oriented toward political economy. Even less so is the work of another author who has considered some of these questions, the Dutch sociologist H. Hoetink (1971). In discussing the two variants of race relations in the Greater Caribbean—the North-West European (the English, Dutch, and French spheres) and the Iberian (the Portuguese and Spanish spheres)—Hoetink concluded that these relations were determined by two factors: intimate relations are regulated by "somatic distance," which is the extent of deviation of the phenotype of the subordinate group from the "somatic norm image" of the dominant group; and public, nonintimate relations are determined by cultural factors that, for the North-West European variant, consist of Protestantism, individualism, and the all-important commercial capitalism (p. 19).

In a later study, Hoetink (1973) further elaborates some of these points. In a decidedly nonmaterialist approach, he attempts to examine what he considers to be the neglected aspect of Tannenbaum's (1946) thesis, that is the alleged correspondence between systems of slavery and systems of race relations. He concludes that black-white relations in the Western Hemisphere cannot be explained as a result of slavery, in as much as there is no correspondence between cruel or benign systems of slavery and tense or loose systems of race relations. What he sees as significant are: (1) cultural factors (e.g., religious differences), (2) numerical factors (objective numbers and their perceptions), and (3) somatic factors (physical criteria of preference in social selection). Except for the second, this appears to be an excessively cultural analysis, one that would seem to be based on dependent variables that themselves need to be explained, rather than on truly causal factors.

Carl Degler has also explored the linkage between slavery and race relations. Taking Tannenbaum's thesis as a working hypothesis, he proceeded from a discussion of slavery in the U.S. and Brazil to a comparative exploration of race relations in the two countries. He concluded that, while the situation in Brazil is different from that of the United States, it is certainly not characterized by racial equality between blacks and whites. The key to the difference is what he calls the "mulatto escape hatch," that is "the presence of a separate place for the mulatto in Brazil and its absence in the United States" (Degler 1971, p. 224). In a review article in a magazine that was shortly thereafter banned by the

120

Brazilian government, Afro-Brazilian sociologist Eduardo de Oliveira e Oliveira (1974), himself a mulatto, took exception. In his judgment, the "escape hatch," while serving as an emergency exit for the system, is also a "prison" for the mulatto (p. 70, note 13). In response to the argument that the recognition of the mulatto as separate from, and above, the black maintains the stability, peace, and harmony of the system, he cites seven of the major leaders of the black social movements in São Paulo in the 1920s, five of whom he classifies as mulattoes.[8] When Oliveira criticizes Degler for mistaking the mulatto as a racial category for the mulatto as a social category (p. 71), he is expressing a reality borne out by research in São Paulo and elsewhere in Southern Brazil, which shows that the actual treatment of the mulatto is not very different from that of the black (Fernandes 1979a, Silva 1978).

There have been other comparative historical studies of slavery and the Afro-Latin American experience by Herbert S. Klein (1967), who compared Virginia and Cuba and attempted to explain the much vaunted Iberian racial tolerance in terms of the system of slavery; by Arnold A. Sio (1964–65, 1967), who related slavery to the larger society; by Franklin W. Knight (1974) who, among other things, discussed critically Brazil's alleged racial democracy; and by Magnus Mörner (1967), who focused on social and physical miscegenation. There have been studies of the same kind for individual countries such as Argentina (Masini n.d.), Brazil (Toplin 1972), Colombia (West 1952, 1957; Escalante 1964), Cuba (Knight 1970), Mexico (Aguirre Beltrán 1974), Uruguay (Pereda Váldes 1965), and Venezuela (Saignes 1975), plus a variety of country studies in volumes edited by Ann M. Pescatello (1975) and Robert Brent Toplin (1974).

However, most studies have focused primarily on the period of slavery and its immediate aftermath, even when this is not indicated in the title (for instance, in Pescatello's volume, *The African in Latin America* [1975], every contribution deals with an aspect of slavery). A major effort to remedy this situation has been made by Leslie B. Rout (1976) in an ambitious book that seeks to encompass the whole Afro-Hispanic experience from the beginning of the sixteenth century on. It succeeds in giving a broad tableau of the early Iberian contact with the New World and the decision to establish African slavery; the development of the slave trade; the trials and tribulations of the black slave; the slave rebellions; the status of freedmen; the black participation in the wars of independence; and the postindependence condition of blacks in the various countries and regions of Hispanic America. It is a straightforward historical work and does not have an explicit theoretical framework, but it is full of valuable insights on systems of racial dominance

121

and mystification. It is unique in bringing together so much material in one volume, and its section on revolutionary Cuba is a useful, though too brief, review of the literature (pp. 308–12).

Whitten, writing about Northwest Ecuador and the southern area of Colombia's Pacific coast, discovered a connection between economic growth, racial conflict, and black disenfranchisement (1969a, 1969b, 1974). Discussing race relations in Cartagena, on the Caribbean coast of Colombia, Sidney Kronus and Maurício Solaún have sought to explain the absence of racial conflict in this old and aristocratic city, in spite of a tradition of racial discrimination, a rapid rate of urbanization, and a history of high levels of political and class violence (Kronus and Solaún 1973, and Solaún and Kronus 1973). They find the answer in the absence of racial bifurcation in the social structure, for while whites tend to be overrepresented at the apex of the social order, persons of color are represented in all the strata. They also "predict that it is improbable that Cartagena will experience major racial problems that will severely complicate continuing urban-industrial modernization," which runs counter to the conclusions about the racial conflict-generating character of modernization reached by Whitten and van den Berghe (1967). However, even some of their data fail to support these conclusions and seem to point to possible conflict. Specifically, their table on enrollment at the Law School of the University of Cartagena (1943–64) shows a sudden and total disappearance of *negros* from its ranks from 1960 on (Kronus and Solaún 1973, p. 107). While this may not be representative of trends occurring elsewhere, it does suggest the possibility of black disenfranchisement and future conflict.

If we turn to Brazil, we find studies that come closest to dealing with the political economy of Afro-Latin America. This is not to say that Afro-Brazilian studies might be characterized uniformly by a political economy approach; far from it. We need not delve into the blatantly racist literature of the late nineteenth and early twentieth century; it has been extensively discussed elsewhere (Ramos 1954; Skidmore 1969, 1974; Mauro 1974). Suffice it to say that, with the discrediting of the European racist theories, Brazilian writers moved away from this pessimist tradition to one that accepts the African origin of most of the Brazilian people, but also believes that they are in the process of "whitening," and that this is a good thing.

Perhaps, the most significant tenet of this school of thought, from our point of view, is that Brazil is a "racial democracy." A quote from Gilberto Freyre (1959, p. 9), the chief exponent of this point of view, excerpted by Toplin (1971, p. 135), expresses it perfectly: "With respect to race relations, the Brazilian situation is probably the nearest approach to paradise to be found anywhere in the world." Armed with this belief, Freyre continued to present Brazil as a model of racial harmony (1966): this being the case, it follows that there is no need to discuss the problem of the Afro-Brazilian, since by definition he does not have any problem qua Afro-Brazilian; thus, there cannot be a political economy of the Afro-Brazilian per se. Therefore, the optimist school was oriented primarily toward folklore and social anthropology, leading toward what has been called the "folklorization" of the Afro-Brazilian: the exclusive preoccupation with religion, rituals, language, diet, and sex that Oliveira calls the "eternal kitchen-bed binomial" (1974, p. 66).

The first and second Afro-Brazilian Congresses, held, respectively, in Pernambuco (Recife) in 1934 and in Salvador (Bahia) in 1937, under the leadership of Gilberto Freyre, were roundly criticized for their patronizing attitude and for being more interested in food, ritual, and music than in the countless socioeconomic problems of the Afro-Brazilians (Levine 1973, pp. 189, 190). This sense of unreality was the more remarkable since all of this was occurring at a time of intense Afro-Brazilian mobilization. The year 1937 marked the high point of the black social movements of the 20s and 30s, especially the Frente Negra Brasileira (Brazilian Negro Front), which had transformed itself into a political party just before it was abolished, together with all other parties, by the Getúlio Vargas dictatorship (the Estado Nôvo).

American sociologist Donald Pierson (1967) was influenced by Freyre in his study of race relations in Bahia, in which he attributes prejudice against blacks to class rather than race, and the low socioeconomic status of such blacks to their slave ancestry, not to racial discrimination. While he provides a detailed breakdown of racial distributions among diverse categories of employment, there is no effort at explaining the larger meaning of these occupation-race correspondences, since the inevitability of black poverty is accepted as a result of historical circumstances (pp. 177–205).

Not surprisingly, an external influence brought about the revolution in the study of the Afro-Brazilian experience, though the revolution was performed by Brazilians themselves, the sociologists of the so-called São Paulo School. It took the form of a UNESCO study whose purpose was to document what was then believed to be the reality of "racial democracy" in Brazil and to use the results of the research in showing the rest of the world how to achieve such an objective. Needless to say, no racial democracy was found, at least in the Center-South region, but our knowledge of black-white relations in Brazil was improved immeasurably, ushering in what has been called the "revisionist" point of view in Afro-Brazilian studies (Toplin 1971).

123

There were two UNESCO teams under the overall direction of the French social scientist Alfred Métraux. One team was led by the anthropologist Charles Wagley (1972) of Columbia University, the Brazilian Thales de Azevedo (1953, 1966) and Luiz de Aguiar Costa Pinto (1953), with the assistance of the American anthropologist Harry W. Hutchinson (1957), Marvin Harris (1964), and Ben Zimmerman. This group contributed greatly to the study of the social dynamics of race and class relations in Northeast and Central Brazil, including Rio de Janeiro. The second team, based in São Paulo, was led by French sociologist Roger Bastide (Bastide and Fernandes 1959) and the Brazilian sociologist Florestan Fernandes (1969a, 1969b), assisted by Oracy Nogueira (1955, 1959), also a sociologist, by psychologists Virginia L. Bicudo and Aniela Ginsberg, and by "the leaders of black associations of São Paulo" (Bastide 1974). This formal interaction and collaboration between academics and leaders of black organizations was occurring during a period of a social ferment among Afro-Brazilians as witnessed by the activities of the Teatro Nacional do Negro and of the black-led First Congress of the Black Brazilian (1950), both organized in Rio de Janeiro by Abdias do Nascimento (1961, 1968), and by Guerreiro Ramos's call for a rejection of white-dominated Afro-Brazilian studies (Ramos 1954). It was from this team that the São Paulo School emerged (Bastide 1974), consisting of Fernandes, Fernando Henrique Cardoso (1962, Cardoso and Ianni 1960) and Octavio Ianni (1962, Cardoso and Ianni 1960).

Fernandes sees himself as a militant sociologist (1975, p. 10) and considers it the responsibility of the social scientist through his scientific work to contribute to the achievement of true democracy in Brazil (1969b, pp. xvi–xvii). His analysis of the racial situation is part and parcel of his overall view of the development of Brazilian capitalism, one that has been self-consciously influenced by C. Wright Mills's perspective and his use of history and structural frameworks. Fernandes' major work on race (1969b) must therefore be read concurrently with his work on the Brazilian "bourgeois revolution" (1975). He sees the abolition of slavery in the last years of the nineteenth century as having been caused by the irresistible pressures of competitive capitalist economic relations. Many of the advocates of abolition were not at all interested in the welfare or fate of the slaves but only in unleashing the productive potential of the society by creating a "free" labor market. It is as if the dominant white group in São Paulo, the locational focus of Fernandes' book, expected the slave to vanish with slavery. The ex-slave was thus rapidly eclipsed by the vast number of new immigrants, who were preferred even in jobs previously held by freedmen. The blacks and the mulattoes were marginalized.

124

The paradox is that this competitive class society retained the traditional views of blacks and mulattoes characteristic of the plantation social order. Thus, the old invidious stereotypes (Carvalho-Neto 1978) still operate to block the access of Afro-Brazilians to jobs, status, and power. Even the black and mulatto protest movements of the 1920s and 1930s did not really challenge the new order. Instead they aimed at eliminating the vestiges of the old order and achieving the fulfillment of an open class society. They were, therefore, doomed to fail under the weight of sheer white indifference. Since then, collective protest movements have been disarmed and continued growth of the industrial economy has allowed industrious "New Negroes" to integrate themselves by filtering in small numbers into the system. The ideological basis of the stability of the existing social order is the whites' "prejudice of having no prejudice," while in fact they continue to subject Afro-Brazilians to subtle, diffuse, and pervasive discrimination. A solution to the problem of deprivation and inequality for blacks and mulattoes will require substituting racial conflict for the prevailing culture of racial accommodation. It will require challenging the extant class system. It will also be a prerequisite to true political democracy in Brazil.

When Bastide criticized the members of the São Paulo School for omitting the study of black culture to the point of even denying it (1974, pp. 119–20), he was in part expressing the preoccupations of a sociologist with strong ethnologic and folkloric interests, as opposed to the others' primary interest in the political economy of race and class. While the accusation is basically correct with respect to Cardoso and Ianni, it is less so in regard to Fernandes who more recently (1972) devoted considerable space to the discussion of cultural issues, both as worthy of consideration in their own right (part four) and as instruments in the search for racial democracy (part three). He also explicitly defended himself from accusations of denying the black and mulatto cultural heritage (p. 10).

The overall preoccupations of Cardoso and Ianni are very close to those of Fernandes, that is to identify and illuminate the roots and dynamics of Brazilian (and Latin American) dependency in the hope of contributing to its elimination. All three have been intellectually influenced by their *paulistano* background of dynamic urbanization and industrialization. In a study of the rise and fall of the slave system in Curitiba, capital of the southern state of Paraná, Ianni (1962) explores the dynamics of the transformation of the "slave" into the "black" and the "mulatto" in a community where slavery was not the dominant form of labor organization and coexisted with free labor. He found that this did not prevent the prevailing racial ideology from being strongly

125

influenced by the legacy of slavery. Discrimination operated as a mechanism to maintain the distance between blacks and whites, as color became a primary social attribute that dominated class relations.

Ianni pursues his examination of the contradiction between the agrarian-slave past and the requirements of an industrial capitalist society in a subsequent volume (1972). Here, he presents the cultural and racial relations as being mere reflections of two fundamental relationships: (a) the regime of private ownership of the means of production, and (b) the domination-subordination generated by the social division of labor. He sees the postabolition history of the blacks as essentially the history of their proletarianization (Ianni, 1970, p. 270). And, like Fernandes, he links the future of race relations in Brazil to the future of true democracy there.[9]

Cardoso is one of the foremost exponents of the dependency model of Latin American underdevelopment (Cardoso and Faletto 1970); his earlier works, however, were in the area of black-white relations. His major study of the subject was a replication in the southern state of Rio Grande do Sul of the work done on slavery by Fernandes in São Paulo and by Ianni in Curitiba (Cardoso 1962). His findings have pretty much confirmed theirs on the consequences of capitalism and slavery for Brazil. One significant point to which he calls attention is that the traditional Brazilian behavior of racial accommodation tends to break down when whites find themselves confronted by blacks with superior professional and social status (1965). Cardoso also shows the transformation of the function of racism, after slavery was abolished, that insured the continued subordination of blacks under the regime of free labor.

Cardoso and Ianni have examined the place of the blacks in the economic development of Florianópolis, the capital of the southern state of Santa Catarina, with emphasis on their location in the occupational structure of the community and the impact of economic change on the transformation of that occupational system. Using questionnaire surveys, they also analyzed the racial ideologies of both blacks (and mulattoes) and whites, the former being identified as an "ideology of compromise" (1960, p. 225).

The principal characteristic of the São Paulo School has been its combining of Marxist dialectics with quantitative research in a context strongly influenced by the historical dimension—in this case, as in the other Latin American cases, the history of slavery and its abolition. Its approach tends to be generally meta-analytical, although, as has been seen, microanalysis of sorts has been used in circumscribed urban contexts. The range of topics has been limited. In part, this is the result of the unavailability of census data after 1950, since countries such as Bra-

126

zil, Colombia, and Peru avoid including racial categories in their censuses. Thus, the time, money, and technical burden make much research practically impossible. This is complicated by the "prejudice of having no prejudice," which casts a shadow of illegitimacy, irrelevance, or even menace on research on black-white relations in Latin America, especially in Brazil.

Unfortunately, Cardoso seems not to have written on this topic since 1965. Fernandes and Ianni have continued producing in this field (Fernandes 1972; Ianni 1972, 1978), but their work is not being renewed empirically. They are putting out reinterpretations based on data collected in the 1950s. Although probably due, in part, to the absence of fresh demographic data, such research is also unpopular in a society that refuses to think critically about its own racial situation. One study worthy of mention is João Baptista Borges Pereira's (1967) work on blacks in the field of radio. But this, too, is based on survey data collected in 1958.

Fortunately, there appears to be a new stage developing in Afro-Brazilian studies, building on and transcending the contributions of the São Paulo School. But before analyzing this new crop, a peculiarity in the writings on the black condition in Brazil should be brought up. It concerns the use of the terms "politics" and "political" in this context. Freyre's *The Racial Factor in Contemporary Politics* (1966), "Political Aspects of the Brazilian Racial Dilemma" by Fernandes (1972, pp. 256–83), "Race and Politics" by Ianni (1978, pp. 127–42), and "Race and Politics in Brazil" by Hasenbalg (1979, pp. 223–60) have one thing in common: they do not deal with political institutions, behavior, or attitudes, or with elections, electoral behavior, or political parties, or even public policy, all of which are the stock-in-trade of political scientists. In fact, in some cases, such as that of Freyre, they do not deal with politics at all. Those that do, do so in a broad sense, at an abstract level of conflict and power imprecisely defined. Or, as in the case of Hasenbalg, they try to explain the historic failure of blacks to mobilize as a group around racial issues.

Of course, these authors are sociologists; but even the political scientist Bolivar Lamounier (1968), who may have made the first attempt at straightforward political analysis of race in Brazil, did so also in a general and schematic way, and he too attempted to explain the blacks' absence from the political field in Brazil. Still, he provided a valuable framework for political research on race and class. Lamounier asked three important questions: (a) To what extent do social inequalities tend to result in political attitudes (beliefs) and behaviors that reflect them? (b) To what extent and under what conditions does a sense of racial or

127

ethnic solidarity capable of expressing itself in collective political behavior develop? (c) How does a biracial or multiracial state operate? (pp.
39–40). While he did not answer these questions, he provided a good
discussion of the role of symbolic politics in race relations in Brazil.

Lamounier was aware of, and made reference to, the then forthcoming work of Amaury de Souza (1971), another seminal contribution
to the political study of blacks in Brazil. To my knowledge, at the time of
this writing, this is the only published study on the subject using survey
research. Both Lamounier and Souza make ample use of the work of
Fernandes in developing the theoretical underpinning of their analyses.
Basically, Souza draws on Fernandes' conclusions to depict a background of "demobilization" of blacks, prevalence of the ideal of "whitening," black acceptance of the Brazilian racial ideology, and loss of
racial identity as the price of social mobility. He then takes up the three
questions asked by Lamounier. Using survey data collected by Gláucio
Ary Dillon Soares in Rio de Janeiro in 1960, he found basically: (a) that
there were strong socioeconomic inequalities between blacks and whites;
(b) that blacks generally thought of themselves as belonging to the lower
strata of society; (c) that, though there was no difference in level of
electoral interest, blacks tended overwhelmingly to support the populist
Brazilian Labor Party (PTB) and whites the centrist National Democratic
Union (UDN); and (d) that the black vote tended to be more homogeneous in this respect, regardless of class. He concluded that, though
there was basis for collective protest action among blacks in terms of the
existence of a racial consciousness, it was unlikely because of their in-
dividualistic approach to social mobility.

The premises of this body of work on black politics are rejected by
Michael Mitchell (forthcoming). Dividing students of Brazilian race relations between those who believe in the fluidity of the racial line and the
ambiguity of racial attitudes and identities, and those who subscribe to a
rigid, structural mode of analysis that resolves race relations into reflections of broad class relations, he rejects both schools of thought. Against
the ambiguity school, he argues that this characteristic is mostly in the
eyes of the outside (generally white) observers and that the blacks themselves are quite clear about their identity. Besides, the number of those
with unambiguous phenotypical characteristics is rather substantial
(Dzidzienyo 1971). Against the structural approach, in both its Marxist
and non-Marxist formulations, Mitchell points out that, while it allows
for the possibility that under certain conditions of social change, racial
consciousness can express itself openly and politically, it fails to take
advantage of this by legitimizing the political study of racial consciousness and its impact.

128

He then proposes an alternative approach that rejects a class focus in favor of a group focus, and whose major assumption is that, within a dominant-subordinate system of relations, groups will act so as to maximize their respective power positions. Needless to say, this model reflects the North American origin and experience of its author. The rejection of class analysis is also a serious departure from the traditions of the São Paulo School, and possibly may have its limitations in terms of the explanatory and predictive capacity of the model. However, this is a political study of Afro-Brazilians based on relatively fresh (1972) survey data generated from a sophisticated questionnaire probing for self-concept, political efficacy, and the like.

Two recent sociological works on Brazil deserve attention, both dealing with the issue of inequality and discrimination (Silva 1978; Hasenbalg 1979). It is difficult to exaggerate the significance of these contributions, for with the use of survey research and quantitative analysis based on tightly argued theoretical models, they have at the very least put to rest the myth of racial democracy. What the Hasenbalg study has sought to discover is the nature of income, educational, and employment inequalities between the races and the mechanisms by which they have managed to exist without disruption or violence. Unlike Mitchell, Hasenbalg accepts most of the premises of the São Paulo School, especially Fernandes'. In fact, he accepts both the thesis of fluidity, which he expresses as "fragmentation of racial identity," and the necessity of class analysis; as he puts it, it is racism that determines the position of the blacks as social agents within the class structure. He differs sharply from Fernandes in the matter of the precise function of racism in a modern capitalist society. Fernandes sees it as an archaic survival from a traditional, quasi-feudal past into the competitive social order; Hasenbalg characterizes it as having evolved and modernized into a structural element of that order. The difference is highly significant, for while Fernandes' position optimistically expects racism to disappear as the competitive social order becomes well established, Hasenbalg sees no such prospect and expects the industrial capitalist order to accommodate a necessary dose of racism. As for the blacks' "acquiescence," he explains it as being due to the absence of a split labor market; the fragmentation of racial identity; the ideology of "whitening" and "racial democracy"; the depressed economic conditions of nonwhites; and the authoritarian nature of the political system.

The study by Silva, though dealing too with discrimination and inequality, is from a different mold. It is further removed from the tradition of Brazilian sociology and is firmly a University of Michigan social research type of study.[10] It is less given to broad-gauged theorizing, is

129

more data-bound, and the quantitative manipulations are more diverse and complex. It is too bad that they had to be based on partial 1960 census data (the 1.27 percent subsample), and not on something as recent as the 1972–73 survey data used by Hasenbalg. Predictably, this study makes no reference to class; it does not even discuss the validity and relevance of class analysis as opposed to group analysis.[11] Thus, while the existence of economic discrimination by race is convincingly demonstrated, we still do not know why it occurs and what can be done about it. But these were not the author's objectives.

What Silva set out to do—and he did it admirably—was to test two hypotheses drawn from a review of Brazilian sociological literature on race. The first was that of clear differentiation between blacks and mulattoes in terms of educational, occupational, and income attainment, with the mulattoes achieving higher levels in all dimensions. The second was that race is largely irrelevant to mobility, which is influenced more by the historically disadvantageous position from which non-whites started. Through meticulous manipulation of the data along the dimensions of educational attainment, marital status, income attainment, and occupational and age discrimination, Silva demonstrated both hypotheses to be implausible. The major strength of this work is the fundamental assumption that "discrimination is not a binary behavioral outcome that one can suffer or not . . . it is exactly in the process of achievement . . . that discrimination has its most vicious impact . . . by preventing people to have [sic] access to a higher position in the social status dimensions . . ." (p. 71). Its principal finding, in this author's judgment, is that "nonwhites suffer increasing disadvantages as they try to go up the social ladder . . . the magnitude of the discrimination coefficient seems to increase with the educational requirements to perform the occupation, and hence with its economic rewards" (pp. 215, 274).

A discussion of the Brazilian contribution would be incomplete without a mention of the relevant work of Abdias do Nascimento (1968, 1978, 1979). The constant in his writings has been an effort to expose the myth of "racial democracy" and the ideal of "whitening," which he characterizes as genocide. There is an implicit framework of "Afrocentricity" and a rejection of "Eurocentricity"; the approach is rather eclectic, encompassing history, folklore, theatre, politics, and transnational relations; the tone is pessimistic, and rejectionist, accusatory at times, and enthusiastic and hopeful at other times. Though the author does not claim to be a "social scientist" in the conventional sense of the term—in fact, he explicitly rejects such a label—his writings are full of unexpected insights into the Brazilian situation, precisely because of his unorthodox

130

style and his activism. Finally, there is a peripheral body of work indirectly relevant here. It does not focus specifically on blacks qua blacks, but the people whom it studies are in great measure, and sometimes in majority, black. This is the case, for instance, in studies of the favelas (Leeds and Leeds 1970, Perlman 1976, Valladares 1976),[12] of criminality and police brutality (Donnici 1978),[13] and of syncretic religious movements (Brown 1974).

In a 1975 conference on applied social science research at the University of the West Indies, George Beckford (1978) made a strong plea for the development of a framework that would incorporate systematically the notion of race into the analysis of the political economy of the Afro-Caribbean region. The same should be said for Afro-Latin America. Norman Girvan (1975) has drawn the basic outlines for such work in a design that includes a taxonomy based on patterns of relations of production and of ethnic/racial composition of labor forces. It distinguishes three geocultural areas based in part on a typology by Marvin Harris (1964): (a) highland America, with the Indian and the hacienda system; (b) tropical lowland America, with the Africans and the plantation system; and (c) temperate lowland America, with the Europeans and modern industrial society. Each area is then analyzed in terms of its role in the evolving international division of labor and production and in the stratification and relations of the races in this division.

The study of the political economy of the Afro-Latin American world must, to be complete, include a full and systematic account of the way in which socialism is coping with the racial problem in Cuba. We need to explore how the nineteenth-century slave society (Knight 1974) was transformed by the wars of independence, the abolition of slavery (brought about by the first war of independence), the American intervention, the incorporation of the sugar plantation system under U.S. control, the political movements of the 30s, the labor movement, the Communist party, the dictatorship, and the Revolution. Here, we need to go beyond a survey of black attitudes to the Revolution (Zeitlin 1967) to an analysis of the objective conditions brought about by the combination of a modified (by intimate U.S. contact) Iberian racial ideology with a Marxian world view and socialist policies.

Unfortunately, while a steadily growing literature on the Afro-Cuban world has appeared since the Revolution (Arredondo 1958, Betancourt 1959, Masferrer and Mesa-Lago 1974), some of it deals with prerevolutionary Cuba (Fermoselle-Lopez 1972, Foner 1970, Martinez-Alier 1974), and much of the rest is polemical (Clytus 1970, Dépestre 1966, More 1967, North 1963, Stearns 1971). One revolutionary era issue that deserves attention is the differential rates and patterns of emigra-

131

tion of blacks and whites as a reflection of their differential responses to the Revolution (Aguirre 1976), and the impact of that emigration on the demographic, socioeconomic, and political position of blacks in revolutionary Cuba. For the pre-Castro period, two issues, among others, should be of interest to researchers. One is the rebellion and massacre of the Association of Black Independents, a frustrated political party, in 1912 (Fermoselle-Lopez 1972). The other is the relationship of blacks to the Cuban Communist party in their search for equality and freedom (Betancourt 1959). For the future, there is a need to analyze seriously Cuban involvement in Africa (Dominguez 1978a, Segal 1978) in terms of its implications for the political economy of blacks in Cuba. But no question is as central as the issue of the comparative importance and mutual relations of race and class consciousness in building a socialist revolution and the resulting implications for public policy.

As Lourdes Casal (1979, p. 26) has pointed out, the problem is that "the view of the status of blacks in prerevolutionary Cuba is closely tied to the ideological commitments, social class and racial membership of the commentator one chooses to read." The same could be said, and more so, about the revolutionary period. Here the passions are even stronger, as demonstrated in particular by Dépestre (1966) on the pro-revolution side and Clytus (1970) and More (1964) on the other. The cleavage appears also in the scholarly literature: thus, one finds Casal (1979) on the prorevolution side; Masferrer and Mesa-Lago (1974) rather on the other side, arguing that things were not as bad before the Revolution as some suggest, though they were not exactly good either; and Domínguez (1978b) somewhere inbetween, but closer to Masferrer and Mesa-Lago. This is probably inevitable, given the issues, class interests, and world views involved.

Perforce, Afro-Brazilian studies have taken up the greatest space in this article. This is, in part, a reflection of the size of the African-descended population of Brazil, the salience of the racial situation there, the myths that still prevail about it, and the influence of the racial question on the development of Brazilian social thought (Skidmore 1974). It is, therefore, not by accident that some of the most interesting work has been, and is being, done in and about Brazil, in spite of obstacles that such studies encounter there. However, there is much left to be done. In particular, there is a need to explore the notion of power in the relations between the races, the relationship between ethnicity and race (the interaction between certain ethnic groups, including the Indians, and blacks), the very meaning of the notion of race in an officially assimilationist society, the dominant Brazilian vision of blackness, Africa, and

132

Africanity, and the socioeconomic and political implications thereof (Dzidzienyo, 1971). One needs to examine the evolving roles being assigned to blacks in relations of production in an increasingly technologized society. For instance, what are the implications of the fact that blacks in Brazil are generally considered to be excellent drivers for heavy trucks, while Japanese are considered terrible drivers, but excellent in work requiring extreme manual dexterity in handling small and complex objects; or of the fact that blacks are not normally hired as waiters or in any other jobs requiring direct contact with customers, though they are considered good as cooks, maids (in private homes, not in hotels, where they might encounter the guests), or stevedores? At a grander level, there is a need to analyze the structural role of the black in the Brazilian economy as a particular social agent of production.

But Brazil is only a special case of a larger situation; the same questions can be raised about other Latin American countries, and these questions should, preferably, be treated comparatively. The concept of forced labor, for example, might be redefined or adapted in such a way as to allow an exploration of the spatial and historical continuity of the black condition in Latin America. The concept of marginalization too, might be useful, provided we keep in mind the counsels of Mintz (Moreno Fraginals 1977) and Perlman (1976). In order for all this work to be done properly, however, more data must be forthcoming. At least in Brazil, the issue of reintroducing the color dimension into the census is being actively debated (in 1978, by the Brazilian Association for the Advancement of Science meeting in São Paulo; in 1979, in a joint meeting of the Brazilian Institute of Geography and Statistics [IBGE] and the Institute for Research on the Black Culture [IPCN] in Rio de Janeiro). The IBGE did a national survey in 1976 that included racial data, the publication of which will be useful to researchers in Afro-Brazilian studies. It is to be hoped that the example will be followed elsewhere in Latin America.

NOTES

1. The term Afro-Latin America is used here to designate all regions of Latin America where significant groups of people of known African ancestry are found. These include not only the obvious cases of Brazil, Colombia, Venezuela, Ecuador, and Panama, but also the Carribean coastal areas of the various Central American countries (including Costa Rica), and as well Uruguay and the Buenos Aires region of Argentina. In addition, the Hispanic Antilles (Cuba, the Dominican Republic, and Puerto Rico) are also encompassed in this designation.
2. Their low socioeconomic and political status has not prevented a significant amount of research on the Indians of Latin America under the auspices of various indigenist institutions and journals, but these too tend to be of an ethnologic or folkloric nature, not generally in the realm of political economy.

133

3. For a serious challenge to the thesis of ambiguity, see Michael Mitchell (forthcoming; chap 1). I am grateful to Mitchell for making relevant parts of this important manuscript available to me.

4. An extensive bibliography of Afro-American anthropology broadly conceived can be found in Whitten and Szwed (1970, pp. 419–49).

5. The phrase "all the others" apparently means all the other trades. The quote is from Gaston-Martin (1931, p. 424), reproduced by Williams (1966, p. 209).

6. The irony of this was underlined by Mitchell in a letter to the author.

7. The Panamanian resistance to the congress points to the continuing operation of strong institutional obstacles to the development of Afro-Latin American studies. The Latin American racial ideology, which is yet to be systematically studied, is strongly contemptuous of everything black or African. This explains the existence of such ideals as *embranquecimento* ("whitening") and of such expressions as *negro com alma branca* ("black with a white soul," that is, a good black). It explains why Dominican blacks are called *indios* and Panamanian mulattoes are called *mestizos* (Bryce-Laporte 1979, p. 13). It is also expressed in the pungency of Latin American stereotypes of blacks, which has been documented by several authors, most recently by Carvalho-Neto (1978). One of the behavioral manifestations of these attitudes and beliefs is the discouragement of, and resistance to, all forms of autonomous black self-expression. Institutionally, it means a pervasive censure, sometimes subtle, sometimes rather crude, against any studies of blacks, especially those that do not conform to the prevailing negative view of blackness and Africanity. Thus, in August 1977, the Brazilian government refused to help the Afro-Brazilian writer Clovis Moura to attend the First Congress of Black Culture in Colombia, which prevented his participation. The same year, the Brazilian government had prevailed upon the government of Nigeria to reject a paper submitted by the Afro-Brazilian writer and artist Abdias do Nascimento (1978) to the Second World Festival of African Arts and Cultures (FESTAC), held in Lagos in January-February 1977. The following year, the authorities in Bahia and Rio de Janeiro repeatedly interfered with a festival and congress organized there by a group of black North American scholars (Richard Long of Atlanta University, John Henrik Clarke of Hunter College, Hoyt Fuller of the *First World*, and others). The resistance and censure extends also to private entities. For instance, according to Roger Bastide (1974), Deoscoredes dos Santos and Juana Elbein dos Santos (1972)—who, incidentally, are among the authors included in the Moreno Fraginals book—were unable for a long time to find publishers for their work on Nagô philosophy, because it was considered too alien to the Brazilian worldview and the Brazilian vision of blacks. Even the respected Brazilian news magazine *Veja* refused in 1978 to publish a report on blacks written by one of its star reporters, Claudio Bojunga (1978). These examples illustrate the Latin American perception of Afro-Latin American self-expression and studies (especially self-studies) as being profoundly and inherently subversive of the existing order, or at the very least incongruous. It is to this situation that Bryce-LaPorte (1979, p. 13) was reacting when he wrote, "Hispanic/Caribbean Blacks now can and, therefore, must be willing to participate *as Blacks* in Latin America without feeling that to do so makes them any less Latin American, nationalist, revolutionary, human or refined."

8. It came as a surprise to this author, however, to learn that two of these leaders, whom he knows personally, are labelled mulattoes, and not blacks.

9. Ianni's more recent work on race (1978) has been discussed above.

10. Hasenbalg's book also has a University of Michigan connection, since the survey data he used has been collected in part by Michigan's Institute of Social Research, which also provided him with technical and methodological assistance. Still, he managed to retain a broadly theoretical, strongly historical, and strictly political economy perspective, in the sense defined by Léons and Rothstein (1979, pp. xv–xviii).

11. It could, of course, be argued in extremis that the occupational dimension is a proxy for class, as American social scientists often discuss class in occupational terms; but Silva does not make the argument.

134

12. Of a random sample of *favelados* who were interviewed for Perlman's (1976) study, 20 percent were identified as blacks, 30 percent as mulattoes, and 50 percent as whites. From the elite sample of 150 leaders, 12 percent were blacks, 23 percent mulattoes, and 65 percent whites. The color identifications were made by the interviewers, who were all Brazilians. This information was given to the author by Janice Perlman in a telephone conversation in Rio (September 1979). If these figures are truly representative of the population studied, they suggest that, even at the level of the favela, the dominant racial patterns of leadership tend to prevail, though to a significantly lesser extent than in the rest of the society.

13. The reader is informed that the majority of violent crimes are committed by poor people, who are usually black or mulatto (Donnici 1978, p. 234) and that in the frequent police raids on the *morros* (the steep hills of Rio de Janeiro where the favelas are usually located), "the presumption of innocence does not exist, *especially for black people*" (Donnici 1976, p. 207) (the italics are mine).

BIBLIOGRAPHY

AGUIRRE, BENIGNO E. "Differential Migration of Cuban Social Races." LARR 11, no. 1 (1976):103–25.

AGUIRRE BELTRÁN, GONZALO. *La población negra de México, 1519–1810*. México, 1974.

ANDERSON, CHARLES W. *Politics and Economic Change in Latin America: The Governing of Restless Nations*. Princeton, N.J.: Van Nostrand, 1967.

———. "The Concepts of Race and Class in the Explanation of Latin American Politics." In *Race and Class in Latin America*, Magnus Mörner, ed., pp. 231–55. New York: Columbia University Press, 1970.

ARCAYA, PEDRO M. *Insurrección de los negros de la Serranía del Coro*. Caracas: Instituto Panamericano de Geografía e Historia, 1949.

ARREDONDO, ALBERTO. *El negro cubano socio-economicamente considerado*. La Habana, 1958.

AZEVEDO, THALES DE. *Les élites de couleur dans une ville brésilienne*. Paris: UNESCO, 1953.

———. *Cultura e Situação Racial no Brasil*. Rio de Janeiro, 1966.

BASTIDE, ROGER. "The Present Status of Afro-American Research in Latin America." *Daedalus* 103, no. 2 (Spring 1974):112–23.

BASTIDE, ROGER AND FLORESTAN FERNANDES. *Brancos e Negros em São Paulo*. São Paulo: Companhia Editora Nacional, 1959.

BECKFORD, GEORGE. "The Plantation System and the Penetration of International Capitalism." In *Methodology and Change*, Louis Lindsay, ed., pp. 23–27. Mona, Jamaica: Institute of Social and Economic Research, University of the West Indies, 1978.

BETANCOURT, JUAN RENÉ. *El negro: ciudadano del futuro*. La Habana, 1959.

BLANKSTEN, GEORGE I. *Ecuador: Constitutions and Caudillos*. Berkeley: University of California Press, 1951.

BOJUNGA, CLAUDIO. "O Brasileiro Negro, 90 Anos Depois." *Encontros com a Civilização Brasileira*, no. 1 (July 1978):175–204.

BROWN, DIANA B. "Umbanda: Politics of an Urban Religious Movement." Ph.D. dissertation, Columbia University, 1974.

BRYCE-LAPORTE, ROY. "On the Presence, Migrations, and Cultures of Blacks in the Americas: Some Imperatives for Afro-Hispanic American Studies." *Caribe* 4, pp. 10–18.

135

CARDOSO, FERNANDO HENRIQUE. "Os Brancos e a Ascensão Social dos Negros em Pôrto Alegre." *Revista Anhembi* 39, no. 17 (Aug. 1960):583–96.

———. *Capitalismo e Escravidão no Brasil Meridional: O Negro na Sociedade Escravocrata do Rio Grande do Sul.* São Paulo: Difusão Européia do Livro, 1962.

———. "Colour Prejudice in Brazil." *Présence Africaine* 25, no. 53 (1965):120–28.

CARDOSO, FERNANDO HENRIQUE AND ENZO FALETTO. *Dependencia e Desenvolvimento na América Latina.* Rio de Janeiro: Zahar, 1970.

CARDOSO, FERNANDO HENRIQUE AND OCTAVIO IANNI. *Côr e Mobilidade Social em Florianópolis.* São Paulo: Companhia Editora Nacional, 1960.

CARDOSO, HAMILTON BERNARDES. "Em Defesa do Marxismo." *Versus*, no. 33 (Aug. 1979):37–38.

CARVALHO-NETO, PAULO DE. "Folklore of the Black Struggle in Latin America." *Latin American Perspectives* 5, no. 2 (Spring 1978):53–88.

CASAL, LOURDES. "Race Relations in Contemporary Cuba." Washington, D.C.: Woodrow Wilson International Center for Scholars, 1979.

CLYTUS, JOHN. *Black Man in Red Cuba.* Coral Gables, Fla.: University of Miami Press, 1970.

COSTA PINTO, L. A. *O Negro no Rio de Janeiro.* São Paulo: Companhia Editora Nacional, 1953.

DAVIS, DAVID BRION. *The Problem of Slavery in Western Culture.* Ithaca, N.Y.: Cornell University Press, 1966.

———. "A Comparison of British America and Latin America." In *Slavery in the New World: A Reader in Comparative History*, Laura Foner and Eugene D. Genovese, eds. Englewood Cliffs, N.J.: Prentice-Hall, 1969.

DEGLER, CARL N. *Neither Black nor White: Slavery and Race Relations in Brazil and the United States.* New York: Macmillan, 1971.

DÉPESTRE, RENÉ. "Carta de Cuba sobre el imperialismo de la mala fé." *Casa de las Americas*, no. 34 (feb. 1966):32–61.

DIX, ROBERT H. *Colombia: The Political Dimensions of Change.* New Haven, Conn.: Yale University Press, 1967.

DOMÍNGUEZ, JORGE I. "The Cuban Operation in Angola: Costs and Benefits for the Armed Forces." *Cuban Studies/Estudios Cubanos* 8, no. 1 (Jan. 1978a):10–21.

———. *Cuba: Order and Revolution.* Cambridge, Mass.: The Belknap Press of Harvard University, 1978b.

DONNICI, VIRGÍLIO LUIZ. "Criminalidade e Estado de Direito." *Encontros com a Civilização Brasileira*, no. 5 (Nov. 1978):201–35.

DUNCAN, W. RAYMOND. *Latin American Politics: A Developmental Approach.* New York: Holt, Rinehart, and Winston, 1976.

DZIDZIENYO, ANANI. *The Position of Blacks in Brazilian Society.* London: Minority Rights Group, 1971.

EBEL, ROLAND H. "Political Change in Guatemalan Indian Communities." *Journal of Inter-American Studies* 6 (1964):91–104.

ELKINS, STANLEY. *Slavery: A Problem in American Institutional and Intellectual Life.* Chicago, Ill.: The University of Chicago, 1959.

ENTRALGO, ELIAS JOSÉ. "Un forum sobre los prejuicios étnicos en Cuba." *Nuestra Tiempo* (May–June 1959).

ESCALANTE, AQUILES. *El negro en Colombia.* Bogotá, 1964.

FERMOSELLE-LÓPEZ, RAFAEL. "Black Politics in Cuba: The Race War of 1912." Ph.D. dissertation, The American University, 1972.

FERNANDES, FLORESTAN. "Religious Mass Movements and Social Change in

136

Brazil." In *New Perspectives of Brazil*, Eric N. Baklanoff, ed., pp. 205–32. Nashville, Tenn.: Vanderbilt University Press, 1966.

_____. "Beyond Poverty: The Negro and Mulatto in Brazil." *Journal de la Société des Américanistes* 58 (1969a):121–33.

_____. *The Negro in Brazilian Society*. New York: Columbia University Press, 1969b.

_____. *O Negro no Mundo dos Brancos*. São Paulo: Difusão Européia do Livro, 1972.

_____. *A Revolução Burguesa no Brasil*. Rio de Janeiro: Zahar, 1975.

FITZGIBBON, RUSSELL. "The Pathology of Democracy in Latin America: A Symposium." *American Political Science Review* 44 (1950):124ff.

FONER, PHILIP. "A Tribute to Antonio Maceo." *Journal of Negro History* 55, no. 1 (Jan. 1970):65–71.

FONTAINE, PIERRE-MICHEL. "The Dynamics of Black Powerlessness in São Paulo." Annual Meeting of the African Heritage Studies Association, Washington, D.C., 1975a.

_____. "Multinational Corporations and Relations of Race and Color in Brazil: The Case of São Paulo." *International Studies Notes* 2 (Winter 1975b):1–10.

_____. "Aspects of Afro-Brazilian Career Mobility in the Corporate World." Symposium on Popular Dimensions of Brazil, UCLA, 2 February 1979a.

_____. "The Brazilian 'Model' and Afro-Brazilian Identity, Mobility, and Mobilization." Annual Meeting, American Political Science Association, Washington, D.C., 1979b.

_____. "Transnational Relations and Racial Mobilization: Emerging Black Movements in Brazil." In *Ethnic Identities in a Transnational World*, John F. Stack, Jr., ed. Westport, Conn.: Greenwood Press, forthcoming.

FREYRE, GILBERTO. *Brazil: An Interpretation*. New York: Alfred Knopf, 1945.

_____. *New World in the Tropics: The Culture of Modern Brazil*. New York: Alfred Knopf, 1959.

_____. *The Mansions and the Shanties*. New York: Alfred Knopf, 1963.

_____. *The Masters and the Slaves*. New York: Alfred Knopf, 1965.

_____. *The Racial Factor in Contemporary Politics*. University of Sussex, England, 1966.

GASTON-MARTIN. *L'Ere des Négriers, 1714–1774*. Paris, 1931.

GENOVESE, EUGENE. "Materialism and Idealism in the History of Negro Slavery in the Americas." In *Slavery in the New World: A Reader in Comparative History*, Laura Foner and Eugene Genovese, eds. Englewood Cliffs, N.J.: Prentice-Hall, 1969a.

_____. "The Treatment of Slavery in Different Countries: Problems in the Application of the Comparative Method." In *Slavery in the New World: A Reader in Comparative History*, Laura Foner and Eugene Genovese, eds. Englewood Cliffs, N.J.: Prentice-Hall, 1969b.

_____. *The World the Slaveholders Made*. New York: Vintage Books, 1969c.

GIRVAN, NORMAN. *Aspects of the Political Economy of Race in the Caribbean and in the Americas*. Working Paper No. 7, Institute of Social and Economic Research, University of the West Indies, Mona, Jamaica, 1975.

HARRIS, MARVIN. *Patterns of Race in the Americas*. New York: Walker and Co., 1964.

HASENBALG, CARLOS A. *Discriminação e Desigualdades Raciais no Brasil*, trans. Patrick Burglin. Rio de Janeiro: Edições Graal Ltda., 1979.

HERSKOVITS, MELVILLE J. "The Negro in the New World: The Statement of a Problem." *American Anthropologist* 32 (1930):145–55.

137

———. "The Negro in Bahia, Brazil: A Problem in Method." *American Sociological Review* 8 (1943a):394–402.

———. "The Negroes of Brazil." *Yale Review* 32 (1943b):263–79.

———. "Problem, Method and Theory in Afro-American Studies." *Afro-American* 1 (1945):5–24; also in *Phylon* 7, pp. 337–54.

———. "The Contribution of Afro-American Studies to Africanist Research." *American Anthropologist* 50 (1948):1–10.

———. "The Ahistorical Approach to Afro-American Studies." *American Anthropologist* 62 (1960):559–68.

———, ED. *The New World Negro*. Bloomington, Ind.: University of Indiana Press, 1966.

HOETINK, HARRY. *Caribbean Race Relations: A Study of Two Variants*. New York: Oxford University Press, 1971.

———. *Slavery and Race Relations in the Americas*. New York: Harper & Row, 1973.

HOROWITZ, IRVING LOUIS, ED. *Masses in Latin America*. New York: Oxford University Press, 1970.

HUTCHINSON, HARRY W. *Village and Plantation Life in Northeastern Brazil*. Seattle: University of Washington Press, 1957.

IANNI, OCTAVIO. *As Metamorfoses do Escravo*. São Paulo: Difusão Européia do Livro, 1962.

———. "Research on Race Relations in Brazil." In *Race and Class in Latin America*, Magnus Mórner, ed. New York: Columbia University Press, 1970.

———. *Raças e Classes no Brasil*, 2d ed. Rio de Janeiro: Editora Civilização Brasileira, 1972.

———. *Escravidão e Racismo*. São Paulo: Editora HUCITEC, 1978.

KLEIN, HERBERT S. *Slavery in the Americas: A Comparison of Virginia and Cuba*. Chicago, Ill.: The University of Chicago Press, 1967.

KNIGHT, FRANKLIN. *Slave Society in Cuba during the Nineteenth Century*. Madison: University of Wisconsin Press, 1970.

———. *The African Dimension in Latin American Societies*. New York: Macmillan, 1974.

KRONUS, SIDNEY AND MAURICIO SOLAÚN. "Racial Adaptation in the Modernization of Cartagena, Colombia." In *Latin American Modernization Problems: Case Studies in the Crises of Change*, Robert E. Scott, ed. Chicago: University of Illinois Press, 1973.

LAMOUNIER, BOLIVAR. "Raça e Classe na Política Brasileira." *Cadernos Brasileiros* 8, no. 3 (May–June 1968):34–50.

LANGONI, C. G. *Distribuição da Renda no Brasil*. Rio de Janeiro: Fondo de Cultura, 1973.

LEEDS, ANTHONY AND ELIZABETH LEEDS. "Brazil and the Myth of Urban Rurality." In *City and Country in the Third World*, Arthur J. Field, ed., pp. 229–85. Cambridge, Mass.: Schenkman, 1970.

LÉONS, MADELINE BARBARA AND FRANCES ROTHSTEIN. "Introduction." In *New Directions in Political Economy: An Approach from Anthropology*, M. B. Léons and F. Rothstein, eds. Westport, Conn.: Greenwood Press, 1979.

LEVINE, ROBERT M. "The First Afro-Brazilian Congress: Opportunities for the Study of Race in the Brazilian Northeast." *Race* 15, no. 2 (1973):185–93.

MARTÍNEZ-ALIER, VERENA. *Marriage, Class and Colour in Nineteenth-Century Cuba*. London and New York: Cambridge University Press, 1974.

138

MASFERRER, MARIANNE AND CARMELO MESA-LAGO. "The Gradual Integration of the Black in Cuba." In *Slavery and Race Relations in Latin America*, Robert B. Toplin, ed., pp. 348–84. Westport, Conn.: Greenwood Press, 1974.

MASINI, JOSÉ LUIS. *La esclavitud negra en Mendoza*. Mendoza: Época Independiente, n.d.

MAURO, FRÉDÉRIC. "Le rôle des indiens et des noirs dans la conscience europeánisante des blancs: le cas du Brésil au XIXe siecle." *Cahier des Amériques Latines*, no. 9–10 (1974):195–211.

MILLS, C. WRIGHT. *The Sociological Imagination*. New York: Oxford University Press, 1967.

MITCHELL, MICHAEL. *Racial Consciousness and the Political Attitudes and Behavior of Blacks in São Paulo, Brazil*. Forthcoming.

MORE, CARLOS. "Le peuple noir, a-t-il sa place dans la révolution cubaine?" *Présence Africaine*, no. 52 (1964):199–230.

MORENO FRAGINALS, MANUEL. "Aportes culturales y deculturación." In *Africa en América Latina*, pp. 13–33. México: Siglo Veintiuno Editores, 1977.

MÖRNER, MAGNUS. *Race Mixture in the History of Latin America*. Boston: Little, Brown and Co., 1967.

NASCIMENTO, ABDIAS DO. *Dramas para Negros e Prólogo para Brancos: Antologia de Teatro Negro-Brasileiro*. Rio de Janeiro: Edições do Teatro Nacional do Negro, 1961.

———. *O Genocídio do Negro Brasileiro: Processo de um Racismo Mascarado*. Rio de Janeiro: Paz e Terra, 1978.

———. *Mixture or Massacre? Essays in the Genocide of a Black People*, trans. E. L. Nascimento. Buffalo, N.Y.: Afrodiáspora, 1979.

———, ED. *O Negro Revoltado*. Rio de Janeiro: Edições GRD, 1968.

NEEDLER, MARTIN C. "Race, Class and Political Development." In *Latin American Politics in Perspective*, pp. 16–22. New York: Van Nostrand, 1963.

———. "Social Structure, 'Race', and Politics. In *Political Development in Latin America*, pp. 98–116. New York: Random House, 1968.

NOGUEIRA, ORACY. "Preconceito Racial de Marca e Preconceito Racial de Origem." *Annais do XXXVI Congresso Internacional de Americanistas*, pp. 409–34. São Paulo, 1955.

———. "Skin Color and Social Classes." In *Plantation Systems of the New World*. Washington, D.C.: Pan American Union, 1959.

NORTH, J. "Negro and White in Cuba." *Political Affairs* (July 1963):34–45.

OLIVEIRA E OLIVEIRA, EDUARDO DE. "O Mulato, um Obstáculo Epistemológico." *Argumento* 1, no. 3 (Feb. 1974):65–73.

PEREDA-VALDES, ILDEFONSO. *El negro en el Uruguay: pasado y presente*. Montevideo, 1965.

PEREIRA, JOÃO BATISTA BORGES. *Côr, Profissão e Mobilidade: O Negro e o Radio de São Paulo*. São Paulo: Livraria Pioneira Editora, 1967.

PERLMAN, JANICE. *The Myth of Marginality*. Berkeley: University of California Press, 1976.

PESCATELLO, ANN M., ED. *The African in Latin America*. New York: Alfred Knopf, 1975.

PIERSON, DONALD. *Negroes in Brazil: A Study of Race Contact at Bahia*. Carbondale/Edwardsville: Illinois University Press, 1967.

PITT-RIVERS, JULIAN. "Race, Color and Class in Central America and the Andes." *Daedalus* 96, no. 2 (1967):542–59.

139

RAMOS, GUERREIRO. "O Problema do Negro na Sociologia Brasileira." *Cadernos de Nosso Tempo* 6, no. 2 (1954):188–220.

ROUT, LESLIE B. *The African Experience in Spanish America: 1502 to the Present Day.* New York: Cambridge University Press, 1976.

SAIGNES, ACOSTA. *Vida de los esclavos negros en Venezuela.* Caracas, 1975.

SANTOS, JUANA ELBEIN DOS. *Os Nagô e a Morte.* Petrópolis: Editora Vozes, 1975.

SEGAL, AARON. "Cubans in Africa." *Caribbean Review* 7, no. 3 (July-Sept. 1978):38–43.

SILVA, NELSON DO VALLE. "Black-White Income Differentials: Brazil, 1960." Ph.D. dissertation, University of Michigan, 1978.

SILVERT, KALMAN H. *Guatemala: An Area Study in Government.* New Orleans, 1954.

———. *The Conflict Society: Reaction and Revolution in Latin America.* New Orleans, 1961.

SIO, ARNOLD A. "Interpretations of Slavery: The Slave Status in the Americas." *Comparative Studies in Society and History* 7 (1964–65):289–308.

———. "Society, Slavery, and the State." *Social and Economic Studies* 16 (1967):330–44.

SKIDMORE, THOMAS E. *Brazilian Intellectuals and the Problem of Race, 1870–1930.* Occasional Paper No. 6, Graduate Center for Latin American Studies, Vanderbilt University, Nashville, Tenn., 1969.

———. *Black into White: Race and Nationality in Brazilian Thought.* New York: Oxford University Press, 1974.

SMITH, T. LYNN. "The Racial Composition of the Population of Colombia." In *Studies of Latin American Societies.* New York, 1970.

SOLAÚN, MAURICIO AND SIDNEY KRONUS. *Discrimination without Violence: Miscegenation and Racial Conflict in Latin America.* New York: John Wiley, 1973.

SOUZA, AMAURY DE. "Raça e Política no Brasil Urbano." *Revista de Administração de Empresas* 11, no. 4 (Oct.–Dec. 1971):61–70.

STEPAN, ALFRED, ED. *Authoritarian Brazil: Origins, Policies, and Future.* New Haven: Yale University Press, 1973.

STEARNS, LEWIS. "White Man's Revolution in Cuba." *National Review*, 12 Jan. 1971, pp. 43–44.

TANNENBAUM, FRANK. *Slave and Citizen: The Negro in the Americas.* New York: Vintage Books, 1946.

TOPLIN, ROBERT BRENT. "From Slavery to Fettered Freedom." *Luso-Brazilian Review* 7, no. 1 (Summer 1970).

———. "Reinterpreting Comparative Race Relations: The United States and Brazil." *Journal of Black Studies* 2, no. 2 (Dec. 1971):135–55.

———. *The Abolition of Slavery in Brazil.* New York: Atheneum, 1972.

———, ED. *Slavery and Race Relations in Latin America.* Westport, Conn.: Greenwood Press, 1974.

VALLADARES, LICIA. "Favela, Política e Conjunto Residencial." *Dados*, 12 Nov. 1976, pp. 74–85.

VAN DEN BERGHE, PIERRE L. *Race and Racism: A Comparative Perspective.* New York: Wiley, 1967.

WAGLEY, CHARLES, ED. *Race and Class in Rural Brazil.* New York: Columbia University Press, 1972.

WARREN, JR., DONALD. "The Negro and Religion in Brazil." *Race* 6, no. 3 (Jan. 1965).

WEST, ROBERT C. *Colonial Placer Mining in Colombia*. Baton Rouge: Louisiana State University Press, 1952.

_____. *The Pacific Lowlands of Colombia: A Negroid Area of the American Tropics*. Baton Rouge: Louisiana State University Press, 1957.

WHITTEN, JR., NORMAN E. *Class, Kinship and Power in an Ecuadorian Town: The Negroes of San Lorenzo*. Stanford, Calif.: Stanford University Press, 1965.

_____. "The Ecology of Race Relations in Northwest Ecuador." *Journal de la Société des Américanistes* 58 (1969a):223–33.

_____. "Strategies of Adaptive Mobility in the Colombian-Ecuadorean Littoral." *American Anthropologist* 71 (1969b):228–42.

_____. *Black Frontiersmen: A South American Case*. New York: Halsted Press, 1974.

WHITTEN, JR., NORMAN E. AND JOHN F. SZWED, EDS. *Afro-American Anthropology*. New York: The Free Press, 1970.

WILLIAMS, ERIC. *Capitalism and Slavery*. New York: Capricorn Books, 1966. Reprint of 1944 edition.

_____. "Race Relations in Caribbean Society." *Caribbean Studies: A Symposium*. __ Mona, Jamaica, 1957.

ZEITLIN, MAURICE. "Race Relations and Politics." In *Revolutionary Politics and the Cuban Working Class*, pp. 66–88. Princeton, N.J.: Princeton University Press, 1967.

141

MINORITY OPPRESSION: TOWARD ANALYSES THAT CLARIFY AND STRATEGIES THAT LIBERATE

by

William Bollinger and Daniel Manny Lund*

THE POLITICAL ESSENCE OF MINORITY QUESTIONS

This Issue takes up the complex questions of minority group oppression throughout the Americas—racism, national oppression, indigenismo, ethnicity and self-determination—questions which are bound up with but also distinct from class oppression. Although capitalist development is far advanced in Latin America compared with many other areas of the world, the attendant processes of proletarianization and cultural homogenization by no means have brought an end to the special oppression of minorities. Latin Americans have only to look north to U.S. society to see that, even in its most advanced stages of development, capitalism still reproduces and reinforces the special exploitation of minorities. Clearly, there must be solid material bases for the continued existence of oppressed minority communities within every nation.

Such complex and enduring forms of oppression often seem to have defied coherent analysis by Marxist and conventional scholars alike. Despite the publication of a vast literature, our theoretical understanding of various minority-related questions is remarkably weak. This in turn has led to all manner of problems in the political sphere. In spontaneous reaction to their oppression, minority group movements often have remained ineffective and divided. Equally weak has been the work of many revolutionary movements in minority communities or regions, where the tendency has been either to promote a conception of class struggle which liquidates the particular importance of minority oppression or to take the most advanced Marxist conceptions and apply them mechanically and dogmatically.

Issues surrounding minority oppression transcend national boundaries and, indeed, unite North and South America in a single set of theoretical-political problems. Although it has been nearly a century-and-a-half since the Southwest was seized from Mexico and over twelve decades since the

*The coordinating editors of *Latin American Perspectives* would like to thank William Bollinger and Daniel Manny Lund, historians and fellow coordinating editors, for editing this issue on minorities in the Americas. The authors are Director of Program Development and Director of Research, respectively, of the Inter-American Center for the Study of History and Culture in Los Angeles.

abolition of slavery, racism continues to be one of the most burning social issues in the United States and the key question dividing the many sectors of the proletariat. The fastest-growing oppressed minority in the United States is, in fact, a Latin American minority.

Both reform and revolutionary movements in Latin America have recognized the importance of the "minority problem" for their struggles. Politicians of every persuasion have promised to resolve the special oppression of minority groups. For socialist revolutionaries, in particular, the oppression of minorities touches on almost every aspect of revolutionary strategy—from questions of the forging of the worker-peasant alliance to the handling of contradictions within the working class.

The political essence of minority questions lies in the method of social struggle which will lead to the elimination of the particular oppressions—national, indigenous, racial and their various combinations. The political questions include: Who is mobilized and around what analysis of the oppression and with what strategy for resolving the oppression? Who can be won to support the minority struggle, and whose interest do the continued relations of oppression serve? How does the struggle intersect with the class struggle, and what is the content of this intersection?

At stake in these political questions are nothing less than the survival or extinction of native peoples, the persistence or ending of the social relations of racism, the success or failure of national liberation struggles as well as the advance or setback of socialist construction. Guatemala (where the indigenous movement has come, after a long process, to merge with revolutionary struggle) and Nicaragua (where the revolutionary government is grappling with national reconstruction and the historically-isolated Northeastern indigenous region) are perhaps the most dramatic contemporary crucibles of struggle within which these questions are pushed to the fore, but the issues are manifested everywhere in the Americas (for Guatemala, see EGP, 1980, and for Nicaragua, see Bourgois, 1981).

Contents and Contributions of this Issue

Despite their different topics and approaches, all of the authors in this Issue are highly conscious of the political import of their work. The first article is Stefano Varese's defense of the contemporary struggles of indigenous peoples. It is a bold description and rationale for modern *indigenismo* as seen by a sympathetic social scientist. Following this is a major critique of indigenismo by Héctor Díaz-Polanco, which attempts to posit a solid Marxist framework for understanding class struggle in the countryside. These two articles help delineate the main poles within the ongoing debates over the oppression and liberation of minority peoples.

One of the most difficult and emotionally-charged issues faced by oppressed peoples in both the United States and Latin America is the question of self-determination. The aspiration to control one's own destiny is integral to the quest for liberation from oppression. But the "right of self-determination" has referred historically to a very specific form of control: the option of achieving liberation through secession from the oppressor nation and the construction of a new independent nation of the minority formation.

Latin American Perspectives: Issue 33, Spring 1982, Vol. IX, No. 2

Marxists have attempted to remove this question from the moral atmosphere in which it is often discussed and to understand whether or not a material basis for a separate nation does (or could) exist.

Juan Gómez-Quiñones takes up the question of self-determination within this materialist framework, but he is deeply dissatisfied with the mechanical approach of those who would reduce a "nation" to a pat set of categories and who would limit their vision of the historical formation of nations to the experience of England, France, and Spain. He argues for a more dialectical understanding of national formation and especially an appreciation of the role of national consciousness in the forging of nationhood among oppressed peoples. For those readers only vaguely familiar with the basic debates and literature on the national question, including the positions of Lenin and Stalin, this thoughtful piece by a leading Chicano historian will provide an initial grounding. While he does not attempt to offer any specific resolutions, it is clear that Latin America and the Southwest region of the United States are on his mind in the critique. For those more versed in the debates on the national question, we believe the article will be stimulating and provocative.

Perhaps the single most pervasive and controversial institution at work among minority peoples throughout much of Latin America is the Summer Institute of Linguistics (SIL). Time and again in recent years newspaper accounts in Latin America and the United States have told of some new episode involving SIL personnel. Several countries have been forced by popular protest to expel this remarkable religious agency of neocolonialism, sometimes only to turn around and rescind the expulsion. David Stoll's article provides a very useful discussion of the background and orientation of the SIL. While he certainly confirms that there is much more going on here than religious proselytizing, his analysis may surprise those who assume that the institution *simply* represents U.S. strategic interests.

Next is a brief interview with Nilo Cayuqueo, an indigenous spokesman from South America. Covering a wide range of contemporary issues, the discussion focuses on the themes of the relation of the Marxist left to indigenismo and of class struggle to indigenous resistance. U.S. readers will especially want to compare and contrast Cayuqueo's views with those of North American Indian leaders on similar subjects (see Means, 1980a and 1980b, and Quinn, 1972).

SOURCES OF MINORITY OPPRESSION

By way of a general overview of the main theoretical issues involved in taking up the study of minority oppression, we advance three basic assertions in this essay: first, that the exploitation and oppression of minority groups in the United States and Latin America cannot be properly analyzed without first distinguishing two distinct types of oppression (racial and national); second, that the oppression of indigenous peoples cannot be understood solely within the categories of racial and national oppression but rather must be taken up as a distinct form of oppression; and, third, that distinct forms of minority oppression may in fact be combined in a given concrete situation and intersect with class contradictions as well. Distinguishing the distinct types of oppression thus becomes a necessary preliminary step in analyzing the particularities of their intersection in a specific context. At the political level, it is most often the particularities of the intersection of aspects of oppression which define the methods of struggle for their resolution.

A Definitional Critique

It is common, especially among movement activists in the United States, to refer to *all* minority groups as "national minorities." In this fashion, explicitly or implicitly, Blacks, Chicanos, Asians, and Native Americans are all understood as being similarly oppressed and having some relationship to their respective separate "nationalities." Similarly, China officially recognizes the existence of fifty-six separate nationalities within the multinational Chinese state. In such broad definitions, every different indigenous group in North and South America, Africa and Asia would probably constitute a nationality.

While the term is so pervasive as to make an objection to its blanket usage almost futile, it is nonetheless an analytical advance to limit or restrict the term "national minority" to those peoples who have some clear relationship to a nation—one which either exists, previously existed, or is in the process of formation.

Later in this essay we will argue specifically that socially defined "racial" groups are not nationalities, although resistance to racism has often been expressed through nationalist and even separatist currents. From a different framework, we will argue that many indigenous peoples are not nationalities, although, again, indigenous resistance has also taken a nationalist form. The Shoshone and Choctaw peoples of North America, the Pipil and Chamula peoples of Central America, the Campa and Mapuche peoples of South America, the Ching and Jinuo peoples of China, and so on, are all distinct peoples who nevertheless may well not constitute nations or nationalities. Of course, whether or not a people do indeed constitute a nation is often the subject of great debate, inquiry, and consequence. This is all the more reason not to compound the dilemmas by pushing all racial groups and every distinct cultural formation into the category of nation or nationality.

Nations and Oppressed Nationalities

Throughout their historical evolution, the peoples of the world have known many forms of unifying social organization. These forms have been based, in general, upon different modes of production, and they have included communes, tribes, estates, domains, fiefs, city-states, nations, and several forms of empire. With some exceptions (such as federations and empires), each social unit is defined by a common economic life, territory, language, and culture. It is the underlying mode of production which most stamps a communal village in the Amazon with a different social character than, say, a European fiefdom.

Nations emerged with the development of capitalism, often accompanied by a long and torturous amalgamation of distinct peoples who formerly lived separately under precapitalist forms of social organization. For example, the Bretons, Gauls, and Teutons were all distinct and viable social groups, *not nations*. But, in the course of the rise of capitalism in Europe, elements of these groups and others were forged into a modern nation (France). Separate cultures were melded in the *nationalist* quest to transform viable nations into capitalist nation-states.[1]

The leading class in national formation has been the incipient bourgeoisie, seeking to establish commodity production, develop a home market, impose a single (or at least hegemonic) language, and forge a single national identity over an entire region. This process has always been fraught with conflict, usually including long periods of warfare. Conflict between distinct peoples and the suppression of "weaker" cultures is inherent in the process of assimilating distinct peoples into a single nation. This conflict has also had international dimensions, because nations arise in competition with each other. They have disputed various territories, redrawn state boundaries, and struggled to control markets as capitalism spread across the globe.

These conflicts have done violence to thousands of distinct cultural and social formations. Most of them have become assimilated into national entities. Yet, for a variety of reasons, some have not been assimilated and, instead, are reproduced generation after generation within nations as minority peoples. Some of these peoples are nations in their own right, but more often they are groups rooted in precapitalist relations which have never evolved into viable nationalities capable of a separate national existence.

Precapitalist Social Formations and Indigenous Peoples

Because of the very *form* of oppression which results from an expanding *nation* attempting to assimilate other social formations, the most obvious and potent form of resistance for any group has often been the raising of an alternative "national" banner. A nation can be opposed by what else but another nation? Faced with extinction as a people, it is logical that indigenous peoples, no matter what their actual social formation, would raise a national banner. If nations are perceived as the form in which a people reproduce their collective life and culture, then separate nationhood would appear to resolve the dilemma of continued existence.

But, the long centuries of the rise and consolidation of capitalism have provided ample illustrations that not every struggle that takes a "nationalist" form is necessarily the struggle of a *nation* for self-determination, nor even an incipient nation calling itself into being. The key test, broadly stated, would seem to be a combination of collective will to national existence plus the material capacity to maintain that existence. Definitional resolutions, however, remain elusive. As late as the mid-1960s, a group of historians, philosophers, ethnographers and others in the Soviet Union engaged in a collective discussion and debate over a definition of nation which could "be applied to all nations." There was no collective agreement (Howard, 1967).

Whether or not a particular social formation is a nation or has the basis to exist as a nation-state, the historical origins of añ *indigenous* formation need to be identified and set forth. Indigenous peoples share a distinguishable

[1]The debates among Marxists over the origin of nations and nation-states and their relation to the mode of production and class formation have been extensive—more extensive than we can possibly summarize or argue with here. The reader is directed to the discussions and references in the Gómez-Quiñones and Díaz-Polanco articles for some of the critical literature.

common origin in self-sufficient precapitalist communities. These communities may have been tribes or more complex formations that, like nations, "once had an all-sided, historically developed, economic, cultural, territorial, and linguistic life" (see Racism Conference, 1981). Crucial to the identification of contemporary indigenous minority groups is that they still have some distinct social economic formation in a common territorial base.

The point of distinguishing the indigenous minority formation is not to define it arbitrarily out of any national project, nor to separate it from the social relations of racism. An indigenous people may, in fact, through a combination of regional capitalist development, class stratification and autonomous cultural identity come to form a nation struggling for self-determination. This is a separable, though related, question. This question, however, will be concretely and specifically conditioned by the indigenous character of a people and its social development. Further, indigenous people in the Americas suffer racial oppression as "indios"—a grouping whose very name is an historic illustration of a socially defined categorization of the type discussed in the next section.

"Self-determination," particularly in the U.S. mass-movement rhetoric of the past two decades, has come to be an umbrella category covering all manner of class demands, community interests, anti-oppression and anti-repression concerns. The analysis and argument can be generally clarified if we limit "self-determination" to its historical definition (rooted in both bourgeois and Marxist scholarship) as referring to the struggle of an oppressed nation for independence or voluntary association, and, at the same time, identify class concerns, group interests and efforts at democratic control by their particular names.

The distinctions are necessary because particular forms of oppression require particular struggles to resolve or overcome them. For example, oppression of a national formation requires a struggle for the self-determination of that nation, while oppression of a national immigrant minority may require a struggle for democratic rights, and class oppression calls for class struggle and social revolution. The fight of an indigenous minority may be for some form of regional autonomy within a nation.

This is not intended as a mechanical schematic, telling us what is to be done in each oppressive situation. But, it can guide us in recognizing that in situations where there is, for example, a combination of class, race, and indigenous oppression, the methods of struggle may be multifaceted, reflecting the complexity of the social relations of oppression.[2] If a group suffers class, racial and indigenous oppression but is not a nation, the struggle for "self-determination" is worse than an erroneous diversion; it may lead to deeper oppression and an isolation from the very forces who can be allied with to overcome the actual oppression.

Socially Defined Racial Groups and Racial Oppression

An analysis of racial oppression needs to explain how and why classes in

[2]The peasantry can be identified as a social grouping subject to class oppression—such peasantry may or may not be an indigenous peasantry or an ex-slave Black peasantry. The class position is related to but distinguishable from the indigenous question and the socially defined racial character.

Latin American Perspectives: Issue 33, Spring 1982, Vol. IX, No. 2

capitalist society remain internally stratified along racial lines and how the racial categories become reproduced and reinforced in spite of the tendency of capitalism to homogenize peoples as proletarianization advances. The essence of racism in capitalist society is the historical assignment of individuals into separate "superior" and "inferior" groupings on the basis of color and other secondary physical characteristics. The superior/inferior dichotomy has become both the form and rationalization for pronounced differential treatment of peoples, including their differential exploitation as workers, differential participation in national life as citizens, and differential valuation of culture and language.

Elements of racial distinction and categorization certainly predated capitalism, but the elaboration of racial theories of historical development and the institutionalization of racial differentiation is bound up with the development of capitalism (Burnham and Wing, 1981). Primitive accumulation in the New World was historically tied to complex processes of land usurpation and labor exploitation. The treatment of indigenous and transported African peoples required, in time, moral justification and legal rationalization. The emerging social relations of capitalism included an appropriation of racial categories and the construction of both a theology and an anthropology of racial differentiation.

Despite the formal ending of slavery for Blacks and differential legal status for the indigenous in the nineteenth century, there was nonetheless a persistance to racial categorization. Perhaps most dramatically apparent in the United States, racism has been a pervasive social relation which has continued to influence patterns of immigrant assimilation and the processes of class stratification. In the elaboration of modern class society, each person has come to have a racial and a class interest. The class lines are divided by race and to a lesser extent the racial lines are divided by class. For the United States, it is no exaggeration to point out that the maintenance of bourgeois class rule has been historically accomplished in part through the promotion of cross-class racial unity, tying together a white racial group of bourgeois, petty-bourgeois, and some working-class forces.

The situations in Latin America are distinct, but the dynamics of race and class are as fundamental (see especially Mörner, 1970: 199-123). In the case of the Black/white dichotomy, there is a revealing difference in the way the distinctions operate between the two regions. In the United States, there are only two categories: unless one can pass as "pure" white, one is socially-defined as Black. In Latin America, there are intermediate racial castes stamped with degrees of inferiority between the two primary Black/white poles.

> A Brazilian child is never automatically identified with the racial type of one or both of his parents, nor must his racial type be selected from one of only two possibilities. Over a dozen racial categories may be recognized in conformity with the combination of hair color, hair texture, eye color and skin color which actually occur (Harris, 1964: 57).

Often this difference between the systems is cited to deny or minimize the existence of a system of racism in Latin America. On the contrary, however, these national differences merely highlight the fact that the racial categories are defined socially, not biologically. All such racial categories (however benign they are painted in some Latin American countries) are antagonistic and embody relations of oppression. To be Black, mulatto, zambo, chino, cholo or mestizo is to be "not white." In class society, such color distinctions mark individuals to experience quite different life destinies. Because these distinctions channel people to different occupations and into racially different life experiences, the resulting stratification of each class on the basis of color constitutes the material social relations of race which reproduce racism in the society quite apart from the will of any individual.[3]

Yet, however much separateness has resulted from the social relations of racism, it is a long step to argue that an oppressed racial group is a national minority or could be the basis for a new nation. In fact, in their analysis of the U.S. experience, Burnham and Wing argue that

> Whites and Blacks have lived and worked together in the same economy and on the same territory for more than 350 years in the course of which they were forged into a single U.S. nationality. However, racism divides the whole society, and hence the U.S. nationality, into antagonistic racial groups: "white Americans" and "Black Americans." Consequently, whites and Blacks experience U.S. national life from opposite ends of the racial contradiction, and these qualitatively different experiences have given rise to distinctive cultural expressions within the U.S. national culture . . . Despite racist discrimination, Blacks have in the past been able and continue to qualitatively appropriate to themselves the broader American nationality and culture. Yet due to the white supremacy dialectic, the process is not reversible. Except as commodities, white Americans cannot appropriate the experience of Black Americans (Burnham and Wing, 1981, II: 51-52).

In other words, racism and racial polarization only *appear* to produce two distinct nationalities. Relegated to the oppressed category, it is logical for Blacks to feel that they are systematically denied a full claim on the U.S. nationality. What they are actually denied is a full claim on the relative privileges (or at least the promise of attainment of the "American Way of Life") which are reserved for whites in the oppressor pole of a single racially stratified nationality. Because these oppressive social relations of race are therefore a part of U.S. capitalist society, it is logical that the Black struggle for liberation often takes the form of a nationalist or separatist struggle against that very nationality which promises oppression to every Black and relative privileges to every white, even when they belong to the same class.[4] The pitfall is to presume that, given that institutionalized racism in capitalist society produces such nationalist responses, there must be a separate Black nationality or nation seeking self-determination (the right to forge a separate nation-state). To do so leads logically to an acceptance of permanent social relations of racism in which the United States is reserved for whites and where the liberation of racial minorities can only be conceived of as a struggle for national liberation against that white nationality.[5] This failure to

---

[3]There is a tremendous need for further scholarship (investigation and theoretical work) on the questions of race, class, and racism in Latin America. We are not denegrating what has been done, but it is sobering to review Magnus Mörner's (1970) charting of scholarly tasks and problems and realize how critical the balance of unfulfilled topics is.

[4]An emerging Black nationalist current in Brazil which offers some interesting parallels to the radical indigenista position can be found in Nacimento (1977 and 1979).

[5]Nationalism among Blacks is not nearly as strong as it is often depicted (or experienced by whites). The struggle against racism in the United States, which found its most advanced expression in the Civil Rights movement, is essentially a struggle to break down and ultimately destroy the social relations of racism. Affirmative action programs were a major gain in the effort to remove the institutionalized relative privileges enjoyed (or promised) to all whites. The banner

distinguish the social relations of race within a single nationality from the very distinct problem of national oppression has plagued the communist movement for decades.

Communist Movement and Racial/National/Indigenous Oppression

Prior to the late 1920s, the infant socialist movements in the Americas tended to minimize the special oppression of minorities by conceiving their liberation as simply a natural by-product of the class struggle against the bourgeoisie. The Communist Party of the United States (CPUSA) initially had no program for leadership of the antiracist struggle in the United States and tended to deny that Black people were subjected to a special form of oppression other than that endured by the working class in general. The Brazilian Communist Party believed that racism was a serious problem in the United States but not significant in Brazil. The parties in countries with large Indian populations tended to see Indian oppression as only a problem of land tenure and feudal exploitation which would be swept away by socialist revolution.

Thus, it was a major advance in the late 1920s when the Communist International prompted the American parties to turn special attention to the condition of oppressed minority peoples. Given the long history of debates within the Marxist tradition over national oppression and nationalism, it was not surprising that the leadership of the Communist International urged the national question framework on the American parties as the perspective through which to analyze local realities and develop political programs. The search for the material basis of oppressed nationalities was launched, and the banner of self-determination for minority peoples was readied.

The most concrete and best-known result was the line adopted at the 1928 and 1930 world congresses of the Communist International to the effect that there was a Black nation in the South of United States.[6] The past white chauvanism of the CPUSA was examined and criticized, the Black struggle for equal rights was taken up extensively, and in November 1930 the U.S. party launched the League of Struggle for Negro Rights with a program of self-determination for the Black Belt. While in retrospect it was a fundamental error to conceive of Black people in the United States as a separate nationality rather than an oppressed racial minority, this line was in fact a major advance for the movement because the party began, with some success, to take up the struggle against Black oppression as a revolutionary struggle.

It is less well-known that these debates over the special oppression of minorities were also projected into Latin America at the same time. At the First Latin American Communist Conference, held in Buenos Aires in June 1929, the Peruvian delegation was given principal responsibility for organizing

of separate nationhood has simply not been the historic rallying point for the masses of Black people in the United States (or Latin America). But the historic reluctance of white workers to seriously commit themselves to the struggle against racism has naturally fostered pessimism and antiwhite hostility among Blacks. It is this failure of the white section of the working class to consistently fight racism (and not the existence of a separate Black nationality) which materially reinforces tendencies toward Black nationalism and separatism.

[6]Associated with the "Black Nation Thesis" were political lines advanced for the Black struggles in South Africa and the West Indies.

discussion and debate on the "Racial Problem in Latin America." The arguments presented and the inability to come to any unity, or to design a strategic perspective, revealed the pitfalls of failing to distinguish clearly between distinct forms of racial, national, and indigenous oppression.

The Peruvians based their presentation on the important theoretical work concerning the indigenous question by José Carlos Mariátegui, one of Latin America's most important Marxist writers, who was too ill to attend the conference. Mariátegui had polemicized both with bourgeois analysts who ascribed the Indians' condition to their racial or ethnic background and with indigenista leaders who defined Indian oppression in moralistic and romantic terms. He asserted that Indian oppression in Peru was the product of the precapitalist bondage in which the peasantry was still held by Peru's semifeudal land tenure system. (The polemic is available in English translation as the second chapter of his famous *Seven Interpretive Essays on Peruvian Reality* [Mariátegui, 1971].) Hugo Pesce, speaking for the Peruvian communists in Buenos Aires, therefore repeated Mariátegui's assertion that the "racial" problem in Peru was not a racial problem at all, but rather an economic and social one. "The problem of the races is, at bottom, that of the liquidation of feudalism" (Martínez de la Torre, 1947: 434). Ninety percent of all Indians, he said, are serfs.

The strength of the Peruvian position was the insistence that the oppression of Latin America's indigenous peoples, especially the Indians of the Andes, lay in the precapitalist relations of exploitation. It was a problem of the land and the peasantry, rather than a racial division within a proletarianized capitalist society. The weakness of the position was that it only spoke to the condition of the Indian peasantry, as opposed to the racial situation in Latin America generally. Indeed, the Peruvians recognized that Indians, Blacks, and Chinese immigrant laborers were *all* subject to the most virulent forms of racism and that racist ideology toward these groups was an important point of unity between the local (white) bourgeois classes and their imperialist allies. The main problem throughout the conference discussions on racism was that none of the delegates possessed a theory of racism or a political program which spoke to the special oppression of people of color in Latin America. For its part, the Peruvian delegation arrived in Buenos Aires ready to clarify the nature of *indigenous* oppression, not racial oppression. The conference organizers realized that the racial question must be taken up (and that it was a universal problem throughout the continent), and apparently, because the Peruvians had already drafted an extensive document on a related topic, those delegates were asked to organize the discussions.

The fact that Indians (serf and nonserf) shared racial oppression with Blacks and Asians and that this oppression was bound up in capitalist social relations was beyond the scope of the Peruvian analysis. For all of the delegates, there seemed to be two obstacles to taking up the question of racism in theoretical and political fashion—one problem shared with their U.S. comrades and another particular to the Latin American movement. Among both U.S. and Latin American socialists who daily had to confront bourgeois propaganda on the supposed racial inferiority of people of color, as well as utopian nationalist and separatist sentiments within the oppressed communities. there was the notion that even to pose oppression in racial

Latin American Perspectives: Issue 33, Spring 1982, Vol. IX, No. 2

terms was a racist concession to bourgeois ideology. In effect, this line of reasoning held that racial distinctions existed only in the minds of people (an ideology or false consciousness imposed by the oppressors) and that racial contradictions can be overcome by appeals to class interest and classwide solidarity. Because the racial question was reduced to an "economic and social" (i.e., strictly class) question, the Peruvian delegation could argue that the duty of communists was to combat any "deviations" which accepted the bourgeois definition of the problem in "strictly racial" terms. In this way, revolutionaries could "destroy racial prejudice." At the same time, the Peruvians also warned of the need to combat "Black Zionism" by fighting for a class perspective within Indian and Black struggles, "giving the [racially oppressed] masses a clear class consciousness . . . and demonstrating their identity with the mestizo and white proletarians" (Martínez de la Torre, 1947: 463). This was quite similar to the classic liquidationist view on race which plagued the U.S. left for so long. The effect of the Peruvian position was to negate the special oppression flowing from the nonclass socially determined racial categories and to negate the need for communists to take up the struggle against racial oppression (as opposed to simply combatting racist ideology).

The second obstacle to the development of a theory of racism was the view expressed throughout the Buenos Aires discussions on the racial question that, by contrast to the United States, racism was not an important problem in Latin America. "The Black in Latin America does not suffer the same scorn as in the United States" (Martínez de la Torre, 1947: 458). "The purely racial aspect of the problem [for both Indians and Blacks] is largely diminished by the great degree of miscegenation" (1947: 462). "Prejudice against the Black [in Latin America] is minimal. In the heart of the working class it does not exist" (1947: 444). "The situation of Blacks in Brazil is not such that our party would be required to organize particular campaigns for their rights with special slogans" (1947: 444). These opinions seemed to go unchallenged. Of course, there are important differences in the forms and degree of racism between the United States and Latin America. But the question of racism is liquidated altogether when indignation toward the stark racism prevailing in the United States is used to minimize or sanctimoniously deny the racism which pervades most Latin American countries.[7]

Overall, the Peruvian exposition in Buenos Aires was an advanced one, speaking to the condition of indigenous groups in Mexico, Guatemala, Peru, and Bolivia, as well as the tribes of the Amazon basin. The failing of the conference was the inability of other delegations or the Communist International (CI) leadership to respond to the limited focus of the Peruvians with an analysis of *racial* oppression. Instead, a Communist International representative spoke at length in opposition to the Peruvian analysis by insisting that indigenous oppression should be understood through the national framework (which had already been applied to explain Black oppression in the U.S. South).

[7]During the last decade there has been renewed interest in the racial question in Latin America which has been reflected in a number of important films: for example, *Chuquiago* (Bolivia), where a working-class youth pitifully attempts to disguise his Indian facial appearance; *Tent of Miracles* (Brazil), a comedy treatment of racial dynamics complicated by U.S. influences; and a number of Cuban films dealing with slavery.

> It seems to me that the working papers confuse the racial question with the national question . . . The Peruvian comrades have correctly reacted against the idealist and petty-bourgeois conception . . . but it seems to me that they have fallen into the opposite error: that of negating the national character of indigenous struggles . . . Lenin said that "every national question is ninety percent an agrarian question" [a fact denied by bourgeois analysts, as the Peruvians show]. But an equally serious error is to reduce the national question to a class question—the agrarian question . . . (1947: 467).

This criticism of the Peruvian position was half correct; but, unfortunately, even the correct half missed the point. The special oppression of peoples of color was not being addressed, partly because the Peruvians did tend to reduce all minority oppression in Latin America to class oppression. The CI delegate correctly emphasized that oppressed peoples had special demands which could not simply be encompassed by the classwide demands of a socialist program. But the missing treatment at the conference was an analysis of racial oppression, along with the development of a framework to take account of the intersections of class, national and racial oppression.[8] Attempting to speak to the racial question in Latin America by counterposing class versus nation frameworks, the discussion took on a sterile and confused character. A delegate from Venezuela called for the right of self-determination for Indians to form their own Indian nation, while another from El Salvador asserted that, "the complete solution of the Indian problem will only come with the dictatorship of the proletariat" (1947: 473-475).

The conference thus wound up with fundamental differences unresolved, and the CI was unable to project a line on racism and the liberation of racial minorities in Latin America. A review of party statements and CI documents on Latin America during the 1930s and 1940s found virtually no attention given to racial oppression, even for countries like Brazil where the indigenous question could hardly account, as in Peru, for such a racial "blind spot."

Intersection of Racial, National, and Indigenous Oppression

Some cases of Black oppression are especially illuminating because they allow analysis of the racial aspect of minority oppression, isolated from complicating factors of indigenous or national heritage. But for many minorities, forms of oppression intersect and become combined, especially when peoples of color migrate from one nation to another or are assimilated (or partially assimilated) from indigenous or national minority groupings into a broader social framework.

As pointed out earlier in this essay, assimilation of diverse peoples, tribes, cultures and "nationalities" into a single nation is a historical process which

---

[8] It should be noted, in defense of the CI representative, that the Black-nation assessment of the U.S. South would logically apply to the Quechua and Aymara peoples of Peru and Bolivia. The cornerstone of the analysis of the Black Belt was the conclusion, plausible at the time, that the plantation system could never be broken up under capitalism. It was only after the Second World War, with the plantation system gone and millions of Blacks employed by capitalist industry, that it became more obvious that the sources of continuing Black oppression would have to be found elsewhere than in the semifeudal conditions of Southern agriculture. Mariátegui's assessment of Peru's feudal structures was quite analogous to the Black Belt nation view, in that he felt that the Peruvian bourgeoisie and foreign imperialist penetration were incapable of rooting out feudalism from Peru.

Latin American Perspectives: Issue 33, Spring 1982, Vol. IX, No. 2

has accompanied capitalist development throughout the world. It is simulta-neously a progressive process (forging a single working class and developing the productive capacity of society) and a very destructive and violent one (subjugating distinct cultures, eliminating regional languages and dialects, etc.). Assimilation takes place as capitalist exploitation removes or qualita-tively undermines the material basis for the separate existence and reproduc-tion of each distinct indigenous group or nationality.

But when a capitalist society has become racially stratified, the process of assimilation is altered substantially. Peoples of color (Indians, Blacks, Asians, mestizos, etc.) undergo a process of assimilation into the oppressed racial minority pole of the society. The trauma of proletarianization is compounded. This can have the appearance of an incomplete integration or acceptance into bourgeois society. It is as if every Black in the United States must carry the visible mark of slavery, while people of distinctly Indian features in Latin America must carry the visible mark of the peasantry—regardless of what class in bourgeois society they are part of. Even in Mexico, where the ideology of national *mestizaje* is deeply implanted, there is strong color differentiation among the petty bourgeoisie and upper class. Indeed, in many Latin American countries sociologists have noted a pronounced tendency for the middle and upper sectors to seek to "whiten" themselves as a means of further upward mobility. Racial dynamics continue to be an important aspect of marriage throughout much of Latin America.

However, differential assimilation does not fully capture the historical process which produces a "cholo" in Peru or a Chicano in the United States. For many groups—and this seems to be the case for many Latin Americans in the United States—the encounter with racism becomes at least a partial barrier to national assimilation. Particularly in the Southwest where there are other factors which contribute to the reproduction of the Mexican nationality (such as continual immigration and the heritage of the territory), racism serves as an additional and powerful barrier to U.S. national assimilation *even when immigrants become integrated into the U.S. proletariat.* Here is a case, then, where the racial aspect actually reinforces the national aspect, keeping alive the national question in the Southwest.[9]

The United States offers numerous examples of complex intersections between the racial and national. Perhaps the most revealing are the frequent cases of racially-mixed Latin Americans (especially from Puerto Rico and the coastal areas of Peru and Colombia) where the children of the same family become assimilated into different racial groups because U.S. society assigns one to the Black category but another to the Latino or white categories.

Racism can also serve as a barrier to the assimilation of indigenous peoples, especially those already resisting proletarianization and loss of their

---

[9]Commentators frequently remark on the national implications of the Southwest. A proposed U.S.-Mexican development program for the border region has been opposed in some U.S. circles for fear of an irredentist movement there. One writer noted that 40 percent of the population of the United States in 2080 could very well be comprised of post-1980 immigrants and their descendants, of whom 85 percent would be from Latin America. "Bilingualism and biculturalism could well tear at the cohesion of America" (Pierce, 1981). Former television commentator Eric Sevareid gravely warned that Latin American cultural influence "could produce greater strain on this country than Black-white relations."

Indian cultural identity. Quite apart from the spectre of racial oppression, many Indians consider assimilation through proletarianization to be a form of cultural genocide. The prospect of also having to join the ranks of racially oppressed minorities makes integration into bourgeois society all the more uninviting. Just as many Andean peasants have "preferred" feudal bondage to proletarianization, many North Americans have remained isolated on reservations rather than join the racially stratified U.S. working class.

INDIAN LIBERATION: A CRITIQUE OF INDIGENISMO

Ever since the Spanish conquest, there have been progressive voices denouncing the oppression of Indians and championing their liberation. Indian communities repeatedly rose in revolt, and on a few occasions entire regions were engulfed in revolution against the systems which taxed the wealth, exploited the labor, and suppressed the culture of America's indigenous peoples. While there was never any common ideology or political outlook to these movements, most projects to defend and liberate Indians fall within one variant or another of what is generally referred to as *indigenismo*. Although indigenismo is as old as the earliest indigenous resistance to European control, the debates over the fate of Indian communities and culture continue to rage today, as manifested in the polemical arguments of several authors in this Issue. Our purpose in this section is to provide English-speaking readers, who may not be well acquainted with the debates, an introductory review of the complex currents of indigenismo.

Rather than trace indigenista movements chronologically, we have attempted to classify different currents according to their underlying objectives and the class outlook of their proponents. Although anthropologists and historians often study and portray them as discrete entities, the struggles of indigenous peoples have never been divorced from the broader societies in which they occur. Indigenous movements have been conditioned by and have in turn conditioned a whole range of national and class struggles.

Officialist or Bourgeois Indigenismo

The most conservative indigenista currents have been those which, since the independence period, have endeavored to glorify the Indian past and romanticize the Indian present for the purpose of forging a unified national identity. This form of indigenismo has been integral to the bourgeois project of nation-building in those Latin American countries with substantial Indian populations. In societies like Mexico, Peru, or Bolivia, still burdened by feudal structures and severe racial and cultural divisions, what we would call "officialist indigenismo" was an appeal to national unity across class and racial lines. Because independence from Europe could only be guaranteed by an anti-Spanish movement, the emergent national bourgeois forces needed non-Iberian symbols of national unity. Thus, officialist indigenismo stressed the shared "identity of birthplace with the now distinguished preconquest rulers of the continent" (Stein and Stein, 1970: 162). In Peru this evocation of the Indian past and aversion for Spain, which were reflected in the popular song and verse of the period, had, in the opinion of historian Raúl Porras Bar-

Latin American Perspectives: Issue 33, Spring 1982, Vol. IX, No. 2

renechea, a false ring in the mouths of republicans.[10] "The most deceitful and insincere of these lyrical exaltations seems to be . . . the sudden 'indigenismo' of all the bards. In the absense of historical memories which enliven national sentiment, at the eleventh hour these Spaniards, decendents of the *conquistadores,* all resort to invocation of the distant Incan spirits" (Porras Barrenechea 1974: 210). The verses portrayed independence as indigenous vengence for three centuries of hateful oppression. The Incan sun, father of the universe, became a common metaphor for the nation. In the ode to the victory over Spain at Junín by the poet José Joaquin de Olmedo, there is an apparition of Huayna Cápac, complete with his retinue of virgins. "La Chica" became the most celebrated popular song of the period, elevating the fermented corn beer of the Indian as the new national libation over imported Spanish wines whose local manufacture had been prohibited by the Crown:

Patriotas, el mate
de chicha llenad
y alegres brindemos
por la libertad.

The ideological break with European values was a weak one. A consistant bourgeois nationalist indigenismo had great difficulty emerging during the predominantly conservative and racist climate of nineteenth century Latin America. The "liberalism" of the early national period was only a partial modification of the rigid racial castes defined by the Laws of the Indies. It emphasized a type of "equal rights" and assimilationism designed to proclaim the legal end of the Indian and the elevation of the mestizaje. European immigration and colonization projects were embraced, in part to dilute the Indian blood and promote what José María Luis Mora in Mexico called "the fusion of all races and colors" (Hale, 1972: 246). Paradoxically, the ultra-racist pro-Iberian conservatives defended the traditional colonial hierarchy with its legal protections of the Indian communities (the base of the tribute system), while the liberals championed reforms which would and did accelerate privatization of Indian lands and the proletarianization of indigenous peoples. The policies of a Benito Juárez, portrayed in bourgeois literature as a liberator of the indigenous masses, were designed to hasten the doom of Indians as a distinct people. And, in the end, whenever the social tensions produced by the advance of capitalism in the countryside broke out in indigenous insurrection, liberals and conservatives quickly put aside these differences to join in massive repression and, if necessary, extermination.

As in North America, extermination was the rule in those countries where rapidly advancing industrial capitalism, riding forward on the railroads, encountered indigenous communities characterized by small units at levels of primitive communism and weak tribal confederations. Uruguay, for example, was able to send its last surviving Indians off to a Paris museum where they died. But in Mesoamerican and Andean regions, where the most advanced Indian civilizations had developed, indigenous societies survived

---

[10]Much of the material presented by the authors is drawn from Peru and Mexico. Our goal was to provide illustrations for a general argument and not a comprehensive review. Thus, we have tended to focus on those areas rich in examples and most familiar to us.

and even flourished, not in some splendid isolation but in direct economic relation to both feudal and capitalist economy. It was here that the need to adjust to (and overcome) this Indian heritage gave rise to forms of bourgeois indigenismo. Instead of mestizaje being articulated as anti-Indian, there was a
gradual shift within bourgeois ideology toward incorporation of the Indian
heritage into the nation-building project. "Pre-conquest cultures provided an
intellectual bond between masters and dependents" (Stein and Stein, 1970:
179). No one in nineteenth-century Latin America better incarnated officialist
indigenismo than did Mexico's President Benito Juárez, a full-blooded
Zapotec Indian.

The illusion that European values and symbols could somehow still
provide the ideological cement to hold the nation together came crashing
down in the social turmoil and violence of the early twentieth century. The
Mexican revolution especially drove home the urgency of what Manuel
Gamio in 1916 called "forjando patria" (forging the nation). A decade later
this leading Latin American social scientist explained the problem with great
clarity:

> It is unquestionably urgent, most urgent, to investigate the indigenous population of
> Mexico scientifically, for until this is done thoroughly, social contacts cannot be
> normalized and orientated authoritatively, a thing by all means desirable since it requires
> convergent racial, cultural, and spiritual fusion to secure unification of tongue and
> equilibrium of economic interests. This, and only this, can place the Mexican nation as a
> nation, upon a solid, logical, consistent, and permanent base (Vasconcelos and Gamio,
> 1926: 127).

José Vasconcelos joined Gamio in amplifying the antiracist dimension of
the integrationist view. Implicitly critiquing the racist limitations of both
liberals and conservatives in the nineteenth century, Vasconcelos argued that
the basis for a united nation was in a mestizaje which embraced the
indigenous heritage, affirmed integration, and rejected the efforts to dilute the
Indian aspect. The indigenous contribution to the mestizaje was seen as
positive, especially when put in a comparative perspective:

> Our Indians then are not primitive as was the Red Indian, but old, century-tried souls who
> have known victory and defeat, life and death, and all the moods of history" (Vasconcelos
> and Gamio, 1926: 79).

It is helpful to see this version of integrative indigenismo as an ideological rationale for extensive capitalist integration. The "gospel of the mestizo" as a
"new race" was to be "conscious of their mission" as a bridge to the future,
"as builders of entirely new concepts of life" (Vasconcelos and Gamio, 1926:
95). Or, as Lázaro Cárdenas so candidly put it in 1940 in his keynote address
to the Pátzcuaro Interamerican Congress, the fundamental role of the
Mexican Instituto Indigenista was "to Mexicanize the Indian" (González
Navarro, 1970: 154).

The projects envisioned particularly by Manuel Gamio found an echo
throughout the Americas, including the United States, where officialist
indigenismo profoundly influenced the ideas and policies of John Collier,

Roosevelt's New Deal Commissioner of Indian Affairs. Collier identified his first and most pressing task in the New Deal asserting:

> . . . Indian societies must and can be discovered in their continuing existence, or regenerated, or set into being *de novo* and made use of. This procedure serves equally the purposes of those who believe the ancient Indian ways to be best and those who believe in rapid acculturation to the higher rather than the lower levels of white life (Collier, 1947: 155).

Out of a series of hemisphere-wide conferences in the 1930s, the Inter-American Institute of the Indian was established in 1940. This crystallized the regional institutionalization of indigenismo. Yet, even within this officialist form, the deep contradictions surrounding indigenous struggle persisted and can be seen in a review over time of the contents of *América Indígena*, the publication of the Inter-American Institute. John Collier (president of the board for the institute in the 1940s) caught a sense of the complex forces even as he commended the programs of the various national affiliated institutes for Indian affairs:

> Now they are reaching below the political level, and across the narrow political boundaries of previous years. They are not as yet Indian revolutions, but they included genuine and deeply intended efforts to free and aid the Indians. Should they fail, it might very well be that Indian-centered revolutions would take their place (Collier, 1947: 179).

And, indeed, rebellions there were (discussed in the next section). By the 1960s, when officialist indigenismo found a new framework in the agrarian reform projects of the Alliance for Progress, the spectre of indigenous insurrection still menaced the nations of Mesoamerica and the Andes. Perhaps the most radical extreme to which the bourgeois indigenistas were driven was embodied in the Velasco-led military regime which came to power in Peru in 1968. Indian peasant, "the landlord will never again feast on your poverty," Velasco dramatically exclaimed. Generals donned the *chullu* (knitted Indian cap) at provicial political rallies and decorated their living room walls with posters of Túpac Amaru. Quechua was declared an official national language (a prominent linguist wryly commented: "This will mark the last stage in the elimination of Quechua"). General Velasco's humble origins as a *soldado de raza* were stressed by government propagandists. A neofascist organization sponsored by the regime adopted Quechua exclamations as battle cries. Of course, in the end the hypocrasy of this indigenismo was exposed, sending most peasants into opposition against the regime. But the contemporary significance of such officialist indigenismo cannot be ignored.

Insurrectionist or Peasant Indigenismo

As the initial advance of capitalism into Latin America was felt in the Indian communities, some indigenous resistance began to take a kind of peasant insurrectionary form. The promises of the independence period went unfulfilled. Indebted governments continued or increased the odious colonial taxes (including the feudal Indian tribute or *contribución de indígenas* in Peru).

Manufactured goods from abroad or from nascent national industries penetrated the countryside, undermining indigenous artisan crafts. The appearance of capital in agriculture brought further pressures to privatize the land and concentrate holdings into larger estates employing wage labor. Governments declared an end to communal land tenure and began to classify landless peasants as vagrants subject to forms of indentured servitude and forced labor. In this context of growing capitalist threat to Indian survival, the 1780-1781 Túpac Amaru rebellion at the close of the colonial period in Peru and the 1810 Indian rebellion in Mexico presaged the sort of peasant insurrections which were to haunt the Indian regions of Latin America well into the twentieth century.

The forms taken by different revolts varied widely even within single countries. Some of the more threatening and dramatic insurrections occurred when national governments were already embroiled in other debilitating conflicts, such as the Yucatan Mayan Rebellion and the Sierra Gorda insurrection of 1847-1848 during the U.S. war with Mexico or the 1885 Atusparia rebellion in the Peruvian department of Ancash on the heels of the War of the Pacific. But, after the consolidation of national governments, Indian revolts tended to diffuse into isolated social banditry or millenarian religious revivals—except where indigenous struggles benefited from linkage to the struggles of other national sectors. The peasant indigenismo manifested in the dress, demands, and orientation of the largely Indian Zapatistas of Morelos was not lost on contemporary observers of the Mexican revolution, but this special indigenista character of the Army of the South could hardly have been created in isolation from the broader forces in Mexican society which produced the revolution (Womack, 1969). Likewise, the Salvadoran oligarchy was shaken by the apparent suddenness of Indian participation in the 1932 rebellion and therefore carried out special punishment of Indian communities. But the revolt itself was a nationally coordinated action, at least partially led by trade unionists and the Salvadoran Communist Party.[11] The last major attempt to lead the Indians of the Andes in the restoration of the preconquest Tahuantinsuyo was organized by a renegade Peruvian army major, Teodomiro Gutiérrez Cuevas in Azángaco in 1915. Major Gutiérrez Cuevas adopted the name Rumi Maqui Ccori Zoncco (Hand of Stone, Heart of Gold) (see Vassallo, 1978: 123-127).

It is important to recognize that we are not making an identification of peasant and indigenous. The struggles of indigenous groups include, among other forms, the resistance of isolated jungle tribes, agricultural laborers striking over wages and work conditions, tenant farmers in spontaneous revolt, land invasions of displaced communeros, as well as efforts at comprehensive rebellion. The point is to acknowledge that the current of indigenismo associated with or taking the form of peasant insurrection has been and still is the current most organically tied to revolutionary challenge.

---

[11]The Salvadoran case is an example of repression so severe that, to escape further attack, Indians completely cast off all visible signs of their Indianness. Traditional Indian dress was abandoned, and the remaining speakers of indigenous dialects switched to Spanish. The terror of the period seems to be still stamped on the western region of El Salvador, the only area of the country without significant peasant participation in the Frente Farabundo Martí para la Liberación Nacional (FMLN)-led revolution.

In Peru, all of the important peasant uprisings since the Second World War have been led by communist forces, from the 1959-1962 rural union movement organized by Trotskyists (Hugo Blanco) to the mid-1970s land seizures led by the Confederación Campesina del Perú (see Palomino, 1978: 187-211). In Mexico, the massive rural unrest of the 1960s was largely located in the regions of indigenous peasants. Radicalized rural school teachers like the Gamiz brothers in Chihuahua, Genero Vasquéz Rojas and Lucio Cabañas in Guerrero, led dramatic foco-style challenges with acknowledged indigenous character.

The active struggles of today are very much rooted in this heritage. In their most advanced form, such as Guatemala, indigenous people have embraced strategic unity with other elements of the oppressed peasantry. Much of the weight and significance of the Guatemala struggle is rooted in the increasing participation of the twenty-two ethnic indigenous minorities who collectively comprise 60 percent of the total Guatemalan population (EGP, 1980: 227).

Radical or Petty-Bourgeois Indigenismo

In the caldron of turn-of-the-century social debate, and against the prevailing bourgeois pessimism over the capacity of the indigenous "races," there emerged an opposite, almost ecstatic redemptive hope focused on the Amerindians. Especially within radicalized petty-bourgeois sectors, in Latin America and the United States alike, there was a rejection of the racist ideology which defined the Indian as an inferior, and a searching for an alternative to the rapacious advance of industrial capitalism which threatened to finally destroy Indian culture and community. And, despite the progressive nature of radical indigenismo, it was often stamped with an anti-Marxist character as well. For many—perhaps most—radical indigenistas, the Marxist vision of the forward march of historical forces, operating apart from the will of individuals, was too sobering, too materialist, and too threatening to the idealist goals of defending indigenous culture from penetration and destruction by international capitalism.

The radicals turned the prevailing bourgeois cynicism upside down. They saw in Indian people and their culture the source of an alternative or even superior value scheme to the conflict and voracious exploitation of industrial capitalism. Bourgeois society pitted individuals against each other in brutal competition, a materialist race which did violence to spiritual values, scarred the earth, and poisoned the environment. In refreshing contrast, the radical indigenistas "discovered" Indian patterns of collectivity, harmony with nature, and celebration of spirituality and passion. These qualities are easily romanticized, especially in the minds of the petty bourgeoisie, a grouping whose members often aspire to higher status but are almost as often frustrated and even face situations of "sliding back" into a proletarian status. Elements of this redemptive vision have also struck responsive chords in those intellectuals who have emerged from Indian society itself, as witnessed by the growing Indian leadership of the radical indigenista movement. Notable recent U.S. expressions were Meredith Quinn's Dakota Proclamation of 1972 ("Keep this in mind: The Indian sitting on his reservation, wrapped in his blanket, has been the only deterrent for the obliteration of mankind.") and Russell Means' 1980 speech at the Pine Ridge Reservation ("And when the catastrophe is over, we American Indian peoples will still be here to inhabit the hemisphere.") (Quinn, 1972: 139, and Means, 1980b: 31).

In less apocalyptic form, this radical current came to intersect with the varieties of institutionalized indigenismo discussed above. As the limitations of the official government Indian institutes and their programs became more and more pronounced, the "Indian-centered" revolutionary thrust foretold by Collier emerged. This intersection is particularly reflected today in the contemporary heirs of Gamio and Collier—the radicalized anthropologists and other social scientists who work among the indigenous peoples. Their views are reflected in Varese's article published in this Issue.

In the case of Peru, the initial appeal of a radical indigenismo among petty-bourgeois intellectuals was undoubtedly facilitated by the profound national trauma which followed the economic collapse of the guano era and the humbling defeat by Chile in the War of the Pacific (1879-1882). If the bourgeoisie lacked confidence in the Indian, now a deep pessimism and cynicism about the bourgeoisie itself set in. Surely it had compromised itself by tolerating feudal exploitation of the indigenous peoples. Manuel González Prada asked rhetorically why a Peruvian army comprised of Indians should want to defend a nation of which they were not apart. "Like the serf of the Middle Ages, he will only fight for the feudal lord . . . [The] haciendas are separate kingdoms in the heartland of the Republic" (Valderrama and Alfajeme, n.d.: 57-58).

Reflecting the growing frustration of the Peruvian petty bourgeoisie, González Prada lost all hope that the non-Indian wealth owners could reform the nation. "The Indian will be redeemed by his own efforts, not by the humanizing of his oppressors. Every white person is, more or less, a Pizarro, a Valverde, or an Areche" (Valderrama and Alfajeme, n.d.: 59). This initial Peruvian radical indigenismo was centered in literary circles in the late nineteenth century and reflected in several remarkable novels, especially Clorinda Matto de Turner's *Aves sin nido.* But in 1909 a handful of progressive intellectuals in Lima founded the Asociación Pro-Indígena to champion Indian rights, and an even broader movement developed in Cuzco at the same time (the "Escuela Cuzqueña"). The Lima movement was impelled by moralistic outrage at the continued feudal exploitation of the Indian in a nominally democratic república. The Asociación was devoted to philanthropic service: defense of Indian rights, support of all claims against abuses, and promotion of the study and popular divulgation of all things indigenous.

Radical indigenismo impacted the political movements of the 1920s, particularly since the Mexican revolution had demonstrated the potential national import of indigenous *reivindicaciones.*[12] It was during his residence in Mexico that the young Peruvian radical Víctor Raúl Haya de la Torre attempted to launch a continental movement based upon an "Indoamerican"

---

[12]The Indian demands for recognition of original land tenure as well as reestablishment of past social, political, and economic rights.

Latin American Perspectives: Issue 33, Spring 1982, Vol. IX, No. 2

ideology. But, as with virtually every *political* expression of petty-bourgeois indigenismo, the pro-Indian rhetoric was soon altered and subordinated to suit the purposes of the quest for national power.[13] Radical indigenismo tended to get swallowed up or coopted in the reformism of mid-twentieth century Latin American politics and the comprehensive institutionalized indigenismo of the nineteen national institutes that were formed in the wake of the 1940 Pátzcuaro Conference.

It is only since the 1960s repolitization of both Latin America and the United States that radical indigenismo has once again emerged as an important ideology and social force. Tribal and cultural leaders from Canada, the United States, and Latin America now meet regularly together in international conferences, which have even broadened to include the op-pressed indigenous minorities of Australia, New Zealand, and other regions. And the radical social scientists who met at Barbados in 1971 and 1977 provide the new Indian proponents of indigenismo with important allies who can sometimes affect government policy. These contemporary indigenous radicals have largely assumed the leadership formerly provided the indigen-ista movement by sympathetic non-Indian intellectuals. But the radical social scientists of the Barbados conferences continue to assist the indigenous leadership in developing theoretical and historical perspectives.[14]

Radical Indigenismo and Marxism

In a fundamental sense, the very fact of indigenous survival and resistance gives the elements of indigenismo a progressive cast. For scores of years, the working assumption of bourgeois development has been that the comparatively weak indigenous social and economic formations would be undermined and overcome by the general strength of the expanding social relations of capital. Of necessity, the indigenous people would then be drawn into the labor force and the dominant patterns of consumption, culture, and language. The incompleteness of this process reflects both unevenness in the development of capitalism and the persistent resistance on the part of indigenous communities.

The survival of large numbers of native peoples is an impressive manifestation of their capacity to reproduce themselves as peoples. Census data, however, must be approached carefully since the methodology is often weak in regard to both compilation of numbers and definitions of categories. The lines between indio, mestizo, and other categories can be blurred and vary from country to country and census to census. While more data are now being published, the statistics are not very meaningful without interpretation.

[13]Once Haya had established the Alianza Popular Revolucionaria Americana (APRA) as a national party in Peru, he was more concerned with the modernizing ambitions of the petty bour-geoisie and described the Indian peasantry as "primitive," "culturally backward," and "without political consciousness." Instead of defending or glorifying indigenous insurrection, Haya began to oppose any rural movements which would destroy the basic social peace of the nation (Valderrama and Alfajeme, n.d.: 213).

[14]The "Declarations of Barbados" (position papers from the meetings) have become important summations of radical indigenismo, theoretically and politically. This is particularly true of the summation paper of the 1977 meeting, known as "Barbados II." The text is available in a variety of publications, including the journal *Arte, Sociedad, Ideología,* (see Declaración de Barbados, 1977).

Both empirical studies and impressionistic observations indicate that significant processes of proletarianization and assimilation are, in fact, going on. But, these processes are by no means universal or consistent. Vast numbers of people are not being effectively proletarianized or assimilated into a nonindigenous culture.[15]

Studies based on census data of 1940 indicated there were from 16 million to as many as 23 million indigenous peoples in the Americas (Lipschutz, 1972: 45). At the present time, statistically informed estimates place the indigenous population at from 26 million to more than 30 million (Rodríguez and Soubié, 1978: 49). Outside the Andean-Mesoamerican chain, the indigenous groups and their overall numbers have been declining, but within the traditional chain there is an overall population increase. In absolute terms, the indigenous "minorities" constitute a majority of whole regions and even a couple of countries.

Yet, just surviving in the face of capitalism's historic tendency to break down indigenous formations does not necessarily make indigenismo anticapitalist. There are many currents—pro- and anti-capitalist, pro- and anti-socialist, pro- and anti-"Spanish" or white—within indigenismo. (See, for example, the discussion of Nicaragua's east coast by Bourgois [1981] and the conflicting indigenous testimony at the 1980 Russell Tribunal in Rotterdam [Luna, 1980: 40].)

There are some who tend to emphasize the unity of all indigenous people in such a way as to blur the very real differences within the population. Clarifying these differences, however, is an invaluable aid to understanding something of the varied currents and shades of differences within indigenismo itself.

The Barbados Declaration of 1977 advances an outline of the three different situations in which the divided Indian peoples find themselves (Declaración de Barbados, 1977: 91). The first is composed of groups who have remained relatively isolated and have been able to "preserve their own cultural schemes" relatively intact. These are mainly the many and varied tribal formations of the Amazon Basin. Such groups are fighting for basic survival, and the guarantee of their territory has become, in effect, the main political demand. The cause of these tribal groups may be championed by the movement; but, in their very isolation, these groups are not generally integrated into the indigenous political formations.

The second general situation identified in Barbados II concerns those groups which have been able to preserve a great deal of their culture but who are nonetheless in relations of "direct domination by the capitalist system." These are primarily the great masses of Indians in the Andean and Mesoamerican regions. Struggling for control of their own resources (according to Barbados II), they represent the most highly-politicized social formations and actively relate to a whole series of social struggles. It is from these groupings that participation in both the broad indigenous movement and national revolutionary struggles come.

---

[15]In the course of capitalist development in some regions, the extraction of surplus value has been accomplished in the utilization of precapitalist forms. Thus, pressures for proletarianization and assimilation vary widely from region to region, depending on a complex set of factors.

The third general situation is identified as the section of the population "de-Indianized" through integration, having lost coherent cultural schemes and gained "limited economic advantages." This Barbados category refers to formations throughout the Americas, but specifically regions of the southern cone and perhaps areas of the United States in which Indians are isolated on reservations or in urban lumpen formations.[16] The task here, according to Barbados II, is immediate liberation from "cultural domination" and recovery of "their own being, their own culture" (1977: 91). It is out of these formations that the most intense embrace of what we have identified as radical indigenismo appears to take place. The redemptive vision is most attractive to those who are closest to being lost and who suffer the most profound alienation.

The left's general historic failure to integrate the struggles of the indigenous people into a viable revolutionary strategy is another important factor. As we discussed briefly above, it would appear that until the recent period many Marxists assumed that a persistent process of proletarianization would take place among the indigenous (a kind of proletarian reflection of bourgeois capitalist assimilationist assumptions). Until the Indians were proletarianized, they (in the eyes of some communists) remained on the margin of history and the sidelines of class struggle. The communist movement seemed to know what to do with workers and peasants, but was less certain about indigenous peoples who didn't quite fit in the categories. Thus, in many quarters there has been and continues to be an estrangement between Marxists and indigenistas.

A beginning point both for understanding the estrangement and for resolving it is to grasp some of the elements of the world-view and orientation of contemporary indigenismo (we will leave an amplified historic critique of the left for another article). What seems to be key at the outset is the historic refusal of many of the indigenous minority groups to die away, to cease to exist as a people. Not only have they refused to give up, but some have embraced a form of national or autonomous project as the only apparent viable alternative to extinction as an identifiable people.

Since the indigenista ideology is not one thing set forth in one place, it is useful for an introductory framework, such as we are attempting, to draw together the elements and present a synthesized summary. The essence of radical indigenista categories lies in turning bourgeois scholarship and ideology on their head. This is apparent in the characterization of central historical processes: the conquest is seen as the invasion; colonization is viewed as an interruption of indigenous history; recapturing the historical process is a necessity to bring an end to the "chapter of colonization" (see Declaración de Barbados, 1977: 91).

---

[16]The indigenous situation in the United States is not, of course, uniform. There is both a commonality and a world of difference between the 160,000 tribal Navahos on 25,000 square miles of Arizona, Utah, and New Mexico (much of which appears to contain potentially valuable deposits of oil, gas, and uranium) and the Shoshone remnants in the Owens Valley of California. The discussion in this issue does not really scratch the surface of the situations of the U.S. native peoples. It is anticipated, however, that the general framework and analyses developed in this Issue will help provide the basis for some illuminating comparative studies of the indigenous peoples of Latin America, Canada, and the United States.

The Europeans are said to see the material as determinative of reality, while the indigenous see the spiritual as determinative. Nilo Cayuqueo argues in the interview given below, that the Europeans mistake the material basis of life as lying in things, while the indigenous identify the material basis as the earth and the land itself.

The Europeans struggled with nature to overcome and transform it, while the indigenous labor to bring themselves into conformity with nature. Such notions find a powerful echo of response among radical middle class currents of opposition in bourgeois society—from anticonsumerist sentiments to the antinuclear and ecology movements.

From the indigenista perspective, what is real is contrasted with what is merely abstract. The very abstractness of non-Indian thought is seen as falsifying mediation, or as masked rationalization. For some, the dichotomy is extended to communication itself: what is real is spoken; what is abstract, and therefore suspect, is written (Means, 1978a: 19).

In regard to social knowledge, indigenismo tends to contrast the drive in western bourgeois thought toward unitary systems of science, religion, and language with the need for recognizing, preserving, and even celebrating a multiplicity of views—an assumption of a reality so complex and rich that only social and intellectual pluralism can provide the necessary correlation.

There is also a tendency to contrast the bourgeois dichotomy between religion and science, and the religiosity of modern bourgeois (as well as Marxist) faith in science with a complex indigenista view of the separation and interpenetration of scientific knowledge and religious verity (Commission on Indianist Ideology and Philosophy, 1980).

In regard to social action, there is a contrasting of revolt in the narrow political sense with resistance in an all-sided, but especially cultural sense. Even Marxist concepts of revolution are seen as continuities of the present order; some argue for "authentic revolution" and "true socialism" reflecting the "indigenous majority" of the working classes of Andean and Mesoamerican countries (CISA, 1981: 6). Others argue for revolution as turning full circle, going back to the beginning and picking up new options for the building of indigenous communities and nations.

Where traditional liberalism assumed assimilation and much of the old left depended on the process of proletarianization to transform the indigenous people, indigenismo counters with a call for the "re-Indianization" of native peoples, ladinos, and mestizos. Guillermo Bonfil Batalla calls mestizos, "indios recuperables" (Bonfil, 1977: 101). Thus, the "colonized" proletarians and other potential allies are to be transformed into Indians again as the basis for a unified struggle. Re-Indianization is a process of reassembling all the indigenous-related peoples so that they may be able to resume the processes of history and nation-building which were interrupted by the European invasions.[17]

Indigenismo tends to reject the "inevitable" subordinate status of alliance

---

[17]At the same time, other indigenous formations who have no need whatsoever to be "re-Indianized" are opening struggling for indigenous organization of peasants and workers. See proposals of the Ayoréode in *Boletin Del Campesino Indigena del Oriente Boliviano*, 1 (January 1981), 11-15.

or coalition with other forces. The key first step in any coordinated struggle is seen instead as the development of an autonomous movement. Complete separation is projected as the immediate basis for the eventual unity of equals in a pluralistic, federated struggle.

There is, without doubt, a liberating process in turning racist, capitalist bourgeois assumptions on their heads. Particularly as the pervasive categorization of superior/inferior are imposed on all aspects of life and culture, the inversion of these very categories makes a profound break with the social relations of racism. It is not a racist orientation to invert the inferior/superior categories. Resistance to oppression is not oppression in reverse; striking back against racist culture is not racism in reverse.

But, in the process of historical social inquiry, inversion of error and the reversal of false categories are not sufficient in and of themselves for an analysis and a strategy. There is a pronounced mechanical tendency in the method of turning things on their head that distorts social reality. It tends to set up dichotomies where the actual social and historical processes are interconnected. Just as Marxism must come to terms with the very persistence of national and indigenous struggles, so indigenismo needs to reckon with historical dialectics and the complex heritage (positive and negative) of the "invasion."

Finally, how does indigenismo actually view the forces and processes of history, particularly the last five hundred years? The indigenismo civilizing or nation-building project assumes a measure of relatively autonomous indigenous development that has, in essence, preserved the material bases for picking up interrupted options of development. The questions then emerge: in spite of the remarkable persistence and reproduction of indigenous communities in the past five centuries, have not there been some profoundly transforming penetrations into the indigenous communities? Are not some historical options not, thereby, foreclosed with the passage of time and the changing of conditions? What, in fact, are the available historical options and what new ones can be called into being through conscious mobilization?

The answers to these questions are not yet clear. Such questions are not raised to impose limits on the aspirations of native peoples, but rather to struggle for an understanding of both the objective and subjective possibilities which actually exist and can be made to exist in the real world. "Realism" is often used as a cover to deny oppressed people their right to act, to decide, to determine their social destiny. Yet, decisions and determinations are social acts which are conditioned by social history. History becomes ultimately most confining when we do not grasp its patterns and processes.

Radical indigenismo is both a political movement and a theory of history. This Issue of *Latin American Perspectives* tends to focus on the political dimensions of minority questions. Our concern in this introductory essay has been to provide an admittedly partisan theoretical framework, especially with regard to initiating critiques of both class reductionist and racial and indigenous separatist views. Carrying these discussions to another level in the future will require much more elaborate efforts to deal directly with the complex historical experiences of the minority formations.

REFERENCES

Bonfil Batalla, Guillermo
1977 "Sobre la liberación del indio," *Nueva Antropología*, II (April), 95-101

Bourgois, Philippe
1981 "Class, Ethnicity, and the State Among the Miskitu Amerindians of Northeastern Nicaragua," *Latin American Perspectives*, VIII, No. 2 (Spring, 1981), 22-39

Burnham, Linda and Bob Wing
1981 "Toward a Communist Analysis of Black Oppression and Black Liberation," *Line of March*; Part I in No. 7 (July-August), 21-88; Part II in No. 8 (September-October), 31-92; Part III in No. 9 (November-December)

Collier, John
1947 *Indians of the Americas: The Long Hope*, New York: New American Library

Commission on Indianist Ideology and Philosophy
1980 *Report of the Commission on Indianist Ideology and Philosophy*, Ollantaytambo, Peru: Mimeographed Report of the First Congress of Indian Movements of South America

CISA (Consejo Ejecutivo de CISA)
1981 "Comunicado Cisa," *Hatun Chaski: Vocero Indio*, 1 (April), 5-6

Declaración de Barbados
1977 "Declaración de Barbados," *Arte, Sociedad, Ideología*, (August-September), 90-91

Degregori, Carlos Ivan
n.d. "Indigenismo, clases sociales y problema nacional," in Degregori et. al., *Indigenismo, clases sociales y problema nacional; la discusión sobre el "problema indígena" en el Perú*, Lima: Ediciones CELATS

EGP (Ejército Guerrillero de los Pobres)
1980 "Manifesto internacional," *Nueva Antropología*, IV (December), 207-235

González Navarro, Moisés
1970 "Mestizaje in Mexico During the National Period," pp. 145-155 in Magnus Mörner (ed.) *Race and class in Latin America*, New York: Columbia University Press

Harris, Marvin
1964 *Patterns of Race in the Americas*, New York: Walker and Company

Howard, Peter
1967 "The Definition of a Nation: A Discussion in 'Voprosy Istorii,' " *Central Asian Review*, XV (1), 26-36

Kapsoli, Wilfredo E.
1977 *Los movimientos campesinos en el Perú: 1879-1965*, Lima: Delva Editores

Lipschutz, Alejandro
1972 *Perfil de indoamerica de nuestro tiempo: antología 1937-1962*, La Habana: Instituto Cubano del Libro

Luna, Lucía
1980 "La de los indígenas, una lucha popular continental," *Proceso*, Año 5, No. 215 (December 15), 40

Mariátegui, José Carlos
1971 *Seven Interpretive Essays on Peruvian Reality*, Austin: University of Texas

Martínez de la Torre, Ricardo
1947 *Apuntes para una interpretación marxista de la historia social del Perú*, Vol. II (we have used the 1974 reprint by the Sociology Department at the UNM de San Marcos, which is mislabled "Tomo I")

Means, Russell
1980a "Marxism as a European Tradition," *Akwesasne Notes* (Summer), 17-19

1980b "Fighting Words on the Future of the Earth," *Mother Jones*, V (December), 22-38

Mörner, Magnus
　　1970 "Historical Research on Race Relations in Latin America During the National Period,"
　　pp. 199-230 in Magnus Mörner (ed.), *Race and Class in Latin America,* New York: Columbia
　　University Press

Nacimento, Abdias do
　　1977 *Racial Democracy in Brazil: Myth or Reality,* Ibaden, Nigeria: Sketch publishing

　　1979 *Mixture or Massacre: Essays in the Genocide of Afro-Brazilians,* Buffalo: Afro Diaspore

Palomino, Abdón
　　1978 "Andahuaylas, 1974: un movimiento de reivindicación campesina dentro del proceso de
　　reforma agraria," *Allapanchis* ((Cuzco), XI, 187-211

Pierce, Neal R.
　　1981 "Our Threadbare 'Welcome Mat'—Immigration, Birth Statistics Draw a Grim Picture of
　　2001," *Los Angeles Times,* November 29

Porras Barrenechea, Raúl
　　1974 *Los ideólogos de la emancipación,* Lima: Milla Batres

Quinn, Meredith M.
　　1972 *Dakota Proclamation,* USA: Published by the Toltecs en Aztlan

Racism Conference
　　1981 *Working Papers of the Racism Conference,* Oakland: Institute for Scientific Socialism

Rodríguez, Nemesio J. and Edith A. Soubié
　　1978 "La población indígena actual en América Latina," *Nueva Antropología,* III (October),
　　49-66

Stein, Stanley J. and Barbara H. Stein
　　1970 *The Colonial Heritage of Latin America: Essays on Economic Dependence in
　　Perspective,* New York: Oxford University

Valderrama, Mariano and Augusta Alfajeme
　　n.d. "El surgimiento de la discusión de la cuestión agraria y del llamado problema indígena,"
　　in Carlos Ivan Degregori et. al., *Indigenismo, clases sociales y problema nacional; la
　　discusión sobre el "problema indígena" en el Perú,* Lima: Ediciones CELATS

Vasconcelos, José and Manuel Gamio
　　1926 *Aspects of Mexican Civilization,* Chicago: University of Chicago

Vassallo, Manuel
　　1978 "Rumi Maqui y la nacionalidad quechua," in *Allapachis* (Cuzco) XI, 123-127

Womack, John Jr.
　　1969 *Zapata and the Mexican Revolution,* New York: Alfred A. Knopf

BRAZILIAN RACIAL DEMOCRACY: REALITY OR MYTH?

Carlos Hasenbalg
Instituto Universitário de Pesquisas do Rio de Janeiro

Suellen Huntington
University of California, Berkeley

ABSTRACT

The Brazilian claim to "racial democracy" is examined historically, and in light of the 1976 Pesquisa Nacional por Amostra de Domicílios data on race, class, and social mobility in Brazil. Racism is seen as limiting upward mobility for all non-white Brazilians, pointing to a potential break in Brazil's "color-class continuum." The interlocking social mechanisms which maintain Brazilian faith in the existence of racial democracy are briefly analyzed.

The popular Brazilian ideology of racial democracy holds that there is no prejudice or discrimination against non-whites in Brazil, certainly not when compared to the United States. This paper examines that ideology in terms of the realities of race, class, and social mobility in contemporary Brazil. We begin by briefly describing the historical background of the ideology of racial democracy as it bears on race relations in Brazil. Second, we summarize and criticize three main theoretical approaches to race relations and their Brazilian variations. Third, we discuss racism as a causal variable in social stratification and compare the evidence of social mobility for white and non-white Brazilians. Finally, we analyze the social mechanisms supporting the Brazilian belief in racial democracy and their effects on equality of opportunity in Brazil. For perspective, we note the most pertinent comparisons to the United States.

HISTORICAL DEVELOPMENT

Brazil's history helps explain the development of the ideology of racial democracy and its strong hold on the Brazilian popular mind. Brazil, colonized under the auspices of the Portuguese crown, remained subject to its strongly authoritarian, paternalistic, and monarchical traditions for three-hundred years. Unlike the United States where slavery was an issue from its very beginning and became a bitter point of contention in the Civil War, slavery was easily accepted by Brazil's Portuguese settlers whose long familiarity with slavery dates to the Moorish invasions. These differences of attitude influenced the racial composition of their respective populations. In Brazil through the 1850s, half the population was enslaved; in the United States, slaves were never more than fifteen percent of the population. The presence of this large slave population in Brazil, along with the relative absence of white women, prompted a high rate of miscegenation resulting in a large group of mixed race and mulatto slaves. In the United States, where miscegenation was both less common and illegal, all offspring of mixed unions were classified as negroes.

Brazil, the last country in the Western hemisphere to relinquish slavery, did so slowly, in a series of compromise reforms which sought to balance the needs of a plantation economy for cheap, plentiful labor against a sporadic, mostly non-violent, abolitionist movement and the force of international condemnation. When the national legislature passed an abolition law in 1888, most slaves in Brazil had been freed, partly by state legislatures acting independently, but also by county governments, by city governments, by city blocks, and by private citizens. Rather than a tumultuous emancipation, Brazilian slavery merely disintegrated. In the United States, the slavery issue was finally settled in 1865 with the Northern victory in the Civil War.

To solve the plantation labor crisis envisioned as the aftermath of abolition and to ease the transition to free labor, the Brazilian government instituted, in 1885, a program promoting the importation of European workers. This program attracted 6500 Italian laborers in 1886, 30,000 in 1887, and 90,000 in 1888, the year of offical emancipation. During the period of emancipation, immigrant labor worked side-by-side with ex-slaves, but most ex-slaves, unable to compete with the relatively more skilled, relatively more literate European workers, were soon relegated to the lowest positions—unskilled labor and domestic service, tenant farming and sharecropping—in the urban and rural workforce. In the United States, skilled black workers were replaced by whites in the post-Civil War South; in the North, they were systematically excluded from the skilled trades, from all but menial labor, and from union membership. In post-emancipation Brazil, however, the replacement of black ex-slaves by white immigrants resulted from hiring decisions by individual employers rather than from any systematic or organized opposition, thus tending to create class rather than racial antagonisms.

In addition, in the United States whites filled the intermediate positions in the occupational hierarchy, leaving blacks only the least desirable, worst paying positions. In Brazil the labor shortage, together with a prejudice in favor of light skin, caused these intermediate positions to be filled by mulattoes. This labor market preference for whites first, mulattoes second, and blacks last created a status and income continuum corresponding to the color continuum, in contrast to the caste-color line created in the United States.

PERSPECTIVES ON RACE RELATIONS

Three historical perspectives—assimilationist, Marxist, and colonial—have dominated the American literature on race relations and, in varying degrees, have influenced Brazilian perspectives. None, however, see racism as a causal variable in social stratification.

General Theoretical Perspectives.

1. *The Assimilationist Perspective.* The assimilationist perspective, from its beginnings in the 1920s (Park, 1950), analyzed the structural requirements of modern industrial societies—universalism, achievement, instrumental efficiency, and individual attainment—within an open structure of opportunities. Given the irreversible logic of industrialism, race, ethnicity, and other ascriptive attributes would become negligible sources of social cleavages, group formation, and allotment of positions in the social structure. The final integration of blacks and other racial minorities becomes inevitable. Assimilation is only a matter of time, and would be accelerated by the moral commitment and increased enlightenment of the dominant white group.

Another version of the assimilationist perspective is the "immigrant analogy," wherein blacks, as the last group to move into urban and industrial settings, would successfully repeat the process of social integration completed by earlier immigrant groups.

Residually, when blacks failed to meet the expectations of assimilationist theories, black social immobility was explained away in terms of the culture of poverty, anomie, social disorganization, incomplete families, and other subcultural traits. Thus, the causes of social immobility were attributed to the minority group itself; the dominant group, usually white, and its institutions were exempted from any responsibility.

In criticizing the assimilationists' implicit assumption that racism and industrialization are incompatible, Blumer and others (Blumer, 1965; Bowles, 1973) assume racism to be an objective feature of society. To the extent that

HUMBOLDT JOURNAL OF SOCIAL RELATIONS — VOL. 10 NO. 1 — FALL/WINTER 1982/83 rational economic decisions are not made in a social vacuum, the industrial structure must comply with the racist logic of the broader social organization, replicating internally the same ideological and political practices which regulate the relations among racial groups in the wider society. When older forms of racial division of labor are renewed and elaborated in the more complex division of labor fostered by industrial development, race is maintained as a symbol of inferior position and continues to provide the rationale to confine members of the subordinate group to their appropriate "place."

2. *The Marxist Perspective.* In the orthodox Marxist perspective, epitomized by the work of Cox (1970), the situation of blacks and other racially subordinated groups is rooted, almost exclusively, in their working class economic position. Racial prejudice and discrimination are manipulative devices used by capitalist ruling classes to exploit racial minorities, and to divide the proletariat. Racism and prejudice are inherent in, and necessary for, the preservation of capitalism. The result is net gains for capitalists and losses for all workers. The counter-prescription is the alliance of workers of all races. This Marxist reduction of racial antagonisms to epiphenomena of economic relations underestimates the independent power of racism and prejudice, and explains away the poor fit between theory and reality as the result of workers' false consciousness.

3. *The Colonial Perspective.* Colonial theory breaks with earlier conceptual frameworks by directly attacking the assimilationist bias of academic theories and the conventional Marxist reduction of interracial dynamics to class exploitation. Colonial theory goes beyond Blumer's view that there is no inherent incompatibility between industrial society and racism to see racially subordinated groups as internally colonized minorities within industrial societies.

Blauner (1972) conceptualized people of color in the United States as an internal colony, based on commonalities among all colonial situations: 1) forced entry into the larger society or metropolitan domain; 2) subjection to various forms of unfree labor, greatly restricting the physical and social mobility of the group, and encompassing the minority's experience of being controlled, administered, and manipulated by members or institutions of the dominant group; 3) subjection to policy that constrains, transforms, or destroys original values, orientations, and ways of life; and 4) subjection to racism, employed as a principle through which a group, seen as "biologically" different or inferior, is exploited, controlled, and oppressed by a dominant group. Colonial theory's central concept of racial privilege suggests that, beyond economic exploitation, the whole dominant group extracts certain psychological, cultural, and ideological "surplus value" from the colonized.

The main limitation of the colonial approach, both theoretically and practically, is two-fold: the lack of an explicit model of 1) class exploitation, and of 2) the relationships between class structure and domination, and racial oppression and stratification. Since both class exploitation and racial oppression coexist in capitalist multiracial societies, when either class exploitation or racial oppression is the exclusive focus, the other remains as a residual and unexplained element. Theoretical developments proceed without coming closer to an integrated explanation of both processes. One solution is to consider the process of social mobility as the crucial link between racism and the class structure.

Brazilian Perspectives

The Brazilian literature on race relations reveals three principal theoretical lines, all basically assimilationist: assimilation through miscegenation; assimilation through expanding opportunity; and assimilation as the result of societal transformation.

1. *Assimilation through Miscegenation.* This now popularly accepted, semi-official interpretation of Brazilian race relations was formulated, in its academic version, by Freyre during the early 1930s. Freyre (1973, 1945) argued that cross-breeding produced hybrid vigor in humans as well as in plants. He also stressed the positive contributions of Africans and Amerindians to Brazilian culture. A double emphasis on the plastic character of the Portuguese colonizers' cultural background and on the widespread miscegenation in Brazil's population gave birth to the notion that Brazilians were giving birth to a new race and culture of formidable potential, a "new world in the tropics." Brazil's interracial, multicultural melting pot would be a racial democracy, without prejudice or discrimination, but with equal economic and social opportunity for members of all races.

2. *Assimilation through Expanded Opportunity.* Freyre's thought influenced a line of research, conducted by students of race relations in rural and urban northern Brazil during the 1940s and 1950s, which focused on the effects of economic development on class position. Despite the strong correlation between color and social status, these scholars (Pierson, 1942; Wagley, 1963; de Azevedo, 1955), impressed by the most noticeable differences between the American caste-color line and the Brazilian class-color continuum, concluded that: 1) the Brazilians' marked awareness of color differences is not related to discrimination; 2) derogatory stereotypes and prejudice against blacks in Brazil are manifested verbally, not behaviorally; 3) what prejudice there is in Brazil is

class, not race, prejudice; and 4) characteristics such as wealth, occupation, and education are more important than race in determining patterns of interpersonal relations in Brazil. In this hopeful formulation, as Brazil transforms itself into an industrial nation, expanding economic and social opportunity, combined with the absence of color barriers, would result in increased social mobility for blacks. In an inconclusive, but representative, statement, Wagley asserts:

> There are no serious racial barriers to social and economic advance and, as opportunities increase, larger numbers of people will rise in the social system. The great contrast in social and economic conditions between the darker lower strata and the predominantly white upper class should disappear. There are dangers, however, along the road to this ideal. There are indications both in the present studies and in reports from the great metropolitan centers of the country that discrimination, tensions, and prejudices based on race are appearing (Wagley, 1969:60).

3. *Assimilation through Societal Transformation.* In São Paulo during the 1950s and 1960s, race relations were analyzed within the more general process of transition from a slave, caste society to a capitalist, class society. Fernandes' influential work (1965, 1972) focused on the integration of blacks into the free labor market and the emerging class society. In his diagnosis of the post-abolition social and economic situation of blacks, the employers' preferences for white European workers is combined with the ex-slaves' cultural unpreparedness for the role of free man and free worker to explain the perpetuation of black social immobility. Racial prejudice and discrimination, though functional requirements of a slave society, are incompatible with the legal, economic, and social requirements of a class society, much as prejudice and discrimination were viewed as incompatible with industrialization. Thus, manifestations of racism are conceptualized as anachronistic survivals of the slave past, a phenomenon of cultural lag.

4. *Critique of Brazilian Perspectives.* In these three major Brazilian theories of race relations, the first completely denies the role of race in the process of social stratification; the second reduces prejudice to a residual of class; and the third makes racial discrimination into a mere cultural residue from the distant past. Relatively ambiguous evaluations of present and future race relations result from the latter approaches. In the assimilation-through-societal-transformation view, the further development of a class society will dissolve the legacy of prejudice and discrimination and favor the incorporation of blacks into "typical class positions." The assimilation-through-economic-development view at least entertains the possibility that the Brazilian parallels between color

and class may become permanent, but prefers to disregard color. None of these approaches seriously considers the possibility of a pacific coexistence between industrial capitalist development and racism.

Freyre's views became the basis of the belief, widely held by Brazilians of all classes, that Brazil is a racial democracy in which prejudice and discrimination based on race no longer exist. Inequalities of social status and position are explained away by calling on the other two theories' conceptualizations of inequalities as residuals of class and history. Finally, all three theories, as well as popular Brazilian thought, are underpinned by notions of individual effort as the basis for individual social mobility.

RACISM AS A CAUSAL VARIABLE IN SOCIAL STRATIFICATION

We propose that race operates as a criterion with an efficacy of its own in filling places in the class structure and the system of social stratification. Poulantzas' (1975:34-35) analytic distinction between the reproduction of class positions, on the one hand, and the reproduction and distribution of individuals among those positions, on the other, is the starting point for clarifying how race operates as an independent selection criterion. Race, as a socially elaborated attribute, is related mainly to the reproduction (formation-qualification-subordination) and distribution of the individuals within the class structure.

In our view, racial oppression benefits both capitalist *and* non-capitalist members of the dominant group, generally whites, but for different reasons. Capitalists benefit directly from the (super) exploitation of minority groups, generally blacks, whereas other whites obtain more indirect benefits. The majority of whites profit from racism and racial oppression because it gives them a competitive advantage *vis-a-vis* black people in filling the positions in the class structure which command desired material and symbolic rewards. Stated more broadly, whites profited and continue to profit from better chances of social mobility and from differential access to higher positions in the several dimensions of social stratification. This notion of racial privilege parallels Stinchcombe's (1968) concept of tenure: a socially defensible right to a flow of rewards which is not dependent on current performances. To be born white in a multiracial society dominated by whites constitutes a kind of tenure. In terms of the structuring of stratification and mobility, if one enters the competitive arena with the same resources, except for racial membership, the result (class position, occupation, income, and prestige) will be detrimental to non-whites.

We contend that racism, through discriminatory practices and cultural stereotyping of the roles "appropriate" for blacks, perpetuates an unequal structure of social opportunities for whites and non-whites. One test of the theoretical notion that the social subordination of blacks is due to the persistence of unequal structures of opportunity is to analyze the patterns of education, employment, and income for whites and non-whites. For this purpose, the Brazilian case, with its official claims to racial democracy and equal opportunity, is particularly interesting, especially in contrast to the American case, with its official acknowledgments of racial discrimination and unequal opportunity (1954 Brown vs. Board of Education; 1964 Civil Rights Act; 1965 Voting Rights Act). Another, finer test of the persistence of unequal structures of opportunity is to compare the patterns of social mobility of whites and non-whites. For this comparison, the Brazilian case, given its claims, is most interesting.

The Brazilian Case: Equal Opportunity or Social Immobility?

1. *Education, Employment and Income.*[1] Assuming that aspirations and abilities are equal, if opportunities are equal, then all non-whites' patterns of education, employment, and income should be similar to those of all whites. In Brazil, where free public education extends through the eighth grade, average years of education were 4.5 for whites, but only 2.9 for non-whites; in the United States, with twelve years of free public education, average years of education were 11.2 for whites, but 10.2 for blacks. In Brazil, non-whites are 3.5 times as likely as whites not to complete nine or more years of school; in the United States, blacks are twice as likely as whites not to complete high school. At the higher end of educational achievement, Brazilian whites are fifteen times more likely to enter college than are Brazilian non-whites, while in the United States, 25- to 29-year-old whites are only twice as likely as blacks of the same age group to have completed college.

The participation of the racial groups in the occupational structure also indicates sharp racial inequalities.[2] For Brazil, the most notable fact is the concentration of non-whites in the minimum wage sectors of agriculture, construction, and personal and domestic services, the sectors readily available to the unskilled and uneducated. These sectors employ 68% of the economically active non-whites and 52% of whites (de Oliveira, 1980). While not strictly comparable, the most notable fact for the United States is that the unemployment rate of blacks has been about twice that of whites since the mid-1950s.

The inequalities between racial categories, in education and employment opportunities, have strong effects on income. In 1976, white males in the Brazilian labor force had an average annual income of Cr$40,716, while non-while males averaged Cr$19,368, less than half the average income of whites. For white males in the United States' labor force in 1978, average income was $15,374, while black males earned $10,278, two-thirds the average income of whites.

2. *Social Mobility in Brazil.* The interracial disparities found in Brazil are commonly interpreted, in Brazilian social thought, as reflecting the different starting points of whites and non-whites at the time of abolition, now manifest as differences of class background and class discrimination in a highly class-stratified society. If the claim of racial democracy is assumed, however, then all persons born into families of the same general occupational status should have the same chance of arriving at the same general occupational destinations regardless of race. To test for equality of opportunity against the alternative hypothesis that whites and non-whites face unequal structures of opportunity, we now examine patterns of social mobility for whites and non-whites in Brazil. Table 1 reports the inter-generational occupational mobility flows for Brazil, which are discussed below.

Table 1. Brazilan Father-Son Occupational Mobility by Race, 1976#

Whites

Father's Occupation*		Son's Occupation							
		Non-Manual			Manual			%	N
		6	5	4	3	2	1		
Non-Manual	6	47.0	11.9	16.4	12.3	10.3	2.1	100.0	(438)
	5	20.4	23.2	13.7	14.0	15.5	13.2	100.0	(643)
	4	22.3	15.1	26.4	17.3	15.0	3.9	100.0	(700)
Manual	3	16.6	10.5	13.8	36.3	20.5	2.3	100.0	(609)
	2	13.8	8.5	15.6	21.7	35.8	4.6	100.0	(1,059)
	1	4.1	5.1	7.1	13.7	24.2	45.8	100.0	(4,054)

(N = 7,503)

Non-Whites

Father's Occupation*		Son's Occupation							
		Non-Manual			Manual			%	N
		6	5	4	3	2	1		
Non-Manual	6	24.2	13.4	15.4	24.8	20.8	1.4	100.0	(149)
	5	8.7	16.9	13.5	17.3	22.2	21.4	100.0	(265)
	4	17.8	11.1	24.5	21.7	21.7	3.2	100.0	(253)
Manual	3	9.2	6.0	13.9	37.2	25.8	7.9	100.0	(368)
	2	6.3	5.4	9.3	22.7	48.5	7.8	100.0	(847)
	1	2.0	2.8	4.8	10.0	27.8	52.6	100.0	(3,537)

(N = 5,419)

*In this table: 6 Upper = professionals, managers and big business owners; 5 Higher non manual = high clerical workers and small farmers; 4 Lower non-manual = lower clerical workers and small owners in commerce and services; 3 Higher manual = workers in modern industries and unskilled workers in services; 2 Lower manual = workers in traditional industies, personal and domestic services, and retail trade; and 1 Manual workers in agriculture.

#From Carlos A. Hasenbalg, "Race and Socioeconomic Inequalities in Brazil," paper presented to the *Symposium on Race and Class in Brazil,* Center for Afro-American Studies, University of California, Los Angeles, February 28-March 1, 1980. The data are from the 1976 PNAD supplemental sub-sample on intergenerational social mobility.

HUMBOLDT JOURNAL OF SOCIAL RELATIONS — VOL. 10 NO. 1 — FALL/WINTER 1982/83

Among the upwardly mobile sons of agricultural workers, the main destination points are urban manual jobs. Whites born in this group experience a small advantage over non-whites: not only is whites' degree of status inheritance (45.8%) smaller than that of non-whites' (52.6%), but only 9.6% of non-whites, as opposed to 16.3% of whites, experience sufficient upward mobility to cross the manual/non-manual line.

Interracial differences in social mobility are greater for those from urban occupational strata. Among men born to lower manual workers, not only do a greater proportion of non-whites remain there, but only 21% of non-whites, compared to 35.8% of whites, move up to non-manual positions. For men whose origins are within the higher manual level, 40.9% of whites, but only 29.1% of non-whites, achieve non-manual occupations. Again, greater proportions of urban-born whites experience sufficient long-distance upward mobility to cross the manual/non-manual line.

For men with origins in the non-manual social strata, among those born to lower non-manual workers, 63.8% of whites and 53.4% of non-whites are in the same or higher occupational levels as their fathers. For men of higher non-manual origins, 43.6% of whites and 25.6% of non-whites are in occupations equal to or higher than their fathers. Finally, 53% of whites, but 75% of non-whites, born to the highest occupational levels are subject to social demotion.

In sum, controlling for father's occupation at birth, Brazilian non-whites have smaller chances of upward social mobility than whites. Interracial differences in the opportunities for upward mobility increase with increases in status of origin. While Brazlian whites born to high social positions enjoy a greater degree of status inheritance, the small group of Brazilian non-whites born in families of high social standing are much more exposed to the risks of social demotion.

On the sequential phases of the process of status transmission, further findings for Brazil are: non-whites consistently obtain less education than whites of the same social background; even with educational achievement controlled, non-whites tend to cluster at lower occupational levels than whites; and, also with education controlled, non-whites consistently earn markedly less than whites. Thus the returns to education, in both occupation and income, show sharp differentials favoring Brazilian whites (Hasenbalg, 1980).

Silva's (1980) model of status attainment applies the structural equations of non-white Brazilians to white Brazilians. Controlling for all life-cycle variables, he found 40% of the difference in educational achievement unexplained; 29% of the difference in occupational scores unexplained; and 50% of the difference in income unexplained. The unexplained differences can be viewed as the consequences of racism and discriminatory practices for non-white Brazilians.

Silva also argues that all non-whites, including mulattoes, are now subject to the same restraints on upward mobility. While mulattoes still continue to occupy slightly better positions than blacks, their chances for upward social mobility are no longer better. The result is a widening social gap between white and non-white Brazilians, and a potential break in the color-class continuum.

In any case, the empirical evidence from recent research clearly indicates that, in comparison to whites, Brazilian non-whites are exposed to a "cycle of cumulative disadvantage" which limits intergenerational social mobility.

THE MYTH OF "RACIAL DEMOCRACY" IN BRAZIL

Given the popular Brazilian belief in racial democracy, how is this structure of cumulative disadvantage maintained? Two major interlocking social mechanisms which helped maintain this structure of discrimination are the color-class continuum and cooptation, and ideological manipulation. Operating together, they structured a system of individual opportunity and individual responsibility which effectively closed off the development of racial identity and of political organization based on race, forces which have been remarkably effective in the United States.

Historically, by filling the intermediate positions in the occupational hierarchy with mulattoes of intermediate color, Brazilian society created its color-class continuum. Whites, in rewarding lightness, also created a system of cooptation, of controlled upward mobility for mulattoes. In such a system, controlled from the top, mobility was always possible for promising individuals: talent and leadership were drained upward. Mulattoes came to see themselves as inferior to whites, but superior to blacks, which, in terms of opportunity for social advancement, was true.

Also, the ideology of "whitening" has always been important in Brazil. The nineteenth-century reasoning, advanced by abolitionists, that the gradual disappearance of blacks would solve the racial problems left by slavery and raise the moral tone of the nation, was augmented by Freyre's twentieth-century argument for human hybrid vigor through miscegenation. In fact, this symbolic reinforcement of a basic racism operated much like "americanization" did for immigrants to the United States. In the search for upward mobility, mulattoes were set against blacks, and against their own families of origin, and all were set in search of lighter marriage partners to "whiten" their children.[3]

Another form of ideological manipulation which plays a role in black subordination in Brazil is symbolic integration. One common form of symbolic integration is expressed in the phrase "money whitens." Brazil's many terms for shades of skin color are used symbolically to indicate wealth and social standing. A wealthy mulatto is called *moreno* (brunette) to indicate superior social status; a poor mulatto is called *preto* (black) to indicate social inferiority. Other forms of symbolic integration have their roots in paternalism and ritual religious kinship, so that poorer, darker Brazilians frequently have much wealthier, whiter godparents. Their mutual obligations unite them in pseudo-familial forms. Also, many aspects of culture—*candomble,* the *samba,* the samba schools that parade at *Carnaval*—have been coopted by whites and are now dominated by them. Without providing social or economic equality, these symbolic forms give non-white Brazilians a sense of contributing to the national culture, of integration with whites, and of social mobility.

Finally, the ideology of racial democracy claims that there is no racism or *de jure* racial discrimination in Brazil. Brazilians have never been subject to any system of legally sanctioned segregation or discrimination. Legally enforced, separate facilities and interracial violence have not existed in Brazil. Social and economic opportunities are seen as equal for whites and blacks. Racial problems are simply denied.

Discrimination and disadvantage are seen as the products of class prejudice, not racism. In addition, if an individual is not successful in improving his social position, it is considered to be the fault of the individual victim. Individualism obscures failures of "racial democracy" much as subcultural traits obscure the predictive failures of assimilationist theory. These views are held by whites and non-whites alike, as well as by political and labor leaders. By the same reasoning, organization along racial lines is open to political attack as racist and, on occasion, has been repressed by government action. Not only are whites consequently relieved of responsibility for the status of non-white Brazilians, but race is prevented from becoming a principle of either collective identity or political action.

Given the combined strengths of the still existing color-class continuum, the desirability of "whitening," the many forms of symbolic integration, the underpinnings of individualism, the potent influence of "racial democracy" in popular Brazilian thought, and the resulting structure of cumulative disadvantage for non-white Brazilians, it appears most unlikely that the ideal of racial equality will be achieved through the market-like processes of individual social mobility.

NOTES

1. The most recent data for assessing racial inequalities are those of the

Pesquisa Nacional por Amostra de Domicílios (Fundacão IBGE, 1976) and the U.S. Census Bureau's 1978 Current Population Survey. For the United States' comparisons, we rely heavily on Farley's summarization (1980:8-22). For Brazil, the PNAD consists of a national probability sample of 120,000 households, and in 1976 included a supplement, consisting of 20% of the sample, on intergenerational social mobility.

Since 1950, race has not been systematically counted in the Brazilian census. In 1950, non-whites were 37.5% of the population. "Non-white" includes the PNAD's self-selected, precoded categories of *preto* (black), *pardo* (brown), and *amarelo* (yellow).

2. In 1950, non-whites comprised 37.9% of the economically active population. In the economically developed Southeast, non-whites were 17% of the economically active, but 15.8% of the total population; in the rest of Brazil, non-whites were 53% of the population and 54.7% of the economically active.

3. Immigration and intermarriage have "lightened" the Brazilian population. Census reports of racial composition were: in 1890, 56% of the population was reported to be non-white, compared to 37.5% in 1950.

REFERENCES

Blauner, Robert. *Racial Oppression in America.* New York: Harper and Row. 1972.

Blumer, Herbert. "Industrialization and Race Relations," in Guy Hunter, ed., *Industrialization and Race Relations.* London: Oxford University Press. 1965, pp. 220-253.

Bowles, Samuel. "Understanding Unequal Economic Opportunity." *American Economic Review 63: (1973) pp. 346-356.*

Conrad, Robert. *The Destruction of Brazilian Slavery 1850-1888.* Berkeley: University of California Press. 1972.

Cox, Oliver C. *Caste, Class, and Race.* New York: Modern Reader. 1970.

de Azevedo, Thales. *As Elites de Cor, Um Estudo de Ascensão Social.* São Paulo: Companhia Editora Nacional. 1955.

de Oliveira, Lucia Elena Garcia *et al.* "O 'Lugar do Negro' na Forca de Trabalho," IV Encontro da Associação Nacional de Pesquisa e Pós-Graduação em Ciencias Sociais, Rio de Janeiro. Paper presented, 1980.

Farley, Reynolds. "Racial Progress in the Last Two Decades." Xerox. 1980.

142

Fernandes, Florestan. *A Integração do Negro na Sociedade de Classes,* 2 vols. São Paulo: Daominus. 1965.

_____. *O Negro no Mundo dos Brancos.* São Paulo: Difusão Européia do Livro. 1972.

Fundação IBGE. *Pesquisa Nacional Por Amostro De Domicílios,* Rio de Janeiro: O Grupo Executivo de Pesquisas Domiciliares. 1976.

Freyre, Gilberto. *New World in the Tropics.* New York: Vantage Books. 1954.

_____. *Casa Grande e Senzala.* Rio de Janeiro: José Olimpio. 1973.

Hasenbalg, Carlos. "Race Relations In Post-Abolition Brazil: The Smooth Preservation of Racial Inequalities." Berkeley: University of California. Doctoral Dissertation. 1978.

_____. "Race and Socioeconomic Inequalities in Brazil," Symposium on Race and Class in Brazil, University of California at Los Angeles. Paper. 1980.

Park, Robert E. *Race and Culture—The Collected Papers of Robert Ezra Park,* ed. Hughes, Everett, *et al.* Glencoe: The Free Press. 1950.

Pierson, Donald. *Negroes in Brazil: A Study of Race Contact in Bahia.* Chicago: The University of Chicago Press. 1942.

Poulantzas, Nicos. *As Classes Sociais no Capitalismo de Hoje.* Rio de Janeiro: Zahar. 1975, pp. 34-35.

Silva, Nelson do Valle. "Cor e o Processo de Realização Socio-Econômica," IV Encontro da Associação Nacional de Pós-Graduação e Pesqûisa em Ciencias Sociais, Rio de Jâneiro. Paper. 1980.

Stinchcombe, Arther. "The Structure of Stratification Systems," in D. L. Sills, ed., *International Encyclopedia of the Social Sciences.* New York: Macmillan and Free Press. 1968, pp. 325-332.

Wagley, Charles. *Race and Class in Rural Brazil.* New York: Columbia University Press. 1963.

_____. "From Caste to Class in North Brazil," in Melvin Tumin, ed., *Comparative Perspectives in Race Relations.* Boston: Little, Brown & Co. 1969.

Race and Class in Brazil: Historical Perspectives*

Thomas E. Skidmore

Our understanding of modern-day race relations in Brazil rests primarily on research done between 1945 and 1965. To appreciate the context of that work, we need to look at the history of Sociology and Anthropology in Brazil. Before 1945 both disciplines were in the early stages of development, centered largely in São Paulo, with clusters of researchers also in Rio de Janeiro and Bahia. The 1930s had seen the influx of influential foreign scholars, such as Donald Pierson, Roger Bastide, And Emílio Willems. All played important roles in the development of graduate faculties at the University of São Paulo (USP) and the Escola Livre de Sociologia e Política, both in São Paulo.[1] One of the most significant publications of this era was by the U.S. scholar, Pierson, whose *Negroes in Brazil* (Chicago, 1942) remains an outstanding research work on Bahia and the Northeast, although its conclusions are now generally rejected.[2]

With the end of the war, there was a new inflow of foreign interest that reinforced the efforts of the still-small community of Brazilian researchers. Prominent among the non-Brazilians were North American Anthropologists, especially from Columbia University, and French scholars. Most knowledgeable among the French was Roger Bastide, who had been in Brazil since 1938 and had already won USP support to begin a large-scale survey research project on race relations in São Paulo. Key Brazilian scholars included Florestan Fernandes (University of São Paulo) and Thales de Azevedo (Federal University of Bahia). Among those who distinguished themselves in this field were Charles Wagley, Marvin Harris, Costa Pinto, René Ribeiro, Oracy Nogueira, Fernando Henrique Cardoso, Octavio Ianni and Arthur Ramos. To these researchers, and their collaborators, we largely owe our present knowledge of race relations.

From this body of scholarship have emerged several themes.[3] Most relevant for our purposes is the direct (sometimes explicit) challenge to the long prevailing view of Brazil as a "racial democracy." In its more extreme form, that belief held that race and skin color make virtually no difference in Brazil. In the

Luso-Brazilian Review XX, 1   0024-7413/83/0104 $1.50

words of one prominent Brazilian writer, "the highest, most significant and most edifying aspect of our culture is racial brotherhood . . . ."[4] If there are few Brazilians of dark color at the
higher levels of society, that simply reflects past disadvantages
—poverty and the lack of education which inevitably accompanied
slavery. The elite belief was well stated by the President of the
National Congress: "In Brazil, access to society depends upon individual effort, intellectual ability, and merit. . . . We have
all inherited common attributes, and what we are building—
socially, economically and politically—proves the correctness of
our rejection of the myths of racial superiority."[5] If race does
play a part in stratification, this view holds, it is small. At
the margin, Brazilians may not give the benefit of the doubt to a
darker person, but the frequency is not great enough to alter the
fact that Brazil is substantially free of racial discrimination.

How did Brazil reach this harmonious state? The answer, say
believers in its "racial democracy," is to be found in Brazilian
history. Almost willy nilly, the Portuguese created a multi-racial
slave-based society with a large free colored population. Portuguese colonization seemed somehow immune to racial prejudice. In
the words of the Congress President, "In our land the three ethnic
groups interacted to produce the union of which we are the expression and synthesis."[6] The Portuguese male was crucial in this
process. At home he had known the charms of dark-skinned Moorish
women, and thus it is not surprising that in the New World he suc-
cumbed to the Indian, and later African, women. This trend was
reinforced by the absence of women among the Portuguese explorers
and colonists. The inevitable outcome was miscegenation. Most
important for future race relations, however, was the fact that
Portuguese men had guilty consciences, as well as strong libidos.
As a result, they often manumitted the mixed-blood offspring they
had sired by their slave women. This affectionate weakness for
the illegitimate progeny led directly to the sharp contrast between the fate of those of color in Brazil and the U.S. This sim-
plistic historical view was well expressed in the 1940s by Waldo
Frank, a minor U.S. literary figure who often travelled to Latin
America: "Why is the difference so great between the exploited
Negro of Brazil and the exploited Negro of the United States?
Because the latter have known lust and greed of their masters;
the former, lust and greed no less, but tenderness also."[7]

This belief in "racial democracy," whether it fitted the historical facts or not, has been the operating racial ideal among
the elite since at least 1920. Faith in "whitening" was the result of the elite's struggle to reconcile the facts of Brazilian
social relations (no clear line between white and non-white) with
the doctrines of scientific racism that had penetrated Brazil from
abroad. It also implied that the inexorable process of whitening
would produce a white (or light tan?) Brazil. Thus would the
legacy of the Portuguese libido "solve" Brazil's race problem.
This remained the elite view through the Second World War—not-
withstanding the fact that "scientific racism" had become discredited in academic circles by the 1930s.[8]

The 1930s were also the years that elsewhere saw the application of one of History's most vicious racisms: anti-semitism. In the aftermath of 1945, the Europeans looked abroad for models of inter-racial peace. Hadn't Brazil for years been disproving the racist shibboleths about miscegenation? In 1950 UNESCO decided to study Brazil's harmonious race relations and share Brazil's secret with the world.[9] International teams of scholars, primarily Anthro-pologists, undertook field research around the country, following common research goals. Such international recognition was a high-water mark of reinforcement for the Brazilian elite's belief in their "racial democracy." In fact, however, this and succeeding research played the opposite role: it raised serious questions about, and partially discredited, their image of Brazilian society.[10]

Other factors were also at work eroding the image. An impor-tant element in the definition of Brazil's "racial democracy" had always been the contrast with the United States.[11] The U.S. phenomena of segregation and racial violence (urban riots, lynch-ings, etc.) were unknown in Brazil. Even if there had once been onerous barriers to black advancement, Brazil had never been in-fected with the race hatred so evident in the U.S. Whatever the precise explanation for the difference, Brazilians could say that their country had the distinction (hadn't UNESCO said as much?) of representing man's best future.

But the U.S. was changing. The Supreme Court decision of 1965 sounded the death knell for racial segregation, and subsequent legislation closed virtually every loophole sought by the die-hard racists. Where once the law had been used to segregate, now it was used to integrate. Both uses assumed a clearly defined bi-racial society. Both stemmed from the assumption that race is a fundamental (the most fundamental?) characteristic of North Americans. From the Brazilian viewpoint, it might at first appear that the North Americans, by finally eliminating legal color bars, were merely catching up to the Brazil of the early nineteenth cen-tury, when its few color bars, inherited from the colonial era, disappeared. The difference in the U.S., however, was the mili-tancy and organization of non-whites. In the non-violent resis-tance movement, led by Southern clergymen such as Martin Luther King, blacks forcefully claimed their "rights." Since final abo-lition (1888) at least, Brazilian non-whites had never shown a comparable degree of initiative. U.S. society, the major point of reference for Brazilians when describing their "racial democracy," had changed in a basic way.

Another shift in the Brazilian elite's foreign points of refer-ence came in Africa. There, as in Asia, the Second World War brought in its wake a cry for decolonization. The remaining em-pires of Britain, France, Holland and Belgium were now an unpleas-ant reminder of the era when white Europeans, using racist lan-guage, had taken control of much of today's "Third World." In Africa, the departure of the empires and their ruling whites paved the way for the appearance on the world scene of nations totally governed by blacks. This trend contradicted one of the central assumptions of the Brazilian belief in "whitening": the closer to his African origins, the less civilized the man of color. Indeed, faith in "whitening" was based on the assumption that the superior racial element, i.e., white, was prevailing. Now Africa had black (not even mulatto) nations. These new peoples wanted no part of "whitening," a doctrine that assumed assimilation, if not liquidation, of African identity. As in the case of U.S. desegregation, history was removing the very landmarks that had helped anchor the Brazilian elite in its racial beliefs.

Brazil's relation to Africa was further complicated by the fact that her mother country, Portugal, was the last European power to relinquish its African colonies. It was a Brazilian, Gilberto Freyre, who had spelled out the most ambitious doctrine ("Luso-tropicalism") to justify Portuguese colonialism. He argued that the Portuguese were the only European colonizers to create a new civilization in the tropics, an accomplishment attributable above all to their racial tolerance. The logical conclusion was that the Lusitanian legacy would spare Portugal the anti-colonial violence found elsewhere in Africa. Freyre himself remained a staunch defender of Portuguese colonial rule.[12]

Thanks to Salazar's repressive regime and an enormous per capita investment of resources, the Portuguese government prolonged its rule over Angola and Mozambique into the 1970s. By the time the armed struggle began in Africa, Brazil had a military government that was completely committed to the Salazar policy. Freyre, an enthusiastic adherent to the 1964 "Revolution" that installed the military, gained increased publicity for his Lusotropical theories. Meanwhile, government censorship presented an open debate over Brazil's African policy.

As Salazar finally faded from power in the early 1970s, it was his Army officers who pushed for withdrawal from Africa. The peoples of Portuguese Africa won independence, and many whites left. After those events were well underway, Brazil also experienced political change. The end of the Geisel presidency (1974-79) brought an "opening," and the possibility for rethinking Brazil's African interests and policies. One recent incident shows how this new relationship can call into question the Brazilian elite's image of their nation's race relations.

Brazil's leading TV network, Rede Globo, had broadcast in 1978-79 a TV series for children, adapted from stories by the famous children's writer, Monteiro Lobato. Brazilians generally considered it a high-level effort for the children's hour. Angolan TV, which is state controlled, decided to take advantage of this Portuguese-language resource by broadcasting the series in early 1979. This was no precedent, since they had shown Globo's version of Jorge Amado's "Gabriela, Cravo e Canela," with no apparent problems. After seven installments, however, the Angolan TV authorities abruptly cancelled the childrens' series. It was "racist," they charged, because Negroes were depicted only in inferior positions. Most offensive was the role of Tia Nastácia, the sixty-year-old black cook whom the Angolans thought a caricature. Reaction in Brazil was rapid. Were the Angolans

justified? How should blacks be depicted? Had Lobato's characterization been faithfully rendered in the TV script? What is the
true meaning of Tia Nastácia's role in the household?, etc.[13]
Brazil is undoubtedly in for more such surprises in its cultural
relations with Africa. It is not the world Freyre had led the
Brazilian elite to expect.

Although Brazil's external points of reference in race relations—the U.S. and Portuguese Africa—changed fundamentally,
there was no immediate rethinking of race relations in Brazil.
That began only in the late 1970s. Why?

First, the Brazilian elite tenaciously defended their image of
Brazil as a racial democracy. They did it in a number of ways.
One was to attack as "unBrazilian" anyone who raised serious questions about race relations in Brazil. Such a tactic was common
among politicians, cultural luminaries, and media controllers.
The usual argument was: the only racial "problems" in Brazil result from the agitation of those who claim there are problems. An
interesting case is the reaction to a small "black is beautiful"
movement, primarily in Rio de Janeiro. In August, 1976, the
prominent Rio daily, *Jornal do Brasil*, ran a feature story on
"Black Rio," with photographs of black men with Afro hairstyles
and platform shoes. This publicity ignited an angry reaction from
readers who denounced the movement and its press coverage.
Critics implied that reporting on such "unBrazilian" groups was
itself divisive and unpatriotic. As for the movement, it was
branded by many whites as a foreign import, illustrating little
more than the "cultural alienation" into which Brazilian blacks
could slip.[14]

Such vigilance by the elite cannot alone, however, explain the
lack of debate. There was a second factor: government repression. After 1965, and especially after 1968, military governments
closely controlled the media and all public events. The government justified repression as necessary to meet the threat of
"subversion," which in the early 1970s did include a guerrilla
movement. But the military branded as "subversive" not only kid-
nappers with guns but social scientists with ideas. That was
bound to include academics who had raised questions about Brazil's
"racial democracy."

One of the most dramatic cases in point was the purge of
faculty at the University of São Paulo in 1969. Prominent among
those involuntarily retired were Florestan Fernandes, and his colleagues Fernando Henrique Cardoso and Octavio Ianni. Given their
well-known (although differing) ideological and political views,
it was not surprising that they were targets for "national security"-minded military. But can it be coincidental that they
were also among the handful of Brazil's researchers into race relations? And, that, by their research, writing and teaching,
they had raised troubling questions about the realities of
Brazilian race relations?[15]

The military government often intervened to suppress news that
contradicted the official image of racial harmony. Under full-
scale censorship from 1969 until gradual liberalization began in

1975, television and radio were closely watched. Vigilance was especially intense on the popular TV soap operas ("telenovelas"), as well as on samba songs. TV scripts rejected by the censors more often than once had to do with race relations.[16]

Such a preoccupation also appeared in the censorship of the print media. In 1973 a new journal of opinion, *Argumento*, appeared on the newsstands in São Paulo. It was quickly confiscated by the authorities. On the cover was an African-looking boy and the title of an article inside which was a comparative analysis of post-abolition race relations in Brazil and the U.S.[17] Although the police gave no explanation, many observers thought the article on race relations had, at least in part, provoked their action. Another example of such action was the Brazilian government's 1978 decision to bar the Inter-American Foundation from further activity in Brazil. Brazilian authorities felt that this foundation, financed by U.S. government-originated funds but operating independently from other U.S. agencies, was supporting "subversive" Brazilian organizations. Among the groups receiving financing were three black organizations whose stated purpose of "consciousness raising" undoubtedly displeased Brasília.[18]

A third example of government sensitivity came in connection with a scholarly conference on blacks in the Americas, scheduled for Bogotá, Colombia in August, 1977. Countries were invited to send delegations, on the usual assumption that each government would finance their delegates' travel. Not so in Brazil. Brasília dragged its feet on the travel authorization until it was too late, and most of the Brazilians missed the meeting.[19]

Another incident of the late 1960s was the most revealing of all: the decision to omit race from the census of 1970. The opponents of racial identification argued that the language of racial categories (*preto*, *negro*, *mulatto*, *moreno*, etc.) was applied so inconsistently that meaningful data collection would be impossible.[20] No responsible observer would dispute the fact that there is a problem. Yet the Census Commission's radical solution of eliminating race altogether precluded *any* data gathering by race. Undoubtedly many Commission members who voted for this policy genuinely believed that race was unstudiable. In doing so, they were reflecting the elite consensus that race was not an independent variable in Brazilian society. Without data, of course, discussion would continue being reduced to the anecdotal level. That is where defenders of Brazil's racial myth have always preferred to operate, dwelling on examples of famous Brazilians whose physical features bore little relation to their station in life.

There was a third factor responsible for muting Brazilian discussion of race relations: the belief on the left that race is insignificant. Social class is the most fundamental variable, leftists argue, both for studying society and for changing it. Spokesmen of this view therefore usually dismissed race as a "false issue."[21] Since the left has remained very strong in the university faculties that produce most Brazilian researchers, its negative attitude toward studying race relations has, ironically, helped contribute to the silence on race which was sought by the authoritarian government.[22]

In the late 1970s this picture began to change. Attention to
race increased, in a small but perceptible fashion. Brazilians of
color began to question publicly the myth of racial democracy.
With the gradual political opening pursued by the government of
President Ernesto Geisel (1974-1979), debate emerged into the
open.

The recent growth of the black movement contradicts everything
the predominant myth would have led us to suspect. Brazil now has
militant groups that may come to rival their most ambitious counterparts of the *Frente Negra* era in the 1930s. The *abertura* allowed many taboo topics to surface, with race relations high on
the list. Dramatic confirmation of this change came in the decision to include race in the 1980 census. Initially, the census
authorities wanted to follow the 1970 precedent of omitting race.
That created a strong reaction among the staff and the public, and
led to reconsideration and a reversal of the decision.[23] The less
repressive atmosphere surrounding the 1980 decision made more
likely the willingness to collect the data (if not wholly reliable) without which no informed discussion of race relations could
take place.

Before looking at the new attention to race in Brazil, it is
worth noting that a more traditional area of interest has never
lacked attention: Afro-Brazilian religion, folklore and art. Interest here centered on African origins and African survival.
Most familiar are the religious cults of *candomblé* in Bahia and
umbanda in Rio de Janeiro, both well known tourist attractions.
Included also are the "exotic" costumes and foods identified with
Africa. The (adopted) patron saints of this world are Gilberto
Freyre and Jorge Amado, who have gained much of their fame by
showing the Afro-Brazilian contribution to Brazilian culture and
national character. Although undoubtedly important and valuable,
the study and preservation of Afro-Brazilian beliefs and customs
has been politically very safe. It fits perfectly with the elite
view that Brazil's historic links to Africa are now essentially
quaint. Thus the recently-founded *Sociedade de Estudos da Cultura
Negra no Brasil* (Society for the Study of Negro Culture in Brazil)
in Brazil represented no threat to the government or elite
figures.[24] Another example was the *Semanas Afro-Brasileiras* held
at the Museum of Modern Art in Rio de Janeiro in 1974.[25] The emphasis of such groups has allowed them to avoid the thorny questions of present-day race relationships among Brazilians.

The new departure of the late 1970s was the promotion of racial
consciousness among Brazilians of color. Some leading activists
were researchers, but they did not sally forth with questionnaires
or interview forms. They felt they *knew* what the facts were.
Themselves of color, they passionately believed that Brazil's
claim to be a racial democracy was a fraud. They wanted Brazilians to know that their country's race relations bore no relation
to the idyllic scene praised by the elite and many foreigners.
This activist explosion has startled many. Is it possible that a
significant "black power" movement is arising in Brazil?

The militant tone of some current leaders, is more aggressive than that of any group since the Frente Negra of the 1930s. They repudiate whitening, still Brazil's dominant ideology of race relations, and argue for the virtues of blackness. Most important, they want to provoke colored Brazilians into racial consciousness. They want to act against what they see as white exploitation—a line of protest which has been taboo for colored Brazilians over the last forty years.

The new black protest movements are denouncing the conditions that Brazilian scholarship has long been documenting. To take one example, Thales de Azevedo, one of the *doyens* of Brazilian Anthropology, attacked the racial democracy myth by publishing a compilation of cases of racial discrimination as reported in the national press. Carlos Hasenbalg's important 1979 monograph used similar sources, and carried the analysis of discrimination to the most systematic level possible with the limited data then available.[26] Nelson do Valle Silva's paper for this symposium shows how important new economic data can be.[26a] Suddenly we seem to be on the threshold of a major debate about the role of race in Brazilian society.

Any debate is bounded by the terms in which it is defined. What will be the definitions for the debate on race? What are the questions to be posed? What is the subject to be studied? If it is race relations in the broadest sense, how should we proceed?

Research effort is needed on all fronts, not least the historical. Surprising as it might seem, our understanding of the history of Brazilian race relations is extremely uneven. Despite the fame of Gilberto Freyre's writing on Brazil's patriarchical past, and much recent work on slavery by many other scholars, we know all too little about some of the most important features of Brazilian social history. One is the historical experience of free persons of color, both in the colonial era and in the nineteenth century.

In the first half of the latter century, there was a strong mulatto movement, even with its own newspapers. An important imperial institution, the *Guarda Nacional*, had become a vehicle for mulatto mobility. By the 1840s the officer corps was heavily mulatto, since they were elected by the predominantly colored ranks. But this channel of mobility was abruptly closed in 1850, when the crown made officers appointive. The command soon turned markedly whiter.[27]

The questions are obvious: How extensive was this mulatto movement? What were its relationships to other Brazilians of color, slave and free? Why did the crown abolish the election of officers? Did the political and social elite see a threat from the mulatto movement? What did they give as the rationale for their actions?[28]

The early decades of the twentieth century provide similar questions. How do we explain the assertion of black/mulatto consciousness in the 1920s and 1930s?[29] Just as a century earlier, black newspapers appeared, aggressively promoting the cause of the Brazilian of color. Why did they appear then, in the 1920s,

and not immediately after final abolition (1888)? Were there unusual economic circumstances in the 1920s and 1930s? Were they
comparable to those of the early nineteenth century?

This twentieth-century movement was snuffed out by the authoritarian coup of 1937. The success in disbanding the black/mulatto
organizations was hardly surprising, given the fact that the Estado
Nõvo government (1937-45) was able to repress all opposition
groups. But the return of open government in 1945 did not see the
movement reappear, and two decades after 1945 saw nothing comparable to the black/mulatto movements of pre-1937, despite the
persistent organizing efforts of a few individuals, such as Abdias
do Nascimento.[30] That did not come until the late 1970s. Why?
Is there a general explanation for the militancy which erupted in
the late 1970s, the 1920s-1930s and the 1820s-1830s-1840s?

Part of the answer lies in a better understanding of the total
dynamics of Brazilian socio-economic history. Most important is a
deeper understanding of the role of the free person of color before slavery expired for good in 1888. Some of the most lasting
forms of interracial social behavior must have been established in
those years. The scholarly consensus has been that Brazil created
a multi-racial society, as contrasted to the bi-racial one in the
United States. In his extended comparison of the U.S. and Brazil,
Carl Degler suggested that the "mulatto escape hatch" was the key
to the difference. Yet Degler's book, the most thoughtful and
exhaustive comparative analysis of race relations in Brazil and
the U.S., gives virtually no hard evidence to support his thesis.
The reader searches in vain for historical documentation to show
that the mixed blood got preferential treatment. How do we know
that the mulatto enjoyed mobility? What are the data (census
records, tax records, court records) that confirm such mobility?
Degler could not provide such information because the necessary
research is only recently beginning to be done. The "escape
hatch" is a *plausible* explanation, but we await the evidence on
what actually happened.[31]

One priority area for investigation is relations between whites
and persons of color in the labor force. In the South of the
United States, for example, there was a period, roughly 1865 to
1900, when poor whites and newly freed blacks might have made common cause against the old agrarian order. Instead, white politicians successfully got poor whites to focus on threatened job competition with the blacks, instead of fundamental questions of
economic structure. As a result, the Jim Crow system became fixed
on the South and the cause of black progress was set back for
decades to come.[32]

Obviously there are perils in carrying historical comparisons
too far. It might well be argued that by the time of the Emancipation Proclamation in the U.S., there was no possibility for the
emergence of a multi-racial society. Yet some of the explanations
given for the U.S. case may suggest questions for the Brazilian
one. What were the racial attitudes of Brazilian workers? Were
they manipulated by employers who used such techniques to maximize
control over the labor force? We know, for example, that racist

sentiments helped divide Rio de Janeiro dockworkers in the 1910s and 1920s.[33] Did this happen in other sectors? Could such patterns be seen in earlier eras? What effect did these patterns have on subsequent race relations? Such questions are implicit in virtually all our attempts to explain present-day Brazilian race relations.

No amount of subsequent research and documentation, however helpful, will answer all our questions. Just as in the study of race relations in the United States, with its avalanche of monographs, symposia, and syntheses, the questions go too deep and in the end their meaning is too elusive for us to be satisfied with the answers provided by conventional social and economic history. In Brazil also, we shall find ourselves drawn toward examining "mentalities," habits of mind, and social beliefs. What is Brazilian about Brazilian race relations? Does it have anything to do with the now oft denigrated idea of Brazilian national character? There has been a long and rich debate over the Brazilian's alleged *cordialidade*.[34] Does that idea furnish any clues in our quest to understand how and why Brazil has created its particular form of multi-racial society? What about those qualities that anthropologists, sociologists and political scientists have explored—patrimonialism, paternalism and clientelism? However slippery these concepts may be for the historian, we must remind ourselves that the most enduring attempt to explain the United States—that of de Tocqueville—was built around a discussion of precisely those kinds of collective traits.[35]

Our efforts to understand Brazilian race relations will necessarily carry us into the ongoing debate about the nature of Brazilian society. It will thus parallel (and sometimes coincide with?) attention to the history of labor relations in Brazil, also inseparably linked to our views about the essence of Brazilian social relations.[36]

We are therefore brought to the elusive relationship between ideas and societies. Seen abstractly, they are socio-economic structures and ideologies. Seen historically, they come down to the many realities of human behavior and human thought. We appear to be on the verge of a new burst of inquiry into those realities. Although we shall ask new questions and produce new evidence, we shall be walking familiar ground.

NOTES

*This article is based on a paper prepared for a Symposium on "Race and Class in Brazil: New Issues and New Approaches" at the Center for Afro-American Studies, University of California, Los Angeles, in February 1980.

[1]For a first-hand description of the early years in the growth of Anthropology and Sociology, see Florestan Fernandes, *A sociologia no Brasil* (Petrópolis: Ed. Vozes, 1977), esp. chapter 8. A useful summary of the most relevant researchers and

institutions may be found in Charles Wagley, "Anthropology and
Brazilian National Identity," in Maxine L. Margolis and William E.
Carter, eds., *Brazil: Anthropological Perspectives* (New York:
Columbia University Press, 1979), 1-18.

[2]Donald Pierson, *Negroes in Brazil: A Study of Race Contact at
Bahia* (Chicago: University of Chicago Press, 1942). It was reprinted with the text unchanged (Carbondale/Edwardsville: Illinois
University Press, 1967), but with a long introduction by Pierson,
where he defended his original approach, which had emphasized
class as perhaps more important than race in determining social
position.

[3]An excellent synthesis of present-day scholarly views on
Brazilian race relations is John Saunders, "Class, Color and
Prejudice: A Brazilian Counterpoint," in Ernest Q. Campbell, ed.,
Racial Tensions and National Identity (Nashville: Vanderbilt
University Press, 1972), 141-169. Barriers to collective mobility
are reviewed in Maria Isaura Pereira de Queiroz, "Coletividades
negras: ascensão sócio-econômica dos negros no Brasil e em S.
Paulo," *Ciência e Cultura*, vol. 29, no. 6 (June 1977), 647-663.
One of the most successful efforts to place Brazil within a frame-
work of world-wide race relations is Michael Banton, *Race Relations* (London: Tavistock Publications, 1967), 258-282. For an
excellent survey, which emphasizes the lack of more recent work
on race in Brazil, see Pierre-Michel Fontaine, "Research in the
Political Economy of Afro-Latin America," *Latin American Research
Review*, vol. XV, no. 2 (1980), 111-141.

[4]The speaker was Vianna Moog, appearing before the highly-
prestigious *Escola Superior de Guerra. Jornal do Brasil*,
August 3, 1972.

[5]The remarks were by Senator Petronio Portella, speaking on the
International Day for the Elimination of Discrimination. *O Globo*,
April 6, 1977.

[6]This comes from Senator Petronio Portella's speech, as
reported in *Correio Brasiliense*, April 6, 1977.

[7]Waldo Frank, *South American Journey* (New York: Duell, Sloan
and Pearce, 1943), 50-51.

[8]The emergence of the "whitening" ideal is traced in Skidmore,
Black Into White (New York: Oxford University Press, 1974).

[9]There is a brief discussion of the UNESCO project, along with
citation of the principal sources, in Pierre-Michel Fontaine,
"Research in the Political Economy of Afro-Latin America," *Latin
American Research Review*, vol. XV, no. 2 (1980), 124; and in
Skidmore, *Black Into White*, 215-216.

[10]It has been argued that one of the senior Brazilian researchers, Florestan Fernandes, believed from the outset that the project
would "show that UNESCO was wrong, that the Negro was not equal in
Brazil." The source is Fernando Henrique Cardoso, a collaborator
in the project, as interviewed in Joseph A. Kahl, *Modernization,
Exploitation and Dependency in Latin America* (New Brunswick:
Transaction Books, 1976), 131. Looking back on the UNESCO-
sponsored research after twenty-five years, Fernandes concluded
that "if the study has done nothing else then, it has unmasked the

myth of racial democracy in the country," Fernandes, "The Negro in Brazilian Society: Twenty-Five Years Later," in Margolis and Carter, eds., *Brazil: Anthropological Perspectives*, 100.

[11]For a discussion of possible approaches in comparing the U.S. and Brazil, see Skidmore, "Toward a Comparative Analysis of Race Relations Since Abolition in Brazil and the United States," *Journal of Latin American Studies*, vol. 4, pt. 1 (May 1972), 1-28.

[12]Gilberto Freyre, *O mundo que o Português criou* (Rio de Janeiro: José Olympio, 1940); Gilberto Freyre, *Aventura e rotina* (Rio de Janeiro: José Olympio, 1953).

[13]Ida Lobato, "Fala, Tia Nastácia!" *Folha de São Paulo*, February 17, 1979; Mirna Pinsky, "Angola x Lobato," Folhetim of *Folha de São Paulo* , March 4, 1979.

[14]The story covered four pages of the widely-read "Caderno B," a highly prized source for publicity on the arts in Brazil. The emotions stirred up by the story can be seen in the letters published in same paper on August 3, 1976. Ten months later "Black Rio" had supposedly won twenty thousand followers in São Paulo, an alarming development in the eyes of some samba composers, *Folha de São Paulo*, June 11, 1977.

[15]Details on the purges at USP, including a number of contemporary documents, may be found in *O Livro negro da USP: o controle ideólogico na universidade* (São Paulo: Ed. Brasiliense, 1979).

[16]For a general account of censorship, see Peter T. Johnson, "Academic Press Censorship under Military and Civilian Regimes: The Argentine and Brazilian Cases, 1964-1975," *Luso-Brazilian Review*, vol. 15, no. 1 (Summer 1978), 3-25. Details on censorship of TV programming are given in a long dispatch on race relations in Brazil by the *New York Times* correspondent, David Vidal, in the issue for June 5, 1978.

[17]*Argumento*, Ano 1, No. 1 (Outubro 1973). The article was my "O Negro no Brasil e nos Estados Unidos," a translation, without the footnotes, of Skidmore, "Toward a Comparative Analysis of Race Relations Since Abolition in Brazil and the United States," *Journal of Latin American Studies*, vol. 4, pt. 1 (May 1972), 1-28.

[18]One of the grants was for an Instituto de Pesquisa das Culturas Negras, which aimed "to assist Brazilian black communities to appreciate their own history, to achieve more effective participation in development, and a more just distribution of wealth," *Journal of the Inter-American Foundation*, Summer 1977, 17.

[19]Letter to the editor from Sebastião Rodrigues Alves in *Visão*, November 28, 1977; *Versus*, October 1977, 34.

[20]A brief discussion of the controversy may be found in Skidmore, *Black Into White*, 218. It should be noted that race was included in the 1976 National Household Survey (PNAD).

[21]A scholar who has offered one of the more subtle approaches emphasizing class is Octavio Ianni. See, for example, his *Escravidão e racismo* (São Paulo: Editora Hucitec, 1978).

[22]For a stinging attack on the Brazilian left because it played into the hands of the "reactionaries" by refusing to see that race is not reducible to class in Brazil, see Abdias do Nascimento, "O Negro e o Brasil na década dos 80," *Singular & Plural*, February

1979, 28-29.

[23]My sources are staff members in the IBGE (Instituto Brasileiro de Geografia e Estatística), who were first-hand observers of these events.

[24]The Sociedade's publication is *Sárépegbé*, the first number appearing dated January/March 1975. The Sociedade was founded in 1974. A conference on Afro-Brazilian religious syncretism, held in Bahia in 1976 was another example. Some of the papers and discussions were published in *Revista de Cultura: Vozes*, vol. 71, no. 7 (September 1977).

[25]Even this group ran into difficulties when they planned a series of public seminars to discuss black culture and Brazilian-African relations. The seminars were vetoed by the authorities, although the art exhibition came off without any problems. Details on the planning and the nature of the exhibits may be found in *Revista de Cultura: Vozes*, vol. 71, no. 9 (November 1977).

[26]Thales de Azevedo, *Democracia racial: ideologia e realidade* (Petrópolis: Editora Vozes, 1975). Carlos A. Hasenbalg, *Discriminação e desigualdades raciais no Brasil* (Rio de Janeiro: Ed. Graal, 1979).

[26a]This paper has now been published: Nelson do Valle Silva, "O Preço da Cor; diferenciais raciais na distribuição da renda no Brasil," *Pesquisa e Planejamento*, vol. 10, No. 1 (April 1980), 21-44. See also the important recent additional analysis by the same author in "Cor e o Processo de Realização socio-econômica," *Dados*, vol. 24, No. 3 (1981), 391-409.

[27]The case of the *Guarda Nacional* is studied in Jeanne Berrance de Castro, *A Milícia cidadã: a Guarda Nacional de 1831 a 1850* (São Paulo: Companhia Editora Nacional, 1977). Castro's emphasis on race is disputed in Thomas Flory, "Race and Social Control in Independent Brazil," *Journal of Latin American Studies*, vol. 9, pt. 2 (November 1977), 199-224.

[28]In his important article on race relations in the three decades after independence (1822), Flory argues that the elite succeeded in obscuring the racial issue in a manner that sounds very twentieth-century: "By 1841 abiding reactionary changes in social attitudes and the structures of authority had taken place in Brazil, and the negative outcomes of the race question was one reason for the changes. Genuine race fear, by definition, could not often be mentioned aloud, while constitutional restrictions and ideology prevented racially exclusive legislation. So in informal attitudes as well as in formal regulation, the race problem shaded into a social problem after 1835, and the full range of reaction was therefore directed at social categories described by behavior and class rather than by skin color." Thomas Flory, "Race and Social Control."

[29]There is no general history of black and/or mulatto movements in modern Brazil, aside from the abolitionist era. That is hardly surprising, since so little research has been done on the subject. The most detailed accounts of the movements of the 1920s and 1930s are in Roger Bastide and Florestan Fernandes, *Brancos e negros em São Paulo* (São Paulo: Companhia Editora Nacional, 1971),

3rd ed., 229-268; and Roger Bastide, *Estudos Afro-Brasileiros* (São Paulo: Editora Perspectiva, 1973), 129-156. Signs of growing interest in this history from "official" cultural quarters could be seen in a June 1977 exhibition on "A imprensa negra em São Paulo, 1918-1965," which received national publicity, as in *Isto E*, June 22, 1977. It was organized and sponsored by the *Secretaria da Cultura, Ciência e Tecnologia* of the São Paulo state government.

[30] In the Constituent Assembly of 1946 one Senator denounced what he saw as widespread racial discrimination. His speech and subsequent efforts, largely unsuccessful, at mobilizing black/mulatto protest are described in Rodrigues Alves, *A Ecologia do grupo afro-brasileiro* (Rio de Janeiro: Ministério da Educação e Cultura, 1966); further details on this period can be found in Abdias do Nascimento, org., *O Negro revoltado* (Rio de Janeiro: Edições GRD, 1968).

[31] Among the most important analyses of the fate of the free person of color until 1888 are A. J. R. Russell-Wood, "Colonial Brazil," in David W. Cohen and Jack P. Greene, eds., *Neither Slave Nor Free* (Baltimore: Johns Hopkins University Press, 1972); Herbert S. Klein, "The Colored Freedmen in Brazilian Slave Society," *Journal of Social History*, vol. 3, no. 1 (Fall 1969), 30-52. Much valuable information on the patterns of manumission has been published in Stuart B. Schwartz, "The Manumission of Slaves in Colonial Brazil: Bahia, 1684-1745," *Hispanic American Historical Review*, vol. 54, no. 4 (November 1974), 603-635; Luiz R. B. Mott, "Brancos, pardos, pretos e índios em Sergipe: 1825-1830," *Anais de História*, vol. VI (1974), 139-184. For evidence of occupational mobility among slaves in Rio (which has great relevance for investigating the mobility of free men of color), see Mary Karasch, "From Porterage to Proprietorship: African Occupations in Rio de Janeiro, 1808-1850," in Stanley L. Engerman and Eugene D. Genoves, eds., *Race and Slavery in the Western Hemisphere: Quantitative Studies* (Princeton: Princeton University Press, 1975). One scholar concluded his recent study of the 1822-1850 period thus: "Although the system's blurred distinctions did provide a way for a few mulattoes to rise—a mulatto escape hatch—too many historians have failed to note that the same set of conditions also placed a trapdoor under Brazilians of all colors," Flory, "Race and Social Control," 224.

[32] The classic work describing this process is C. Vann Woodward, *The Strange Career of Jim Crow*, 2nd rev. ed. (New York: Oxford University Press, 1966).

[33] Sheldon L. Maram, "Anarcho-syndicalism in Brazil," in *Proceedings of Pacific Coast Council on Latin American Studies*, vol. 4 (1975), 101-116; Maram, "Labor and the Left in Brazil, 1890-1921, A Movement Aborted," *Hispanic American Historical Review*, vol. 57, no. 2 (May 1977), 254-272; Maram, "Urban Labor and Social Change in the 1920s," *Luso-Brazilian Review*, vol. 16, no. 2 (Winter 1979), 215-223.

[34] The best introduction to the historic debate over the essential nature of Brazil's "social personality" is Dante Moreira

Leite, *O caráter nacional brasileiro* (São Paulo: Livraria
Pioneira Editôra, 1969).

[35]Alexis de Tocqueville, *Democracy in America* (Garden City:
1969).

[36]It cannot be coincidental that the political opening brought
a burst of attention to previously taboo topics—race relations
and labor relations.   I have discussed the latter in a comparative
framework in "Workers and Soldiers: Urban Labor Movements and
Elite Responses in Twentieth-Century Latin America," in Virginia
Bernhard, ed., *Elites, Masses, and Modernization in Latin America,
1850-1930* (Austin: University of Texas Press, 1979).

Peasant Politics and the Mexican State: Indigenous Compliance in Highland Chiapas

George A. Collier
Stanford University

Se trata de la política de indígenas Tzotziles y Tzeltales de Chiapas dentro del marco del estado. Alternaciones en la política indigenista y agraria del estado Mexicano influyen al caracter fragmentario y faccional de la vida política de pueblos indígenas, deprimiendo conciencia de clase y subrayando un clientelismo y un caciquismo bastante restringidos en su poder.

In her incisive review of recent approaches to the problem of "What Makes Peasants Revolutionary?" Theda Skocpol (1982:373) cautions that "Too close a focus on peasants themselves, even on peasants within local agrarian class and community structures, cannot allow us to understand peasant-based revolutions." Peasants are only ever part of a revolutionary story whose plot hinges critically on such factors as internal and external sources of weakness of the state and the role of military and other outside organizing forces in mobilizing peasantries.

Many of the same admonitions are apt in considering the related question of "What makes peasants *un*-revolutionary?" Peasant conservatism has to be understood in a broad context. Jeffrey Paige (1975), for example, relates the world-market context of export enclaves to relations among agrarian classes that make landholding peasants conservative within them. Another important dimension of peasant conservatism is the political context of national states. Here again, holistic approaches to the study of peasants in states, such as Warman's (1980) groundbreaking analysis of the peasants of Morelos and the Mexican national State, are required to discern how national States bring about the political subordination of peasantries.

Mexican Studies/Estudios Mexicanos 3 (1), Winter 1987. © 1987 Regents of the University of California.

This is a study of the political involvement of Indians in the highlands of Chiapas in the post-Revolutionary Mexican State up through the late 1960s. In the wake of the Mexican Revolution, an increasingly powerful State promulgated policies that semi-proletarianized the peasantry throughout central and southern Mexico. These policies also effectively shaped and controlled grass-roots politics and contained the potential for organized dissidence.

The political subordination of the peasantry to the national State evolved along several dimensions. First, as the State grew in power through its increasingly redistributive role, it effectively coopted one, then another sector of Mexican society. Villagers at the margins of haciendas and agrarian workers returning to them from debt labor on haciendas were among the earliest groups coopted, through land reform. Land reform elicited and legitimated local-level peasant leaders who would be beholden to the State even as it shifted the emphasis of political involvement to groups such as commercial farmers whose interests countered those of peasants.

Second, State policies segmented agrarian workers in a variety of ways tending to blunt their consciousness and potential for con-certed political action. Because of their partial control of means of production, peasant smallholders and *ejidatarios* distinguished themselves from agrarian proletarians even though they themselves grew increasingly dependent on laboring for exploitive wages to supplement ever more intensive subsistence cultivation. In areas of dense indigenous population, Indianist policies of the 1940s and 1950s segmented Indian communities one from another and from the larger agrarian working class.

Finally, the shift in state policy from one to another strategy for rural development parochialized and factionalized local-level po-litics by displacing the leaders who had brokered one program with rivals willing to broker the next.

State Agrarian Policy and the Peasantry

Throughout the post-Revolutionary period the State pursued policies with profoundly cyclical consequences for peasantries in an overall trend toward their increasing semi-proletarianization.[1] There were several periods—the early 1920s, the 1934–40 Cárdenas presidency, the opening of the 1950s—in which specific policies fa-

---

1. Reynolds (1970) presents the most authoritative analysis of economic trends of Mexico in this century. I have drawn from Warman (1980) and De la Peña (1981) in characterizing political and economic policy.

vored small-scale, increasingly intensive peasant production, and there were interludes favoring the alternative interests of commercial agriculture. Peasants experienced the ebb and flow of the State's political involvement of various interest groups that seems to have attained certain regularity in the post-Revolutionary period, the rhythm of which Lomnitz Adler (1984), following Skinner and Winckler (1969) and Etzioni (1961), relates to cycles of coalition in the compliance of interest groups within the dynamics of Mexican government.

Certain *caveats* must be borne in mind in so characterizing the post-Revolutionary period. To speak of the "State" and its "goals" and "accomplishments," as I will, glosses over the struggles that took place for control of government and the sometimes fortuitous ways in which historical circumstances complicated the interplay of forces resulting in what in retrospect seems to have been the State's course. For example, in the decade following the Mexican Revolution, Mexico's regions, dominated by local strongmen, were interconnected but poorly, and national government had fallen into the hands of military and ideological figures of the Revolution, many of whom were in competition with one another; yet in important ways the State began to assert a centralizing role then. Through time, as the State grew in power, the multivocality of those striving to control it increased, and contending coalitions struggled for power within it.

With this in mind, one can yet discern the State's initial, fundamental accomplishments, which were to consolidate its political power as a central actor in the economy. The State revived the entrepreneurial sector oriented toward export agriculture while placating the opposed interests of those agitating for agrarian reform, and established the central government as paramount over the revolutionary *caudillos* who governed various regions and federal states for their personal benefit.

The demands for agrarian reform were the first to be quieted by Obregón's distribution of land, primarily as restitution to villages of lands lost to *latifundias* under 19th-century liberal policies. By invalidating the earlier Zapatista redistributions in Morelos, and then redistributing in the name of the State,[2] Obregón's policies converted peasant recipients of land reform into loyal subordinates of the central State. But restitution was not allowed to undermine the

---

2. Reynolds (1970:138) characterizes the Zapatista redistribution as "anarchic reform," followed by "decentralized institutional reform" of Obregón and his successors. Only after 1934 did redistribution become "centralized institutional reform," with full support of the State apparatus.

integrity of the export agriculture on large estates thought to be indispensable for attracting foreign capital for investment and for financing imports and foreign debt. Left largely intact under Obregón, the latifundias were strengthened under Calles through public irrigation works and through the establishing of institutions for extending agrarian credit within a new State banking system. Meanwhile, after Obregón and Calles had put down the De la Huerta insurrection of 1924, and as former caudillos themselves began to emerge as a capitalist class based in export agriculture, the State successfully forced the compliance and won the involvement of another interest group, the military.[3]

The era of the peasant quickened with Mexico's responses to the collapse of world-market demand for exports after 1929. The collapse of the export sector curtailed the flow of foreign exchange to pay for industrial imports and of foreign investment to capitalize extractive industries and commercial agriculture. Under the six-year plan embraced by the Cárdenas presidency of 1934–40, the State responded to the collapse by trying to build up an internal economy in which new domestic industry would be subsidized by agrarian production, not of commercial exports, but of wage foods (Warman 1980: 159–161, 167–170). The State began to expropriate land from stagnant commercial estates to turn over to *ejidos* for peasant families to farm with family labor, or collectively so as to get by with minimal capital investment. The huge scale of peasant production thus stimulated[4] would keep down the price of foodstuffs, and hence wages could be kept low enough in the urban sector for industry to start up. At the same time, peasants' income from sale of crops would finance consumption of manufactures sufficiently to secure a domestic market for new industries, promulgated in key instances with State management.

The program required and engendered a powerful political apparatus, the populist Partido Revolucionario Mexicano, through which the State orchestrated the support of urban and agrarian labor and the peasantry against the owners of private estates (Warman 1980:186–190). Cárdenas did in fact redistribute millions of hectares to peasants in pursuit of this policy, leading to a veritable renaissance of peasant village life throughout central and southern Mexico based on subsistence cultivation with surplus crops sold into the marketplace.

3. Warman (1980:133–158) presents an excellent overview of these developments of the 1920s.
4. By the early 1940s, "much of the smallholder agriculture that had been eliminated during the Porfiriato was restored" (Reynolds 1970:141).

In the 1940s[5] the State began to favor a revival of commercial agriculture and development of import-substitution industrialization at the expense of the peasantries, policies leading to semi-proletarianization of the peasantry whose dynamics intensified during the 1950s.

The return to favor of commercial agriculture[6] began during World War II with revived U.S. demand for Mexican fruits, vegetables, fibers, and textiles. The flow of foreign exchange helped the State accelerate investment in large-scale infrastructure for commercial agriculture such as irrigation, mostly in the North, which had begun under Cárdenas (Reynolds 1970:142–3; Warman 1980:193–194). These developments favored capitalist farming on large estates of the sort against which Cárdenas had directed land reform in the 1930s. Under Avila Camacho and Alemán, the revival of commercial agriculture brought land reform to an abrupt halt, leaving peasants unrequited in their expectations of further redistribution if not setting back their gains under Cárdenas.

Meanwhile, the State promulgated import-substitution industrialization at the expense of the peasantry (Warman 1980:238–240; see also de Janvry 1981:123–125). Here too foreign revenues helped capitalize industrialization, but fiscal policies holding down the relative prices of foodstuffs and hence the level of wages stimulated industry's growth even more. The stimulus came about through ever greater extraction of surplus from peasant agriculture. Peasants could produce food cheaply in the first instance by farming with unpaid family labor.[7] Under Cárdenas, peasants had given up many traditional crafts when given land to farm, substituting manufactured wares. Now, as fiscal policy allowed manufactures to rise in price more rapidly than foodstuffs, peasants intensified their production simply to make ends meet.[8]

5. During this decade, the South Pacific region (in which Reynolds includes Chiapas) led the nation in growth of production both of commercial crops (such as coffee, cotton, etc.) and of staples (such as corn, beans). Reynolds attributes the growth in part to increased inputs of land and labor (1970:111) but also more significantly to road building and the incorporation of formerly uncultivated territory into cropping through use of underemployed local labor (1970:125).

6. Many *latifundias* had been left with their choice hectarage and production facilities intact (Reynolds 1970:149) after expropriation of less productive lands. Thus plantations were less disrupted than might otherwise have been the case.

7. Warman (1970) repeatedly argues that symmetrical, redistributive relations among peasants enabled them to produce without their labor being paid as a factor of production. This is something of an oversimplification. Peasant stratification also enabled some peasants to exploit others so as to produce crops cheaply.

8. Warman (1980) discusses this intensification in Morelos. Direct statistics on labor inputs are not generally available, but Reynolds (1970:147–148) infers intensification of labor in production on small holdings from his analysis of ejidal efficiency.

First they cultivated to the limits of the capacity of their land holdings; then they augmented income by working part-time, in the reviving sector of commercial agriculture, usually for wages of less-than-subsistence level as their own cultivation assured subsistence. This in turn held down wages throughout the economy much as did fiscal control of the price of foods. Thus peasants were partially proletarianized and increasingly exploited.[9]

As the dynamic of semi-proletarianization complementary to in-dustrialization and the growth of commercial agriculture intensified in the 1950s, the State began programs of rural community develop-ment to sustain peasant production and contribution to rural labor. Among these were the Indianist programs such as those established in central Chiapas to improve conditions of public health, build rural infrastructure, and draw Indians more fully into the economy.

Indians and the State in Chiapas 1920–1960

In examining how political organization in the Indian commu-nities of Central Chiapas responded to mid-twentieth century State policies and programs in the region, it is important not to lose sight of the Mexican State's political and economic policy at the most general level. State action in Chiapas, far from being particular to the region or distinctive for Indians, was at one with the most gener-alized agrarian policy. Like other regions, Chiapas experienced "peasantization" of the countryside through land reform of the 1930s and community development and *indigenismo* of the 1940s and 1950s. This is not to say that Central Chiapas and other regions experienced State policy identically; for example, the character and timing of impact varied with regions' centrality in the Mexican econ-omy.[10] The point is rather that the pertinent State policies and programs grew out of and participated in Mexico's most general po-litical and economic realities. Far from being a carryover of a back-ward, marginal existence, peasant life and politics as known to us in mid-20th century ethnography of Chiapas was quintessentially a product of its era.

9. As Reynolds puts it, "the rural smallholdings served as a sponge of unskilled labor that could be squeezed to provide workers when needed for growth of indus-try, services, and commercial agriculture at relatively constant real wages" (1970:154). See also de Janvry (1981:129).

10. See Reynolds (1970) for analyses differentiating five regions of Mexico in terms of the economic trends they experienced from 1900 to 1960. Chiapas falls in Reynolds' South Pacific region, which, with the Center region, has experienced rela-tively low levels of rural per-capita output because, in part, of the greater expansion of commercial cultivation in other regions (1970: 100–101).

At the outset of the 1920s, the victors and heirs of the Revolution had already radically altered the situation of Indians in central Chiapas by weakening regional elites who dominated them. Among these elites, lowland ranchers and plantation owners had gained the upper hand over conservative landowners of the central highlands during the Porfiriato, drawing highland Indian labor into debt servitude. But the revolutionaries abrogated lowland ranch and plantation owners' control of Indian labor by abolishing debt servitude and sending indentured Indian laborers back to their homes. They suppressed the head tax through which municipal officials had collaborated with ranchers in recruiting labor, and they instituted the *municipio libre* under which villages were to be self-governing through elected officials (Casahonda Castillo 1963; Wasserstrom 1983:156–157, 175–176). They also undercut conservative highland landowners' attempts to involve Indians in counter-revolutionary measures.[11]

While these developments relieved Indians of the domination they had experienced at the hands of the region's elites, Indians evidently were not important enough for the government to include in efforts to strike alliances with agrarian workers and peasant groups. For example, there is no evidence that politicization and grass-roots agitation for land reform encompassed Indians of the highlands in the same way as rural workers in the coffee-rich Soconusco zone, whose agitation and incorporation into socialist labor politics led the Obregón presidency to appease them with ejidos expropriated from coffee *fincas* (García de León 1979; Wasserstrom 1983:160–161). Although Indians of the highlands drew up a number of petitions for restitution of communal lands in the early 1920s, the State took almost no positive action on any of these petitions. In this respect Chiapas differed from Morelos.

Life in the Indian municipios thus turned in on itself during the 1920s much more so than in the case of more politicized peasantries that the State appeased and coopted early on elsewhere. There was a hiatus of ladino manipulation of municipal affairs, during which elders bulwarked their own positions of power as native leaders,

---

11. Under a Maderista banner, conservatives had involved a large number of Chamulas under the leadership of Jacinto Press Chixtot ("Pajarito") in an abortive move against lowlanders in 1911 (Wasserstrom 1983:157), and continued to court Indians in the counterrevolutionary endeavors of the decade that followed, notably those led by Alberto Piñeda (see Moscoso Pastrana 1960). Thus, like their counterparts in Oaxaca (Waterbury 1975), Indians were sometimes drawn into what proved to be reactionary alliances and did not emerge as a revolutionary force, as in Morelos.

emphasizing traditionalism (Rus 1976:12; Wasserstrom 1983:172–3). This also served as a defense against outside interference, as traditionalists were least likely to speak Spanish and thus could not collaborate with outsiders such as labor recruiters. Although the recruitment of labor through *enganchadores* did make inroads against these defenses (Rus 1976:8–10; Wasserstrom 1983:164, 166), nonetheless the traditionalists remained in charge of the civil-religious hierarchies and other municipal affairs.[12]

Not until the crisis of the post-1929 depression did the State begin directly to involve Indians of the Chiapas highlands, first in electoral politics, then in labor and land reform. In Chiapas, as elsewhere in Mexico, Cárdenas set out first to consolidate political control through his Partido Revolucionario Mexicano (PRM) into which organized labor and peasantries of the Confederación de Trabajadores Mexicanos and the Confederación Nacional Campesina had been amalgamated.

In the instance of Chiapas, this was done so as to undercut lowland ranching and coffee interests with whom Cárdenas's predecessors had accommodated. Choosing the gubernatorial elections of 1936 as the arena for this demonstration of power, Cárdenas put up his own candidate against that of the lowland interests, whipping up the agrarian and labor vote through the PRM. The delivering of the highland Indian vote was assigned to Erasto Urbina, a petty functionary whose peddler-class origins facilitated contacts with Indian towns throughout the region. The political situation thrust Urbina and Indians to prominence in the distribution of State rewards. Urbina became director of the region's new Departamento de Protección Indígena and quickly installed henchmen as *Secretarios* in Indian communities of the highlands, recruiting young Indian bilinguals through them to head up labor and land reform.[13]

Setting up the Sindicato de Trabajadores Indígenas was Urbina's major labor initiative (Rus 1976:23–26; Wasserstrom 1983:162–167). The STI took over from enganchadores the legal supplying of highland Indian labor to coffee fincas, regulating employment contracts, wages, and work conditions. It gave the government both clout over coffee interests by monopolizing access to Indian labor and power over Indians of the several highland municipios who re-

12. Rus (1976), focusing principally on Chamula, and Wasserstrom (1983), emphasizing Zinacantan, differ in the degree of autonomy they accord to indigenous traditionalists in their control of town governments in the 1920s, with Rus making a persuasive case for substantial ladino intervention in Chamula affairs (1976:10–13).

13. See Rus (1976:20–23) for the most cogent account of the politics leading to Urbina's ascendance during 1936–37. See also Wasserstrom (1983:162).

lied on seasonal wage labor to supplement subsistence. At the same time, it coopted young leaders of the municipio of Chamula to whom Urbina entrusted the STI's key posts.

Simultaneously, Urbina and his cadres initiated land reform in the highlands in a manner distinguishing Indians from other peasant groups as special clients of the State. This effort coincided both in timing and in goals with the Cárdenas presidency's national impetus for agrarian development through redistribution of land to peasants under the ejido. But in the highlands, bureaucratic intervention on behalf of Indians was withheld from federal agrarian agents that promulgated the ejido elsewhere and turned over to Urbina's agency. By the end of Cárdenas's term, only a fraction of former finca lands remained in non-Indian hands, and thousands of Indians had received use rights in ejidos through their leaders' collaboration with the State through its Indianist agency. Local-level ejido organizations, incorporated into the PRM, had emerged as the channels through which the State controlled indigenous municipal politics (Edel 1962; Rus 1976:25).

The State's attention to Chiapas's Indians waned during the 1940s' effort to stimulate import-substitution industrialization and then waxed during the 1950s in programs of rural community development. Once again the State worked through an Indianist organization, the Insituto Nacional Indigenista (INI), that heightened Indians' status as special clients of the State.

INI officials acknowledged that their goals—rural development through education, improved health, and extension agriculture— were the same as for *campesinos* generally, but that the special characteristics of Indians in regions such as central Chiapas necessitated distinctive efforts to integrate Indian communities into the national agrarian sector. INI sought out Indian leaders to train as *promotores* of community development and used them to organize work crews for road construction, to teach curriculum designed specially for Indian school children, to run small clinics and promote public sanitation, and to demonstrate new crops and techniques of cultivation. Effectively, Indian promotores became brokers with a good deal of discretion over who would receive development resources, and through them the State sustained its control over local-level politics.[14]

14. See Rus (1976) for a critical analysis of the interaction of *indigenismo* and the discipline of Anthropology and their role in Mexican Indianist policy of this era. Aguirre Beltrán (1955) and De la Fuente (1953) represent the official position of INI at the time.

The Community Context of State Programs

State policies shaped the domains over which emergent Indian brokers were to exercise their control. The jurisdictional entities that State policies reinforced tended to be Indian municipalities, constituted not only as territorial domains, but as entities segmented from one another on ethnic lines, among which State policy imposed a kind of mechanical solidarity by disregarding and even undercutting class differences of Indians within them. This in turn undercut the potential for politics in the region to develop along lines of class that might have given Indians access to the State other than through local-level brokers. In effect, State policies reestablished the "corporate" characteristics that Indian communities had exhibited in different ways in an earlier epoch.

Nineteenth-century developments had fragmented older corporate Indian communities. The disintegration followed the divestitures of Indian communities' lands by mid-century legislation. Although the region's competing elites had left intact structures of municipal government helpful in recruiting labor (Rus 1983:159; Wasserstrom 1983:115)—for example, handpicked officials charged with collecting the head tax—Indian communities were substantially bereft of integrity. The encroachment of ladino-owned fincas had fragmented their territories. Debt indenture and *baldiaje* had moved their populations down from the highlands into or around the fringes of lowland estates (Wasserstrom 1983:116–126), leaving behind a minority of wealthier Indians in the patchwork of land that they had managed to acquire and hold onto as private property. When Indians were returned to the highlands by the 1914 *Ley de Obreros*, they returned to isolated hamlet settlements held together by little more than the residual structures of town government and religious hierarchy controlled by the propertied indigenous minority. The centrifugal tendencies within municipalities were strong, and indeed had been heightened by the different ways hamlets of a given *municipio* were drawn into the three-way contest among the region's highland and lowland elites and the new Revolutionary State.

Both the norms and the practice of land reform and Indianist development worked powerfully in central Chiapas to counteract these centrifugal tendencies, to reconstitute the integrity of the Indian municipalities, and, in effect, to parochialize them.

Land reform not only restored but actually amplified territorial integrity within Indian municipios beyond its mid-nineteenth century extent. The provisions of Article 27 for restitution to communities of corporate lands divested in the 19th century, legally affected lands many fincas had absorbed within the municipalities. Even though the State allowed Chiapas Indians many petitions for restitution to langour in the 1920s, the later efforts of Cárdenas's protagonization of the ejido recaptured these holdings within municipios in the highlands. On the one hand they amalgamated petitions started up earlier on behalf of separate hamlets within municipios into larger claims based on municipios' former corporate holdings. Additionally, they instituted claims against former national lands within municipios that fincas had absorbed. The pressure put upon finca owners within the highland municipios was sufficient to bring many to sell out their holdings. This meant that Indians not only regained control of former communal lands but also extended control within municipios to national lands to which they had not formerly held title (Edel 1962, 1966; Collier 1975).

At the same time the practice of land reform generally limited territorial integrity to municipal jurisdictions within the highlands. Although the agrarian laws in force during the Cárdenas presidency allowed for donation of expropriable lands to peasant communities within seven kilometers on the basis of demonstrable need, the practice of donation was generally restricted to already-formed settlements of tenants on the affectable lands. Indians who had returned to the highlands after the Revolution were not able to seek donation of lands outside their municipios. Land reform thus generally restricted benefits for Indians to land in their municipios of origin.

The Indianist programs of development begun in the 1950s also accentuated the Indian municipio as an integral entity. By that time, *indigenismo* had absorbed then-current anthropological approaches to the community as an integrated functional system. Julio de la Fuente (1953), in explaining the philosophy of the Centro Coordinador Tzeltal Tzotzil of the Instituto Nacional Indigenista shortly after it had been established on the outskirts of San Cristobal de las Casas, emphasized Indian municipios as basic units, each with its characteristic personality, within which health, education, and economic infrastructure had to be developed integrally.

As the basis for programs of the Centro Coordinador, Gonzalo Aguirre Beltrán (1953) also elaborated a theory of regional integration based on the idea of the Indian municipio as a functionally integrated entity. He interpreted highland Chiapas as a functional regional system in which San Cristobal de las Casas, as a metropolis, depended upon a constellation of such satellite Indian municipios through trade. Accepting the idea behind Robert Redfield's folk-urban continuum (1953) that development diffuses from the metropolis to the peasant community, Aguirre (1955) argued that INI should stimulate regional development by linking isolated satellite municipios more effectively to the metropolis through the construction of roads, while fomenting both commerce in the metropolis and new enterprise in Indian municipios through Indian promotores (development agents, usually drawn from within a municipio). Because of the functional integration of municipios, changes that promotores introduced would set off a chain reaction reverberating on other aspects of their total structure to bring about acculturation, better integration into the region, and ultimately of the region into national rural development.

Both land reform and INI development implemented programs in the highlands in a manner tending to reinforce municipios as parochial domains within which the Indians brokering them could exercise their power. The administration within a municipio of an ejido was turned over to a governing body, the *Comisariado ejidal*, through whose officials the State party generally controlled municipal politics. INI coordinated programs throughout a municipio via a small number of promotores drawn from within it and also used promotores as a cadre to control key municipal posts.

In addition to accentuating the Indian municipio as a community entity, State programs tended to disregard class differences among Indians spanning municipios while tacitly encouraging patronage-based stratification within them.

When Indians returned to the highlands from the lowland ranches where they had served as *mozos* or *baldios* in 1914, they returned as landless poor. Some were able to find employment working for other Indians, often kin, fortunate enough to own highland property (Collier 1975:149). Others gravitated back toward seasonal wagework in the lowlands, sometimes even working for other Indians who took up rental farming there. Thus there were important differences of economic position among Indians and many situations in which some Indians exploited others. Yet, partly because of State policy, these differences did not develop along regional lines of class.

Land reform, for example, disregarded differences between propertied and landless Indians of a municipio in distributing as much land in an ejido to wealthy participants as to poor ones.[15] It also masked the differences by appearing to swell the category of small holders whose households might subsist autonomously by

15. If anything, wealthier Indians benefited disproportionately in the distribution of ejidal parcels because they wielded greater power in the organizing of ejidal petitions. This was true in Zinacantan, for example.

farming. In practice, ejidal holdings alone were usually insufficient for more than temporary reprieve from having to work for others, and poor Indians continued to do so. When they worked for one another within a municipio, however, their unequal relation was all too easy to subsume in other terms given shared perception of one another as small holders.

Indianist development policy, like land reform, also tended to misconstrue asymmetries in the economic relations of Indians of a municipio to one another. As Gonzalo Aguirre Beltrán and Ricardo Pozas (1954:219) pointed out, indigenismo embodied a contradiction in seeking to modernize the economy while promoting the supposed positive values of Indian cultures, among them cooperative and communal organization whose seemingly egalitarian and collective principles contrasted favorably with the competitive values of "mercantile" economy. Some Indianist programs attempted to promote communal or collective organization in development. For example, INI called on Indian municipios to come up with communal work crews in its road-building programs, and it set out to stimulate small businesses as cooperatives. These policies failed to recognize how asymmetrical relationships underlay Indian leaders' ability to call up work gangs or organize cooperatives and how both endeavors heightened the asymmetry by making leaders the brokers for employment and enhancing their economic position through the credits made available to cooperatives.

Thus State policies tended to segment Indian municipios one from another as though they were integral domains, with relatively little internal differentiation. As a consequence, Indians in the full sway of the modern Mexican State were as parochial and as prepolitical as Hobsbawm's (1959) pre-modern primitive rebels of an earlier epoch. Other policies might have evoked political participation of Indians of the region along lines of shared class position. Instead, the policies evoked political brokerage.

Indigenous Brokerage of State Programs and Factional Politics

Programs directed toward the peasantry from the arena of national politics also tended to draw factionalism into the politics of brokerage within municipios through their ebb and flow. Essentially, there were two ways the ebb and flow of federally-initiated programs factionalized politics. Political careers built upon brokering specific programs such as land reform in the era of their rise risked being swept away by a change in the tide of policy. At the same time, the swelling of alternative currents of public policy engendered political competition among those seeking to broker them. Because the Mexican State periodically shifted its policies to secure the compliance of different sectors, programs of land and labor reform and Indianist development did indeed ebb and flow. Only unusual circumstances allowed central, stable municipal leadership to emerge on the basis of brokerage of these programs.

The consequences of land reform for indigenous politics in Chiapas illustrate this particularly well. On the one hand, land reform elicited brokerage as higher-level bureaucrats sought out avenues through local leaders to secure the participation of relatively inaccessible Indian populations. On the other hand, the dramatic shifts through time in State commitment to land reform undermined the position of specific brokers and tended to stimulate competition for their positions of leadership.

A certain number of Indian groups in Central Chiapas initiated petitions for land reform in the 1920s but became discouraged when their early efforts brought no results. It was not until the Cárdenas presidency of 1934–40 committed itself to extensive land reform that federal bureaucrats sought out and cultivated Indian organizers capable of getting their fellow Indians to set aside reluctance stemming from earlier failures and to submit new petitions. As they did so, Indian petitioners relied on leaders to press their claims forward.[16] A petition would lead the state-level agrarian commission to investigate the legal standing of the petitioning group, sending out an engineer to census it and to survey the land it held or might expropriate. Meanwhile the petitioners might have to hire a lawyer or devise other tactics to offset landowners' attempting to invalidate their claims. All these activities called for extraordinary skills. The brokers who undertook them began with literacy and some familiarity with *ladino* life, cultivated working relationships with agrarian officials, and shared gossip with one another about how to forge strategies for their role.

If all went well for the petitioners and their leaders, the state commission would recommend that the governor make them a provisional award, passing their claim on to the federal Agrarian Department to review and to transmit to Mexico City for approval there prior to the President's making a definitive award. These steps often lasted many additional years and required Indian leaders to

16. Edel (1962) has a helpful summary of the steps petitioners and various agencies had to follow to initiate and implement petitions for restitution or donation in the era of Cárdenas.

travel to the capital to press their suit. Not infrequently they led to failure. In the meantime brokers still had to administer the ejido for recipients in accordance with the law. Thus, the brokering of land reform, initially advancing leaders' careers, often left them vulnerable to growing disillusion and sometimes disaffection of their followings. As we shall see, opportunities for brokering other programs also threatened an ejido brokers' career by encouraging competition from factional rivals.

For example, the career of the principal land reform broker for Zinacantan,[17] Mariano Zárate, while advancing with the national tide of land reform in the 1930s, suffered setbacks with deflections and reversals of the tide in the 1940s as well as from the political competition within Zinacantan for brokering INI programs of community development in the 1950s and 1960s.

Mariano Zárate was from one of the better off Zinacanteco families which had controlled municipal posts in the 1920s.[18] He was among the handful of literate Zinacantecos sought out by federal officials in 1934 to help initiate petitions for land reform. Zinacantan was strained at that time by centrifugal tendencies, and several of its settlements wanted to initiate independent petitions;[19] but federal officials amalgamated all the petitions into two and consolidated the organizing of them, giving Zárate a major role (Edel 1962).

Zárate took on the job of drawing up a census in each settlement to determine who would be eligible for land. He accompanied the engineer sent to survey former communal lands and the various private fincas within Zinacantan. He transacted much of the other agrarian business with bureaucrats in the state capital. In 1939, he was selected to be *Presidente Municipal*, and one year later, when Zinacantan was provisionally awarded its ejido, Zárate was appointed to head up the *Comisariado Ejidal* to govern it. This gave

17. For the history of land reform in Zinacantan, and of Mariano Zárate's role in it, see Collier (1975), Edel (1962, 1966), Guarnaccia (1972), and Wasserstrom (1983:170–178).

18. Wasserstrom (1983:172) discusses how Zárate's father participated in the control of political and religious posts in Zinacantan during the 1920s.

19. The centrifugal strains date at least to the 1920s when Obregón installed Petul Zu, a leader from Navenchauk (one of the outlying settlements) in Zinacantan's presidency (Wasserstrom 1983:172). Zu proceeded to eliminate mandatory religious service, one of the mechanisms whereby elders of the *cabecera* sustained control of outlying hamlets. The cabecera elders ousted Zu and kept their control. But by 1934 seven settlements within Zincantan had drawn up separate petitions for land reform, and the western portion of the municipio was eventually granted an ejido of its own (Edel 1962).

him the power to decide which Zinacantecos would receive which parcels of ejido land, and thus a loyal following in every settlement. Zárate wielded substantial control of municipal politics. During 1942, when anthropologist Sol Tax visited Zinacantan, Zárate was the power behind both the municipal presidency and the Comisariado Ejidal (Edel 1962:50–52).

But by the 1940s, federal enthusiasm for land reform had waned. Zinacantan had only received provisional donation of its lands, and its petition had made no further progress. The ejidal archives show that during this decade Zárate kept up a steady but futile correspondence with agrarian bureaucrats to get them to advance the petition. Meanwhile, opposition to him within Zinacantan had arisen among Zinacantecos who had not received ejidal awards and an attempt was made to oust him from the Comisariado Ejidal (Edel 1962:63). Zárate still had the support of agrarian officials and of Zinacanteco ejidatarios, however, and the ouster attempt failed.

During the 1950s, the climate for land reform warmed once again, and Zárate was persuaded by other Zinacantecos to begin a new petition for an award of national lands in the Grijalva Valley below Zinacantan. He did so, but the petition was not immediately successful.[20] In 1957, however, Zinacantan's provisional award of ejido was finally advanced to the stage of federal approval, reconsolidating Zárate's stature.

Meanwhile, opposition had arisen from another quarter, INI, which had begun its projects of community development in Zinacantan, found that Zárate had little interest in collaborating.[21] Although he and his supporters supplied labor for one of the first construction projects, they withdrew their support when they discovered they were building a clinic rather than an office for the Comisariado Ejidal. INI tried to coopt Zárate by hiring him as a promotor to teach school in one of the hamlets. But they also sought out new leaders from among Zárate's opponents within Zincantan, eventually managing to win control of offices in municipal government through them. Zárate's opponents had him jailed on charges of political assassination, but he hired a lawyer to get him released. Though he remained a force in municipal politics, his domination had eroded. When a colonization movement revived the defunct 1952 petition for national lands, it was younger leaders who pressed it forward.

20. Guarnaccia (1972) and Collier (1975:198–202) discuss the later colonization effort based on this initiative.
21. See Edel (1962:63) on Zarate's resistance to INI programs.

Statistics on how the twenty-three municipios of substantially Indian populace in central Chiapas participated in land reform show that the timing of Zárate's successes and setbacks was not fortuitous but rather inherent in the ebb and flow of land reform throughout this era.[22]

The curve in Figure 1a shows the approximate number of petitions for land reform filed state-wide in Chiapas by year of filing. Statistics on the average number per month of hectares awarded nationally[23] for each presidential term show up as a bar graph. The two sets of data are not comparable directly, petitions being initiatives in the quest of future awards. They are juxtaposed here to indicate that land reform in Chiapas roughly paralleled that in the nation, with initiatives peaking in the 1930s and 1950s and awards cresting shortly thereafter.[24]

Initiating of petitions from the twenty-three municipios of substantial Indian populace in central highland Chiapas shows up in Figure 1b. Comparing these to initiatives for the state as a whole, we see, first, a comparatively larger early spurt of initiatives in the 1920s, second, a slightly later and longer-lasting surge in the 1930s, and finally, a resurgence much milder in the 1950s than for the state as a whole.

The first small spurt of these municipios' petitions was for restitution of lands in the 1920s and was part of the wave of such petitions initiated nationally in anticipation of early federal implementation of land reform following the Revolution. The central highlands was the core region of the state of Chiapas in which Indians lost control of former communal lands when 19th-century liberal laws divested Indian municipios of corporate holdings. After the Revolution, Indian municipalities nation-wide petitioned for restitution of former corporate holdings. The bulge of national awards shown in the 1920s in the first bar graph was of awards for restitution. Indian municipios in Chiapas evidently followed suit, whereas non-Indian groups in other regions, not ever having had corporate holdings, did not.

22. The analysis which follows is based on data I compiled in 1973 from the archives of the federal Departamento Agrario at its offices in Tuxtla Gutiérrez. The data include all petitions submitted from 23 municipios after 1920 and the responses to them. The collection of these data was made possible by a grant form NICHD, No. HD–06265, to study land reform and demography in highland Chiapas.

23. The national data are from Wilkie (1967:188).

24. The Southern Pacific Region, in which Reynolds classifies Chiapas, lagged behind all other regions in the proportion of total hectarage of cultivation corresponding to production on ejidal holdings (1970:145). Ejidal distribution was not as extensive in Chiapas as in other areas.

Map 1 *State of Chiapas, Mexico: 23 Study Municipios**

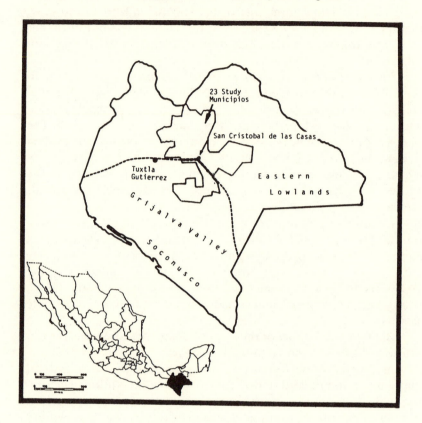

**See notes 26 and 27.*

Figure 1 *Land Reform Petitions from 23 Study Municipios** *

A) Land Reform, State of Chiapas, Mexican Nation

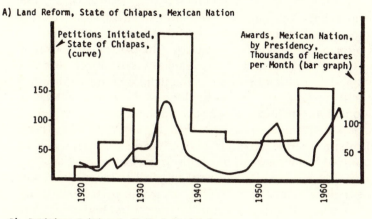

B) Petitions Initiated, 23 Study Municipios

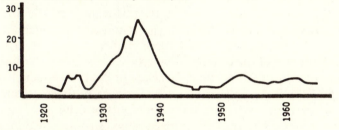

C) Petitions Awarded, 23 Study Municipios

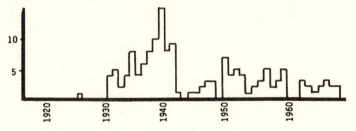

D) Proportion of Petitions Denied, 23 Study Municipios

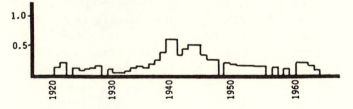

See notes 22 and 23.

During the 1930s, as the Mexican state strove to solve the crisis of the collapse of its exports, it invigorated agrarian reform as the rural counterpart of a hoped for industrialization. Federal bureaucrats of the Cárdenas presidency helped revive old claims for agrarian reform and invited new ones. In Chiapas, Erasto Urbina's Departamento de Protección Indígena initiated the surge of initiatives among those of the twenty-three municipios along major roadways or with ceremonial centers having some mestizo as well as Indian population. Their efforts then spread to more isolated municipios lacking such linkages to the larger region.[25] Petitions now sought the expropriating of land from overly large properties as well as restitution of former communal tracts. It took longer for land reform to elicit the participation of these more isolated municipios and longer for their populace to overcome barriers to participation, accounting for why the surge continued in the central highlands after it had begun to subside state-wide.

Finally, expropriations resulting from the surge of the 1930s claimed most of the land available for ejidos in the central highlands. This is why the 1950s inaugurated relatively fewer initiatives there than in other parts of the state, particularly the east, where colonizing accounted for much of the resurgence of claims. Indians from the highlands surely participated in the forming of these colonies, but no longer as members of their municipios of origin.

Examining the fate of these initiatives gives some sense of the risks and timing of rewards for brokering land reform to build a political career. The records for the twenty-three study municipios show that the proportion of initiatives left unresolved, without any rewards for brokers to pass on to petitioners, never dropped much below .75. Only one out of about four petitions ever met with any resolution. The business of organizing petitions was always risky. Regardless of when they were begun, initiatives met with reward primarily in the 1930s and 1950s (see Figure 1c). In contrast to brokers organizing initiatives in other eras, however, brokers doing so in the 1930s were much more likely to win rewards for their followers quickly. On the other hand, the 1940s were most unrewarding for land reform. The 1940s bulge in the proportion of new initiatives flatly denied, shown in Figure 1d, suggests how dangerous the political brokering of land reform may have been during this ebb until the return of its tide in the 1950s. Thus, throughout the highlands, as in Zinacantan, political careers built on brokering land

25. The spread is reflected in the dating of petitions for land reform.

reform faced risks of initial failure, but also the frustration of having efforts to capitalize on initial success stymied by turns in the tide of land reform's fortunes.

Land reform was not the only federally-initiated program to elicit and then frustrate local-level political brokering. Several other programs affected local-level politics not only through their ebb and flow, but also by multiplying the political resources over which local brokers could compete.

I confine my attention to the federal organizing of Indian labor and the programs of INI as those principally affecting indigenous politics. The second set of graphs (Figure 2) pertains to these programs. At their head is the now-familiar temporal pattern of land reform initiatives from these municipios. Next comes a short run of statistics on workers recruited by the federally-organized Native Workers' Union.[26] Finally, four more graphs delineate trends in the road building, legal aid, medical care, and schooling engaged in by INI after it opened its Tzeltal-Tzotzil Coordinating Center in Chiapas in the early 1950s.[27]

The Union of Native Workers arose as part of Cárdenas's nationwide organizing of labor into the machinery of the state party.[28] The union was set up by Erasto Urbina to be run by Indian leaders. It monopolized the legal recruiting of Indians from the central highlands to cultivate and harvest coffee on the Pacific coastal slopes. Brokering employer-employee contracts as well as citizen-party relationships opened new avenues for union leaders to develop political power, distinct from and competing with those opened by land reform in that Indians forming the reserve army of unemployed for other regions' production sought jobs as well as land to farm for subsistence.

INI established its center as part of a national Indianist policy during the 1950s[29] and began programs for development and culture change of Indians in the highlands. I see at least three ways that INI's programs engendered factionalism in local-level political brokerage.

First, INI's use of Indian promotores to implement its programs added new positions of brokerage. Promotores were Indians trained

26. Data on the Union are drawn from Pozas (1959:124).
27. Data on INI programs are drawn from Aguirre Beltrán, et al. (1976: 187–266).
28.. Rus (1976:20ff) is an excellent source on the forming of the Union and its consequences for Chamula politics. Pozas (1959:151ff) and Aguirre Beltrán and Pozas (1954:220–226) give more contemporary accounts.
29. See De la Fuente (1953) and Aguirre Beltrán (1955) on the philosophy and implementation of these programs in Chiapas.

Figure 2 *Government Programs Affecting 23 Study Municipios* *

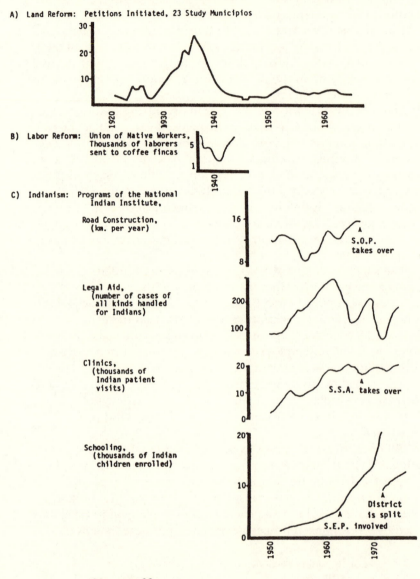

A) Land Reform: Petitions Initiated, 23 Study Municipios

B) Labor Reform: Union of Native Workers,
                   Thousands of laborers
                   sent to coffee fincas

C) Indianism: Programs of the National
                Indian Institute.

    Road Construction,
    (km. per year)

    S.O.P.
    takes over

    Legal Aid,
    (number of cases of
    all kinds handled
    for Indians)

    Clinics,
    (thousands of
    Indian patient
    visits)

    S.S.A. takes over

    Schooling,
    (thousands of Indian
    children enrolled)

    District
    is split
    S.E.P. involved

*See note 22.

to involve their fellow citizens in various aspects of development and culture change (Aguirre Beltrán 1955:39–41). INI deliberately sought out influential individuals and those who aspired to lead to promote its programs. Sometimes INI nurtured these individuals' political roles, for example, by seeing to it that they assumed administrative positions in their municipio's civil governments. INI trained sizeable numbers of promotores, over four hundred of them, by 1976 (Aguirre Beltán et al. 1976:190).

At the same time, the programs that INI implemented changed through time in a manner tending to undercut the promotores who had brokered them.[30] Particular programs were not long-lived—the program of legal assistance, for example. Some programs moved out through the countryside, first bringing and then restricting opportunity for brokerage. Road construction is an example. Supplying labor crews for constructing the Pan American highway already had nurtured brokering in the 1940s. The first surge of INI road building in the 1950s spread through the municipios closest to the coordinating center in San Cristobal, bearing a measure of brokerage with it. The second surge, in the 1960s, carried road building into remoter areas. Finally, programs through which brokers could remunerate followers gradually gave way to programs such as schooling that burdened brokers with the purveying of ideology alien to most Indians.

Third and finally, INI itself ebbed, and the turning of its functions over to other agencies forced brokers to adjust to and compete for new avenues to external political resources. INI's fortunes changed with the wane of Indianism as a force in national politics. In Chiapas, agencies lacking an explicitly Indianist mandate took over one, then another of its functions. Road building shifted increasingly to the Secretaría de Obras Públicas, clinics to the Secretaría de Salubridad y Asistencia, and so forth. In the 1970s a new Chiapas development agency, PRODESCH, subsumed many of INI's remaining functions as well as some of its staff of indigenous promotores. In so far as promotores and other brokers were pawns in a larger game, these changes in who controlled the play undermined relationships they had developed with higher-level players while opening up opportunities for competitors to displace them.

Only exceptional circumstances enabled local-level leaders to circumvent the unsettling political consequences of these programs' ebb and flow. For the most part, the succession of brokering for land reform, for labor organizing, for the development of economic infrastructure, and for schooling called forth a succession of leaders

30. For trends, see Aguirre Beltrán, et al. (1976:187–266).

and considerable political competition. One of the few exceptions was Chamula, in which young, literate town scribes who rose to power brokering land reform in the early 1930s formed a coalition, consolidating their power by taking on higher positions in the Union of Native Workers.[31] Chamula was the most populous Indian municipio, yet it had limited lands. It stood to gain most from a combining of land and labor reform. In addition to providing this, the Chamula scribes came to control the plantation labor opportunities for Indians of other municipalities. During World War II, when the government ran coffee plantations owned by Germans, the union run by Chamula brokers supplied the plantation labor. These leaders took advantage of INI road building and commercial cooperatives by starting up a lucrative trucking monopoly (Wasserstrom 1983:176–177). Their growing power enabled them to exile political competitors, something that is continuing to this day with the exiling of Chamula Protestants. These leaders were successful because Chamula's circumstances enabled them to capitalize upon the shift from land reform to labor policy without suffering the ebb in other leaders' political fortunes in the 1940s.

What we have seen, then, is that with rare exceptions the multiplicity of avenues for brokering that opened and closed with the cycling of federal programs for Indians in Chiapas contributed to the factional and impermanent character of indigenous local-level leadership. In closing, I wish first to make clear that I do not believe these federal programs were the *only* forces thus shaping indigenous politics. In most instances the factions coalescing around the brokering of State programs grew out of preexisting cleavages within an indigenous population.[32] Segmentary indigenous kinship and social organization engendered by the heightened boundaries around these "closed-corporate" ethnic communities also contributed to factionalism because leaders built discrete followings largely by accumulating rights in people organized as distinctive clusters of kin. Furthermore, lacking a clearcut mechanism for political succession other than along lines of segmentary lineage, informal leadership inherently engendered competition from the young for the power

31. See Prokosch (1963) for a description of the positions of power these scribes had attained by the 1960s. Rus (1976) discusses how *indigenismo* and labor policy manipulated these positions of Chamula leadership.

32. As Rush (1971) has documented, for example, the political factions in the Zinacanteco settlement of Navenchauk can be traced forward in their evolution from before 1920 to the present. Although the divisions in Navenchauk shifted gradually, the political issues over which the factions fought were closely attuned to development policy and its brokerage.

held by the old. I do not mean to ignore these factors but rather to point out how external political forces molded and heightened them.

Second, while I have emphasized the explicitly political consequences of State programs of the era for Indians of Chiapas, I would not claim that these political mechanisms were the only external factors at work. Though politically contained by State programs, Indians of the highlands were profoundly affected by their involvement in the economy of other regions of the state of Chiapas, and this involvement affected indigenous life, including local-level politics, in many ways.[33] My goal has been specifically to focus attention on the political consequences of land reform and Indianist development and to indicate how these programs and their consequences flowed from the fundamental evolution of the post-Revolutionary Mexican national State.

In their analyses of the articulation of the Morelos peasantry to the Mexican national State, Warman (1980) and De la Peña (1981) have delineated how land reform initiated sustained market exploitation of the peasantry, enabling dependent industrial capitalism to develop on the basis of cheaply fed and cheaply paid labor in a country no longer troubled by peasant revolution. The Indians of central Chiapas shared in this articulation in many respects. Like the Morelos peasants of the 1920s, a decade later Indians of Chiapas were major beneficiaries of land reform undertaking in the name of the national State. As in Morelos, land reform initiated a resurgence of peasant farming in Chiapas, which Indians intensified, much as peasants did elsewhere, as State fiscal policies subsequently restrained the value of agrarian commodities relative to that of industrial goods. In Morelos, land reform forged in peasants the illusion of having political strength in the State and won their compliance to growing exploitation managed by the State. So too, through land reform and Indianist development, the State forged a quintessentially mid-20th century political compliance among the indigenous municipios of highland Chiapas.

33. For example, Adams' general ideas (1970) about how broad economic cycling affects brokerage has pertinence for the more recent opening up of avenues by which Indians circumvent the political monopoly of former brokers. Economic changes such as those resulting from road building and federal intervention in the grain market (Cancian 1972:111–17, Wasserstrom 1983:181) have also significantly affected Indians' participation in regional economy in a manner tending to open up "closed-corporate" communities such as Zinacantan.

Bibliography

Adams, Richard N.
  1970a Brokers and Career Mobility Systems in the Structure of Complex Societies. *Southwestern Journal of Anthropology* 26:315–27.
  1970b *Crucifixion by Power: Essays on Guatemalan National Social Structure, 1914–1966.* Austin and London: University of Texas Press.
Aguirre Beltrán, Gonzalo
  1955 A Theory of Regional Integration: The Coordinating Centers. *América Indígena* 15(1):29–42.
Aguirre Beltrán, Gonzalo and Ricardo Pozas A.
  1954 Instituciones Indígenas en el México Actual. In Caso, Zavala, Miranda, et al. 1954, pp. 171–268.
Aguirre Beltrán, Villa Rojas, Romano D., et al.
  1976 *El Indigenismo en Acción: XXV Aniversario del Centro Coordinator Indigenista Tzeltal-Tzotzil, Chiapas.* México, D. F.: Instituto Nacional Indigenista y Secretaría de Educación Pública.
Cancian, Frank
  1965 *Economics and Prestige in a Maya Community.* Stanford: Stanford University Press.
  1972 *Change and Uncertainty in a Peasant Economy: The Maya Cornfarmers of Zinacantan.* Stanford: Stanford University Press.
Casahonda Castillo, José
  1963 *50 años de revolución en Chiapas.* Tuxtla Gutiérrez: Instituto de Ciencias y Artes de Chiapas.
Caso, Alfonso, Silvio Zavala, Jose Miranda, et al.
  1954 *Métodos y resultados de la política indigenista en México.* Memorias del Instituto Nacional Indigenista, Vol. 6. México, D. F.: Instituto Nacional Indigenista.
Collier, George A.
  1975 *The Fields of the Tzotzil: The Ecological Bases in Highland Chiapas.* Austin: University of Texas Press.
Edel, Matthew D.
  1962 Zinacantan's Ejido: The Effects of Mexican Land Reform on an Indian Community in Chiapas. Mimeographed report of Columbia-Cornell-Harvard-Illinois Summer Field Studies Program, Harvard College.
  1966 El Ejido en Zinacantan. In *Los Zinacantecos*, E. Z. Vogt, ed. México, D. F.: Instituto Nacional Indigenista.
Etzioni, Amatai
  1961 *A Comparative Analysis of Complex Organizations: On Power, Involvement, and Their Correlates.* New York: The Free Press.

De la Fuente, Julio
  1953   El Centro Coordinador Tzeltal Tzotzil: Una realización del
         México de hoy. *América Indígena* 13(1):55–64.
García de León, Antonio
  1979   Lucha de clases y poder político en Chiapas, *Historia y Sociedad* 22: 57–87.
Guarnaccia, Peter Joseph
  1972   Land and Tortillas: Land Reform in a Maya Indian Village in
         Mexico. Honors thesis for Committee on Degrees in Social
         Studies, Harvard College.
Hobsbawm, Eric
  1959   *Primitive Rebels*. New York: Norton.
de Janvry, Alain
  1981   *The Agrarian Question and Reformism in Latin America*.
         Baltimore and London: Johns Hopkins University Press.
Lomnitz Adler, Claudio
  1984   Compliance and Coalitions in the Mexican Government:
         1917–1940. In *Five Centuries of Law and Politics in Central
         Mexico*, edited by Ronald Spores and Ross Hassig. Nashville:
         Vanderbilt Publications in Anthropology.
Modiano, Nancy
  1973   *Indian Education in the Chiapas Highlands*. New York:
         Holt, Rinehart and Winston, Inc.
Moscoso Pastrana, Prudencio
  1960   *El Pinedismo en Chiapas, 1916–1920*. México, D.F.: Editorial
         Cultura.
Paige, Jefferey M.
  1975   *Agrarian Revolution: Social Movements and Export Agriculture in the Underdeveloped World*. New York: The Free
         Press.
De la Peña, Guillermo
  1981   *A Legacy of Promises: Agriculture, Politics, and Ritual in the
         Morelos Highlands of Mexico*. Austin: University of Texas
         Press.
Pozas A., Ricardo
  1959   *Chamula: Un pueblo indio de los altos de Chiapas*. Memorias
         del Instituto Nacional Indigenista, Vol. 8. México, D. F.: Instituto Nacional Indigenista
Prokosch, Eric
  1963   Chamula Government. Unpublished manuscript prepared at
         the London School of Economics.
Redfield, Robert
  1953   *The Primitive World and its Transformations*. Ithaca: Cornell University Press.
Reynolds, Clark
  1970   *The Mexican Economy: Twentiety-Century Structure and
         Growth*. New Haven and London: Yale University Press.

Rus, Jan, III
1976 Managing Mexico's Indians: The Historical Context and Consequences of Indigenismo. Manuscript prepared for Department of Anthropology, Harvard University.
1983 Whose Caste War? Indians, Ladinos, and the Chiapas "Caste
War" of 1869. In *Spaniards and Indians in Southeastern
Mesoamerica*, Murdo J. MacLeod and Robert Wasserstrom,
eds. Lincoln: University of Nebraska Press.

Rush, Timothy Nevins
1971 Navencauk Disputes: The Social Basis of Factions in a Mexican
Indian Village. Honors thesis for Committee on Degrees in Social Studies, Harvard College.

Skinner, G. William and Edwin Winckler
1969 Compliance and Succession in Rural Communist China: A Cyclical Theory. In *A Sociological Reader on Complex Organizations*, edited by Amitai Etzioni. New York: Holt, Rinehart
and Winston.

Skocpol, Theda
1982 What Makes Peasants Revolutionary? *Comparative Politics*
14(3): 351–375.

Warman, Arturo
1980 *"We Come to Object." The Peasants of Morelos and the National State*. Translated by Stephen K. Ault. Baltimore and
London: The Johns Hopkins University Press.

Wasserstrom, Robert
1977 Land and Labour in Central Chiapas: A Regional Analysis, *Development and Change* 8:441–463.
1978 The Exchange of Saints in Zinacantan: The Socioeconomic
Bases of Religious Change in Southeastern Mexico. *Ethnology*
17:197–210.
1978b Population Growth and Economic Development in Chiapas,
1524–1975. *Human Ecology* 6:127–143.
1983 *Class and Society in Central Chiapas*. Berkeley, Los Angeles,
and London: University of California Press.

Waterbury, Ronald
1975 Non-revolutionary Peasants: Oaxaca Compared to Morelos in
the Mexican Revolution. *Comparative Studies in Society and
History* 17: 410–442.

Wilkie, James W.
1970 *The Mexican Revolution: Federal Expenditure and Social
Change since 1910*. Berkeley and Los Angeles: University of
California Press.

Black Political Protest in São Paulo, 1888–1988*

GEORGE REID ANDREWS

Beginning with Brazil's origins as a nation, and continuing to the present, the relationship between race and politics in that country has been a close and integral one.[1] Portuguese state policy made black slavery the very foundation of Brazil's social and economic order during three centuries of colonial rule. That foundation remained in place even after independence, with the paradoxical result that Brazil became 'the last Christian country to abolish slavery, and the first to declare itself a racial democracy'.[2] Indeed, perhaps nowhere is the connection between race and politics in Brazil more evident than in the concept of 'racial democracy', which characterises race relations in that country in explicitly political terminology.[3]

* The research on which this article is based was supported by grants from the Fulbright Programme and the Social Science Research Council (USA).

[1] For some examinations of that relationship, see Gilberto Freyre, 'A escravidão, a monarquia, e o Brasil moderno', *Revista Brasileira de Estudos Políticos*, vol. 1, no. 1 (1956), pp. 39–48; Bolivar Lamounier, 'Raça e classe na política brasileira', *Cadernos Brasileiros*, no. 47 (1968), pp. 39–50; Amaury de Souza, 'Raça e política no Brasil urbano', *Revista de Administração de Empresas*, vol. 11, no. 4 (1971), pp. 61–70; Pierre-Michel Fontaine, 'Research in the Political Economy of Afro-Latin America', *Latin American Research Review*, vol. 15, no. 1 (1980), pp. 111–41; George Reid Andrews, 'Race and State in Colonial Brazil', *Latin American Research Review*, vol. 19, no. 3 (1984), pp. 203–16; Pierre-Michel Fontaine (ed.), *Race, Class and Power in Brazil* (Los Angeles, 1985); Glaucio Ary Dillon Soares and Nelson do Valle Silva, 'Urbanization, Race, and Class in Brazilian Politics', *Latin American Research Review*, vol. 22, no. 2 (1987), pp. 155–76. On Brazilian race relations more generally, see Donald Pierson, *Negroes in Brazil: A Study of Race Contact in Bahia* (Chicago, 1942); Roger Bastide and Florestan Fernandes, *Brancos e negros em São Paulo* (3rd edn., São Paulo, 1971); Florestan Fernandes, *A integração do negro na sociedade de classes*, 2 vols. (3rd edn., São Paulo, 1978), and *O negro no mundo dos brancos* (São Paulo, 1972); Carl Degler, *Neither Black nor White: Slavery and Race Relations in Brazil and the United States* (New York, 1971); Clóvis Moura, *O negro: De bom escravo a mau cidadão?* (Rio de Janeiro, 1977), and *Sociologia do negro brasileiro* (São Paulo, 1988); Carlos Hasenbalg, *Discriminação e desigualdades raciais no Brasil* (Rio de Janeiro, 1979); George Reid Andrews, *Blacks and Whites in São Paulo, Brazil, 1888–1988* (Madison, 1991).

[2] Hélio Santos, 'O presidente negro', *Veja* (31 Oct. 1984), p. 138.

[3] On the concept of racial democracy, see Thales de Azevedo, *Democracia racial* (Petrópolis, 1975); Emília Viotti da Costa, 'The Myth of Racial Democracy: A Legacy

George Reid Andrews is Professor of History at the University of Pittsburgh.

This article explores some of the connections between race and politics in Brazil by examining four moments in the history of black political mobilisation in that country. Geographically, it focuses on the south-eastern state of São Paulo, which by the time of emancipation, in 1888, housed the third-largest slave population in Brazil (after neighbouring Minas Gerais and Rio de Janeiro), and which has formed a centre of black political action from the 1880s through to the present.[4] Chronologically, it focuses on: the struggle for the final abolition of slavery in the 1880s; the rise and fall of the Frente Negra Brasileira in the 1930s; the black organisations of the Second Republic; and the most recent wave of black protest, from the mid-1970s to 1988.

The purpose of such an exercise is twofold. First, placing these moments of black mobilisation in a century-long time-frame makes it possible for us to see them not as isolated episodes, but as chapters in a long-term, ongoing history of black protest and struggle in Brazil. Secondly, this article seeks to relate the history of black protest to the larger history of state–society relations in Brazil during the last hundred years. Recent work in this area has suggested how the character and institutional structure of the regime in power at any given moment have directly influenced the organisational forms through which popular forces, including Afro-Brazilians, have mobilised to assert themselves in politics.[5] At the same time, movements originating in civil society have had significant reciprocal impacts on state policies and institutions, and have helped drive forward the repeated regime transitions which Brazil has experienced since 1889: from monarchy (1822–89) to oligarchic republic (1891–1930) to corporatist dictatorship (1937–45) to populist republic (1946–64) to military dictatorship (1964–85) to the Third Republic. The history of black protest is very much a part of this state–society dialectic,

---

of the Empire', in *The Brazilian Empire: Myths and Histories* (Chicago, 1985), pp. 234–46; and Florestan Fernandes, 'O mito da "democracia racial"', in *Integração do negro*, vol. I, pp. 249–68.

[4] On black political organisation in São Paulo, see Michael Mitchell, 'Racial Consciousness and the Political Attitudes and Behavior of Blacks in São Paulo, Brazil', unpubl. PhD diss., Indiana University, 1977; Clóvis Moura, 'Organizações negras', in Paul Singer and Vinicius Caldeira Brant (eds.), *São Paulo: O povo em movimento* (São Paulo, 1980), pp. 143–75.

[5] See, for example, Richard Graham, *Patronage and Politics in Nineteenth-Century Brazil* (Stanford, 1990); John D. French, 'Industrial Workers and the Origins of Populist Politics in the ABC Region of Greater São Paulo, Brazil, 1900–1950', unpubl. PhD diss., Yale University, 1985; and Maria Helena Moreira Alves, *State and Opposition in Military Brazil* (Austin, 1985). This article thus provides additional support for Michael Mitchell's observation that 'styles of Black political activity will be determined by the prevailing political environment'. Michael Mitchell, 'Blacks and the *Abertura Democrática*', in Fontaine, *Race, Class and Power*, p. 96.

although its centrality has varied substantially over time: high in the 1880s, low in the first half of the 1900s, and then increasing in the 1970s and 1980s.

Moment 1: The Empire and Abolition

Reflecting the tensions between colonial state and local elites which had produced independence, the Brazilian Empire divided political power between a centralising national monarchy and provincial landowning elites.[6] Imperial policy was for the most part supportive of the landowners and their needs, but conflicts inevitably arose between the monarchy and those regional oligarchies who saw themselves neglected or actively harmed by its policies. During the last decades of the Empire the most serious such conflict revolved around the institution of slavery. As that conflict reached its climax, it increasingly took the form of a confrontation between slave-owning planters and a popular abolitionist movement tacitly supported by a monarchy whose policy initiatives had over time effectively undermined the institution of slavery.

During the first half of the century the Empire had resisted British efforts to terminate the Atlantic slave trade; by 1851, however, the monarchy had reversed course and began actively to prosecute slave traders, a policy which eliminated the trade in a matter of months.[7] By the late 1860s Emperor Dom Pedro II was expressing public support for the idea of a gradual, indemnified emancipation of the nation's slaves, and had instructed his Council of State to explore means of carrying this out. The result was the Rio Branco Law of 1871, which decreed the freedom of all slaves owned by the national state, the eventual freedom (at the age of majority) of all children born of slave mothers after 28 September 1871, and the purchase of the freedom of other slaves through a state-administered emancipation fund.[8]

The Rio Branco Law was a compromise measure which provided for the eventual termination of slavery, but at the cost of maintaining forced

[6] On the political dynamics of the Empire, see Roderick J. Barman, *Brazil: The Forging of a Nation, 1798–1852* (Stanford, 1988); Graham, *Patronage and Politics*; José Murilo de Carvalho, *A construção da ordem: A elite política imperial* (Rio de Janeiro, 1980), and *Teatro de sombras: A política imperial* (São Paulo, 1988); and Leslie Bethell and José Murilo de Carvalho, '1822–1850', Richard Graham, '1850–1870', and Emília Viotti da Costa, '1870–1889', all in Leslie Bethell (ed.), *Brazil: Empire and Republic, 1822–1930* (Cambridge and New York, 1989).

[7] Leslie Bethell, *The Abolition of the Brazilian Slave Trade* (Cambridge and New York, 1970), pp. 327–59.

[8] The terms of the law, as well as the story of abolition more generally, are laid out in Robert Conrad, *The Destruction of Brazilian Slavery, 1850–1888* (Berkeley, 1972); Robert Brent Toplin, *The Abolition of Slavery in Brazil* (New York, 1971); Emília Viotti da Costa, *Da senzala à colônia* (2nd edn., São Paulo, 1982), and *A abolição* (São Paulo, 1982).

labour in Brazil well into the twentieth century.[9] Immediate and definitive abolition was a political impossibility in a Parliament dominated by slave-owning interests. And the likelihood of such abolition was further reduced in 1881 by a sweeping electoral reform passed by planter interests fearful of the dangers posed by an expanding electorate which they were finding increasingly difficult to control. At a stroke the voting population was reduced from a million adult males to fewer than 150,000, effectively reinforcing the control of the propertied classes over Brazilian politics.[10]

If slavery were to be eliminated before the turn of the century, the effort would have to come from outside the formal political system, and this is precisely what happened. Immediately following the electoral reform of 1881 a new and more radical abolitionist movement began to appear in Rio de Janeiro and São Paulo states, a movement which advocated civil disobedience and non-violent resistance, by both slaves and free people, to the institution of slavery. Abolitionist agitators, the *caifazes*, circulated through the countryside urging slaves to flee the plantations and make their way to urban centres, where abolitionist groups would provide them with shelter and protection and prevent slave-hunters from pursuing them.[11]

The radical abolitionism of the 1880s sparked a massive response among a slave population which over time had displayed considerable sensitivity to, and canniness in exploiting, changes in public and official attitudes toward slavery. Rising abolitionist sentiment after 1860, and the monarchy's openly critical attitude toward slavery, had prompted a growing number of slaves to explore possible protections in the royal court system, where not infrequently they received a sympathetic reception. Mulatto lawyer Luis Gama won freedom for a number of slaves in São Paulo whose age indicated that either they or their parents had been imported after the first abolition of the slave trade, in 1831. The courts also proved receptive to slaves appealing for protection against abusive masters. State officials and landowners both commented on a series of cases in the 1860s and 1870s in which slaves had assaulted their masters or overseers and had then voluntarily turned themselves over to the police, claiming self-defence and demanding a court trial.[12]

---

[9] Female slaves born prior to 28 Sept. 1871 would still have been of childbearing age in the early 1910s. Under the 1871 law, their children would not have acquired full freedom until reaching the age of majority, in the late 1920s – at which time their mothers would have been in their late 50s, and still slaves.

[10] The reform and its effects are discussed in Graham, *Patronage and Politics*, pp. 182–206.

[11] See works cited in note 8.

[12] On slaves appealing to royal justice during this period, see Maria Célia Marinho de Azevedo, *Onda negra, medo branco: O negro no imaginário das elites – século XIX* (São Paulo, 1987), pp. 180–99; Maria Helena P. T. Machado, *Crime e escravidão: Trabalho, luta, resistência nas lavouras paulistas, 1830–1888* (São Paulo, 1987), pp. 114–23: Suely Robles

Such acts of resistance, and subsequent appeals to royal justice, tended to involve individuals or small groups. Not until the 1880s did the radical abolitionists provide a level of public support which emboldened the slave population to act *en masse*. When the opportunity for such action presented itself, thousands of slaves in São Paulo state seized it, fleeing the plantations in 1887 and 1888 in a massive, non-violent exodus which neither the plantation owners nor the state proved able to stop.[13] Indeed, a key moment in the process of abolition took place in October 1887, when the president of the Club Militar formally petitioned the monarchy to relieve the armed forces of responsibility for capturing escaped slaves, a mission which the officers rejected both as immoral and impossible to carry out.

The withdrawal of the armed forces from the enforcement of slavery removed the last major impediment to slave flight, and it was at this point that São Paulo's coffee planters abruptly changed course and embraced 'planter emancipationism'. Forty thousand slaves, over a third of the province's slave population, were freed by their masters during slavery's last twelve months of existence, and on 13 March 1888 the province's Legislative Assembly unanimously petitioned Parliament to abolish the institution. By 13 May 1888, when Princess Regent Isabel signed the Lei Aurea, the Golden Law which definitively abolished slavery throughout Brazil, São Paulo's planters were congratulating themselves on having anticipated the inevitable and ended slavery 'through the spontaneous will of the masters, without the intervention of the authorities', as a contemporary report prepared by the provincial government put it.[14]

As we have seen, however, abolition was precipitated not by the masters, but by the slaves. This was clearly perceived by most of the participants at the time. A French visitor to São Paulo at the turn of the century was informed by his hosts that slavery had been abolished because

---

Reis de Queiroz, *Escravidão negra em São Paulo: Um estudo das tensões provocades pelo escravismo no século XIX* (Rio de Janeiro, 1977), pp. 144–62; Sidney Chalhoub, 'Slaves, Freedmen, and the Politics of Freedom in Brazil: The Experience of Blacks in the City of Rio', unpubl. paper presented at the Conference on the Meaning of Freedom, Greensburg, Penn., Aug. 1988.

[13] Abolitionist Ruy Barbosa's description of the slaves' flight from the plantations suggests the tactics and moral tone of the US civil rights movement of the 1960s: 'the "I refuse" of the slaves, that glorious exodus of São Paulo's slaves, solemn, Biblical, as divine as the most beautiful episodes of the Scriptures...'. Quoted in Azevedo, *Onda negra*, p. 213, n. 52.

[14] *Relatório apresentado ao Exm. Sr. Presidente da Província de São Paulo pela Comissão Central da Estatística* (São Paulo, 1888), p. 245.

'the situation of such owners as had retained their slaves was becoming difficult; and discipline on the plantations was becoming impossible. The abolition law merely ratified the already profound disorganisation of slave labour' – a disorganisation produced, of course, by the slaves themselves.[15] An 1898 editorial commemorating the tenth anniversary of emancipation explained the event in almost identical terms:

Had the slaves not fled en masse from the plantations, rebelling against their masters... Had 20,000 of them not fled to the famous *quilombo* of Jabaquara [outside the port city of Santos], they might still be slaves today... Slavery ended because the slave didn't wish to be a slave any longer, because the slave rebelled against his master and the law that enslaved him... The May 13th law was no more than the legal sanctioning, so that public authority wouldn't be discredited, of an act that had already been consummated by the mass revolt of the slaves....[16]

Though planters might try to claim credit for the achievement of emancipation, contemporary and subsequent observers acknowledged it as 'a victory of the people and, we may add, a victory by the free blacks and slaves'.[17] Describing the abolition of slavery as 'the most genuine popular conquest' in Brazilian history, the *Diário de Campinas* stated flatly that 'the people made Abolition'. 'Quite rare in our land, the executive branch being the mere executor of a decree by the people,' mused São Paulo's *Diário Popular* on 14 May. And writing four years after the event, an editorialist in *O Estado de São Paulo* observed that popular opinion tended to attribute abolition to Princess Isabel's decision to free the slaves, but that in fact it had been the first expression of democracy in the country's history. 'A mass-based movement, deeply and profoundly of the people, and spread over the entire vastness of our country, we have but one example in our history, and that is the movement that on 13 May 1888 achieved its glorious ratification, and its recognition by the government.'[18]

For the first time in Brazilian history, a grassroots political movement had triumphed against oligarchical interests. The implications of such an event were literally revolutionary, as more than one observer noted at the time.[19] It also signalled to landowners the potential dangers posed by a political alliance between the monarchy and the masses – an alliance which

[15] Pierre Denis, *Brazil* (London, 1911), p. 183.   [16] *Rebate* (3 June 1898), p. 1.

[17] Costa, *Abolição*, p. 94.

[18] Cleber da Silva Maciel, *Discriminações raciais: Negros em Campinas (1888–1921)* (Campinas, 1988), p. 86; 'Liberdade, um compromisso assumido pelo "Diário Popular"', in *Abolição: 100 anos, Diário Popular* (12 May 1988), p. 5; 'Dia a dia', *O Estado de São Paulo* (13 May 1892), p. 1. President José Sarney echoed such judgements during the celebrations marking the centennial of Brazilian abolition, when he described abolition as 'the greatest civic campaign ever undertaken in this country'. 'Maestro acusa a Bossa Nova de racista', *Folha de São Paulo* (12 May 1988), p. 14.

[19] See, for example, Toplin, *Abolition*, pp. 239 and 245.

had been tacit and informal during most of the decade, but which took concrete form in late 1888 with the creation of the Black Guard, a para-military organisation of former slaves headed by mulatto abolitionist José do Patrocínio, the members of which were sworn to defend the monarchy against Republicanism.[20]

The Republican Party had been created in 1870 by São Paulo coffee planters responding in part to the threat represented by Dom Pedro's calls for gradual emancipation.[21] Now the reality of emancipation, and additional demands by the abolitionists for agrarian reform, land grants for former slaves, and 'democratisation of the soil', further alienated the landowning elite and pushed growing numbers of them into the Republican ranks. As a Rio newspaper noted at the time, 'the pact between the monarchical regime and the classes which formerly defended and upheld it was destroyed' by abolition.[22] São Paulo Republicans were now actively conspiring with discontented members of the officer corps to overthrow the monarchy; and when the armed forces struck, just a year and a half after abolition, landowners either stood aside or actively rejoiced in the fall of the Empire.

The only development that might have saved the monarchy was the formation of a new political pact in which rural and urban masses replaced the landowners as the monarchy's base of political support. Certainly such support was not lacking. Several historians note that, largely because of emancipation, the monarchy's popularity was at an all-time high in 1889, and monarchist sentiment continued to run strong among poor and working-class Brazilians well into the twentieth century.[23] Given the

[20] June Hahner, *Poverty and Politics: The Urban Poor in Brazil, 1870–1920* (Albuquerque, 1986), pp. 71–2. For alarmed reports in the São Paulo press on the Black Guard, see 'Santos 13', *A Província de São Paulo* (15 Jan. 1889); 'Guarda Negra', *A Província de São Paulo* (13 Jan. 1889); 'Contra a Guarda Negra', *A Província de São Paulo* (30 Jan. 1889); 'Os defensores da rainha', *A Província de São Paulo* (25 April 1889); 'Loucos ou ineptos', *A Província de São Paulo* (9 May 1889); 'Cartas do Rio', *Diário Popular* (13 May 1889); 'Cartas do interior', *Diário Popular* (22 May 1889).

[21] Conrad, *Destruction*, pp. 94–5.

[22] Quoted in Stanley J. Stein, *Vassouras: A Brazilian Coffee County, 1850–1900* (2nd edn., Princeton, 1985), p. 275. See also Richard Graham, 'Landowners and the Overthrow of the Empire', *Luso-Brazilian Review*, vol. 7, no. 2 (1970), pp. 44–56; Carvalho, *Teatro*, pp. 78–9.

[23] José Murilo de Carvalho, *Os bestializados: O Rio de Janeiro e a República que não foi* (São Paulo, 1987), pp. 29–31; Gilberto Freyre, *Order and Progress: Brazil from Monarchy to Republic* (New York, 1970), pp. 8–9 and 171; Chalhoub, 'Slaves, Freedmen...'. As late as the 1930s São Paulo's black press still carried news of monarchist clubs and social organisations. 'Gentileza', *Progresso* (24 Feb. 1929), p. 2; 'D. Pedro Henrique', *Progresso* (28 Sept. 1930), p. 1. When São Paulo's Vai-Vai samba school, today one of the city's most important, first incorporated itself in 1930, it opted to place a crown at the centre of its flag as an homage to the monarchy: 'Símbolos do samba, sem origem exata', *Folha de São Paulo* (20 Jan. 1985), p. 24. Arlindo Veiga dos Santos, the founder

institutional structure of the Empire, however, it proved impossible to bring the non-elite population into the political system at this late date as a source of support. The Empire had been based on the principle of either excluding non-elites from political participation, or admitting them only under conditions of tight control. In such a political environment, it was little short of a miracle that slavery had actually been brought down by a mass-based political movement; and once that movement's goal had been achieved, it was hardly surprising that abolitionism 'lacked the means of political reproduction' and proved unable to sustain either itself or the political system under which it had triumphed.[24] Nor was it surprising that Brazil's next constitutional experiment, the First Republic, would be structured in such a way as to prevent popular movements from ever again posing such a direct threat to elite interests.

Moment 2: *The First Republic, Vargas, and the Frente Negra Brasileira*

'It was only with the fall of the Empire', notes historian Sérgio Buarque de Holanda, 'that the empire of the planters began.'[25] Reacting to the Empire's concentration of authority in the hands of the monarch, the Republican Constitution of 1891 called for a decentralised federal structure in which the state governments retained substantial autonomy. Elite control of those governments, and of the federal Congress, was assured by levels of suffrage lower than those which had obtained during most of the Empire (i.e. until 1881). The result, as French observer Pierre Denis noted at the time, was a system in which

the sovereign people, before delegating its sovereignty to its representatives, confides to the ruling class the duty of supervising its electoral functions. The large landed proprietors choose the candidates, and their instructions are usually obeyed. They form the structure, the framework, of all party politics; they are its strength, its very life; it is they who govern and administer Brazil.[26]

---

of the Frente Negra Brasileira, discussed later in this article, was an ardent monarchist who in the 1960s was still editing a bi-monthly newspaper, *Monarquia*.

[24] Seymour Drescher, 'Brazilian Abolition in Comparative Perspective', *Hispanic American Historical Review*, vol. 68, no. 3 (1988), p. 460.

[25] Quoted in Carvalho, *Teatro de sombras*, p. 21.

[26] Denis, *Brazil*, pp. 21–2. See also Joseph Love's description of the Republic as a highly effective 'arrangement for the mutual support of incumbent elites at all levels of government...From 1889 through 1930, interparty competition was almost meaningless and usually nonexistent': Joseph L. Love, *São Paulo in the Brazilian Federation, 1889–1937* (Stanford, 1980), pp. xv and 139. See also Boris Fausto, 'Society and Politics', in Bethell, *Brazil*, pp. 265–79. On the extremely low levels of voter turn-out in the Republic, usually between one and three per cent of the population, see Joseph L. Love, 'Political Participation in Brazil, 1881–1969', *Luso-Brazilian Review*, vol. 7, no. 22 (1970), pp. 3–24; Carvalho, *Bestializados*, pp. 66–90.

Under the Republic, as under the monarchy, popular opposition again had to assert itself outside the tightly controlled institutional channels of the state. Such opposition took a variety of forms. One was a series of riots and uprisings, often with strongly monarchist overtones, which took place both in the backlands of rural Brazil and in the national capital of Rio de Janeiro between 1897 and 1916.[27] A second form of resistance to the Republic was the labour movement, which between 1917 and 1920 subjected São Paulo and Rio to several general strikes, and an abortive anarchist uprising in the national capital.[28] And a third form of protest was the *tenente* uprisings of the 1920s, revolts by young officers disgusted with the corruption and stagnation of the Republic. The first three of these revolts were successfully repressed by the government; the fourth, in 1930, was supported by agrarian elites in the south and northeast who felt that they had been locked out of national political power by their colleagues in São Paulo and Minas Gerais. With this civilian backing, the fourth *tenente* uprising brought the Republic to an end and introduced a new era in Brazilian politics, one dominated by the civilian leader of the so-called Revolution of 1930, Getúlio Vargas.[29]

Black people had particular reason to join in the agitation against the Republic. In addition to its open favouring of the planter class, whose interests were in direct and frequent conflict with those of the newly freed *libertos*, the Republic had embraced the doctrines of scientific racism and Social Darwinism, and launched Brazil on a national campaign intended to transform it from a colonial backwater into a 'tropical *belle époque*', a European society transplanted to the tropics. A major part of this national

[27] On the rural uprisings, see Euclides da Cunha, *Rebellion in the Backlands* (Chicago, 1944): Robert M. Levine, '"Mud-Hut Jerusalem": Canudos Revisited', *Hispanic American Historical Review*, vol. 68, no. 3 (1988), pp. 525–72; Todd Alan Diacon, 'Capitalists and Fanatics: Brazil's Contestado Rebellion, 1912–1916', unpubl. PhD diss., University of Wisconsin, 1987. On the 1904 Revolta da Vacina in Rio de Janeiro, see Carvalho, *Bestializados*, pp. 91–139; Jeffrey D. Needell, 'The *Revolta Contra Vacina* of 1904: The Revolt Against "Modernization" in *Belle Epoque* Rio de Janeiro', *Hispanic American Historical Review*, vol. 67, no. 2 (1987), pp. 223–70; Teresa Meade, '"Civilizing Rio de Janeiro": The Public Health Campaign and the Riot of 1904', *Journal of Social History*, vol. 20, no. 2 (1986), pp. 301–22. On the 1910 Revolta da Chibata, in which black sailors in Rio de Janeiro rebelled to protest against brutal punishments by their white officers, see Alvaro Bomilcar, *O preconceito de raça no Brasil* (Rio de Janeiro, 1916); Freyre, *Order and Progress*, pp. 400–2; Hahner, *Poverty and Politics*, pp. 171–2.

[28] On the labour movement during this period, see Boris Fausto, *Trabalho urbano e conflito social (1890–1920)* (São Paulo, 1977); Sheldon Leslie Maram, *Anarquistas, imigrantes e o movimento operário no Brasil, 1889–1930* (Rio de Janeiro, 1979); and Paulo Sérgio Pinheiro and Michael M. Hall (eds.), *A classe operária no Brasil, 1889–1930: Documentos*, vol. 1, *O movimento operário* (São Paulo, 1979).

[29] On the Revolution of 1930, see Boris Fausto, *A revolução de 1930* (São Paulo, 1970); and Silvio Duncan Baretta and John Markoff, 'The Limits of the Brazilian Revolution of 1930', *Review*, vol. 9, no. 3 (1986), pp. 413–52.

campaign was a conscious attempt to replace Brazil's racially mixed population with a 'whitened' population 'fortified' by European immigrants. The national government made the promotion of European immigration one of its primary policy objectives, and the state government of São Paulo invested millions of dollars in a programme to bring Europeans to the state by subsidising their steamship passages to Santos.[30]

Afro-Brazilians thus found themselves politically excluded by the Republic's limitations on suffrage and other forms of political participation; socially and psychologically excluded by the doctrines of scientific racism and the 'whitening thesis'; and economically excluded by the employment and other preferences granted to European immigrants over their black competitors.[31] Particularly in São Paulo, this racial exclusion extended to the various opposition movements as well. Though some elements of the labour movement made an effort to reach out to Afro-Brazilians, the domination of the movement by immigrant members and leaders tended to have a discouraging effect on black participation.[32] And when disgruntled members of São Paulo's middle and planter classes joined in 1926 to create the Democratic Party, they made no effort to bring Afro-Brazilians into their ranks, or to address any of the racial issues raised in the active black press of the 1920s.[33]

The failure of either the Republicans or the Democrats to consider the needs of the state's black population led members of São Paulo's black middle class to think about the possibility of entering *paulista* politics by means of a racially defined party or movement. As early as 1925 the capital's leading black paper, *O Clarim da Alvorada* (The Clarion of Dawn), had called for 'a political party comprised exclusively of men of colour'.

---

[30] On the campaign to Europeanise and 'whiten' Brazil during the Republic, see Jeffrey D. Needell, *A Tropical Belle Epoque: Elite Culture and Society in Turn-of-the-Century Rio de Janeiro* (Cambridge and New York, 1987); Thomas Skidmore, *Black into White: Race and Nationality in Brazilian Thought* (New York, 1974). [F. J. Oliveira Vianna], 'Evolução da raça', in Directoria Geral de Estatística, *Recenseamento do Brasil realizado em 1 de setembro de 1920*, vol. 1 (Rio de Janeiro, 1922), pp. 312–44, reviews in highly positive terms the progress of the campaign as of 1920.

[31] On the economic position of black workers during this period, see George Reid Andrews, 'Black and White Workers: São Paulo, Brazil, 1888–1928', *Hispanic American Historical Review*, vol. 68, no. 3 (1988), pp. 491–524; and Sam C. Adamo, 'The Broken Promise: Race, Health, and Justice in Rio de Janeiro, 1890–1940', unpubl. PhD diss., University of New Mexico, 1983.

[32] Andrews, 'Black and White Workers,' pp. 497–502. The situation was different in Rio de Janeiro, where the smaller size of the immigrant population and the larger number of non-whites made it possible for Afro-Brazilians to assume leadership roles in the labour movement there. See Hahner, *Poverty and Politics*, pp. 98–102 and 282–3; Fausto, *Trabalho urbano*, p. 55; Francisco Foot Hardman, 'Trabalhadores e negros no Brasil', *Folha de São Paulo* (16 May 1982).

[33] On the black press, see Miriam Nicolau Ferrara, *A imprensa negra paulista, 1915–1963* (São Paulo, 1986); *Imprensa negra* (São Paulo, 1984).

In 1929 it returned to this theme, posing the question, 'should the black man be a politician?', and responding with a strong affirmative. 'We have no knowledge of a single Governor who in his political platform has included a single line of interest to black people...If we could put together a voting bloc, then the black would see his position change, without having to bow down at every step to the will and commandments of others.'[34]

By overturning the Republic and its system of one-party rule, 1930 seemed to open the door to the realisation of this dream, and black activists were not slow to respond. Within a year, and following a series of well-attended public meetings, they had organised the Frente Negra Brasileira, a black political party which quickly spread throughout São Paulo state and into Minas Gerais, Espírito Santo, Bahia, and Rio Grande do Sul.[35]

In explaining the reasons for the initial rapid expansion of the Frente, contemporary observers stressed the widespread sense among black people of the new opportunities for political participation created by the change in regime. A report in the mainstream press on one of the Frente's organising meetings noted the palpable atmosphere of hope and expectation among those present. 'Last night's meeting was truly noteworthy, both in terms of attendance, which was enormous, and of the speeches given...One visibly feels the awakening of a national con-sciousness among the black Brazilians, driving them toward more direct participation in the social and political life of the country....' Recalling those meetings years later, one who took part in them stressed the same theme: 'the blacks wanted to participate because they felt themselves to be the greatest beneficiaries of the revolution [of 1930]. The slavocracy had been deposed from power, the men who always scorned and despised the blacks. Now it was time for the blacks to take part.'[36] Even relatively conservative black papers, such as *Progresso*, which had spent the 1920s trying to downplay the extent of discrimination and racism in the city, and urging moderation and accommodation on its readers, could not resist the excitement:

In the hour in which Brazil prepares to convene its Constitutional Assembly [of 1933], setting the tone for the new Brazil, the men and women of the black race

[34] 'A esmola', *O Clarim da Alvorada* (15 Nov. 1925); 'O negro deve ser político?', *O Clarim da Alvorada* (27 Oct. 1929).

[35] The definitive history of the Frente Negra remains to be written. For accounts of its activities, see Fernandes, *Integração do negro*, vol. 2, pp. 29–87; Moura, 'Organizações negras', pp. 154–7; Mitchell, 'Racial Consciousness', pp. 131–9; Ferrara, *Imprensa negra*, pp. 62–77.

[36] 'Movimento de arregimentação da raça negra no Brasil', *Diário de São Paulo* (17 Sept. 1931), p. 5; 'Depoimentos', *Cadernos Brasileiros*, no. 47 (1968), p. 21.

must prepare to fight so that in that Assembly black people are represented by their legitimate racial brothers... Men and women of the black race, struggle bravely so that in the highest councils of the nation the voice of the blacks will lift like a clarion, imposing on Brazil the splendours of Justice for our race.[37]

The public reaction to the Frente exceeded any of its organisers' expectations. In later years, former leaders recalled their amazement at the outpouring of enthusiasm in the community, and their uncertainty as to how to proceed in the face of such a response. Francisco Lucrécio, who joined the organisation in his early twenties, recalls how 'we were exhausted, we used to come out of [Frente headquarters] sick because we were dedicated, we were fanatics. I didn't do anything else: just study, go home, and go to the Frente. I never went to the movies, never went to the theatre.' São Paulo papers covering the organisation's first political campaign (in 1933 its founder and president, Arlindo Veiga dos Santos, ran for the city council) interviewed youths who had been working for 48 hours without rest, covering the city with posters for their candidate.[38]

Despite this prodigious expenditure of effort and energy, the Frente never succeeded in electing a single one of its candidates, or in becoming a significant factor within São Paulo politics. This was in part a function of the continuing restriction of suffrage to literates. Furthermore, the great majority of the state's black population still lived in the countryside during the 1930s, its vote subject to close control by rural landowners and *coroneis*.[39]

Also contributing to the Frente's political weakness, however, was a process of internal political conflict and eventual self-destruction which replicated in microcosm the larger trajectory of Brazilian politics during the 1930s. As in a number of other European and Latin American nations weathering the economic crisis of that decade, Brazilian politics became polarised between a Communist-dominated Popular Front movement, the Aliança Nacional Libertadora, and the Brazilian variant of European Fascism, the Integralist movement, founded in São Paulo in 1932.[40] The Frente Negra had initially drawn support from a broad spectrum of political opinion within the black community, but within months of its

---

[37] 'Frente Unica', *Progresso* (15 Nov. 1931), p. 3.
[38] Fernandes, *Integração do negro*, vol. 2, p. 19; 'Frente Negra Brasileira' (unpubl. collaborative *trabalho de pesquisa*, Pontifícia Universidade Católica – São Paulo, 1985), anexo 3 (unpag.); 'A Frente Negra Brasileira trabalha pela victória do seu candidato', *Correio de São Paulo* (1 May 1933), p. 7.
[39] Despite the provisional government's rhetoric of expanded political participation, voter turn-out as a percentage of the total population actually declined between the elections of 1930 (under the Republic) and 1934, from 5.7% of the adult population to 5.5%. Love, 'Political Participation', p. 16.
[40] The political history of this period is covered in Robert M. Levine, *The Vargas Regime: The Crucial Years, 1934–1938* (New York, 1970).

founding it had moved into a close relationship with the Integralists.[41] Both organisations espoused an unrepentant xenophobia, and repeatedly denounced foreign domination of Brazilian life, as personified by foreign capitalists, foreign landlords, and 'the pro-foreigner policies which marked the ominous dominion of the Paulista Republican Party'. In their speeches and publications, the Frente's leaders called for 'a hard nationalist campaign, against the foreign or semi-foreign slime that engineers divisions, Bolshevism, Socialism, and other vile and infamous things', and urged the Vargas regime to 'close the doors of Brazil [to foreigners] for twenty years or more' so that black people could reconquer their rightful position in the country.[42]

The Frente Negra shared with Integralism a contemptuous disdain for liberal democracy and, despite both organisations' frequently voiced rejection of foreign political philosophies, an open admiration for European Fascism. In a 1933 editorial saluting Adolf Hitler's rise to power, Arlindo Veiga dos Santos congratulated him for rescuing Germany from the hands of 'Jewish cosmopolitanism' and 'the narcotic opiate of fourteen years of liberal-democratic republicanism'. Essays in the Frente's newspaper, *A Voz da Raça* (The Voice of the Race) reported in highly positive terms on the achievements of Nazism and Fascism in instilling discipline and patriotism in their people. This admiration for authoritarianism extended to the Frente's own system of internal governance: officers were chosen not by election but rather by incumbent officeholders, and the organisation as a whole was policed by a 'militia' modelled on the Integralists' Green Shirts and commanded by Pedro Paulo Barbosa, a dedicated anti-Communist and supporter of Mussolini.[43]

The Fascist orientation of both the Integralists and the Frente reflected the anxieties of São Paulo's middle and lower-middle classes, and their fear of powerful pressures from above and below. They had deeply resented their exclusion from politics by the planter-dominated Republic; and they feared as well the fierce competition for jobs, education and upward mobility which they faced from the European immigrants and the

---

[41] The Frente's founder, Arlindo Veiga dos Santos, had been active in several of the proto-Fascist organisations in São Paulo which preceded the establishment of Integralism. Hélgio Trindade, *Integralismo: O fascismo brasileiro na década de 30* (2nd edn., São Paulo, 1979), pp. 114 n. 72, 118 n. 85.

[42] Quotes from 'Apelo à economia', *A Voz da Raça* (28 Oct. 1933), p. 1; 'A afirmação da raça', *A Voz da Raça* (10 June 1933), p. 1. As Fernandes correctly notes, the Frente's paper, *A Voz da Raça*, offers 'abundant material' along these lines. Fernandes, *Integração do negro*, vol. 2, p. 49 n. 40.

[43] 'Afirmação da raça'; 'Apreciando', *A Voz da Raça* (Oct. 1936), p. 1; for essays by Pedro Paulo Barbosa, see 'Apreciando' and 'O perigo vermelho', *A Voz da Raça* (Nov. 1936), p. 1.

immigrants' children. Many responded by embracing the strident nationalism and xenophobia of Integralism, and by rejecting the liberal democracy discredited by the corruption and fraud of the Republic.[44]

To judge by its rhetoric, the Frente Negra's middle-class leadership shared these feelings and frustrations.[45] However, the Frente's Fascist orientation proved of limited appeal to the black population as a whole. As the organisation allied itself ever more closely with Integralism (it even adopted as its own the Integralists' motto of 'for family, for country, and for God', modifying it slightly by adding 'for race'), it progressively alienated both working-class and middle-class support within the black community, driving moderate and left-wing dissenters in São Paulo city to create the Clube Negro de Cultura Social and the small Frente Negra Socialista.[46] The Frente chapter in the port city of Santos cut ties with the central organisation to enter into an electoral alliance with the Socialist Party (which, characteristically, the São Paulo headquarters dismissed as 'a horde of undesirables from other countries'). The Frente responded to such dissidents with vicious attacks in *A Voz da Raça* on 'Judases to their race' and by sending its militia to wreck the offices of a black newspaper critical of its orientation.[47]

Such conflicts prevented the Frente from achieving its goal of becoming a significant political force in São Paulo or anywhere else in Brazil. And similar Left–Right polarisation at the national level prevented Brazil as a whole from realising 1930's promise of expanded participation and broad-based democracy. An abortive Communist uprising in 1935, and allegations of a planned Integralist putsch, led Getúlio Vargas in 1937 to suspend the new constitution and institute the New State, a corporatist dictatorship closely modelled on Portuguese and Italian Fascism. The Frente saluted the new regime as 'the reaffirmation of *brasilidade*' and pledged its full support.[48] Shortly thereafter it was banned by the New

[44] On middle-class nativism and support for Fascism during the 1920s and 1930s, see Steven Topik, 'Middle-Class Nationalism, 1889–1930', *Social Science Quarterly*, vol. 59, no. 1 (1978), pp. 93–103; Trindade, *Integralismo*, pp. 130–49.

[45] All members of the Frente leadership for whom professions could be ascertained were professionals or white-collar office workers. These include Arlindo Veiga dos Santos (clerk-secretary), Raul Joviano Amaral (accountant), António Martins dos Santos (engineer), Francisco Lucrécio (dentist), and others.

[46] On the organisation's difficulties in retaining both working- and middle-class support, see 'Por acaso', *A Voz da Raça* (31 Aug. 1935), p. 4; 'Alvorada da "Frente Negra"', *A Voz da Raça* (July 1936), p. 2.

[47] On these splits within the movement, see Mitchell, 'Racial Consciousness', pp. 135–7. On the Socialist Party, 'É o cúmulo', *A Voz da Raça* (20 Jan. 1934), p. 1; on the attacks on the anti-Frente newspaper *Chibata*, 'Foi empastellado o jornal "Chibata"', *Diário Nacional* (20 March 1932), p. 8; 'O empastellamento d'A Chibata', *Diário Nacional* (22 March 1932).

[48] 'O negro na face da situação atual', *A Voz da Raça* (Nov. 1937), p. 1.

State's blanket proscription of all political parties. Reduced to a handful of members, it struggled on for several months as a non-political civic organisation but then formally dissolved in May 1938, shortly after the fiftieth anniversary of emancipation.

Moment 3: The Second Republic

The New State came to an end with the military coup of 1945, and the inauguration the following year of the Second Republic. The resulting restoration of civil liberties and party politics seemed at first glance to open the doors for a resurgence of the black movement. São Paulo's black press, which had disappeared under the dictatorship, promptly resurfaced with the appearance of *Alvorada* in September 1945, *Senzala* in January 1946, and *O Novo Horizonte* in May 1946. The Convenção Nacional do Negro Brasileiro was hastily convened in the state capital a month after the fall of the dictatorship, work began on the creation of a new Associação do Negro Brasileiro, and community leaders began to prepare for the elections of 1946.[49]

All of these efforts (save the black papers, which continued into the 1950s and were joined by several additional publications) failed, and no racially defined political movement comparable to the Frente Negra appeared during the Second Republic. In part this was due to bitter memories of the Frente's failings.[50] Probably more important in explaining this development, however, were the changes which Brazil had undergone during the Vargas years, and the marked differences between the Second Republic and the First.

The New State had actively promoted Brazilian industrialisation, which led to the rapid growth of the industrial economy and a corresponding increase in the industrial labour force. Vargas' policies had also imposed a new system of organisation on that labour force, mobilising it into state-sponsored unions subject to close government supervision and control. Under the New State, the unions were expected to maintain a high level of workplace discipline and quiescence among factory workers, and to provide a solid base of political support for the government.[51]

These new developments were particularly visible in São Paulo, the heartland of the Brazilian industrial economy, and had powerful implications for the state's black population. Afro-Brazilians had been

[49] Fernandes, *Integração do negro*, vol. 2, pp. 88–115.
[50] See, for example, 'Advertência', *Senzala* (Jan. 1946), pp. 14, 28; 'Problemas e aspirações', *Diário Trabalhista* (12 July 1946), p. 4; 'Nem tudo que reluz é ouro', *Alvorada* (April 1946), p. 4.
[51] The Vargas system of labour relations is discussed in Kenneth Paul Erickson, *The Brazilian Corporative State and Working-Class Politics* (Berkeley, 1977). On how that system functioned in practice in São Paulo, see French, 'Industrial Workers…'.

systematically excluded from the opportunities created by the economic growth of the 1890–1930 period, when blue-collar employment had been dominated by European immigrants. After 1930, however, restrictions on immigration into Brazil (part of Vargas' efforts to combat the Depression and to win support among Brazilian workers) combined with conditions in Europe greatly to reduce immigration into the country. As industrial growth accelerated, Afro-Brazilians no longer had to face job competition from the immigrants, and were now able to start entering the industrial economy and obtain the factory jobs that had previously been denied them.[52]

This entry of black workers into the industrial labour force had direct political consequences. First, by lowering previous barriers to black participation in the industrial economy, it considerably reduced the sense of grievance among the black population. Secondly, by enlisting black workers in the state-controlled labour movement, it integrated Afro-Brazilians into the Brazilian political system in a new and unprecedented way. Those black workers who could vote (suffrage was still restricted to literates, though this requirement was often circumvented for union members) were openly courted by the labour-based political parties which competed for power in the new Republic. The Communist Party, Getúlio Vargas' Partido Trabalhista Brasileiro (PTB), and, in São Paulo, Adhemar de Barros's Partido Social Progressista (PSP) – each of these parties, and the labour movement from which they drew their support, was aggressively seeking black support and welcoming black voters into its ranks.[53]

The receptiveness of the populist parties to black voters substantially reduced sentiment in the black community for racially defined political activity along the lines of the Frente Negra. The result was that the black organisations of the 1946–64 period were almost exclusively cultural in their orientation, focusing on literacy and other educational projects, the fostering of black literary, theatrical and artistic activities, and so on. Indeed, the pre-eminent black organisation in São Paulo during these years, in terms of membership and visibility, embodied this orientation in its very name: the Associação Cultural do Negro, founded in 1954 by

[52] By 1950 Afro-Brazilians comprised 11.3% of São Paulo's industrial labour force, a figure virtually identical to their 11.2% representation in the population as a whole. Instituto Brasileiro de Geografia e Estatística (hereafter IBGE), *Censo demográfico: Estado de São Paulo, 1950* (Rio de Janeiro, 1954), p. 30.

[53] The PSP, for example, maintained close ties with the black newspaper *O Novo Horizonte*; see 'Mensagem aos negros' (Sept. 1954), p. 5, and numerous other articles in the issues prior to the elections of 1954. The smaller Partido Socialista Brasileiro had a similar relationship with *Mundo Novo*. On black support for Getúlio Vargas and the PTB during this period, see Souza, 'Raça e política'.

journalist Geraldo Campos de Oliveira, which functioned into the late 1970s.[54]

By admitting Afro-Brazilians to political participation, the populist institutions of the Second Republic greatly reduced the perceived need for a racially separate, black political movement. As those class-based institutions asserted themselves in Brazilian politics, however, they provoked stiffening opposition on the part of the elites and a substantial proportion of the middle class, both of which felt increasingly threatened by the demands and power of the populist parties. This opposition culminated in the military coup of March 1964, which closed down the Second Republic and inaugurated a twenty-one-year period of military dictatorship.

Moment 4: redemocratisation and the modern black movement

During its years in power, the military sought to restructure Brazil both politically and economically: to replace the 'irresponsible, corrupt' democracy of the Second Republic with reformed institutions less vulnerable to populist excesses; and economically, to move Brazil further down the road of industrialisation and modernisation on which it had embarked during the Vargas years and continued during the Second Republic.

The officers enjoyed considerable success in achieving their second goal. Economic growth averaged more than 10% per year during the 'miracle' years of 1968–74; by 1980, Brazil's industrial output was the seventh-largest in the capitalist world.[55] However, the benefits of economic expansion were grossly maldistributed, flowing disproportionately to the upper and middle classes (the top 20% of the population), and bypassing the working class, which saw the real value of the state-determined minimum wage shrink to between 50 and 60% of the purchasing power it had achieved at its height in the late 1950s.[56]

Within the middle class as well, the benefits of economic growth were by no means evenly distributed. Much like their grandparents during the early decades of the century, though now at a quite different level of the economy, black high-school and university graduates seeking white-collar

---

[54] On the association's activities, see its monthly newspaper, *O Mutirão*, which began publication on the seventieth anniversary of abolition, in May 1958. See also Moura, 'Organizações negras', pp. 157–9; and 'Embora perto (e às vezes junto), o negro está muito longe do branco', *Última Hora* (17 Oct. 1973).

[55] George Thomas Kurian, *The New Book of World Rankings* (New York, 1984), p. 199.

[56] Margaret Keck, 'The New Unionism in the Brazilian Transition', in Alfred Stepan (ed.), *Democratizing Brazil: Problems of Transition and Consolidation* (New York, 1987), table 3, p. 270. On the 'wage-squeeze' of the 1970s, see also Charles H. Wood and José Alberto Magno de Carvalho, *The Demography of Inequality in Brazil* (Cambridge and New York, 1988), pp. 104–24.

and professional jobs in São Paulo's booming economy found themselves relegated to the least desirable positions, or rejected for employment altogether. The initial evidence of racial barriers in the white-collar job market was largely anecdotal; but government data gathered in the national household survey of 1976 made clear that racial exclusion was not a random phenomenon, confined to scattered individuals. Those data conclusively demonstrated the existence of racial inequities at all levels of the work force, and particularly severe inequality in white-collar and professional jobs. Furthermore, those data indicated that the higher the level of education attained by Afro-Brazilian jobseekers, the greater the disparity, both in absolute and percentage terms, between the salaries which they and their similarly prepared white competitors were receiving.[57]

Even before these findings became available to the public, a younger generation of Afro-Brazilians, many with one or more years of university study, were starting to organise a new black movement in response to the economic and political exclusion which they were experiencing under the dictatorship. This movement, most vividly symbolised by the Movimento Negro Unificado, created in São Paulo in 1978, was considerably more militant than any of its predecessors, reflecting in part the influence of its foreign models – the national liberation movements in Portugal's African colonies, and the civil rights and black power movements of the United States – and in part the strongly leftist orientation of much of the political opposition to the dictatorship, especially in southeastern Brazil.[58]

[57] These findings are presented in Francisca Laíde de Oliveira et al., 'Aspectos da situação sócio-econômica de brancos e negros no Brasil', internal rpt., IBGE, 1981; Carlos Hasenbalg, '1976 – as desigualdades revisitadas', and Nelson do Valle Silva, 'Cor e o processo de realização sócio-econômica', both in *Movimentos sociais urbanos, minorias étnicas e outros estudos, Ciências Sociais Hoje*, vol. 2 (1983), and both published in English translation in Fontaine, *Race, Class and Power*; Lúcia Elena Garcia de Oliveira et al., *O lugar do negro na força de trabalho* (Rio de Janeiro, 1985). For studies that draw similar conclusions on the basis of the national censuses of 1960 and 1980, see Nelson do Valle Silva, 'Black–White Income Differentials: Brazil, 1960', unpubl. PhD diss., University of Michigan, 1978; and Peggy A. Lovell, 'Racial Inequality and the Brazilian Labor Market' unpubl. PhD diss., University of Florida, 1989.
    The pool of Afro-Brazilian high-school and college graduates in São Paulo increased substantially between 1950 and 1980, from 3,898 to 101,148. In 1950 only 0.3% of São Paulo's Afro-Brazilians had graduated from high school, and 0.03% from college; by 1980 1.5% of the state's black population had graduated from high school, and an additional 0.7% had completed one or more years of university study. Among the white population in 1980, 5.4% were high-school graduates, and an additional 5.1% had taken one or more years of university study. IBGE, *Censo demográfico: São Paulo, 1950*, table 20, p. 24; IBGE, *Censo demográfico – dados gerais, migração, instrução, fecundidade, mortalidade – São Paulo, 1980* (Rio de Janeiro, 1982), table 1.5, pp. 12–13.
[58] Joel Rufino dos Santos, 'O movimento negro e a crise brasileira', unpubl. ms., 1985; Mitchell, 'Blacks and the *Abertura Democrática*'. On the Movimento Negro Unificado in particular, see Lélia Gonzalez, 'The Unified Black Movement: A New Stage in Black

This new movement of the 1970s and 1980s was to a large degree the expression of frustration among upwardly mobile Afro-Brazilians denied admission to the middle-class status to which their education and qualifications entitled them. Its activists worked hard at recruiting support in the slums and *favelas* of the urban *periferia*, but their rhetoric and aspirations often seemed somewhat removed from the lives of poor and working-class blacks facing the immediate, grinding problems of poverty, crime and hunger.[59] Still, despite its resulting difficulties in attracting a mass following, the black movement had major impacts on Brazilian life during the 1980s, exercising a degree of political influence out of all proportion to its actual membership, and provoking more state response in the area of race than at any time since 1888.

A major part of the explanation for this success may be found in the 'party reform' of 1979. Prior to that time, the dictatorship had permitted the existence of only a single opposition party, the Movimento Democrático Brasileiro. Eventually recognising that such a policy provided the perfect mechanism for its opponents to join forces, in 1979 the government freed the opposition to return to multi-party competition. The Movimento Negro Unificado had been founded just the year before and, inspired by its example, local-level black organisations were coming into existence throughout Brazil.[60] As the newly created opposition

---

Political Mobilization', in Fontaine, *Race, Class and Power*, pp. 120–34; 'Negro: A luta continua', *Cadernos do CEAS*, no. 72 (March–April 1981), pp. 18–28; Movimento Negro Unificado, *Programa de ação* (Campinas, 1984).

For examples of literature and analysis produced by activists and intellectuals associated with the black movement, see Abdias do Nascimento, *O genocídio do negro brasileiro: Processo de um racismo mascarado* (Rio de Janeiro, 1978), and *Quilombismo* (Petrópolis, 1980); Moura, *O negro*, and *Sociologia do negro brasileiro*; Joel Rufino dos Santos, *O que é racismo* (São Paulo, 1980); Sueli Carneiro and Thereza Santos, *Mulher negra* (São Paulo, 1985); Quilombhoje, *Reflexões* (São Paulo, 1985); Paulo Colina (ed.), *Axe: Antologia contemporânea da poesia negra brasileira* (São Paulo, 1982); and the literary annual *Cadernos Negros* (São Paulo, 1978–).

[59] For a discussion of the problems middle-class activists experienced in working with poor and working-class blacks, see 'Avaliando nosso movimento', in Grupo Negro da PUC, Boletim 3, *A luta continua* (São Paulo, 1984), pp. 16–26. For survey data on the attitudes of black voters, by education and income level, toward the black movement, see Ana Lúcia E. F. Valente, *Política e relações raciais: Os negros e as eleições paulistas de 1982* (São Paulo, 1986), pp. 125–43.

[60] Two separate estimates suggest that 200–250 such organisations were in existence in Brazil by 1984. Santos, 'Movimento negro', p. 1; Cándido Mendes, 'O quilombo urbano pede passagem', *Folha de São Paulo* (6 Aug. 1984), p. 3. A study carried out during 1986 and 1987 found 343 such organisations in Brazil as a whole: 138 in São Paulo, 76 in Rio de Janeiro, 33 in Minas Gerais, 27 in Bahia, and the rest scattered throughout the country. Caetana Damasceno et al., *Catálogo de entidades de movimento negro no Brasil, Comunicações do ISER* [*Instituto de Estudos da Religião*], no. 29 (1988).

parties competed among themselves for electoral support, they directed particular attention to this burgeoning black movement, inserting anti-racism planks into their platforms, and creating special working groups and commissions to investigate racial problems in Brazil.

This inter-party competition for black electoral support was particularly visible in São Paulo, where fifty-four Afro-Brazilian candidates were nominated for municipal, state and national-level offices in the elections of 1982.[61] Reflecting the movement's inability to mobilise mass support, only two of those candidates were elected (one to the state Legislative Assembly, and the other to the São Paulo city council); nevertheless, when the leading opposition party, the Partido do Movimento Democrático Brasileiro (PMDB), swept the government party from power that year, it proceeded to establish a new state agency, the Conselho de Participação e Desenvolvimento da Comunidade Negra, charged, in the words of the executive decree which created it, with 'carrying out studies on the condition of the black community and proposing measures aimed at defending its rights, and eliminating the discrimination which affects it'.[62] Following the elections of 1986, in which the PMDB was again victorious, anti-discrimination offices were created in the Secretariats of Education and Labour, and black union activist Oswaldo Ribeiro was appointed to head the newly created Special Secretariat of Social Relations.[63]

These new agencies are small, fledgling organisations occupying minute niches within the colossal structure of the Brazilian state, and critics of the PMDB, and of the black activists associated with the party, have been quick to denounce them as purely cosmetic entities with no real political influence or significance.[64] Viewing these developments from a

---

[61] João Baptista Borges Pereira, 'Aspectos do comportamento político do negro em São Paulo', *Ciência e Cultura*, vol. 34, no. 10 (1982), pp. 1,286–94; João Baptista Borges Pereira, 'Parámetros ideológicos do projeto político de negros em São Paulo', *Revista do Instituto de Estudos Brasileiros*, no. 24 (1982), pp. 53–61; Valente, *Política e relações raciais*.   [62] *Diário Oficial. Estado de São Paulo* (12 May 1984).

[63] Similar developments took place in Rio de Janeiro, where Governor Leonel Brizola, who had campaigned on a platform of 'socialismo moreno' (literally, 'brown socialism'), appointed three Afro-Brazilians to his cabinet (the Secretaries of Labour and Housing, Military Police, and Social Affairs – all areas of particular interest to his Afro-Brazilian constituency) and undertook a number of policy initiatives aimed at benefiting the city's poor population, which is heavily black. On Afro-Brazilian support for Brizola and his party, the Partido Democrático Trabalhista, see Soares and Silva, 'Urbanization, Race, and Class'.

[64] See, for example, the criticisms reported in 'Conselho busca adesões e apoio', *Caderno C, Diário do Grande ABC* (24 Nov. 1985).

historical perspective, one must disagree. Never before, to my knowledge, had a state or national government in Brazil ever officially contradicted the country's image of itself as a racial democracy. Nor had a Brazilian government ever taken the step of creating a set of state agencies with a vested interest in publicising, and stimulating public debate on, the issues of discrimination and inequality. In 1984 the Secretariat of Culture initiated Projeto Zumbi, a month-long programme of lectures, concerts, art exhibits, public debates, and TV and radio programmes which takes place each November. The following year the Conselho de Desenvolvimento e Participação da Comunidade Negra began to publish a bimonthly newspaper distributed free of charge in black neighbourhoods and the central business district, as well as inexpensive booklets on black history, black literature, and racial problems in Brazil.[65] The anti-discrimination office at the Secretariat of Labour focused its efforts on union leaders and on personnel administrators in São Paulo firms, trying to enlist both groups in a campaign to eliminate discrimination in hiring and promotion. And in 1988 the Secretariat of Education's Grupo de Trabalho para Assuntos Afro-Brasileiros produced 200,000 copies of a special magazine on the centennial of emancipation, which was distributed to students and teachers in the São Paulo public schools and used as a basis for class discussions of the event.[66]

These state initiatives combined with the consciousness-raising work and lobbying of the black movement more generally to stimulate a broad debate and discussion in Brazilian society on the nature of race relations in that country, and the degree to which the image of racial democracy accurately reflects racial realities. Carried out in the print and electronic media, and in venues ranging from elementary schools to samba schools, from prestigious universities to humble Christian base communities, this debate reached a climax of sorts in the festivities marking the centennial of Brazilian emancipation in 1988, during which the concept of Brazil as a racial democracy was roundly criticised. The Catholic church devoted its annual Lenten Brotherhood Campaign to the theme of race relations, distributing a *texto base* which condemned past Church complicity in slavery, and present-day racial discrimination.[67] Federal Minister of Culture Celso Furtado, whose ministry was responsible for coordinating the centennial activities, stated flatly that 'the idea that there is racial

[65] On the activities of the Conselho and the other black agencies, see the *Jornal do Conselho da Comunidade Negra*.

[66] Interviews, Grupo de Orientação e Interferência em Situações de Discriminação Racial no Trabalho, Secretária de Relações do Trabalho, May–June 1988; *Salve o 13 de maio?* (São Paulo, 1988).

[67] Comissão dos Religiosos, Seminaristas e Padres Negros – Rio de Janeiro, '*Ouvi o clamor deste povo*'...*negro!* (Petrópolis, 1988).

democracy in Brazil is false'.[68] The nation's two leading news weeklies both concurred, *Istoé* noting that 'the myth of racial democracy appears to be definitively in its grave', while *Veja* implicitly dismissed the concept by opening its cover story on the centennial with the observation that 'one hundred years after Abolition, in Brazil there are two distinct citizenships – white and black'.[69] Similar observations appeared in other prominent newspapers and magazines, and even in a somewhat unexpected quarter: the nationalist and politically centrist *The Brasilians*, a monthly newspaper published in New York by Brazilian *émigrés*. In its editorial commemorating the centennial, the paper reviewed recent statistical data documenting racial inequality in Brazil, strongly condemned the history of racial discrimination in that country, and saluted the 'new and long overdue openness in dealing with racial issues there'. As far as racial democracy was concerned, the editors' attitude was succinctly expressed by the editorial's title: 'Another Myth Bites the Dust.'[70]

The future in light of the past

At the very moment, however, that it was redefining the national discourse on race, the black movement of the 1980s was visibly receding, losing political influence and weight. Just as the Frente Negra's Fascist orientation had antagonised initial supporters in the 1930s, the Marxist militancy of the Movimento Negro Unificado had a similarly alienating effect in the 1980s. One of the MNU's founders described in 1984 how the movement 'kept getting narrower and narrower ideologically, characterising itself increasingly as a movement of the left... After a year, it started to lose militants and strength.'[71] As the MNU faded in importance, no comparable organisation emerged to replace it, and by 1988 *Istoé* observed that the black movement as a whole was in a state of 'dramatic pulverisation... Ten years after the boom of the black movements, much of the initial euphoria has dissipated.'[72]

[68] 'Vem ai cem anos de ebulição', *A Gazeta* (13 May 1988), p. 13.

[69] 'Cem anos, sem quasi nada', *Istoé* (20 April 1988), p. 30; 'Na segunda classe', *Veja* (11 May 1988), p. 22.

[70] 'Another Myth Bites the Dust', *The Brasilians* (May–June 1988), p. 2. See also 'Cem anos depois', *Folha de São Paulo* (13 May 1988), p. 2; 'Cem anos de solidão', *Caderno B, Jornal do Brasil* (8 May 1988); 'Brasil: Os negros, hoje', *Manchete* (21 May 1988), pp. 4–9.

[71] 'Movimento negro avalia sua importância', *Folha de São Paulo* (15 April 1984); see also 'Avaliando nosso movimento', p. 16. Even a sympathetic observer describes the MNU's ideological orientation as 'notoriously rigid'. Joel Rufino [dos Santos], 'IPCN e Cacique de Ramos: Dois exemplos de movimento negro na cidade do Rio de Janeiro', *Comunicações do ISER*, vol. 7, no. 28 (1988), p. 6.

[72] 'No rastro de Zumbi', *Istoé* (20 April 1988), p. 42.

This decline can be traced in part to the pressures, both political and economic, which were undermining all popular movements in Brazil by the mid-1980s.[73] However, a comparative examination of the instances of black mobilisation summarised in this essay suggests some additional factors specific to the history of black movements in Brazil. In all four cases, middle-class militants experienced enormous difficulties in bridging the gap between themselves and the poor and working-class blacks whom they sought to organise. This divergence between middle- and lower-class interests and aspirations contributed directly to the demise of the Frente Negra, and was one of the major obstacles facing the black movement of the 1980s. The alliance between slaves and middle-class abolitionists, both black and white, in the 1880s appears at first glance to constitute an exception to this generalisation. But the middle-class abolitionists were most important, not in providing leadership to the slave population, but rather in creating a climate of public opinion opposed to slavery, and in providing protection for fleeing slaves in the state capital, Santos and other urban areas. The actual leadership of that mass flight fell to the slaves themselves, or to black and white *caifazes* who were predominantly of working-class background.[74] Once emancipation had taken place, the abolitionist movement soon dissolved, and the black middle class devoted itself either to the pursuit of upward mobility through cultural and biological whitening or, failing that, to a tightly circumscribed world of clubs and dances which excluded *libertos* and members of the black proletariat. Not until the 1930s, nearly fifty years after emancipation, did its members venture forth again to play the role of leaders of the black masses.[75]

Thus in Brazil, as in the United States and other multiracial societies, class divisions within the black population have posed a significant obstacle to political mobilisation along racial lines. Those divisions can occasionally be overcome, however, by conditions of racial and/or political oppression sufficiently powerful to force black elites and masses into alliance, even if only temporarily. Our four cases suggest that those experiences of black mobilisation which have had the greatest societal and political impact have been those which developed under exclusionary, anti-democratic regimes, and in response to highly visible forms of racial injustice.

[73] 'O pais muda e os movimentos sociais perdem muitos adeptos', *Folha de São Paulo* (23 Sept. 1984); Scott Mainwaring, 'Grassroots Popular Movements and the Struggle for Democracy: Nova Iguaçu', in Stepan, *Democratizing Brazil*, pp. 168–204.

[74] Alice Aguiar de Barros Fontes, 'A práctica abolicionista em São Paulo: Os caifazes, 1882–1888', unpubl. *tese de mestrado*, University of São Paulo, 1976.

[75] On São Paulo's 'black bourgeoisie' during the earlys 1900s, see Andrews, *Blacks and Whites*, pp. 129–43.

The first such instance, both chronologically and in terms of its social and political ramifications, was the struggle against slavery, the most extreme form of racial oppression in Brazilian history. Despite the sympathetic attitude of the monarchy, abolitionism was radicalised and forced outside the formal political system by Parliament's drastic reduction of suffrage in 1881. The result was a mass-based popular movement which succeeded in destroying the institution on which Brazilian society and economy had been based for more than three hundred years. Such a movement was profoundly threatening to the planters, who responded by withdrawing their support from the monarchy and replacing it with the oligarchical, decentralised First Republic.

The next two instances of black mobilisation, the Frente Negra and the cultural organisations of the Second Republic, both had negligible political impacts. They also both took place during periods of political 'opening' and of efforts by *Varguista* populism to integrate black people, as part of the urban working class, into the state-dominated labour unions and, during the Second Republic, into labour-based political parties. Racial mobilisation might not have taken place during the 1930s at all had it not been for the recent memory and concrete legacies of the racial exclusion of the First Republic, and the continuing hostility of the mainstream parties to black participation. By the 1940s and 1950s the integration of the black population into the industrial work-force and the creation of new populist parties actively seeking black support had removed the need for a racially defined political movement. As a result, the Second Republic produced no black political movement comparable to those of the 1880s, 1930s or 1980s.

This brings us to the movement of the 1970s and 1980s, which has had an impact on state politics and national racial ideology second only to the abolitionism of the 1880s. This recent movement arose under conditions of marked political exclusion and authoritarianism, and formed part of the larger, society-wide protest against the military dictatorship. It was responding specifically, however, to the visible exclusion of black people from white-collar and middle-class employment. Succeeding where the black movements of the 1930s, '40s, and '50s had failed, the Movimento Negro Unificado and its sister organisations forced the issues of racial discrimination and inequality on to the national political agenda and provoked a society-wide debate on how to deal with them. Several state governments, and to a lesser degree the national government, formally committed themselves to combating racial inequality, and the state of São Paulo followed this up with concrete measures toward that end.

We conclude, therefore, that it is exclusionary regimes which have tended to provoke the most effective instances of black political mobilisation.[76] Inclusionary regimes, by contrast, which have actively sought to integrate Afro-Brazilians into their institutions, have greatly reduced the impulse toward mobilisation along racial lines. As Brazil made the transition from military dictatorship to electoral democracy in the 1980s, this tendency asserted itself in the Third Republic as well, perceptibly weakening, and perhaps bringing to an end, the most recent cycle of Afro-Brazilian protest.[77]

As the historical moments covered in this article suggest, however, the end of each wave of black protest has always been followed, even if at some remove in time, by the beginnings of another. And while our analysis suggests that inclusionary regimes are less conducive to racial mobilisation, it is important to recognise that the events of the 1980s profoundly altered the national discourse on race, making it an overt political issue in a way never before seen in Brazilian history. Whether race will emerge as a focus for renewed struggles in the 1990s remains to be seen; but one doubts that we have reached the 'end of history' for black political protest in Brazil.

[76] This generalisation applies to the southern United States and South Africa as well, where a combination of highly visible racial injustice, in the form of segregation, and exclusionary political regimes, eventually produced massive racial mobilisations in opposition to the status quo.

[77] Though it is to borrow a characterisation from the (in some ways) analogous case of Brazilian feminism, 'dispersion rather than disappearance would be a more accurate way to describe the state of the movement in the late 1980s'. Sonia E. Alvarez, *Engendering Democracy in Brazil: Women's Movements in Transition Politics* (Princeton, 1990), p. 228. Numerous organisations continued to exist (see note 60), and some new ones were being created, such as SOS Racismo in Rio de Janeiro.

Challenging the Nation-State
in Latin America

Rodolfo Stavenhagen

Are we Europeans? So many copper-colored faces deny it! Are we indige-nous? Perhaps the answer is given by the condescending smiles of our blonde ladies. Mixed? Nobody wants to be it, and there are thousands who would want to be called neither Americans nor Argentinians. Are we a nation? A nation without the accumulation of mixed materials, without the adjustment of foundations?[1]
   — Domingo Faustino Sarmiento, Argentine writer and statesman, 1883

When most Latin American countries achieved political independence from Spain in the early nineteenth century, the ideas of nationalism and the formation of national states were just beginning to emerge as central forces in Western thinking. Under the influence of the Enlightenment and the American and French revolutions, leaders of independence movements in Latin America were clearly inspired more by concepts of liberty and sovereignty than by the ideal of creating a "cultural nation-state" that fired the imaginations and struggles of the romantic European nationalists in later decades. Once independence had been obtained by force of arms (Bolivar, O'Higgins and Hidalgo), the rulers of the new states were faced with the daunting task of building new nations. Forging viable polities that might serve the interests of the new ruling groups out of the fragmented remains of the Spanish empire was no small matter, particularly in view of the highly stratified and hierarchical nature of the social system inherited from the colonial period and the ethnic and racial diversity of the population. Thus it became necessary to invent and create nations and to construct national identities. The intellectuals set this task for themselves in

---

1.   Quoted in Leopoldo Zea, *Discurso desde la marginación y la barbarie* (México DF: Fondo de Cultura Económica, 1990) p. 102. Translation by the author.

Journal of International Affairs, Winter 1992, 45, no. 2. © The Trustees of Columbia University in the City of New York.

the nineteenth century: By some accounts it has not yet been completed, for the search for national identity is still a principal concern of Latin American intellectuals to this day.[2]

It is no wonder, then, that post-colonial Latin American elites adopted a nationalist ideology as the guiding orientation in their search for legitimation. Once the new republican political units had been established, true nations would have to be constituted as an act of state and government. In Latin America, as in so many other post-colonial societies, the state and its intellectual and political elites created the nation; the sociological nation itself did not struggle to create its own state, as happened — and is happening again — in Europe.[3]

The purpose of this essay is not to retrace the story of nationalism in Latin America but rather to suggest that one of the unresolved issues of the nationalist debate in the region is the relationship between the model of the unitary state, which was adopted after the wars of independence and developed during the republican period, and the ethnic and cultural diversity of the societies of Latin America. This contradiction has contributed to the weakness of political institutions in the area and to persistent tension between the political structure and the various social forces, occasionally leading to protracted and sometimes violent social conflict as in Guatemala and Peru.

HETEROGENEOUS SOCIETIES: THE PERPETUATION OF A COLOR-CLASS CONTINUUM

The leaders of the independence movements recognized the importance of the various ethnic components that made up the populations of Latin America: European, African and indigenous. Simón Bolivar, the "liberator of America," realized early on the difficulties of creating unified nations out of extremely heterogeneous populations. He warned in 1819:

> We must keep in mind that our people are neither European nor North American: rather, they are a mixture of Africans and the Americans who originated in Europe...It is impossible to deter-

---

2. See Pablo González Casanova, ed., *Cultura y creación intelectual en América Latina* (México DF: Siglo XXI, 1979); Hugo Zemelman, ed., *Cultura y política en América Latina* (México DF: Siglo XXI, 1990); Leopoldo Zea, *The Latin American Mind* (Norman, OK: University of Oklahoma Press, 1963).

3. See Anthony D. Smith, *National Identity* (Harmondsworth, UK: Penguin, 1991).

mine with any degree of accuracy where we belong in the human family. The greater portion of the native Indians have been annihilated; Spaniards have mixed with Americans and Africans, and Africans with Indians and Spaniards.[4]

Bolivar, himself of mixed origin, was not alone in expressing qualms about his ethnic identity and his place in "the human family." Others doubted that civilized nations could emerge at all from such diverse racial and ethnic backgrounds, as the opening quote by the Argentine Sarmiento aptly illustrates. Bolivar, and many others after him, expected these various population groups to mesh into a new amalgam: the mixed or *mestizo* population for which Latin America is widely known. Racial mixture did take place over the centuries, but not to the extent that its early proponents had foreseen. Nor did it bring about the social and political consequences with which it has been associated in so many writings about Latin America.[5]

Since the colonial period, the various ethnic categories of the population have been related to each other within the framework of a polarized social class system based on race, color and ethnicity. Thus, racial and ethnic integration took place only to the extent that changes in the socioeconomic structure allowed. The abolition of slavery in Brazil towards the end of the nineteenth century, as in the United States, did not lead directly to a "racial democracy," although institutionalized segregation and racism were not part of the Brazilian experience. As in the Caribbean, a pervasive color-class continuum continues to exist in Latin America, in which the lighter-skinned population of European descent is at the top of the social structure and the darker-skinned people of indigenous or African descent are to be found at the bottom.

The Place of Indigenous Peoples in Latin American Society

The European invasion of the sixteenth century produced a disastrous demographic decline of the continent's indigenous peoples. Within 50 to 60 years after the first contact, it is estimated that the total population of around 100 million fell by 80 percent, due to epidemics hitherto unknown to the indigenous peoples,

---

4. Quoted in Winthrop R. Wright, *Café con Leche, Race, Class and National Image in Venezuela* (Austin, TX: University of Texas Press, 1990) p. 27.

5. See Magnus Mörner, *Race Mixture in the History of Latin America* (Boston, MA: Little and Brown, 1967).

423

the breakdown of the native subsistence economies, harsh living and labor conditions imposed by the colonial overlords and, as a lesser causal factor, the casualties of war and conquest.[6] By today's standards, this would be labeled genocide, and it is considered as such by indigenous organizations of the continent. Slowly, demographic growth picked up again, and by about the beginning of the twentieth century the total population had reached the same level as three centuries before. Over the last hundred years, at least until the 1960s, overseas immigration has also played an increasingly important role in the composition of Latin America's populations.

This process of demographic growth implies the expansion of the *mestizo* population, but it has not resulted in the disappearance of indigenous peoples and communities. Despite the political, economic and cultural aggressions that the latter suffered at the hands first of the colonizers and their direct descendants, and later of the ruling classes of the independent nation-states, a deeply-rooted "culture of resistance" has ensured the survival of over four hundred distinct ethnic groups (there were of course many more in precolonial times). These groups today represent more than 35 million people, over one-tenth of Latin America's total population.[7]

The pacification of the Pampas in the South was similar to the conquest of the West in North America. Indigenous societies were practically wiped out, or reduced to the status of dependent, vulnerable minority groups whose survival depended on the generosity of a national state that had appropriated their sovereignty and land; a state that they could hardly consider as their own. Elsewhere, the *criollo* self-perception of cultural and racial superiority over the indigenous peoples led to policies designed to accelerate the disappearance of the indigenous peoples and their rapid incorporation into the so-called national mainstream, that is, into the model of the nation-state as defined by the *criollo* upper class.

The inferior status accorded indigenous peoples was most pronounced in regions such as the Andean highlands, the Antil-

---

6. William N. Denevan, *The Native Population of the Americas in 1492* (Madison, WI: University of Wisconsin Press, 1976).

7. Latin American Center, *Statistical Abstract of Latin America*, 28 (Los Angeles, CA: University of California Press, 1990) table 658.

les and Mesoamerica, where the majority indigenous peasantries and the minority *criollo* upper classes were integrated into a single economic system and where a deep social and cultural chasm separated the two groups. In these parts of the continent, a much larger proportion of the original indigenous population survived the arrival of colonizers and a majority indigenous population continued to exist alongside the European colonialists. A colonial policy established a system of economic exploitation based primarily on the concentration of landholdings and various forms of servile peasant labor. This in turn led to a highly hierarchical social structure in which vertical mobility between the horizontal strata was almost completely absent. The lowest strata were made up of the indigenous peasantries. Political independence from Spain aggravated the situation of these peasant populations as the *criollo* elites, white upper classes of Spanish ancestry, were able to consolidate their position by concentrating land, riches and political power.

When economic growth took off again toward the end of the century, stimulated by the industrial world's demand for Latin America's cash crops and mineral exports, the situation of the indigenous peasantries deteriorated once more. Much of their remaining land was taken from them, working conditions deteriorated and the expanding monetary economy weakened the formerly self-sufficient agricultural communities and fostered an increasing flow of labor migrations out of the subsistence sector. This process lasted well into the middle of the twentieth century, at which time growing population pressure on limited resources also played a role. Contemporary analysts have long debated whether to call this system feudal, colonial or capitalist.[8] Regardless, it persisted over several centuries and was able to adjust to a number of different political regimes.

As elsewhere in the world, it was the ruling class and the intelligentsia who imagined and invented the modern Latin American nations, trying to shape them in their own image. The indigenous peoples were excluded from the "national projects" that emerged in the nineteenth century. They have remained in the background since then, shadowy figures which, like Greek

---

8. See André Gunder Frank, *Capitalism and Underdevelopment in Latin America* (New York: Monthly Review Press, 1967); Rodolfo Stavenhagen, *Social Classes in Agrarian Societies* (New York: Doubleday, 1975).

choruses, step into the historical limelight during revolutions, rebellions and uprisings, only to recede again into a forgotten world.

The Argentine statesman Sarmiento and many others were convinced that as long as indigenous peoples continued to constitute any substantial portion of the population, the Latin American countries would be unable to join the civilized nations of the world. Just as the political constitutions were drawn from the American Constitution, so were the legal institutions, the educational system and varieties of cultural policies taken from European models to serve the *criollo* upper classes. While the indigenous peoples were recognized as distinct and separate cultures, their languages and their social, religious and political institutions were not incorporated into the dominant mode of governance. The indigenous cultures were at best ignored and at worst exterminated. Thus, while lip service was at times given to the indigenous roots of modern Latin American societies, the cultural and political leaders of the independent republics were reluctant to recognize the indigenous peoples as part of the new nations. Indeed, the indigenous peoples were explicitly rejected and excluded. As long as they were geographically isolated and numerically insignificant, this approach did not threaten the self-image of the elites, who first affirmed their new-found national identities against the former colonial power Spain, and later, against the upcoming continental hegemonic power, the Anglo-Saxon United States.[9]

European immigration was stimulated to further *criollo* objectives. A number of countries not only opened their doors to immigration, but sought it actively. Latin American governments sent agents to European countries in order to recruit likely prospects. Colonization and transportation companies were set up, and land grants and economic facilities offered. European immigrants were expected to contribute to economic development, bring skills and capital, teach the local populations how to improve agriculture and industry and enhance the biological stock of the country by intermarriage with the local population. Through immigration, it was held, the Latin American nations would finally be recognized as equals by their European and

---

9. Zea.

North American counterparts. In fact, immigration did play a considerable role in changing the demographic profile of numerous Latin American countries, in some of which Asian migrants also arrived, but in lesser numbers and under less auspicious circumstances. Immigration flows continued until after the Second World War and into the 1950s. It has fallen off during the last two decades due to military dictatorships, political instability and economic crisis. Nevertheless, it did contribute to the process of *mestizaje*: the building of a *mestizo* race.

Mestizaje: A New "Cosmic Race" and the Politics of Indigenismo

During the early colonial period, the *mestizo* population had only a slightly higher status than the indigenous peoples and was usually rejected by both the Spanish upper strata and the indigenous communities. Marginal to both cultures, the *mestizos* lacked a coherent identity of their own, a problem that has preoccupied intellectuals, psychologists and sociologists to this day. The racial theories of the nineteenth century, which Latin America's elites willingly imported from Europe and the United States, considered not only the indigenous peoples but also the mixed-breed *mestizos* as inferior human groups. What kind of a modern nation could be built upon such flimsy human material? No wonder so many intellectuals despaired of their nations and their continent. The indigenous groups were rejected outright as being passive, dependent, fatalistic, docile, stupid, incapable of higher civilization, lacking in emotions and sensitivity, impervious to pain and suffering, unable to improve their miserable conditions of living and therefore generally a major obstacle to the progress of the Latin American countries. The *mestizos*, in turn, were said to embody the worst elements of both their ancestors: They were hot-headed, violent, unreliable, dishonest, shiftless, opportunistic, passionate, power-hungry, lazy and generally considered incapable of ruling their countries.

Nevertheless, over time the *mestizos* came to occupy the economic and social space that neither the reduced *criollo* upper classes nor the indigenous peasantries were able to control. With the capitalist expansion of the economy and the growth of cities, trade, services and industry during the nineteenth century, the *mestizo* soon became identified with the national mainstream, as the driving force of economic, social and, most recently, political

427

progress. The earlier doubts about *mestizo* biological and psychological capabilities vanished, except among some foreign observers who still carried the old stereotypes well into the twentieth century.

By now, the *mestizos* had developed their own distinct culture; they became the bearers of truly nationalist sentiments. Moreover, they became identified with the burgeoning urban middle classes and thus with progress, change and modernization. An ideological reversal had occurred. *Mestizo* intellectuals sang the virtues of *mestizaje* as not only a biological process, but rather as a cultural and political condition leading to economic development and political democracy. *Por mi raza hablará el espíritu* — "The spirit will speak for my race" — proclaimed the 1920s slogan of the National University of Mexico, coined by José Vasconcelos, Minister of Education in one of Mexico's postrevolutionary governments and standard-bearer of the *mestizos* as a new "cosmic race" in Latin America.[10]

While Europe was regressing to the myth of racial purity and superiority and while white supremacy was still legally enshrined in the United States, the idealization of the mixed-blood *mestizo* in Latin America during the 1920s and 1930s could be considered as something of a heterodox, if not a revolutionary, position. The identification of the mestizo population with national culture, the middle classes and economic progress soon became the ideological underpinning of various kinds of government policies designed to strengthen the unitary nation-state and the incorporation of the "nonnational" elements, namely, the indigenous peoples. By the 1940s a set of government policies, known as *indigenismo*, had been devised to carry out the "national integration" of the indigenous communities through forcing the social and cultural changes necessary for their assimilation into the *mestizo* national model. Various states established departments or institutes of indigenous affairs that promoted educational and economic development projects at the local level, designed to "integrate" the indigenous peoples. By then, indigenous cultures had already changed considerably, and many observers considered that they were no longer viable and would soon disappear of their own accord. Thus, the argument ran,

---

10. José Vasconcelos, *La raza cósmica, misión de la raza iberoamericana* (Paris: Agencia Mundial de Librería, 1925).

government policy would only hasten their demise and accelerate a natural and inevitable process.

The supposed inferiority of the indigenous peoples was now no longer phrased in biological terms, but rather in the fashionable language of the times — culture and levels of socioeconomic development. Indigenous cultures were deemed to be underdeveloped, archaic, backward, traditional and simple rather than complex, communalist rather than individualist and parochial rather than universalist. Social-science theories were invoked to explain the differences between the indigenous communities and the national societies, providing the parameters for public policy. The writings of Durkheim, Spencer, Tönnies, Weber, Parsons, Boas and Redfield were gleaned for insights that would then justify *indigenista* policies.[11]

In 1940, after several years' preparation, the first continental Inter-American Indianist Congress was held in Mexico. Here, the governments of the Americas laid down general guidelines for dealing with their "Indian problem" and agreed to coordinate their activities in the field of Indianist policies. To be sure, respect for indigenous cultures and values was expressed, but the dominant idea was integration, incorporation and assimilation. The Congress set up the Inter-American Indianist Institute, subordinate to the Organization of American States, as a coordinating agency. Those national governments that had not already done so were invited to establish their own bureaus of Indian affairs.

Before the late 1950s and 1960s, Latin America's political parties and movements had not dealt with the Indian question to any great extent, a position that reflected the marginality of these issues in the body politic and the fact that politics itself was still the domain of a relatively small "political class."

THE "INDIGENOUS PROBLEM" AND LATIN AMERICAN DEVELOPMENT

The two principal ideological currents of the times had rather clear ideas about how to deal with *el problema indígena*. Neoliberal thinkers considered the problem of the indigenous populations as one of underdevelopment, technological backwardness, tradi-

---

11. For an assessment of *indigenismo* in Mexico, see Alan Knight, "Racism, Revolution, and *Indigenismo*: Mexico, 1910-1940" in Richard Graham, ed., *The Idea of Race in Latin America, 1870-1940* (Austin, TX: University of Texas Press, 1990).

429

tionalism and marginality. Within the generally accepted framework of modernization politics, conceiving economic and social development as a unilinear progression along a series of necessary stages, economists, anthropologists and politicians thought that the so-called Indian problem would disappear by way of community development, regional planning, education, technological innovations and paternalistic acculturation. The responsibility for carrying out these policies lay in the hands of the state, which played a tutelary role. Through such policies, indigenous subsistence peasants would become modern farmers. Traditional values, which were considered to be inimical to progress, would have to be changed through modern education; the virtues of individualism and entrepreneurship would have to be learned, and the bonds of the local community would have to broken so that the outside world could penetrate and impart its bounties. For many observers during the heyday of developmentalism, the indigenous problem was an economic problem to be solved by technological change, investments, cash crops, wage labor, profit maximization and the monetarization of the local subsistence economy.

Development policies targeted at the indigenous populations had two principal justifications. First, it was thought that only by means of such policies would the quality of Indian life improve. Second, it was felt that as long as the indigenous peoples lived in poverty and backwardness, isolated from the centers of modernization and growth, the country as a whole would remain backward and underdeveloped. Such countries would be particularly vulnerable to foreign interference and interests, especially economic imperialism coming from the North. As long as the Latin American nations were internally fragmented and polarized, embodied in the concept of the "dual society," they would be weak and unable to assert their sovereignty and independence in the world.

Another point of view was put forward as early as the 1920s by Marxist-oriented writers such as José Carlos Mariátegui in Peru. They considered the indigenous peoples to be a part of the exploited peasantry, whose interests lay in making common cause with other segments of the toiling classes. Indeed, they were viewed as the most exploited and backward element of the working class, lacking in class consciousness precisely because of their community-centered, traditional world outlook. Moreover, their cultural distinctiveness in areas such as language, dress, religious organization, family and community structures — all of which set them apart from the *mestizo* population — facilitated their exploitation by the bourgeoisie and the landholding oligarchies. Through depressed wages and the retention of different kinds of forced and servile labor arrangements, such as peonage, the indigenous peoples were prevented from joining forces with the revolutionary proletariat in the class struggle. Indeed, it was held that the maintenance of indigenous cultural specificity was actually in the interests of the bourgeoisie, or at least its more backward factions, within the framework of underdeveloped and dependent capitalism for which Latin America became notorious in the 1960s.[12]

The Marxist controversy regarding the indigenous peoples — sometimes framed as "the national question" in reference to the debates among Marxists in Central and Eastern Europe before the First World War — continued well into the 1980s. While much of the debate initially took place in the academic environment, it progressively filtered into leftist political movements and the revolutionary guerrilla activities, which emerged in many parts of the continent as a consequence of the Cuban revolution. Che Guevara's attempt to spark a revolutionary uprising in Bolivia in the 1960s probably failed, among other reasons, because Guevara was unaware of, or insensitive to, the national question in that country. Revolutionary theory at that point did not find such issues relevant.

A number of revolutionary guerrilla groups in Guatemala from the 1960s onward were easily isolated and eliminated by repressive, American-backed military regimes because they had not been able to deal adequately, in theoretical or political terms, with the fact that the majority of Guatemala's population is indigenous. One of the reasons that revolutionary activity has continued despite brutal repression is that the revolutionary organizations have now revised the "class" approach of traditional Marxist analysis and have framed their struggle in terms of a national question, challenging not only class rule but also the

---

12. Fernando Henrique Cardoso and Enzo Faletto, *Dependence and Development in Latin America* (Berkeley, CA: University of California Press, 1979).

dominant view of the nation-state. With this concept they have been able to acquire a foothold among the indigenous peoples.[13]

More widely known, because of the media attention it received, was the conflict between the Miskito Indians and the Sandinista government in Nicaragua during the 1980s. This conflict arose because the Sandinistas, basing their policies on class analysis, assumed that the indigenous peoples of the Atlantic coast had a natural interest in joining forces with them. It came as a surprise to the Sandinistas that the indigenous organizations had a different agenda, and they quickly attributed counterrevolutionary intentions to them. This unnecessary, if inevitable, confrontation had disastrous consequences in terms of lives and resources lost, and weakened the political position of the Sandinista government both at home and abroad. The Reagan administration was quick to take up the Miskito cause as a major human-rights issue in its undeclared war against Nicaragua. By the time the Sandinistas recognized their mistakes in the mid-1980s, the damage had been done.[14]

Though originating in different intellectual traditions and based on different analyses and interpretations of social and economic dynamics, the neoliberal and the orthodox Marxist approaches to the indigenous question in Latin America have held one view in common: that indigenous peoples constituted an obstacle to development and progress. Both approaches set out to devise policies to overcome such obstacles. In the former it became "acculturation" and "modernization"; in the latter, the "class struggle." In both scenarios, indigenous cultures would have to disappear eventually, and the sooner the better. These two intellectual traditions also shared the belief that indigenous peoples had not participated in the formulation of either scenario.

From the sixteenth century through the 1960s, indigenous peoples have been written about, but rarely have they been listened to. They have been the object of scholarly research, but they have yet to become the active subjects in rewriting their own history. Except for brief flashes, such as the uprising of Tupac Amaru in Peru or the Caste War in Mexico, countless localized revolts and

---

13. See Arturo Arias, "Changing Indian Identity: Guatemala's Violent Transition to Modernity," Carol A. Smith, ed., *Guatemalan Indians and the State, 1540-1988* (Austin, TX: University of Texas Press, 1990).

14. See Carlos Vilas, *State, Class and Ethnicity in Nicaragua* (Boulder, CO: Lynne Reinner Publishers, 1989).

rebellions have not found their way into official historiography. As scholars now acknowledge, indigenous opposition to domination took the form of passive resistance, of turning inward and building protective shells around community life and cultural identity. This mode of resistance enabled many indigenous cultures to survive into the twentieth century, although countless others did disappear in time.

NEW PRESSURES, NEW FORMS OF RESISTANCE

As a result of economic growth, technological changes and the increasing internationalization of the Latin American economies, social and cultural transformations accelerated during the twentieth century. The remaining indigenous peoples have been put under enormous pressure since the Second World War in their attempts to retain their traditional lifestyle and resist integration into mainstream modern life. The numerous conflicts arising in the Amazon basin illustrate these pressures profoundly: Among the world's last natural frontiers, the Amazon rain forest has increasingly become the target of massive invasions by economic and political pressures, national and international, such as giant mining or hydroelectric projects, strategic road building, deforestation and uncontrolled human settlements. Observers agree that what is happening in the Amazon is ecocide and ethnocide on a massive scale, all in the name of state nationalism, modernization and economic growth.[15]

As the indigenous peoples became the victims of renewed assaults on their lands, resources and cultures in the latter half of the present century, they began to adopt new forms of resistance and defense. Though scattered attempts at political organization had occurred before, the beginnings of a coherent and forceful indigenous political movement began in earnest in the 1970s. Various organizations began to express claims about indigenous rights that had only been stated occasionally and unsystematically before. Congresses, coalitions and federations were set up at the national and local levels, followed by international organizations advocating indigenous rights. As in other forms of social and political mobilization, factionalism, divisions and rivalries appeared. Grassroots organizations sprang up in different areas;

---

15. See Susana Hecht and Alexander Cockburn, *The Fate of the Forest: Developers, Destroyers and Defenders of the Amazon* (New York: Harper Perennial, 1990).

local groups merged to structure organizations along ethnic-group lines, as in the case of the Shuar federation in eastern Ecuador. Professional interest groups were also formed for such groups as indigenous plantation workers, bilingual schoolteachers and indigenous lawyers.

Attempts to form political parties centered on the mandate of furthering indigenous rights have met with mixed success: Indigenous political parties such as *Katarismo* in Bolivia and an indigenous political party in Guatemala have not yet been able to garner large-scale support among the wider population. In other states, indigenous "sectors" of existing parties appeared: The Institutional Revolutionary Party (PRI) in Mexico organized a National Council of Indigenous Peoples. A number of organizations, particularly at the national and international levels, were structured from the top down. In the 1960s, not more than a smattering of indigenous organizations existed; by the beginning of the 1990s, dozens of such groups have been identified as established and representative associations in every country. Hundreds probably exist continent-wide. The emergence of these interest groups is due to a number of factors including: the growth of an indigenous elite or intelligentsia out of the ranks of those who received formal schooling in official or missionary establishments; the widespread disillusionment with development policies that did not bring benefits to the indigenous peoples; the neglect by traditional political parties or class associations of issues of specific interest to indigenous peoples; and the dissemination of information about liberation struggles among colonized peoples in other parts of the world.

In all of these efforts, a newly emerging indigenous intelligentsia has played a fundamental role, aided by indigenous advocates from the social sciences, the churches and a number of political formations. In earlier years, the indigenous intelligentsia would have been siphoned off and assimilated into the dominant society. While this process continues today, indigenous professional people, intellectuals and political activists are consciously embracing their ethnic heritage and providing leadership to their communities. This new leadership is also displacing the more traditional community authority that has played a fundamental role in the period of passive resistance and retrenchment, when, as anthropologists would have it, indigenous peoples lived in closed, corporate communities. As indigenous communities are also internally differentiated according to socioeconomic criteria, so the new indigenous leaders often reflect different interests in the community itself. Whether this leadership represents the interests of the indigenous ethnic groups at large, or only those of an emerging "indigenous bourgeoisie," is currently a topic of widespread debate.

These organizations articulate various sorts of demands relating to the fundamental problems that indigenous peoples face at the present time. Heading the list, no doubt, is the land question. They demand that indigenous land rights be respected and restored, either through agrarian reform (Mexico, Guatemala and Peru), territorial demarcation (Brazil and Panama) or land-titling (Argentina, Chile and Costa Rica). In addition to land, traditional rights to natural and subsoil resources are also claimed. These demands sometimes face stiff opposition by large landholders, mining and lumber companies, the military — which sees claims for territorial demarcation as a threat to national security — and their respective representatives in government.

A second major set of claims that indigenous organizations have been pursuing relates to cultural and legal identity and deals with educational and linguistic policies. Until very recently, most Latin American countries did not recognize themselves as multiethnic. Demands for bilingual and bicultural education in indigenous communities were considered irrelevant, even subversive, by the proponents of the unitary nation-state. In the past few years this opposition has eroded, and most countries now have bilingual and intercultural educational programs that cater to an increasing number of indigenous populations. The Inter-American Indianist Congresses, which are usually held every three years, have gone on record in support of such programs and have urged their member states to take adequate measures.

The third major area that has been widely discussed by indigenous organizations concerns the questions of local and regional autonomy, respect for traditional forms of authority and government, recognition of customary alternative legal systems and, more recently, the right to self-determination. These are usually quite controversial issues, to the extent that even by raising them, the indigenous organizations are challenging the hegemonic concept of the Latin American nation-state. Some sort of local autonomy for indigenous peoples does exist in several countries, such as Panama. As a result of the ethnic conflict in the 1980s, the

435

National Assembly of Nicaragua adopted a Statute for the Autonomy of the Communities of the Atlantic Coast, which was later
incorporated into the new national constitution. The question of
legal pluralism is widely discussed: Some changes have been
made in the legal systems of a number of countries, but progress
in this field is slow because too little is known about customary
legal systems of the indigenous peoples.[16]

Self-determination, considered both a basic human right and a
political issue, is a much more complex matter. Here, indigenous
peoples have clashed with the state on more than one occasion.
Indigenous organizations have put forward claims to the right of
peoples to self-determination, as contained in the United Nations
human rights conventions. Governments, which fear territorial
break-up and secessionist movements, have rejected such demands outright. Generally, indigenous movements do not see the
exercise of self-determination as a secessionist proposal. Rather,
they see it as a move toward greater participation in the political
system on an equal basis with whites and *mestizos* and, above all,
as the right to decide for themselves which issues relate to their
welfare and survival.[17]

International law has established that self-determination refers
to a single political decision usually involving independence. As
used here, however, self-determination may be seen as a process
involving different levels and multiple decisions over a period of
time. First, a distinction may be made between "internal" and
"external" self-determination, the former referring to the economic, social and political arrangements that a people wish to
abide by and the latter to the kinds of links binding a specific
people to another entity, which may or may not be a nation-state
of which they are a part. Generally, when the right of a people to
self-determination is invoked, external self-determination is
thought of. When the indigenous peoples of Latin America speak
of self-determination, however, they usually refer to internal self-
determination, that is, the right to preserve and develop their own
cultures, the right to land and territory and the development of

---

16. See Rodolfo Stavenhagen and Diego Iturralde, eds., *Entre la ley y la costumbre. El derecho consuetudinario indígena en América Latina* (México DF: Instituto Indigenista Inter-americano and Instituto Interamericano de Derechos Humanos, 1990).

17. See Rodolfo Stavenhagen, *Derecho indígena y derechos humanos en América Latina* (México DF: El Colegio de México and Instituto Interamericano de Derechos Humanos, 1988).

economic resources on their own terms, yet all within the context of existing nation-states.

INDIGENOUS POLITICAL MOBILIZATION TODAY

The extension and intensity of indigenous mobilization all over the continent in the past few years has put the indigenous question on the political agenda. A number of countries have adopted legislation relating to indigenous populations. In some cases, entirely new constitutions have been drafted that, for the first time, include the question of indigenous rights. Chapter 8 of the Brazilian constitution, entitled "The Indians," was adopted after much public debate in 1988. It recognizes the permanent rights of the indigenous peoples to their traditional lands and obligates the government to demarcate them within five years of ratification. It also acknowledges indigenous communities and organizations as legal entities. In Nicaragua, the autonomy of the communities of the Atlantic Coast has been incorporated in the new constitution of 1988. Guatemala's constitution of 1985 stipulates the state's obligation to protect indigenous lands and cultures. In 1991, Colombia adopted a new political constitution, drafted over several months by a special constituent assembly in which several indigenous representatives took part. It also includes articles on the rights of indigenous communities. Despite the fact that Mexico has the largest indigenous population in Latin America (over 12 million) and can boast a long history of official *indigenismo*, the Mexican constitution of 1917 did not acknowledge the legal existence of indigenous peoples. From 1990 to 1991, the Federal Congress debated the text of a constitutional amendment which would finally recognize indigenous rights.

By enacting legislation that in some way establishes or acknowledges the rights of indigenous peoples, leaving behind the earlier paternalistic and tutelary legal approaches, the countries of Latin America are beginning to change their national self-image. Of course, as the experience of Guatemala shows, just changing the legislation does not by itself guarantee the effective enjoyment of indigenous peoples' rights. But it may herald changes to come.

The rights that are being reassessed through these processes in Latin America are individual and collective human rights. Due to the inferiority imposed on them by society, indigenous groups have often been the victims of human rights abuses. These have

437

been more than occasional and regrettable excesses by over-zealous agents of the state. Because they are embedded in the social structure, they should be regarded as structural violations of the human rights of the indigenous peoples. Human-rights violations in Latin America have been widely documented in recent years by nongovernmental organizations such as Amnesty International and Americas Watch, whose yearly reports and special studies constitute an importaant contribution to our knowledge about these issues. Also, the Department of State country reports, though sometimes acknowledged to be politically biased, have provided significant information. Reports prepared by the Inter-American Commission of Human Rights and the U.N. Human Rights Commission are also revealing.[18]

The civil and political rights of the indigenous peoples have been too readily neglected and abused precisely because the collective rights to cultural survival, identity and self-determination have been ignored and denied. Thus, the emerging indigenous movement has been placing an emphasis on the collective rights of ethnically specific indigenous peoples.

These issues have also been taken up by intergovernmental organizations, such as the United Nations, the International Labor Organization (ILO) and the Organization of American States (OAS). The U.N. Sub-Commission on Prevention of Discrimination and Protection of Minorities, a subordinate organ of the Human Rights Commission, established a Working Group on Indigenous Populations in the early 1980s. Its sessions have been attended by numerous indigenous nongovernmental organizations, and it is currently drafting a Universal Declaration of the Rights of Indigenous Peoples to be adopted, perhaps as early as 1993, by the General Assembly. The issue of collective rights, including the right of indigenous peoples to self-determination, figures prominently in these discussions. Whether the member states of the United Nations will adopt such a declaration remains an open question, but the indigenous organizations that are actively engaged in promoting the declaration are already looking

---

18. See Amnesty International, *Mexico: Human Rights in Rural Areas, 1986*; Americas Watch, *Rural Violence in Brazil, 1991*. For a critique of the Department of State reports, see Lawyers Committee for Human Rights, *Critique: Review of the Department of State's Country Reports on Human Rights Practice for 1990*, July 1991.

ahead toward the adoption of an international convention of indigenous rights.

The Sub-Commission has also initiated a study on the situation of treaties between indigenous peoples and nation-states. North American Indians are particularly interested in this issue, because the treaties that their ancestors signed in the name of then-independent, sovereign nations were unilaterally abrogated by the U.S. government in the nineteenth century. The Indians consider this to be related to international law and of interest to the United Nations. In most of Latin America, the relations between indigenous peoples and states were never governed by bilateral treaties: Nevertheless, a number of such treaties were signed by the Spanish crown and also by some republican governments in the nineteenth century. They have been similarly ignored by contemporary governments.

In 1957 the ILO adopted Convention 107 on the protection of indigenous and tribal populations in independent states, which has been ratified by 26 states. In 1985 the ILO initiated a process of revision of this international instrument, which resulted in the adoption in 1989 of a revised convention, now known as Convention 169. The issue of land rights and territorial rights figures prominently here also, as does the concept of indigenous "peoples" rather than populations. The ILO Convention disclaims any political intention with the use of the term peoples, but for the indigenous it represents a victory of sorts in that it is peoples, and not populations, who have the right of self-determination as set out in the two international human rights covenants.

More recently, the General Assembly of the OAS requested the Inter-American Commission of Human Rights to initiate consultations which might lead to the drafting and adoption of a new human rights legal instrument in the Inter-American system pertaining to indigenous peoples. While governments are not enthusiastic about it, this development reflects the growing concern and awareness of states regarding the issues pertaining to indigenous rights.

INDIGENOUS PEOPLES AND NATIONAL IDENTITY IN LATIN AMERICA: LOOKING FORWARD

In conclusion, the indigenous peoples are achieving a new political presence in Latin America, and this has led to a reexamination of Latin America's national societies. At the same time, they present a challenge to the traditional ideologies of nationalism and the concept of the nation-state itself.

The legal recognition of indigenous rights in the new constitutions of Brazil, Colombia, Nicaragua and other states is opening the way for new legal and political arrangements between the states and the indigenous peoples. Brazil and Venezuela have both recognized the autonomy of the Yanomami Indians on their common border. "National security ideology" does not disappear so easily; but while "hard-line" nationalists in these countries may not like the idea, such changes may be a harbinger of things to come. Public opinion has begun to recognize that earlier concepts of the culturally homogenous nation-state may no longer apply. The struggle for political democracy in Latin America now also includes the need to recognize indigenous peoples' specific collective rights and their position within the wider society. As these transformations occur, it is inevitable that the perception of national identity will also change, and that the earlier idea of the nation-state will make way for a wider concept of the multicultural, multiethnic society.

❖

Rethinking Race in Brazil*

HOWARD WINANT

Introduction: the Repudiation of the Centenário

13 May 1988 was the 100th anniversary of the abolition of slavery in Brazil. In honour of that date, various official celebrations and commemorations of the *centenário*, organised by the Brazilian government, church groups and cultural organisations, took place throughout the country, even including a speech by President José Sarney.

This celebration of the emancipation was not, however, universal. Many Afro-Brazilian groups staged actions and marches, issued denunciations and organised cultural events repudiating the 'farce of abolition'. These were unprecedented efforts to draw national and international attention to the extensive racial inequality and discrimination which Brazilian blacks – by far the largest concentration of people of African descent in any country in the western hemisphere – continue to confront. Particular interventions had such titles as '100 Years of Lies', 'One Hundred Years Without Abolition', 'March for the Real Liberation of the Race', 'Symbolic Burial of the 13th of May', 'March in Protest of the Farce of Abolition', and 'Discommemoration (*Descomemoração*) of the Centenary of Abolition'.[1] The repudiation of the *centenário* suggests that Brazilian racial dynamics, traditionally quiescent, are emerging with the rest of society from the extended twilight of military dictatorship. Racial conflict and mobilisation, long almost entirely absent from the Brazilian scene, are reappearing. New racial patterns and processes – political, cultural, economic, social and psychological – are emerging, while racial inequali-

---

* Early versions of this work were presented at the Universidade Federal do Rio de Janeiro in October 1989 and at the Latin American Studies Association meetings in Miami, December 1989. Thanks are due to Maria Brandão, Heloisa Buarque de Holanda, Michael Hanchard, Carlos Hasenbalg, Gay Seidman, Tom Skidmore and George Yudice, and to an anonymous reviewer at the *Journal of Latin American Studies*. Research for this article was supported in part by a Fulbright grant.

[1] Yvonne Maggie (ed.), *Catálogo: Centenário da Abolição* (Rio de Janeiro, 1989).

Howard Winant is Associate Professor of Sociology and Director of the Latin American Studies Center, Temple University, Philadelphia.

ties of course continue as well. How much do we know about race in contemporary Brazil? How effectively does the extensive literature explain the present situation?

In this article the main theories of race in Brazil are critically reviewed in the light of contemporary racial politics. I focus largely on postwar Brazilian racial theory, beginning with the pioneering UNESCO studies. This body of theory has exhibited considerable strengths in the past: it has been particularly effective in dismantling the myth of a non-racist national culture, in which 'racial democracy' flourished, and in challenging the role óf various elites in maintaining these myths. These achievements, appreciable in the context of the analytical horizon imposed on critical social science by an anti-democratic (and indeed often dictatorial and brutal) regime, now exhibit some serious inadequacies when employed to explain current developments.

This article accepts many of the insights of the existing literature but rejects its limitations. Such a reinterpretation, I argue, sets the stage for a new approach, based on racial formation theory. This theory is outlined below, and it is suggested that it offers a more accurate view of the changing racial order in contemporary Brazil. Racial formation theory can respond both to ongoing racial inequalities and to the persistence of racial difference, as well as the new possibilities opened up by the transition to democracy; it can do this in ways in which the established approaches, despite their considerable merits, cannot.

Theoretical perspectives: the debate thus far

Until quite recently Brazil was seen as a country with a comparatively benign pattern of race relations.[2] Only in the 1950s, when UNESCO sponsored a series of studies – looking particularly at Bahia and São Paulo – did the traditional theoretical approaches, which focused on the concept of 'racial democracy', come under sustained attack.[3] The work of such

---

[2] Relevant examples here include Donald Pierson, *Negroes in Brazil: A Study of Race Contact in Bahia* (Carbondale, IL, 1967 [1942]); Frank Tannenbaum, *Slave and Citizen: The Negro in the Americas* (New York, 1947); Gilberto Freyre, *New World in the Tropics: The Culture of Modern Brazil* (New York, 1959). For reasons of space this article focuses on contemporary issues of race. I do not discuss the origins or history of racial dynamics or ideas in Brazil. For good sources on these topics see Thomas E. Skidmore, *Black Into White: Race and Nationality in Brazilian Thought* (New York, 1974); Emilia Viotti da Costa, *Da Monarquia a República: Momentos Decisivos* (São Paulo, 1977); *Da Senzala a Colónia* (São Paulo, 2nd edn. 1982); and *The Brazilian Empire: Myths and Histories* (Chicago, 1985), esp. pp. 234–46.

[3] Thales de Azevedo, Roger Bastide, Florestan Fernandes, Marvin Harris and Charles Wagley, among others, were associated with the UNESCO project. Charles Wagley (ed.), *Race and Class in Rural Brazil* (New York, 1972), is a convenient collection of papers from the rural phase of this research. The work of Bastide and Fernandes is the

UNESCO researchers as Thales de Azevedo, Roger Bastide, Florestan Fernandes and Marvin Harris documented as never before the prevalence of racial discrimination,[4] and the persistence of the ideology of 'whitening', supposedly discredited in the 1930s and 1940s after the interventions of Gilberto Freyre and the advent of the more modern 'racial democracy' view.[5] In sum, the UNESCO-sponsored research set new terms for debate, constituting (not without some disagreements) a new racial 'revisionism'.

Racial revisionism was full of insights into Brazilian racial dynamics, but it also had significant limitations. Chief among these was a tendency to reduce race to class, depriving racial dynamics of their own, autonomous significance. In the space available here, I offer only a summary critique of this perspective, concentrating on the leading members of the revisionist school.

In Florestan Fernandes' view, Brazil's 'racial dilemma' is a result of survivals from the days of slavery, which came into conflict with capitalist development and would be liquidated by a transition to modernity. 'The Brazilian racial dilemma', Fernandes writes, 'constitutes a pathological social phenomenon, which can only be corrected by processes which would remove the obstruction of racial inequality from the competitive social order'.[6] Fernandes's work probably remains the most comprehensive sociology of race relations in Brazil. The greatness of his work lies in his recognition of the centrality of race in Brazil's development, not only in the past or even the present, but also in the future. However, race remains a 'dilemma', the 'resolution' of which will signify socio-political maturity. In other words, Fernandes still understands race as a problem, whose solution is integration. Implicitly there is a new stage to be achieved in Brazilian development, in which racial conflict will no longer present an obstacle or diversion from class conflict.

Fernandes at least recognised the continuing presence and significance of race; other revisionists tended to dismiss or minimise it. While

---

chief product of its urban phase. The importance of these studies for Brazilian social science, and more indirectly for racial dynamics themselves, cannot be overestimated.

[4] Key works in this monumental series of studies include: Thales de Azevedo, *Cultura e Situação Racial no Brasil* (Rio de Janeiro, 1966); Roger Bastide, 'A Imprensa Negra do Estado de São Paulo', in his *Estudos Afro-Brasileiros* (São Paulo, 1973), and *The African Religions of Brazil: Toward a Sociology of the Interpenetration of Civilisations* (Baltimore, 1978); Florestan Fernandes, *A Integração do Negro na Sociedade de Clases*, 2 vols. (São Paulo, 3rd edn., 1978); Roger Bastide and Florestan Fernandes, *Brancos e Negros em São Paulo* (São Paulo, 1959); Marvin Harris, *Patterns of Race in the Americas* (New York, 1964).

[5] Gilberto Freyre, *O Mundo Que o Portugues Criou* (Rio de Janeiro, 1940); Skidmore, *Black Into White*.   [6] Fernandes, *A Integração do Negro*, vol. 2, p. 460.

Fernandes' basic optimism was tempered by the question of whether the full modernisation of class society could be achieved, Thales de Azevedo saw evidence that this process was already far advanced: according to him class conflict was *replacing* racial conflict in Bahia.[7] Marvin Harris, who worked closely with Azevedo, suggested that the Brazilian system of racial identification *necessarily* subordinated race to class.[8] Comparing Brazilian and US racial dynamics, Harris argued that the absence of a 'descent rule' by which racial identity could be inherited, and the flexibility of racial meanings, led to a situation in which '[r]acial identity is a mild and wavering thing in Brazil, while in the United States it is for millions of people a passport to hell'.[9]

Actually, there are various theoretical accounts of the process by which race is supposedly subordinated to class. For the original revisionists, the question was whether this process was a social fact, already in progress and perhaps even well advanced, or a mere possibility. For Azevedo, it was already well under way; for Fernandes, it was a tendency which might – tragically – never come to pass unless the Brazilian people exhibited enough political will to transcend the racial dilemma and modernise their social order.

Later work, such as that of Carl Degler and Amaury de Souza, suggested various ways in which racial dynamics could *persist* while still remaining subordinated to class conflicts. Degler, in a rich comparative analysis of Brazil and the United States, concluded that because Brazil distinguished mulattoes from blacks, and afforded them greater social

---

[7] Azevedo, *Cultura e Situação Racial*, pp. 30–43. Azevedo presents the process of transition as a shift from racially identified status or prestige groups to classes. Formerly, whites were identified as a superior status group and blacks, conversely, as an inferior group. Race served as an indicator of status, but the deeper, more 'objective' category of class is a matter of economics, not of colour or prestige. Thus race becomes less salient as class formation proceeds:

> From this structure of two levels social classes are beginning to emerge, which may be identified from an economic point of view by property differences, income levels, consumption patterns, levels of education and rules of behaviour, and even by their incipient self-consciousness. The system of classes is organised in part by the older status groups and is still very much shaped by the old order. Its three elements are an upper class or *elite*, a middle class, and a lower class or *the poor* (*ibid.*, p. 34; original emphasis).

This view thus combines class reductionism (what is ultimately important about race is how it fits people into the economic system) with an implicit optimism about its transcendence in and by an emerging class system.

[8] These arguments led Eugene Genovese to defend the admittedly conservative Gilberto Freyre (as well as Frank Tannenbaum and others) from the admittedly radical and 'materialist' attack of Harris. Genovese (correctly in my view) perceived in Freyre a far more complex and 'totalizing' view of the meaning of race in Brazil than he found in Harris (Eugene D. Genovese, *In Red and Black: Marxian Explorations in Southern and Afro-American History* (New York, 1971) pp. 41–3).

[9] Harris, *Patterns of Race in the Americas*, p. 64.

mobility – the so-called 'mulatto escape hatch' – racial polarisation had been avoided there. Pointing to the same flexibility of racial categories that Harris had documented, Degler found ample evidence and logic for the 'escape hatch' in Brazilian racial history. If there was an 'escape hatch', then the United States pattern of growing racial solidarity would not occur; thus at least for some blacks (that is, mulattoes) questions of class would automatically take precedence over those of race. Other blacks, recognising that mobility was available to the lighter-skinned, would seek this possibility, if not for themselves then for their children.[10]

Besides tending to confirm the traditional wisdom about 'whitening' as the preferred solution to Brazil's racial problems, this analysis also saw economic mobility (and thus, integration into class society) as the key question in Brazilian racial dynamics. Because the 'escape hatch' already provided this opportunity for the light-skinned blacks, the task was to extend it to blacks in general.

Amaury de Souza made a similar argument which had less recourse to historical data and instead focused on 'whitening' as a sort of rational choice model, in which blacks had to weigh the costs of individual mobility against those of racial solidarity; consequently a type of 'prisoner's dilemma' confronted any effort to organise black political opposition.[11]

While the UNESCO studies offered an unprecedented wealth of empirical detail about Brazilian racial dynamics, the racial theory they employed was less innovative. They consistently practised reductionism; that is, they understood race epiphenomenally, as a manifestation of some other, supposedly more fundamental, social process or relationship. In the vast majority of studies, *race was interpreted in terms of class*. Racial dynamics were seen simply as supports for (or outcomes of) the process of capitalist development in Brazil.

While it is certainly not illegitimate to examine the linkage between race and class, reductionism occurs when the independence and depth of racial phenomena goes unrecognised. As a consequence of centuries of inscription in the social order, racial dynamics inevitably acquire their own autonomous logic, penetrating the fabric of social life and the cultural system at every level.[12] Thus, they cannot be fully understood, in the manner of Fernandes, as 'survivals' of a plantation slavocracy in which capitalist social relationships had not yet developed. Such a perspective ultimately denies the linkages between racial phenomena and

---

[10] Carl N. Degler, *Neither Black Nor White: Slavery and Race Relations in Brazil and the United States* (New York, 1971).

[11] Amaury de Souza, 'Raça e Política no Brasil Urbano', in *Revista Administração de Empresas*, vol. 11, no. 4 (1970); see also Bastide, 'A Imprensa Negra'.

[12] I return to this point below in discussing racial formation theory.

post-slavery society. There can be little doubt that since abolition the meaning of race has been significantly transformed; it has been extensively 'modernised' and reinterpreted. To grasp the depth of these changes, one has but to examine the intellectual or political history of the race concept itself. Late-nineteenth-century racial vocabularies and assumptions about white supremacy are as repugnant in contemporary Brazilian discourse as they would be in the present-day United States.[13]

Nor is it tenable to suggest that in Brazil racial distinctions are ephemeral, mere adjuncts to class categories, as do Harris and Azevedo. Substantial racial inequality may be observed in levels of income, employment, and returns to schooling, in access to education and literary rates, in health care, in housing and, importantly, by region.[14] In order to substantiate the thesis of 'transition from race to class', it would be necessary to demonstrate that inequality levels were tending to equalise *across* racial lines; the fact that 100 years after the end of slavery blacks are still overwhelmingly concentrated in the bottom strata certainly suggests that race is still a crucial determinant of economic success.

Degler's and de Souza's emphasis on the distinction between blacks and mulattoes – and the consequences of mobility for mulattoes – is more difficult to evaluate. On the one hand Nelson do Valle Silva's detailed study of racial stratification reveals no significant difference between black and mulatto mobility. Looking at a variety of indicators (income, returns to schooling, etc.), and using 1960 and 1976 census data which distinguish between blacks and mulattoes, Silva finds that 'blacks and mulattoes seem to display unexpectedly familiar profiles...'. Further,

These results lead us to reject the two hypotheses advanced by the Brazilian sociological literature. Mulattoes do not behave differently from Blacks, nor does race play a negligible role in the process of income attainment. In fact it was found that Blacks and mulattoes are almost equally discriminated against... This clearly contradicts the idea of a 'mulatto escape-hatch' being the essence of Brazilian race relations.[15]

On the other hand, the significance of this finding may be overstated,

[13]   For examples of this language, and analyses of its significance, see Celia Marinho de Azevedo, *Onda Negra, Medo Branco: O Negro no Imaginario das Elites – Século XIX* (Rio de Janeiro, 1987); see also Skidmore, *Black Into White*.

[14]   Thus, the impoverished northeast – the traditional locus of Brazilian poverty and underdevelopment, and the focus of Harris' and Azevedo's studies – is also disproportionately black, while the urbanised and industrialised southeast is disproportionately white. Manoel Augusto Costa (ed.), *O Segundo Brasil: Perspectivas Socio-Demográficas* (Rio de Janeiro, 1983); Charles H. Wood and José Alberto Magno de Carvalho, *The Demography of Inequality in Brazil* (New York, 1988).

[15]   Nelson do Valle Silva, 'Updating the Cost of Not Being White in Brazil', in Pierre-Michel Fontaine (ed.), *Race, Class, and Power in Brazil* (Los Angeles, 1985), pp. 54–5; *idem*, 'Cor e Processo de Realização Socioeconómica', *Dados*, vol. 24, no. 3 (1980).

vitiated by Afro-Brazilian practices of racial classification. For example, a recent black movement campaign, *Campanha Censo 90*, sought to counteract the tendency toward 'auto-embranqecimento' ('self-whitening') in responding to the national census questions on race.[16] Thus, Silva's claim that the traditional notion of mobility no longer holds may be statistically correct, but false in terms of Afro-Brazilian perceptions. The 'mulatto escape hatch', an absolutely central theme in Brazilian racial ideology, might thus retain an ambiguous, if weakened, relevance.

Perhaps the most striking limitation of the revisionist literature is its nearly exclusive focus on racial inequality. This is not to deny the importance of the economic dimensions of race. However, the pre-occupation with inequality to the near total exclusion of any other aspect of race is a logical feature of approaches which treat racial dynamics as manifestations of more fundamental class relationships. These approaches tend to take the meaning of race for granted, and to see racial identities as relatively rigid and unchanging.[17]

To summarise, despite their success at exposing racial inequalities in Brazil and thus destroying the 'racial democracy' myth, the revisionist approaches encountered difficulties when they had to explain transformations in racial dynamics after slavery, and particularly the persistence of racial inequality in a developing capitalist society. Their tendency to see the persistence of racial inequality as a manifestation of supposedly more fundamental class antagonisms (reductionism) resulted in an inability to see race as a theoretically flexible, as opposed to an *a priori*, category. In writing about racial dynamics the revisionists tended to ignore the changing socio-historical meaning of race in Brazil.[18]

Beginning in the 1970s, and with greater frequency in later years, a 'post-revisionist' or structuralist approach to race in Brazil began to emerge. This perspective saw race as a central feature of Brazilian society. 'Structuralist' authors sharply refocused the problem of racial theory. They did not seek to explain how racism had survived in a supposedly 'racial democracy', nor how true integration might be achieved. Rather they looked at the way the Brazilian social order had maintained racial inequalities without encountering significant opposition and conflict.

[16] 'Campanha Censo 90' was announced in July 1990 by a broad coalition of Afro-Brazilian organisations of various political and cultural tendencies. Its slogan was 'Não deixe a sua cor passar em branco: responda com bom c/senso' ('Don't let your colour be passed off as white: respond with good sense', thus punning on 'sense/census').

[17] Even Harris (*Patterns of Race in the Americas*), whose research was directed quite specifically at the problem of racial categorisation, is susceptible to this criticism.

[18] This tendency is not confined to Brazil or to the United States; it is global, and only recently has come under sustained scrutiny. The recognition that the meaning of race is a significant political problem implies a racial formation perspective. See below.

In a brief essay originally published in 1971, Anani Dzidzienyo combined a critique of racial inequality with a discussion of both the macro- and micro-level cultural dynamics of race in Brazil. He challenged the

...bias which has been a hallmark of the much-vaunted Brazilian 'racial democracy' – the bias that white is best and black is worst and therefore the nearer one is to white, the better.

Further, he noted that

The hold which this view has on Brazilian society is all-pervasive and embraces a whole range of stereotypes, role-playing, job opportunities, life-styles, and, what is even more important, it serves as the cornerstone of the closely-observed 'etiquette' of race relations in Brazil.[19]

Here in embryo was a far more comprehensive critique of Brazilian racial dynamics. Dzidzienyo argued that racial inequalities were both structural and linked to a formidable racial ideology. This 'official Brazilian ideology achieves *without tension* the same results as do overtly racist societies'.[20] Structural inequality and the system of racial meanings were linked in a single racial order; each served to support the other. In this connection between structure and culture the structuralists saw a pattern of racial hegemony. But how was this hegemony attained and maintained, 'without tension'?

In a contribution of great importance, Carlos Hasenbalg developed a new synthesis of race and class, building on but also departing from the work of Fernandes.[21] Post-*abolição* racial dynamics, Hasenbalg argued, have been steadily transformed as Brazilian capitalism has evolved; thus, far from being outmoded, racial inequality remains necessary and functional for Brazilian capitalism.[22] The essential problem, then, is not to account for the persistence of racism, but rather to explain the absence of serious racial opposition, what Hasenbalg calls 'the smooth maintenance of racial inequalities'.

Both Dzidzienyo and Hasenbalg recognised that neither the powerful cultural complex of 'whitening' and 'racial democracy', nor the brutal

[19] Anani Dzidzienyo, *The Position of Blacks in Brazilian Society* (London, 1971), p. 5.
[20] *Ibid.*, p. 14; original emphasis.
[21] My own critique of Fernandes draws on the one presented by Hasenbalg, which centres on Fernandes' treatment of racial dynamics as survivals of slavery, of a pre-modern, pre-industrial epoch. See Carlos A. Hasenbalg, *Discriminação e Desigualdades Raciais no Brasil* (Rio de Janeiro, 1979), pp. 72–6.
[22] This analysis has strong parallels with Pierre van den Berghe's views on Brazil; van den Berghe argues that in the early post-*abolição* period racial dynamics were 'paternalistic', but later (as capitalism developed), became 'competitive'. In other words there was a shift from a non-antagonistic pattern of racial inequality toward a more conflictual one. Pierre van den Berghe, *Race and Racism: A Comparative Perspective* (New York, 1967).

structural inequalities between black and white would have been sustainable on their own. Both writers analysed the racial order in Brazil in terms of the linkage between culture and structure, between ideology and inequality. In this sense, these writers adopted early versions of a racial formation perspective.

Yet their analyses still bore some of the marks of class reductionism. To be sure, Dzidzienyo and Hasenbalg granted Brazilian racial dynamics a significant degree of autonomy *vis-à-vis* class dynamics. But their structural approach was still limited by the one-dimensionality of a view which explained the shape of the Brazilian racial order almost entirely in terms of its 'management' by white elites. Few constraints are recognised as limiting white 'management', either in the form of social structures inherited from the past, or in the form of resistance on the part of the racially subordinated group. Inequality is 'smoothly' maintained by a combination of ideological manipulation and coercion, all with the objective of maximising elite (i.e. capitalist) control of the developing Braziliaṅ economy.

In Hasenbalg's view, for example, the crucial action which permitted the system of 'smooth maintenance' to evolve occurred when the elites decided to encourage massive European immigration, thus displacing black labour after *abolição*.[23] Plentiful supplies of white labour prevented the emergence of a racially split labour market, such as developed in the U.S.A., and effectively defused racial antagonisms. The infusion of white labour ensured that class divisions among whites, rather than competition between whites and blacks, would shape the pattern of Brazilian capitalist development. It also fuelled the cultural/ideological complex of 'whitening', and later the ideology of 'racial democracy'. Thus, the system of racial categorisation, as well as the ideological and political dynamics of race in general, were shaped by capitalist development in the post-*abolição* years.

This approach does not deviate very far from that of Fernandes. It simply assumes the primacy of capitalist development, and the secondary character of race. It does not take into account the fact that racial ideology was entirely present at the supposed foundations of Brazilian capitalist development. Indeed it was in part because of their fear of blacks that the Brazilian elite turned to European immigration in the first place.[24] Hasenbalg recognises this empirical fact, but cannot incorporate it into his theory.

In fact, Hasenbalg's argument would operate equally well in reverse; in place of his suggestion that capitalist development demanded the smooth

[23] Hasenbalg, *Discriminação e Desigualdades*, pp. 223–60.
[24] Skidmore, *Black Into White*, pp. 130–1, 136–44.

maintenance of Brazilian racial inequality, it would be equally logical to suggest that the course of development followed by Brazilian capitalism was shaped in significant measure by pre-existing racial patterns.[25] However significant the absence of a split labour market was to the development of Brazilian racial dynamics, it was clearly not determining; at most it was one factor among others. Indeed the political authoritarianism – the *coronelismo*, paternalism, clientelism, etc., which characterised elite–mass relationships in the first republic and beyond – was a carry-over from slavery into the post-*abolição* framework in which capitalist development began in earnest. Thus not only the framework of Brazilian class relations, but also in large measure the traditional political structure, may be said to have their origins in racial dynamics.[26]

Without derogating the importance of the structuralist contributions, it may be worthwhile to note that they were written during the most repressive phase of the Brazilian military dictatorship (1968–74), when all opposition, including black movement activity, was at its nadir. The mobilisation which did exist largely took the form of cultural and 'identity' politics, typified most centrally by the 'black soul' movement (see below). It is not unreasonable to suggest that the structuralist problematic – of a frozen racial inequality, 'smoothly maintained' by an all-powerful elite – stemmed from the conjuncture in which it emerged.

[25] This is close to Fernandes' argument, although his understanding of racism as a 'survival' antagonistic to full capitalist development limits his appreciation of the point. See Florestan Fernandes, 'The Weight of the Past' in J. H. Franklin (ed.), *Color and Race* (Boston, 1969).

[26] This reversibility in the structural argument suggests a certain residual functionalism. Certainly a measure of class reductionism survives in the structuralist perspective. In Hasenbalg's study the functionalist moment may be attributable to reliance on Poulantzas. Adopting the latter's approach to class formation, Hasenbalg writes:

> Race, as a socially elaborated attribute, is principally related to the subordinated aspect of the reproduction of social classes, that is, to the reproduction (formation – qualification – submission) and distribution of agents. Therefore, racial minorities are not outside the class structure of multiracial societies in which capitalist relations of production – or any other relations of production, in fact – are dominant. Likewise, racism, as an ideological construct incorporated in and realised through a pattern of material practices of racial discrimination, is the primary determinant of the position of non-whites, in the relations of production and distribution (Hasenbalg, *Discriminação e Desigualdades*, p. 114).

> Note how little autonomy racial dynamics are granted in this model. A series of functional requirements for the reproduction of the capitalist class structure sets the pattern of racial formation. The qualification 'or any other relations of production' is irrelevant, because in these other modes of production (slavery, feudalism?) racial minorities presumably will also be subordinated to class structures which are granted logical priority, as well as historical precedence, over racial dynamics. For a more recent statement of Hasenbalg's position, see Carlos Hasenbalg, untitled presentation, *Estudos Afro-Asiaticos* 12 (Rio de Janeiro, August 1986), pp. 27–30.

Furthermore, despite their recognition of important cultural dimensions in Brazilian racial politics, the structuralists still theorised these elements as strictly subordinate to those of inequality and discrimination. Their view was that Brazilian racial discourse largely served to mask inequality; they did not see the cultural dynamics – the racial 'politics of identity' – as conflictual, contested terrain. Perhaps this residue of class reductionism also limited their ability to recognise potential flexibility and changing patterns in Brazilian racial dynamics.

Summarizing once more, we can say that despite its considerable strengths, the literature on race in Brazil suffers from a series of debilitating problems, including a neglect of the discursive and cultural dimensions of race, an exaggerated belief in the omnipotence of elites where racial management is concerned, and a tendency to downplay the tensions and conflicts involved in Brazilian racial dynamics. These limitations largely derived from a deep-seated tradition of class reductionism, which is manifest in the classic studies of the early postwar period (the revisionists), but latent even in more recent work (the structuralists). Such criticisms point to the need for a new approach, one which would avoid treating race as a manifestation of some other, supposedly more basic, social relationship. I therefore propose an alternative in the form of racial formation theory.

Racial formation theory seems particularly well suited to deal with the complexities of Brazilian racial dynamics. Developed as a response to reductionism, this perspective understands race as a phenomenon whose meaning is contested throughout social life.[27] In this account race is both a constituent of the individual psyche and of relationships among individuals, and an irreducible component of collective identities and social structures. Once it is recognised that race is not a 'natural' attribute but a socially and historically constructed one, it becomes possible to analyse the processes by which racial meanings are decided, and racial identities assigned, in a given society. These processes – those of 'racial signification' – are inherently discursive. They are variable, conflictual and contested at every level of society – from the intra-psychic to the supra-national. Inevitably, many interpretations of race, many racial discourses, exist at any given time. The political character of racial formation stems from this: elites, popular movements, state agencies, religions and intellectuals of all types develop *racial projects*, which interpret and reinterpret the meaning of race.

The theoretical concept of *racial projects* is a key element of racial formation theory. A project is simultaneously an explanation of racial

[27] Michael Omi and Howard Winant, *Racial Formation in the United States: From the 1960s to the 1980s* (New York, 1986).

dynamics and an effort to reorganise the social structure along particular racial lines. Every project is necessarily both a discursive or cultural initiative, an attempt at racial signification and identity formation on the one hand; and a political initiative, an attempt at organisation and redistribution on the other.[28]

The articulation and rearticulation of racial meanings is thus a multidimensional process, in which competing 'projects' intersect and clash. These projects are often explicitly, but always at least implicitly, political. 'Subjective' phenomena – racial identities, popular culture, 'common sense' – and social structural phenomena such as political movements and parties, state institutions and policies, market processes, etc., are all potential sources of racial projects.

Racial formation in contemporary Brazil: the impact of democratisation

When we ask why the Brazilian black movement is newly stirring after a relative absence of half a century, an important part of the answer must be the impact of democratisation. It was the *abertura*, the painfully slow re-emergence of civil society, which created the conditions under which black political opposition could reappear. At first tentative, and still marginalised relative to black movements in the United States and Europe, the black movement in Brazil now occupies a permanent place on the political stage. Of course the process of democratisation is still far from consolidated, and the room for manoeuvre available to an explicitly race-conscious movement remains quite limited. But as the various protests against the *centenário* showed, not since the days of the *Frente Negra Brasileira* in the 1920s and 1930s has so explicit a racial politics been possible.[29]

The reappearance of the black movement also demonstrates the limits of the various analyses of Brazilian racial dynamics which I have reviewed. Nothing about the current upsurge squares with either the revisionist or the structuralist accounts. From the revisionist perspective, one would have expected a diminution of racial conflict as Brazil became a more fully capitalist society, less characterised by the residues of its slave-holding past. The experience of rapid industrial growth under the military dictatorship, the 'miracle' which made Brazil the eighth largest national economy in the world (in terms of GNP) by 1985, should also have made

---

[28] Only a brief statement of the racial formation framework is possible here. For a more extensive discussion, see Omi and Winant, *Racial Formation in the United States*. For more on racial projects, see Howard Winant, 'Postmodern Racial Politics: Difference and Inequality', *Socialist Review* 90/1 (Jan.–March, 1990).

[29] The Frente was the most significant Afro-Brazilian organisation of the 1920s and 1930s. It was repressed by Getúlio Vargas in 1937 after transforming itself into a political party. See Fernandes, *A Integração do Negro*, vol. II, pp. 10–87.

race a less salient marker of political identity. In fact, the reverse occurred.

From the structuralist perspective, one would have expected the elite's 'smooth maintenance' of racial inequality to be nowhere more efficiently carried out than under the military dictatorship. This was a system of elite rule *par excellence*, and one which managed quite 'smoothly' the excruciatingly slow return of democracy during the 1970s and 1980s;[30] furthermore, the military had been at pains to deny, in quintessentially Brazilian style, the existence of racism in the country.[31] Yet, not long after the *abertura* began in earnest (in 1974), the first attempts at national black movement-building were initiated by the *Movimento Negro Unificado* (MNU),[32] and throughout the later transition period a slow but steady build-up of black opposition voices, actions and organisational initiatives was underway.

From a racial formation perspective, by contrast, these developments do make sense. The black upsurge was a combination of two factors: the *re-emergence of civil society*, which necessarily opened up political terrain for social movement activities, and the *politicisation of racial identities* upon that terrain.

The re-emergence of civil society

The *abertura* took place as a conflictual dialogue between democratic opposition forces and the military dictatorship. It was a gradual relaxation of repression both promoted by and fuelling opposition forces. The Brazilian democratic opposition, traditionally compromised and co-opted by elite control, *coronelismo* and corporatism, faced enormous difficulties in the atmosphere of military dictatorship. The decades-long process of military rule rendered ineffective many of the traditional sources of political opposition in Brazil; others it eliminated outright. Thus the popular strata had to adopt new forms of struggle. Here the new social movements – human rights groups, women's groups, residential associations and, very importantly in the Brazilian context, ecclesiastical base committees (CEBs) – became important political actors.

The new social movements *recreated civil society* by expanding the

[30] See Alfred Stepan, *Rethinking Military Politics: Brazil and the Southern Cone* (Princeton, 1988), for a detailed account of the military's sophistication in handling the pace of the *abertura*.

[31] Thomas E. Skidmore, 'Race and Class in Brazil: Historical Perspectives', in Pierre-Michel Fontaine (ed.), *Race, Class, and Power in Brazil*.

[32] The Movimento Negro Unificado Contra Discriminação Racial (later simply Movimento Negro Unificado – MNU) was the most significant movement of the 1970s. See Lelia Gonzalez, 'The Unified Black Movement: A New Stage in Black Political Mobilisation', in Pierre-Michel Fontaine (ed.), *Race, Class, and Power in Brazil*; Maria Ercilia do Nascimento, *A Estratégia da Desigualdade: O Movimento Negro dos Anos 70* (unpubl. master's thesis, PUC – São Paulo, 1989).

terrain of politics. They addressed issues which had formerly been seen as personal or private – i.e. not legitimate themes for collective action – as public, social and legitimate areas for mobilisation. In these groups a range of radical democratic themes – religious, feminist, localist, but chiefly 'humanistic' – were encountered in new ways (or for the first time). For many people, particularly those of humble origin whom the traditional political processes had always been able to ignore, the new social movements provided the first political experiences of their lives.[33] For those of the middle classes – priests, journalists, lawyers, health workers, educators and others who shared explicit democratic and egalitarian aspirations – the new social movements offered a political alternative to leftist and populist traditions which the military dictatorship had effectively stalemated.[34]

Brazilian blacks were intimately involved in the quest for democracy.[35] They were among the *favelados*, the landless *boias frias*, the metalworkers. In the early phases of the *abertura* they did not organise *qua* blacks, but the interrogation of social and political reality and the quest for *citizenship* emphasised in many movement activities placed a new focus on racial themes. By the later 1970s, with the consolidation of democratic opposition politics, a new generation of black movement organisations began to emerge.

It would be impossible to list all the political influences which blacks encountered in this process, nor can the variety of positions and currents within the nascent black movement be elaborated here. Certainly by participating in the panoply of opposition social movements which confronted the dictatorship, many blacks acquired fresh political skills and awareness. Among those mobilised were black activists in *favela* associations, in CEBs, and in rural struggles for land (especially in the

[33] In no small measure due to the ideas popularised by the Brazilian educator and activist Paulo Freire, these primordial political experiences were in themselves acts of reinterpretation.

[34] Ilse Scherer-Warren and Paulo J. Krischke, *Uma Revolução no Cotidiano? Os Movimentos Sociais na América do Sul* (São Paulo, 1986); Theotonio dos Santos, 'Crisis y Movimientos Sociales en Brasil', in Fernando Calderón Gutierrez (ed.), *Los Movimientos Sociales ante la Crisis* (Buenos Aires, 1985), pp. 47–8; Renato R. Boschi, 'Social Movements and the New Political Order in Brazil', in John Wirth et al. (eds.), *State and Stability in Brazil: Continuity and Change* (Boulder, 1987); Marianne Schmink, 'Women in Brazilian Abertura Politics', in *Signs*, 7 (Autumn 1981); Ruth C. L. Cardoso, 'Movimentos Sociais Urbanos: Balanço Crítico', in Sebastião Velazco e Cruz et al., *Sociedade e Política no Brasil pos-64* (São Paulo, 1983).

[35] The following discussion relies heavily on Joel Rufino dos Santos, *O Movimento Negro e a Crise Brasileira* (mimeo, São Paulo, 1985); Michael Mitchell, 'Blacks and the *Abertura Democrática*' in Pierre-Michel Fontaine (ed.), *Race, Class, and Power in Brazil*; Clovis Moura, *Brasil: As Raizes do Protesto Negro* (São Paulo, 1983); Muniz Sodre, *A Verdade Seduzida* (Rio de Janeiro, 1983).

northeast), blacks who participated in strike activity (especially in the
ABC region of São Paulo), blacks involved in cultural activities and
organisations,[36] black students,[37] blacks concerned with issues of African
liberation, black researchers and intellectuals involved in studying Afro-
Brazilian history and culture, and black women involved in feminist
activities.[38]

Thus, as the *abertura* advanced and democratic opposition consolidated
and expanded, blacks began to mobilise and organise as blacks. With the
creation of the MNU in 1978 a national black political movement was
brought into being.[39] More recently still other black organisations have
appeared, notably the *Grupo União e Consciência Negra*, which claims
organisations in 14 Brazilian states, the *Centro de Articulação de Populações
Marginalizadas* (CEAP), the *Centro de Referência Negromestiça* (CERNE), the
Instituto Palmares de Direitos Humanos (IPDH), and the publication *Jornal da
Maioria Falante*. These are the means by which blacks are participating in
the struggle to create democracy and social justice in Brazil.

A variety of political projects can be identified in the black movement
upsurge that accompanied the *abertura*. 'Entrism' (the effort by
marginalised groups to operate in the political mainstream), socialist
positions, and 'nationalist' currents are all clearly in evidence.[40] Strong
debates and dissension characterised the development of the MNU. For

[36] Such as the Palmares group, *terreiros* of *candomblé*, *afoxes* and *blocos africanos*, etc.
Cultural and religious groups are entirely central in black organisational efforts in
Brazil, and in recent years have more frequently linked their traditional vocations with
political themes. For example, *afoxes* are groups of religious orientation, based in
Candomblé. They dance and sing in African languages, and participate in Carnaval.
Formerly outlawed, they were legalised in the late 1970s. In Salvador the *afoxes* have
formed *blocos* which are not only active in Carnaval, but also serve as 'nationalist'
organisations, performing educational tasks (racial *conscientização*), organising *favelados*
and *moradores* groups, etc.

[37] J. Michael Turner, 'Brown Into Black: Changing Racial Attitudes of Afro-Brazilian
University Students', in Pierre-Michel Fontaine (ed.), *Race, Class, and Power in Brazil*.

[38] As in the United States and many other countries, black women play a crucial role in
many social movements in Brazil (Sueli Carneiro and Thereza Santos, *Mulher Negra*,
São Paulo, 1985). They have challenged both sexism in the black movement and racism
in the women's movement. The topic of Afro-Brazilian women and feminism has
generated much debate and several significant studies. The MNU included anti-sexist
points in its statement of principles, for example. (See Gonzales, 'The Unified Black
Movement', pp. 129–30.) On other aspects of these issues see Lucia Elena Garcia
Oliveira, Rosa Maria Porcaro, and Tereza Cristina Nascimento Araujo, 'Repensando
o Lugar da Mulher Negra', *Estudos Afro-Asiaticos*, 13 (Rio de Janeiro, March 1987),
idem, O Lugar do Negro na Força de Trabalho (Rio de Janeiro, 1985); Carmen Barroso
(ed.), *Mulher, Sociedade, e Estado no Brasil* (São Paulo, 1982).

[39] The MNU was, however, riven by regional and ideological divisions, and was unable
to maintain its cohesion at a national level. See Maria Ercilia do Nascimento, *A
Estratégia da Desigualdade*, pp. 112–17.

[40] For US comparisons, see Michael Omi and Howard Winant, 'By the Rivers of Babylon:
Race in the United States', Part II, *Socialist Review*, 72 (Nov.–Dec. 1983), pp. 38–40.

example, major sectors of the organisation rejected Abdias do Nascimento's project of *Quilombismo*:[41] his effort to develop an 'afrocentric' ideology for the black movement. There have also been major debates about the role of feminism within the movement, and about the relationship of race, sex, and class in general.

Alongside such 'nationalist' currents as that of *Quilombismo*, 'entrists' in the movement, oriented both to mainstream and left parties, have urged greater organised black participation in trade unions and political parties. Nascimento himself has been a PDT (Democratic Workers' Party) activist and served a term as a Federal Deputy from Rio, although he failed to win re-election. Many radical blacks have joined the PT (Workers Party); within that organisation they have created a *Commissão de Negros* which operates both at the national and regional levels. One of the few national black leaders, Benedita Souza da Silva, is a PT Federal Deputy.[42] There are also blacks in the PMDB (Brazilian Democratic Movement Party), PSDB (Brazilian Social Democratic Party), and even rightist political parties such as the PDS (Social Democratic Party). Many blacks, however, even among those most committed to 'entrism', continue to criticise political parties, as well as unions and other popular organisations, for being insufficiently committed to racial equality.

Additionally, a pronounced tendency towards co-optation of movement activity exists, for which Brazilian politics is notorious. 'Entrist' groups are particularly susceptible to this. Whether effective or largely symbolic, various government entities have established mechanisms of liaison with the black community.[43] At the national level, there is now an *Assessoria para Assuntos Afro-Brasileiros* in the Ministry of Culture. Several state governments, particularly those of São Paulo and Rio de Janeiro, also have established agencies to foster cultural events and to investigate complaints of discrimination.

[41] Gonzalez, 'The Unified Black Movement', p. 130; a recent representative statement on *quilombismo* is Abdias do Nascimento, '*Quilombismo*: The African–Brazilian Road to Socialism', in Molefi Kete Asante and Kariamu Welsh Asante (eds.), *African Culture: The Rhythms of Unity* (Westport, 1985).

[42] 'Bene' often combines her anti-racist polemic with defence of women's rights. For a particularly strong statement, see Benedita Souza da Silva, 'A identidade da Mulher Negra – a Identidade da Mulher India', presented at the Conferência Nacional Saude e Direitos da Mulher, October 1986 (mimeo).

[43] In the USA, black movement successes were met with sophisticated state strategies which I have elsewhere analysed in terms of 'absorption' and 'insulation' (Omi and Winant, *Racial Formation*, p. 81). Predictably, in Brazil there are big debates about the extent of service, versus the degree of co-optation, offered by such organisations. The state tendency to establish a bureaucracy when confronted by opposition is very strong.

The politicisation of racial identity

Today the meaning of race and the complexities of racial identity are contested far more intensely than ever before in Brazil. We have only to look at the mobilisation against the *centenário* to see this debate in progress. To understand this point it is useful to contrast expressions of black identity articulated at the repressive peak of the military dictatorship and in the present climate of relatively free expansion. The 'black soul' upsurge of the 1960s is used here to exemplify the first period, and the development of the *afoxes* in the 1980s to illustrate the second. Although many examples of public discourse on the subject of black identity could be cited, these two are not arbitrarily chosen: they are the most important manifestations of black cultural politics in their respective epochs.[44]

During the most repressive periods of military rule, when overt political mobilisation against racism was almost impossible, cultural movements sustained black awareness and challenged racial stereotypes, making use of 'identity politics'. Probably the most effective (or controversial) of these currents was 'black soul', which flourished in the later 1960s, drawing inspiration from the black cultural and political upsurges then engulfing the U.S.A.[45] 'Black soul' was a youth-oriented current; it had little appeal beyond the big cities (most notably Rio). To describe it as a movement probably overstates its political resonance.

Yet because it identified the interests of blacks in Brazil with those of blacks elsewhere, because it addressed issues of racial identity, 'black soul' drew considerable attention from the military, and from other official custodians of Brazilian racial ideology. For example, its obvious inspiration by cultural developments in the United States – where the black movement was entering its militant nationalist phase – prompted considerable unease. It was denounced as 'un-Brazilian', implicitly anti-nationalist. In terms of racial formation theory, this reaction can be understood as a conflict over the meaning of race prompted by the 'black soul' phenomenon. The fact that its rather superficial aspects (Afro hairstyles, dashikis, a taste for Motown and Stax/Volt records) became cause for official harassment indicates that, at least in the eyes of its opponents, 'black soul' represented a challenge to Afro-Brazilian isolation from the global assertion of black identity. By drawing attention to blacks *qua* blacks, this current echoed the sporadic efforts of previous

[44] For surveys of debates about racial identity during the 1960s and 1970s, see Skidmore, 'Race and Class in Brazil'; Mitchell, 'Blacks and the *Abertura Democrática*'.

[45] Carlos Benedito Rodrigues da Silva, 'Black Soul: Aglutinação Espontanea ou Identidade Etnica: Uma Contribuição ão Estudo das Manifestações Culturais no Meio Negro', presented at the Fourth Annual Meeting of the Associação Nacional de Posgraduação e Pesquisas em Ciencias Sociais (ANPOCS), 1980.

generations to highlight and discuss the nature of race in Brazil. Thus 'black soul' raised the same hackles that the *Frente Negra Brasileira* had done decades before, and that the *Movimento Negro Unificado* was to do a decade later. In this way it contributed to debate over the nature of black identity in Brazil, at a moment (the mid-1960s to early 1970s) when repression was increasing. 'Black soul' was important, then, in ways which transcended mere style or musical tastes. It was a transitional moment, a bridge between the limited but important black mobilisation taking place in the pre-dictatorship periods (I am thinking of such organisations as the *Comité Democrático Afro-Brasileiro* and the *Congresso Brasileiro de Negro*), and the activities of the MNU in the 1970s.

More recently, black identity has been stressed in the work of the groups known as *afoxés*. These are groups whose roots are religious, lying deep in the Afro-Brazilian traditions of *Candomblé*, in the West African language (Nagô) that slaves of Yoruban origin spoke. Originally the *afoxés* acted largely through *Carnaval*, consciously seeking to accentuate and focus black awareness through the powerful (and frequently subversive) discursive framework offered by this annual popular festival. Largely because of their subversiveness, the *afoxés* were outlawed, and were legalised only under the impact of *abertura* in the late 1970s.

In the northeast, and particularly in Bahia, the 'black capital' of Brazil, *afoxés* are not only active in *Carnaval*, but also serve as political organisations, performing educational tasks (racial *conscientização*), or-ganising *favelados* and *moradores* groups, etc. Salvador is also the home base of the group *Olodum*, which began as an *afoxé*, but has become an important 'nationalist' influence through its recordings. *Olodum*'s music is con-sciously and complexly afrocentric, drawing on the *afoxé* tradition, addressing Afro-Brazilians about their history, their links to Africa and to blacks in the diaspora, and their collective racial identity. Not only in their lyrics, but also in their incorporation of musical forms such as reggae, *Olodum* presents a concept of black identity which radically challenges traditional concepts of race in Brazil. Its deliberate evocation of the African diaspora explicitly refuses the official Brazilian racial ideology in all its forms, from Freyre's 'Lusotropicalism' to 'racial democracy'. Acting through popular music, *Olodum* attempts to reinterpret the question of race, and to valorise black identity, in a manner which addresses millions of Brazilians. Certainly this rearticulation of black identity is not unprecedented. It bears important resemblances to the message of Abdias do Nascimento, for example; in its treatment of Zumbi, the hero of black resistance to slavery, it resonates with many other efforts at mobilisation and analysis. But what distinguishes the project of *Olodum* from those of many other Afro-Brazilian militants past and present is its immense appeal to the masses of blacks. Because it is a popular musical group, indeed *the* black band in Brazil, *Olodum* has become a sort of national *afoxe*.[46]

Conclusion: rethinking race in Brazil

The issue of race is making a belated but inexorable entrance on to the Brazilian political stage. Because today there is – at long last and with all its warts – political democracy in Brazil, there is an upsurge of overt racial conflict. There are two major themes to this conflict: the first is about racial inequality, mobility and redistribution along lines of race, and racially based political action. The second is about the meaning of race, the nature of racial identity, the logic of racial categories, the centrality of the African currents in Brazilian culture and history, and the links between blacks in Brazil and elsewhere in the African diaspora.

Certainly none of these themes is absolutely new – how could it be? Nor do I mean to suggest that a radical transformation of Brazilian racial dynamics is about to take place. There are many reasons to think that a far more incremental process than that which occurred elsewhere in the Americas – in the U.S.A., say, or in the Caribbean – is at work. Many factors in Brazil's history point to a more gradual politicisation of race than occurred, for example, in the U.S.A. In Brazil there has been no apocalyptic national conflict over racial slavery, such as the US civil war; there has been far less state-enforced racial segregation, so that race is inherently less politicised than elsewhere. Further, there are far fewer established and independent black institutions, such as universities or media. The fact that Brazil lacks a viable democratic tradition, capable of incremental extension to previously excluded groups, is also of great importance. This list could be extended, and of course the comparison has been made far more systematically in other literature. I simply offer it here to suggest that no explosive racial upheaval is to be expected in Brazil.

Still, while traditional patterns of race and racism have by no means been invalidated, a qualitative change is evident in the socio-political dynamics of race in Brazil. The many examples I have cited in this article demonstrate that this shift is underway: the protests against the *centenário*, the proliferation of black organisations, the attempts of established institutions – political parties, state agencies, unions, etc. – to address racial issues, and the arrival on the national cultural scene of black consciousness-raising efforts.

If indeed these changes are taking place at the socio-political level, they must be accompanied by changes in the theoretical and analytical tools with

---

[46] *Olodum*'s intervention is not free from the limitations which traditionally afflict popular Afro-Brazilian figures however. The group's appearance in 1990 on videos made for Paul Simon's record *Rhythm of the Saints* has provoked criticisms for 'selling out'.

which we view race in Brazil. Just as we can no longer accept the premodern biologistic racism of the nineteenth century, or the idyllic panorama of tropical racial harmonies imagined by Freyre in the 1930s, so we can no longer agree with the class reductionism which the UNESCO studies, for all their merits, generated in the 1950s and 60s. Brazilian racial dynamics cannot be understood as reflections of an underdeveloped political economy which failed to attain full capitalist status. No transition 'from race to class', however elaborate, is underway.

Nor can we accept the argument of the 'structuralist school' that racial politics are, in essence, permanently marginalised. While there can be no question that the diffusion and denial of racial conflict has operated as effectively in Brazil as anywhere in the world, the *abertura* and its aftermath are providing extensive evidence of the proliferation and deepening of racial conflict and racial consciousness. The argument that effective elite management of racial conflict could continue was refuted by the events of the *abertura* itself, an elite management scheme of unprecedented sophistication, which nevertheless resulted in the upsurge of racial opposition we have seen since the late 1970s.

Rethinking race in Brazil, then, means thinking about racial formation, about a process of permanently contested social institutions and permanently conflictual identities. Racial formation theory tells us that in Brazil the full range of racially salient socio-political and cultural dynamics has not yet even been identified. Language, geography, science, dress, farming, style, food, education, sports, media, literature, medicine, religion, the military – all these topics contain a wealth of hitherto unidentified racial dimensions, even those which have attracted significant research. Can anyone imagine that Bastide, as estimable a writer as he was, has exhausted the field of Afro-Brazilian religion? Or that Stephens's excellent English dictionary of Afro-Brazilian Portuguese has completed etymological and socio-linguistic investigation?[47] Academic research is driven by popular activity, cultural demands and political mobilisation. If democracy can truly take hold, the racial dimensions of many spheres of Brazilian life will be questioned and examined by those who must live them out. This is the heart of the racial formation process.

[47] Thomas M. Stephens, *Dictionary of Latin American Racial and Ethnic Terminology* (Gainesville, 1989).

ACKNOWLEDGMENTS

Borah, Woodrow. "Race and Class in Mexico." *Pacific Historical Review* 23 (1954): 331–42. Courtesy of Yale University Sterling Memorial Library.

Wagley, Charles. "On the Concept of Social Race in the Americas." *Actas del XXXIII Congreso Internacional de Americanistas* 1 (1959): 403–17. Courtesy of the editor.

Cardoso, Fernando Henrique. "Colour Prejudice in Brazil." *Presence Africaine* (English Edition) 25 (1965): 120–28. Courtesy of Yale University Seeley G. Mudd Library.

Germani, Gino. "Mass Immigration and Modernization in Argentina." *Studies in Comparative International Development* 2 (1966): 165–82. Reprinted with the permission of Transaction Publishers. Courtesy of Yale University Seeley G. Mudd Library.

Pitt-Rivers, Julian. "Race, Color, and Class in Central America and the Andes." *Daedalus* 96 (1967): 542–59. Reprinted by permission of *Daedalus, Journal of the American Academy of Arts and Sciences.* Courtesy of Yale University Sterling Memorial Library.

Fernandes, Florestan. "Beyond Poverty: The Negro and the Mulatto in Brazil." *Journal de la Société des Américanistes* 58 (1969): 121–37. Reprinted with the permission of the Musée de L'Homme. Courtesy of the *Journal de la Société des Américanistes.*

Bastide, Roger. "The Present Status of Afro-American Research in Latin America." *Daedalus* 103 (1974): 111–23. Reprinted by permission of *Daedalus, Journal of the American Academy of Arts and Sciences.* Courtesy of Yale University Sterling Memorial Library.

Do Nascimento, Abdias. "African Culture in Brazilian Art." *Journal of Black Studies* 8 (1978): 389–422. Reprinted with the permission of Sage Publications, Inc. Courtesy of Yale University Sterling Memorial Library.

Wong, Bernard. "A Comparative Study of the Assimilation of the Chinese in New York City and Lima, Peru." *Comparative Studies in Society and History* 20 (1978): 335–58. Reprinted with the permission of Cambridge University Press. Courtesy of Yale University Sterling Memorial Library.

Maeyama, Takashi. "Ethnicity, Secret Societies, and Associations: The Japanese in Brazil." *Comparative Studies in Society and History* 21 (1979): 589–610. Reprinted with the permission of Cambridge University Press. Courtesy of Yale University Sterling Memorial Library.

Fontaine, Pierre-Michel. "Research in the Political Economy of Afro-Latin America." *Latin American Research Review* 15 (1980): 111–41. Reprinted with the permission of the *Latin American Research Review*. Courtesy of Yale University Social Science Library.

Bollinger, William and Daniel Manny Lund. "Minority Oppression: Toward Analyses that Clarify and Strategies that Liberate." *Latin American Perspectives* 9 (1982): 2–28. Reprinted with the permission of Sage Publications, Inc. Courtesy of Yale University Sterling Memorial Library.

Hasenbalg, Carlos and Suellen Huntington. "Brazilian Racial Democracy: Reality or Myth?" *Humboldt Journal of Social Relations* 10 (1982): 129–42. Reprinted with the permission of *Humboldt Journal of Social Relations*. Courtesy of *Humboldt Journal of Social Relations*.

Skidmore, Thomas E. "Race and Class in Brazil: Historical Perspectives." *Luso-Brazilian Review* 20 (1983): 104–18. Reprinted with the permission of the University of Wisconsin Press. Courtesy of Yale University Sterling Memorial Library.

Collier, George A. "Peasant Politics and the Mexican State: Indigenous Compliance in Highland Chiapas." *Mexican Studies* 3 (1987): 71–98. Reprinted with the permission of the University of California Press. Courtesy of the editor.

Andrews, George Reid. "Black Political Protest in São Paulo, 1888–1988." *Journal of Latin American Studies* 24 (1992): 147–71. Reprinted with the permission of Cambridge University Press. Courtesy of Yale University Sterling Memorial Library.

Stavenhagen, Rodolfo. "Challenging the Nation-State in Latin America." *Journal of International Affairs* 45 (1992): 421–40. Published by permission of the *Journal of International Af-*

fairs and the Trustees of Columbia University in the City of New York. Courtesy of Yale University Law Library.

Winant, Howard. "Rethinking Race in Brazil." *Journal of Latin American Studies* 24 (1992): 173–92. Reprinted with the permission of Cambridge University Press. Courtesy of Yale University Sterling Memorial Library.